# ARCHIVES
### AND
# JUSTICE

# ARCHIVES
## AND
# JUSTICE

*A South African Perspective*

VERNE HARRIS

with a foreword by Terry Cook

**SOCIETY OF**
**American**
**Archivists**

Chicago

**The Society of American Archivists**
527 South Wells Street, 5ᵗʰ Floor
Chicago, IL 60607 USA
312/922-0140   Fax 312/347-1452
www.archivists.org

Printed in the United States of America

**Library of Congress Cataloging-in-Publication Data**

Harris, V. S.
  Archives and justice : a South African perspective / by Verne Harris ; with a foreword by
Terry Cook.
     p. cm.
  Includes bibliographical references and index.
  ISBN 1-931666-18-0 (alk. paper)
  1. Archives--Political aspects--South Africa. 2. Archives--Social aspects--South Africa. 3.
Archives--South Africa--Philosophy. 4. Social justice--South Africa. 5. South Africa--Politics
and government--1989-1994. 6. South Africa--Politics and government--1994- 7. South
Africa--Social conditions--1961-1994. 8. South Africa--Social conditions--1994- I. Title.

CD2451.H36 2006
027.0968--dc22

                                                    2006103304


Cover design: Matt Dufek
Book design: Bruce P. Cutter
Font: Perpetua

for kerry and ben
who have lived the dangers of hospitality with me

# TABLE OF CONTENTS

# Foreword

## Archival Music: Verne Harris and the Cracks of Memory

by Terry Cook

   In this remarkable collection of essays, speeches, and other writing, Verne Harris plays archives as a fine musician plays a beloved instrument, searching for harmonies, improvising new sounds, inviting engagement. In the opening epigraph to his Introduction that follows, Verne evokes Canadian singer, songwriter, and poet Leonard Cohen for the animating focus of this book: "There is a crack in everything. That's how the light gets in." While Verne footnotes this to a volume of Cohen's poetry, the poem was also set to music as the well-known Leonard Cohen song "Anthem," from the album *The Future,* and both titles offer initial contexts for understanding Verne's exploration of archive.

   An *anthem* is (by dictionary definitions) an uplifting song normally associated with a group or cause, such as an anthem adopted by a country as an expression of its national identity, or now, in popular parlance, a "rock anthem," where musical supergroups perform their signature song to a massive sing-a-long, accompanied by arms pumping in the air (or lighting of flames) as a sign of enthusiastic audience engagement. *Anthem* carries also the more traditional meaning of a musical performance where a religious text is sung by a choir during a church service. And in this sense, let us remember that "religion," in the words of Verne's intellectual hero, Jacques Derrida, "is responsibility, or it is nothing at all."

Like an anthem, Verne's music in these pages is similarly inspiring, carrying archivists up out of their traditional rhythms and set scores, to envision a new *Future* for our profession, and for those who interact with us and with the archives we make. The anthem Verne would have us sing as the "group" called archives is one for justice, to find in the inexorable calling to justice our central "responsibility," or else *we* as archivists are "nothing at all." Archives is not just something we do; it is something we must deeply believe, or we become hollow *archons*, functionaries without soul, without wider societal responsibility, or relevance. This is not "justice" only in the sense of archival records, more judiciously appraised, acquired, described, and made available, allowing citizens to seek justice in righting past wrongs, from aboriginal displacements to war crimes, from medical neglect to ethnic discrimination. Nor is it only "justice" in promoting records as the underpinning of just governments, through transparency, accountability, and freedom of information, indeed, underpinning democracy itself, all resting on the creation of reliable records and their sensitive appraisal and controlled destruction. In addition to these, Verne extends the notion of "justice" into the open, hospitable welcoming of "story" into archives, the telling and retellings of stories by archivists and by multiple users, multiple ways of seeing and knowing being invited in, rather than excluded from, the archives. Let's go back to the music.

There is, of course, more to Cohen's "Anthem" than the famous chorus lines that Verne evokes:

> You can add up the parts
> but you won't have the sum

For all of our archival methods and functions, procedures and manuals, standards and templates, the sum of archives, Verne insists, is more than all we do, more than the functions performed across a continuum or along a life cycle, more than all our finely honed methodologies, for the sum is not the parts added together, but, for Verne, the inspiring vision of our "responsibility," our personal engagement with the rhythms of memory and justice.

You can strike up the march,
there is no drum.
Every heart, every heart
to love will come
but like a refugee.

The refugee is the "other," those outside our professional insularities against which Verne argues so effectively, those who (if we show them hospitality) will enlarge our hearts, lead us inexorably to the call for justice that is central to Verne's (and Derrida's) conceptions of the archive of memory and forgetting, of our role as mediators of past, present, and future. The refugee, the other, is also inside, our suppressed interior selves, our longing for justice that is stilled by convention, regulation, peer pressure. And by such professional (and personal) reorientation will come the warmth of love rather than the cold march of method, the bonding with social relevance rather than professional (and personal) detachment.

Ring the bells that still can ring
Forget your perfect offering

Again, we hear the music, through bells, the ringing, the placing aside (or at least in their proper and subordinate place) of our professional desire for the perfect offering—the masterful model, the consummate metadata, the absolute theory. Such offerings are but positivist illusions, reflecting a desire for controlling power that remains blind to always changing contexts of time, place, language, and tradition. Rather than perfection in standards and models, Verne urges us to recognize that

There is a crack, a crack in everything
That's how the light gets in.

Using deconstruction, inspired by Derrida's hope of an ever-coming justice, Verne's refracting telescope, as with Cohen's metaphor, explores these "cracks" to let the light into archives. His essays do three broad things, and his view of archivy counsels all archivists to do the same. First, we must identify in our monolithic professional mantras these existing but unacknowledged cracks (which might involve exposing systems of power shaping records; language and classification conventions that have been "naturalized" as normal; media and textual blindnesses; archival theories and traditions accepted as universal rather than contingent; record-keeping models or descriptive standards applied as professional mantras). Secondly, we must have (or develop) the will to let the light of difference in through these cracks, now exposed and widened by the analysis of deconstruction, so archives may move from the oppressive to the liberatory, from straitjackets of convention to fountains of creativity. Finally, with such enlightened mindsets and practices, we then invite through hospitality an engagement with the other, the marginalized, those who are not us (creators, managers, many types of users, other professions' heritage curators), in order to break down those insularities that plague most professions and all ideologies. This, ultimately, invites an archive always opening to justice. These are neither easy concepts nor uncontested terrain, but Verne argues them in these pages with a novelist's clarity of prose and a musician's sense of rhythm, making the results intellectually palatable and emotionally satisfying.

*     *     *     *     *

Verne Harris's writing deserves the recognition and celebration that this Society of American Archivists' volume affords. In the past decade, almost single-handedly, he has brought a South African consciousness to the annals of English-speaking archival literature on a worldwide basis. More importantly, he has transformed archival thinking in that wider world in some fundamental ways. This goes well beyond the eloquent force of his prolific ideas about archives in our time. His personal openness and warm support have encouraged many to rethink their unquestioned assumptions, their routinized responses, their traditional ways of seeing and knowing. Rather than suppress ideas within accepted professional discourse, colleagues are encouraged by him—freed by him—to turn the interior "other" into public articulations, inner imaginings into exterior actions.

This book is not, however, easy to categorize. In one sense, given the admirable transparency of its author, it is a professional autobiography of how one archivist has been shaped by experiences, in Verne's case the end of apartheid and the growth of a new democracy in South Africa, and the part that archives can play (and have played) in these momentous changes. And the autobiography is still very much in process, for Verne's career is far from over. It is also a book of advanced archival theory, both a sustained and devastating critique of most of our inherited assumptions and beliefs and an inspired articulation of an alternative path to shape quite different archives for the new century. Part of this reflects lessons Verne learned the hard way in the archival transformation in South Africa; part of it from his Derridean deconstruction of almost every aspect of accepted, "naturalized," mainstream archival thinking. It is also a book about the politics of archival work, and such related public policies as freedom of information, privacy, records destruction, and records for accountability. Ultimately, it is a very ethical book, delineating a philosophy of archives, of how an "examined" profession, like the philosopher's examined life, could act morally in the world by repositioning archives for justice.

To me, Verne personifies the archivist as humanist. From his youthful exploration of the existentialism of Albert Camus and Bob Dylan to his mature engagement with Jacques Derrida's plea for justice for the other; from his long, personal struggles against apartheid in his native land to his tearful horror standing alone at Auschwitz, Verne wears nakedly his deep concern for his fellow human beings. For justice. For sharing. For mentoring. For caring. For reaching across generations, genders, races, peoples, hemispheres, traditions, ways of knowing, of remembering, of forgetting. For listening responsibly to our inner goodness and making moral choices rather than depending on (hiding behind?) standards, rules, models, templates, and codes. For our rich connections with others that alone, as he said in one of his novels, give "a semblance of significance to our lives."

Despite Verne's impressive record of judicious administration of archival programs and much practical accomplishment, there is to him much more of the soulful spirit than senior manager. Because, for Verne, archives are not so much about paper and diskettes, boxes and storerooms, buildings and budgets, standards and procedures. Archives are about memory, continuity, linkages, community, heritage, humanity—about allowing the solace of remembering and the balm of forgetting to move the spirit, to open us evermore sensitively to the possibilities of justice. Archives for Verne are a passion, not a profession or a job—a feverish heat, a sensuous partner—*mal d'archive* indeed. Beyond this passionate humanism, perhaps intrinsic to it, archives for Verne are also about politics; indeed, in one essay that follows, he argues that the archive *is* politics: issues of freedom of information, accountability, ethics, illegal record destruction, respect for the other ways and means of seeing, organizing, describing, accessing, knowing, indeed, direct participation in lobbying, fighting for change, addressing society through popular media rather than staying safely within our comfortable archival cloisters. This is not politics as in left wing or right wing, liberal or conservative, Republican or Democrat, but politics as engagement, as committing the archives to societal interventions for justice rather than curatorial passivity under the guise (and illusion) of professional neutrality.

To support the above rather broad (!) assertions, I could take this preface in one of two directions. For those who know my work (but not my relationship with Verne), perhaps the expected one would be a critical analysis of Verne's publications and lectures that follow, against the background of his career positions and education; a kind of mini-deconstruction of his own ideas in light of the general conditions of postmodernity and South African liberation, accompanied by scores of footnotes and an avalanche of quotations from his many works and those who support and criticize him. But that is not the magical level on which Verne and I interact in our almost continual personal connection, and so, in keeping with the spirit of this volume, and its author, I offer instead another approach: an archival rave, a medley of metaphors, an improvisation of impressions. When Verne resigned from the National Archives of South Africa, I was invited to prepare some comments for an internal publication on the theme, "jazz and the archive—all that jazz," in relation to Verne's career, to improvise new rhythms, new phrasings, new beats, new ways of finding Verne and his writing. I want to revisit that theme, back to those musical roots.[1]

---

[1] For this earlier source, see Terry Cook, "Archival Jazz: Verne Harris and the Rhythm of Memory," in Ethel Kriger, ed., *Wresting the Archon From the Arkheion—A Question of Right(s) and a Call for Justice to Always Come? A 'Festschrift' Celebrating the Ongoing Life-Work of Verne Harris* (Pretoria: National Archives of South Africa, 2001), xi–xxi. I acknowledge and thank again Ethel Kriger for assigning me what I first thought was an impossible topic, and later realized was perfect to capture Verne's spirit and mindset.

*   *   *   *   *

Jazz plays a central role in Verne's life and an important one in South Africa. Jazz started out as the classic "other," in its origins in North America and in the black townships under apartheid. Rooted in African-American culture, product of the Deep South, legacy of slavery, jazz initially offended middle-class, moralistic, white America. Jazz was perceived by mainstream America as nonsense, alarming, even dangerous. So, too, was its earlier contemporary, the Mississippi Delta blues, and so, later on, would be their combined progeny, rock-and-roll. Township jazz in South Africa was similarly born in oppression, used by blacks there to voice the sounds of liberation and group identity, and it not surprisingly alarmed white conservatives in power.

Jazz was sensual—the product, its early critics said, of New Orleans's brothels and savage barbarism. Black racial power and physical sensuality were then very frightening to mainstream America. So was the music itself. Unlike any previous popular music, let alone "serious" classical music, jazz was not written down. Jazz was of the heart, not the head. Usually unrehearsed, intensely improvisational, highly individualistic, alive with new syncopated rhythms, and animated by a new driving beat, jazz violated the norms of traditional symphonic music, where many instruments came together in unison to play a preset score. Jazz soloists instead "blew up a storm" of individuality that somehow came together to make new harmonies. Jazz was performer's art rather than composer's art, making up and telling one's own story rather than playing the stories others had written/archived. The conservative majority of white America neither liked blowing storms nor such unabashed individualism. No less a mainstream voice than industrialist Henry Ford lashed out at jazz as a symbol of all that was wrong, in his view, in the postwar period after 1918; Ford characterized jazz as

> ...waves upon waves of musical slush that invade decent parlors and set the young people of this generation imitating the drivel of morons....The mush, the slush, the sly suggestion, the abandoned sensuousness of sliding notes ... monkey talk, jungle squeals, grunts and squeaks and gasps suggestive of cave love are camouflaged by a few feverish notes.

The fear and racism in Ford's words are palpable. No wonder that the liberated, hedonistic period of the postwar 1920s was labeled the "Jazz Age" in the United States. Yet although young white America soon embraced jazz as an original American art form, this happened only after jazz was watered down, smoothed out, made palatable to white audiences and danceable to white rhythms. To do this, jazz was transformed by the 1930s into "swing" and later into the "Big Band" and "boogie-woogie" sound of the 1940s. Bands became larger, there was more teamwork among band members; the music became "cooler" compared to the original "hot jazz," the singers more melodious and more white, and the famous band leaders all white: Glenn Miller, Artie Shaw, Benny Goodman, the Dorsey Brothers. Initially inspired by jazz, Big Band jazz became nonjazz. And while raw jazz had later revivals with Charlie Parker, Miles Davis, John Coltrane, and others, especially with black performers migrating north to Chicago and New York (Harlem), jazz never regained its dominance as "the" sound of American music. That was only achieved from the 1950s onward by rock-and-roll in its many variations.

Jazz has been intensely important to Verne Harris on a personal level. While the Verne I have known since 1994 is a rocker who grooves on Elvis Presley, the Rolling Stones, the Grateful Dead, Led Zeppelin, and Bob Dylan, long before I knew him, Verne was plugged into Township Jazz—for its music and its politics, and its soul. He studied and wrote about jazz. Jazz was in fact bred in his bones. "My earliest memories," he writes in an essay partly on his father, "are infused with the magical chaos of a household moving to the rhythms of jazz. Music was his life, and the rest of us were caught up in a kaleidoscoping of parties, gigs, practising and people hanging out. I saw my father as a wild happy god dispensing music." An accomplished photographer who played drums in a jazz band, Verne's father had little patience for the nuances of academic argument that Verne would bring home from his schooling. When things at home came to a father-son impasse on that front, Verne would "suggest we rather listen to a Charlie Parker recording."

Both of Verne's novels (each national-level prize nominees in South African literature) show him working out the meaning of jazz through his own and his characters' psyches. *Where They Play The Blues* (1990) and *A Cool Anger Blowing* (1994) have obvious musical titles and, in both books, musicians are the central characters coping with life, creativity, and passion against the background of violence that was apartheid South Africa. Both novels interestingly have saxophones as their cover illustration, the first book with a cool dude blowing the instrument against the hills of the novel's setting in Verne's native Pietermaritzburg, the second featuring the instrument alone in a square frame below the title. The saxophone itself, invented by Adolphe Sax in Brussels in 1840, only came into its own with jazz at the beginning of the twentieth century. The loudest, brassiest, and jumpiest, but also the coolest and smokiest of metal wind instruments, it perfectly suited the early jazz, just as it pumped up wonderfully the instrumental breaks in many of the best early rock-and-roll songs of the 1950s. Note, too, that Verne and his father's choice of favorite recording artist, Charlie Parker, was a famed saxophonist.

Jazz. Verne. Archives. Does it mean anything? The spirit of jazz is the opposite of the soul-destroying, uptight archons of archival bureaucracy that Verne detests. Jazz liberates. Jazz is a metaphor for freedom, sexuality, emotion, and passion, for realizing that archives and memory must engage right-brain intuition as well as left-brain logic, for feminine as well as masculine sensibilities, for black as well as white experiences, for oral as well as written stories, and for the other as well as ourselves. Like much of Verne's archival writing, jazz is innovative, improvisational, creative. Jazz is individualistic, but also finds rhythms and harmonies with others as the playing goes on. Jazz is fusion of yesterday and tomorrow, uniting past trauma and future hope in a soul-expanding present. Jazz challenges power, breaks patterns, blows free. Jazz is Verne. Verne is jazz. Archival jazz: blowing wild, blowing free, blowing up a storm, blowing away the tired shibboleths of archival positivism, blowing down the walls of institutional insularity, blowing out pretentious iterations of narrow dogma, blowing with creativity, innovation, imagination, blowing in new rhythms for a new country at home and a new archival era internationally. "The answer, my friend, is blowin' in the wind," Bob Dylan once wrote, adding in a later song, that "You don't need a weather man, To know which way the wind blows."

But if we did need one, Verne would be our ideal weatherman showing which way the archival winds are blowing. His archival sax blows strongly for rhythms of inclusiveness, mystery, imagination, equality in pluralisms. He plays with sparkling creativity and warm emotion. He knows intuitively that jazz and rock are music of the heart, the guts, the loins, far more than of the head, despite the profound meaning present in the lyrics of a Bob Dylan, a Leonard Cohen, or a Billie Holiday. But no amount of intellectualizing can find meaning in the lyrics of "Hound Dog," "Louie Louie," "Get Off My Cloud," or in the scat singing of jazz. But meaning (in a logical, rational, intellectual way) is not the point of such songs. Feeling is. Emotion is. Sexuality is. Yet our archives cut out feeling, frown on emotion, suspect passion. As Bonnie Smith showed so convincingly in her book, *The Gender of History: Men, Women, and Historical Practice* (1998), the rise of "professional" history in the nineteenth century (which coincided exactly with the professionalization of archivists—who were trained as such historians) squeezed out the storytelling, the ghostly and psychic, the spiritual and the feminine (and of course all "amateur" women practitioners), in favor of men (exclusively) pursuing a "scientific" and "professional" history within the cloister of the archives and the battleground of the highly competitive university seminar. Such historians (and archivists) ignored in their work the real life in families, farms, factories, and local community in favor of national politics, administration, diplomacy, and war. They also venerated their "scientific" methods as fact-based, objective, dispassionate—a means to recover the Truth about the past.

By contrast, listen to Verne, the archival musician, blowing hard and blowing sweet on archival appraisal, a topic dear to my own heart:

> For the feverish, the only people a self-respecting archival institution would want in its appraisal programme, appraisal is an impossible challenge. But they tackle it with passion, believing in the impossible. They tell their story, the vigorous exercise of reason not diminished by the dancing of their imaginations. They tell their story, jealous of its beauty but knowing that there are other tellings, other stories which they might have chosen instead. And their story … has no ending. For the story has been archived; it is the archive. And there is no closing of the archive. In the words of Jacques Derrida, "it opens out of the future."

Making this crystal clear, Verne asks, "Who would want to be an appraiser? Only the feverish, or those too stupid to realise what they are letting themselves in for." What is this "fever"—this *Archive Fever*? Verne answers that "appraisal is a fever characterised by obsessive remembering and forgetting." This insight actually came to Verne long before he was exposed to Jacques Derrida or my ideas about macroappraisal. In his first novel back in 1990, he has a character at the end reflect on "an instinctive realisation that all remembering is a reworking of the past; nothing is retrieved exactly as it was experienced. And consequently, forgetting is unavoidably part of remembering."

This early insight reflects an important stop along the road Verne has traveled from Camus's rebel outsider to Derrida's feverish archivist. He was much influenced in this middle period by Jungian psychology (and I believe this still is at the emotional and intellectual heart of the man, although integrated with both his earlier existentialism and later deconstructionism). Whether Carl Jung's exploration of universal myths and the repetition of societal archetypes across place and time, Thomas Moore's neospiritual enchantment with the mysteries of daily life, or James Hillman's soulful dance with the daemons of our psyche and the role of storytelling in shaping healthy personalities, Verne's deep reading of these authors and strong attraction to their ideas is reflected in his advocacy of the poetry as well as the politics of archives, the emotive psychology as much as the epistemological philosophy of memory, the dance of imagination as much as the exercise of reason.

For an example of "archival jazz," listen to psychologist James Hillman, with my [archival editorializing added]:

> They who still hold to the rationalist and ... positivist theory of man will argue that there can be too much fantasy, that it is a flight from reality, and that the task of therapy [or archives] ... is the gradual trimming of imagination and bringing it into service of realistic goals [traditional archival theory and professional standards]. What makes a man or woman insane, they say [or makes a document unarchival, or fictional], is precisely being overwhelmed with fantasy. Too much story, story confused with history, realities gone [evidence of transactions lost].

> But the imaginative schools of therapy [or archives] ... are workers in story.... we recognize [story as] ... an authentic expression

of the soul … the historicizing activity of the psyche … a new language, a new style of ritual, and of loving … a narrative of the inner workings of the soul through time, a history of memories, dreams, reflections, sometimes disguised, but not necessarily, in empirical realities …. They move us from the fiction of reality to the reality of fiction.

In story can be found, for any individual, "my image, my dignity, my monument." Yet Hillman reminds us, too, that "there is no part of my personal record that is not at the same time the record of a community, a society, a nation, an age." The image in stories—imagination—stands half-way between "the world of now and the imperceptible eternalities of the spirit," that is, the archetypes of myth. In Greek imagining, behind Clio who was the muse of hi-story, was her mother, Mnemosyne, goddess of memory, "the imaginal, mother of historicizing, the soul's archetype," who connects us to the transcendent, to the gods, to the universal-ness of our humanity. This new therapy [as Verne also recommends for the new archives] "picks up again the oral tradition of telling stories; therapy re-stories." In this mytho-poetic context, Verne suggests, as did Hugh Taylor before him, that archivists can find new rhythms to transcend their procedural *mentalité* derived from storing paper artifacts in the stacks, new rhythms for restoring psychic health to, and so call onward justice for, individuals, communities, nations. Like Verne's feverish appraisal archivists, can we learn again to be comfortable telling our own and our communities' stories, rather than collecting evidence of the powerful? Can we become once more the narrative remembrancers of old rather than rule-bound curators? Can we blow our memory saxophones wild and free?

For possible answers, listen to Verne on archival description and descriptive standards, to which he applies an equally feverish energy as he does to appraisal:

> Our dream is of a descriptive standard which is liberatory rather than oppressive, one which works as a touchstone for creativity rather than as a straightjacket. What would the attributes of such a standard be? … A liberatory descriptive standard would not seek to hide the movements of its construction. In particular, it would not obscure the dimensions of power which it reflects and

expresses …. A liberatory descriptive standard cannot emerge from a process which is exclusive, opaque, and beyond the demands of accountability …. standards writers need to seek inclusivity and transparency. Such a standard … would seek to affirm a process of open-ended making and re-making …. It might mean providing space for researchers to embed their own stories of use within the descriptive layerings. Such a standard would, in other words, be permeable to the naming work of users, and respect (rather than banish) prior namings when new ones are articulated … would acknowledge that different categories of user deploy different semantics and require different paths into the record. It would seek to allow different ways of searching, different ways of interrogating records, different ways of organizing and manipulating representations. It would, in short, place a premium on flexibility …. A liberatory descriptive standard would … require engagement with the marginalized and the silenced. Space would be given to the sub-narratives and the counter-narratives. It would strive for an openness to other tellings and re-tellings of competing stories … a politics of ambiguity and multiplicity.

In that paragraph alone are enough stimulating ideas to set the research agenda for the profession for a generation! And as important, there are enough probing (if implicit) criticisms of how we generally do this important function to shake our comfortable self-satisfaction with approved or inherited approaches. And, as it is for Verne's questioning archival description, so too is it in his writings on appraisal, ethics, freedom of information, records destruction, and much else affecting the practical, daily concerns of archives, but now taken to a new level. We can find in Verne, just like his father, "a wild happy god dispensing music," the new archival rhythms that can free our practice and profession of the heavy, often irrelevant, dead weight of the past. Listen. Carefully.

\*　　\*　　\*　　\*　　\*

Among English-speaking archival theorists, Verne Harris most resembles Hugh Taylor. They excel in imagining what archives could be by thinking outside the box of inherited tradition and bureaucratic complacency. Yet, like Hugh, Verne is no idle or idealistic dreamer. Underpinning the language and vision of the perceptive theorist rests two decades of experience at the archival coal-face—much of it in responsible senior positions. Following undergraduate and graduate education in history at the University of Natal, Verne rejected doctoral work at Cambridge (and several lush scholarships) to pursue an archival career, starting full time as an archivist in 1985. Employed first in archives and records management positions, plus training functions, for the regional archival offices of the State Archives Service (the national archives, under apartheid) located in Natal, Transvaal, and the Orange Free State, Verne soon won positions at the head office in Pretoria, eventually rising to deputy director. With the end of apartheid in 1994, Verne's past resistance to that regime, his work for the African National Congress, and his intellectual acumen earned him the principal responsibility for writing new legislation that created the National Archives of South Africa. With the new act and institution in place, Verne became the deputy director charged with changing everything about his institution, from policy to staffing, appraisal to outreach, Eurocentric and positivist assumptions to postmodern and postcolonial sensitivities—moving, in short, a well-established institution from an exclusionist, white, racist, patriarchal archives to one striving for multicultural inclusiveness and pluralistic programs. Verne is not merely an eloquent and stimulating writer about the postmodern archive; he lived (and practiced) its central tenets through one of the great periods of turmoil in modern history. Surely the two are connected: life and ideas, biography and ideology, actions and words. His small, insightful book, *Exploring Archives: An Introduction to Archival Ideas and Practice in South Africa* (2000, second edition), encapsulates this exciting transformation of archives under the emerging South African democracy in that astonishing decade of change. The headlines that galvanized the world played out in the archival sphere as well, with Verne being the principal architect for change and its main storyteller. Verne also influenced his new country's freedom of information legislation and was the key archival voice (and a committee member) before the famous Truth and Reconciliation Commission when it explored illegal records destruction by the security forces of the old regime.

The legacy of the commission led to Verne's personal meeting and sharing a speaking platform with Jacques Derrida, the actual exchange and its impact forming the central motif of another book that Verne co-edited, *Refiguring the Archive* (2002). Derrida's influence on Verne's ideas is enormous, as the essays in this volume bear witness. More than Derridean ideas per se, or Derridean deconstruction as a way of widening those cracks and letting new light into dark or unquestioned places, it was Derrida's liberating example that inspired Verne: of seeing justice as always coming, never completely arrived; democracy ever growing, never fully achieved; the archive always opening, ever changing, never fixed or closed. Archives, Verne insists, are about dynamic record-*making*, and remaking, re-remaking, over and over, without end, rather than the traditional record-*keeping*, looking after and keeping safe some fixed recorded product as a sacred artifact. The correct stance for archivists, then, is ever questioning, never complacent; always searching for the grail of memory, while allowing forgetting, always celebrating the ever-changing contingent, which continually reinvents (remakes) the archive. In this, there is, as with Derrida (and Hugh Taylor, and James Hillman as well) something deeply spiritual, profoundly transcendent, about archives, memory, story, and their transformative powers for justice. On this point especially, Verne bristles when Derrida (or his own) writing is labeled "postmodern," with its implications of endless relativism, destructive criticism, and mindless subjectivity, all without advancing any positive alternatives. For Verne, Derrida is anything but the caricatured relativist. The reader should not be frightened away, then, I truly hope, by Verne's evocation of Derrida or deconstruction, for Verne makes these admittedly difficult ideas and this complex thinker utterly understandable.

Verne left the National Archives in the spring of 2001 to serve for three years as director of the South African History Archive (SAHA), a nongovernmental human rights organization dedicated to documenting the struggles against apartheid and to promoting freedom of information, all while building up an archives of FOI-released and otherwise-restricted materials. In many ways, SAHA has a documentation strategy to build an archives focused on the most sensitive records of the state that, for many reasons, the state did not wish to be made public. Typical of this advocacy work was another publication, *Unlocking South Africa's Nuclear Past* (2003): finding and telling alternative stories to those of power. While maintaining strong formal links to SAHA, Verne accepted his current position in June 2004 on the senior management team of the Nelson Mandela Foundation, serving as project manager of the Nelson Mandela Centre of Memory, an actual and virtual archives of Mandela's records around the world. Here so much of Verne's archival music comes together in archives for stories, for human rights, for justice, for redemption. In his personal interactions with Nelson Mandela—Madiba is the fond sobriquet for the nation's grand old man—Verne is exploring the power of memory carried by and through this twentieth-century icon, and he is using that power—supported by the images and words from the Mandela Archive—with foundation colleagues to raise funds and launch projects to fight AIDS, poverty, and illiteracy. An early product of this new work is an international bestseller by a team of authors that Verne led: *A Prisoner in the Garden: Opening Nelson Mandela's Prison Archive* (2005). An ongoing feature is a series of history comic books, based on Madiba's life and his archives, aimed at those with limited literacy skills; over one million copies of the first issue are circulating.

Since the late 1990s, Verne has been teaching, on a part-time basis, postgraduate courses on archives, memory, and society for the University of the Witwatersrand's Graduate School for the Humanities and Social Sciences. During most of the 1990s, he was editor of South Africa's scholarly archival journal. And through all this myriad of accomplishment and senior positions, he wrote scores and scores of published articles and conference speeches, newspaper columns and government reports, advocacy position papers and lobbying briefs, to say nothing of two novels, published poetry, and, yes, even three years of columns as the jazz music critic for a major Pretoria newspaper. Such richness from an archivist not yet fifty years old offers inspiration and wisdom, and, not surprisingly, Verne's influence has been felt by personal visits, powerful lectures, and wise conversation with colleagues in Canada, the United States, the United Kingdom, Australia, and New Zealand as well as in Germany, Norway, the Netherlands, and in several African countries—and of course at home in South Africa.

Verne's work is not above criticism; even fine musicians will occasionally sound a wrong note, or misinterpret a colleague's cue in a jamming session. His breadth of vision can overlook the painful work in creating and implementing the (often prosaic) minutiae of archivy, such as the necessity of having very detailed, rule-based approaches to descriptive standards if computers are to communicate with each other, details that Verne's wider publics will need to share the riches of the archives. Like Derrida, he tends to see electronic record-keeping issues in terms of memory metaphors or power politics, with little acknowledgment in his writing of the kind of elaborate metadata schemas necessary if reliable records are to exist to make governments, as he wishes them, more accountable, transparent, and democratic. Even macroappraisal—which finds his hearty endorsement—is seen in part by him as a revivifying of Schellenbergian evidential values, despite its originator's vigorous denial that such was not the intent or result, nor indeed contained in the wording of any of the accompanying procedural documents. These examples may suggest an impatience with the working out of archival methodologies and detailed procedures, intellectually challenging as these are to accomplish, and necessary as they are to achieve Verne's own visions of archives for justice. Here is a difficult line to negotiate, between means and ends, between methods and ideals, and there is sometimes a disconnection between Verne's criticizing of the former and extolling the latter.

Verne's love affair with Jacques Derrida has generated wonderful insights into the archive, as the pages in this book make clear in so many places, but what of Derrida's faults, his blindspots? Of these we hear little. What of parallel thinkers, such as Michel Foucault, whose insights—long before Derrida addressed the archive directly in the mid-1990s—situated archives in the nexus of power, exposed "naturalized" language and classification conventions as contingent on time and place, highlighted the neglect of the marginalized and the other. Verne does not explore these connections. This focus on Derrida perhaps exposes a larger concern where Verne has more recently eschewed the terms *postmodern* and *postmodernism*—despite using them in several articles and titles himself—as too vast a musical score to allow the sounds of deconstruction to be heard, or Derrida's gorgeous melodies to soar. At one level, this is fair enough, and a symbolic distinction is appropriate, but at another level it excludes those "postmodern" archivists who make common cause with Verne—often inspired by him, and inspiring him, too—against the traditional, rule-based, procedure-bound, technocratic nostrums of still far too much of modern archivy. Where is the hospitality of forcing a semantic division between like-minded colleagues? Of course, *postmodernism* as a catch-all term is sweeping and distorting, and there are many postmodernisms, but, like *Marxism, feminism,* or *imperialism,* these terms still do mean something. To criticize postmodernism generally on several key points, as Verne does, and his comments are typically right on target, implies, since he does not say otherwise, that archival theorists advocating postmodern archives subscribe to these criticized points, and that is both unfair and inaccurate. Of course, postmodern archivists—Verne included—are a mass of contradictions: advocating inclusive, diverse, multiple-voiced archives; reaching out to the other; exposing "power" behind allegedly objective curatorial practices; extolling hospitality to welcome so much into a redefined archivy that traditionally has been rejected; and yet, at the same time, disdaining, excluding, even mocking (or coming very close to doing so) the "other" that is neopositivist or neo-Jenkinsonian, those who are continuum and metadata modelers, as archons of bureaucracy and procedure. Is that hospitality? Or merely the ideal inevitably meeting the always-flawed human pursuing any grail? Can one draw lines in the sand against ideas that seem fundamentally flawed or outdated, and yet at the same time welcome into dialogue colleagues holding those very ideas? Where, then, lies the duty of hospitality and that of honesty to one's own beliefs? There are no easy answers, only a continual inviting to opening, to including both or many sides, not with the intent to achieve some watery bland consensus, but to welcome justice in the broadest senses outlined above. In this opening the archive, and reaching across traditions and archival mindsets, Verne sets an admirable example in his person and writing, but not an unflawed one.

For Verne, ultimately, archives—and archiving—are profoundly spiritual, involving conceptual and emotional frames where he finds himself "hopelessly (in Derridean terms) religious." This is not the fundamentalist Calvinist Christianity in which he was raised in white South Africa, and which he rejected utterly for its dogma and literalism, its exclusivity and moralism. But it is about embracing spiritual essences, finding (as does Hugh Taylor) spirituality in the very traces of our common humanity preserved in archives, especially in the newly inclusive, pluralistic archives Verne (and Derrida) challenges us to accept as our responsibility to create, all in the transcendent faith that tomorrow will care about the records we preserve today. In a recent personal message (capitalization corrected!), Verne asserted that my religion is about an embrace of otherness ... defined by one other, by a community of others, by society. The embrace is not about a new age existential subjectivism. It is an embrace FOR justice, and THROUGH story. Such an embrace is about re-spect [as in seeing again, seeing anew]. It is about neighbourliness .... It holds uncertainty, and mystery. It speaks, if it speaks, in the language of poetry. It learns the possible and does it better than anyone else, even while it yearns for the impossible. It never rests. But it is always profoundly at rest. It knows, concedes, discloses the contingent. But it believes in the transcendent .... The test is archive. The test is in archive. The voice of the other.

That is the challenge—the test—that Verne sets for us in these essays and the example of his career.

Despite his own important work, and that of others, in addressing this challenge and actually designing successful archival programs to further some of these goals, this is no time for resting on any archival laurels. Derrida is clear that democracy, or justice, or the perfect archive, is always coming, always in process, never arrived, never achieved. The "test" of archive is always changing, for the "other" by definition is always changing. One reviewer of this book's manuscript summarized Verne's message: "We must continually seek to question our values and methods in order to pursue societal well being and justice. Harris's foregrounding of this aim for archives is bracing and challenging. It is not what we usually hear in archival circles. It is a challenge we need to heed....Harris offers a valuable roadmap for doing so, based on his extraordinary experience at the heart of archival responses to a historic moment in world political and social history."

And that is where archives, jazz, deconstruction, music, poetry, spirituality, and justice all come together for imagining relevant archives for a new millennium—in Verne's "roadmap" in the following pages, his own songbook, where through the many cracks he opens much more widely, "the light gets in."

\* \* \* \* \*

Verne gives us the poetry and music of a new archive, and so many rich arguments for freeing ourselves from constraining shibboleths so that archives may be transformed for justice. In the new archive, ever opening, never fixed or closed, respecting story, inviting multiple stories, people in society will in turn be freer from the metanarratives of power. Thereby communities may be restored through memory and hi-story to spiritual health. Not surprisingly given his own involvement at many levels in South Africa's long march to freedom, freeing archives for justice is Verne's passion as well as his argument. Let me end, then, keeping to the theme of this preface, by giving Verne's career and writing their appropriate musical encapsulation, with the lyrics from Leonard Cohen as they might—with much justification—emerge from Verne's own songbook:

> Like a bird on the wire
> Like a drunk in a midnight choir
> I have tried in my way to be free.

Join him in archival song.

TERRY COOK
*Ottawa / Winnipeg, Canada*
January 2007

# INTRODUCTION

## Reaching for Hospitality

> There is a crack in everything.
> That's how the light gets in. [1]

## INSULARITIES

I find it difficult to understand professional discourses that do not at least seek to engage with broader public discourses. Such insularity is something I regard as both inappropriate and misguided. No doubt this has a lot to do with my experience as an archivist working in the contexts of struggle against apartheid and the subsequent transition to democracy in South Africa. I would argue, however, that in any set of contexts, such insularity assumes a privilege and an elevation impossible to justify. The work collected in *Archives and Justice* expresses, in this sense, a resistance to insularity. The op-eds reproduced in section

---

[1] Leonard Cohen, *Stranger Music: Selected Poems and Songs* (Jonathan Cape, London, 1993), 373.

5 illustrate my deliberate endeavors to bring awareness of archive to popular debates in South Africa.

As with all professionals, archivists are challenged by many layers of insularity. It is tempting, for example, to ignore dimensions of power, of politics, and of ethics when engrossed in the minutiae of method, technique, and procedure. In section 2, I have included essays that explore the degree to which the nuts and bolts of archival work are permeable to and, arguably, determined by the tracing of power. Another example: dominant discourses in the West are shaped by the assumption of a hard boundary between "fiction" and "non-fiction," making it difficult for archivists to allow what I call (more or less loosely) poetry into their domain. To a great degree, professional archival discourses are insulated from the energies of imagination, passion, mystery, and wonder. Amongst other prices paid is a dryness relieved only by a small (but growing) number of voices. (This is the root, I would suggest, of the boredom that infuses archives conference sessions around the world.)

We all have what I call our insularities. I am painfully aware of the extent to which I have been shaped, both as a human being and as an archivist, by the specificities and contingencies of space and time. My work, if you like, is strongly *located*—"South," "Africa," "global margins," "South Africa," "transition from apartheid to democracy." It needs to be read, then, along and against the grain of its contexts. Like any archives. Throughout the essays in *Archives and Justice,* I have strained to make it relatively easy for readers to find the grain.


## SELECTIONS

Before the formal transition to democracy in South Africa (1990–1994), I worked in the apartheid-era State Archives Service with my head well down and my energies focused around the role of mole. It was important for my bosses not to perceive me as subversive. My professional writings of necessity, then, were geared to a space defined by acute insularities. Consciously and deliberately I wrote with passion only in terrains outside the professional—fiction, jazz reviews, and historiography.

Two other layers of insularity in my pre-1994 professional writing are worthy of note. (These I explore briefly in the essay "Concerned with the Writings of Others" in section 1.) The cultural and related boycotts of apartheid South Africa effectively isolated South African archivists. While I read foreign publications, until 1994 I never traveled outside the country in my professional capacity, never wrote for a non–South African audience, and was denied active participation in international archival discourses. Connected to this insularity was my own schooling in positivist frames of reference, which were dominant in the academy and beyond in South Africa through the 1980s. So-called postmodernisms were given short shrift, and my own readings in these frames were hesitant and dilettantish. That changed, as did my international isolation, with the visit of Terry Cook to South Africa in 1994. For me, that visit was a major crack (in Leonard Cohen's terms), and Terry has remained a close friend and inspiration ever since.

*Archives and Justice* is a selection of work from the post-1994 period. For South Africa, that year marked the formal ending of apartheid. For me, as an archival thinker and writer, it marked my release from a straitjacket. I have included two pieces that carry strong tracings of earlier insularities—"Exploratory Thoughts on Current State Archives Service Appraisal Policy and the Conceptual Foundations of Macro-appraisal" (section 2) and "Toward a Culture of Transparency" (section 4). I invite readers to contrast them with the essays that follow in each section respectively—the juxtaposition, I think, contours the strait-jacket and sounds the release.

In selecting pieces, I have looked deliberately for those that best express a deconstructive frame of reference, the frame with which I am most comfortable now. Damascus road experiences, of course, are rare, and in my case deconstruction has seeped steadily into my work, especially after my 1998 meeting with Jacques Derrida in Johannesburg (recounted in the section 1 essays "A Shaft of Darkness" and "Something Is Happening Here and You Don't Know What It Is"). As far as possible, I have avoided reworking pieces, concentrating on adding footnotes, ensuring consistent spelling and layout, and removing parts that duplicate inordinately material used in other pieces included in the collection. (In the pre-editing for *Archives and Justice,* I discovered how readily overburdened schedules had drawn me into the temptation of electronic technologies' cut-and-paste option!)

I have grouped the work selected into five section containers, with a chronological sequence followed within each container. None of these containers is, or can be, impermeable. Individual pieces have been assigned a placing in terms of the primary locus of my intention (as I can best remember it) in each case. Section 1 groups pieces in which I have grappled with particular discourses around archives. Section 2 explores the stories archivists tell in certain domains of professional work—appraisal, electronic recordmaking, and arrangement and description. Section 3 groups pieces in which I have dealt directly with the politics and ethics of archives. Section 4 documents my sustained engagement with the tightly interlinked issues of troubled pasts, "the secret," and freedom of information in South Africa. The rationale for section 5 was outlined at the beginning of this introduction.

I would like to record my gratitude to the people who collaborated with me on some of the pieces included in the book (and who agreed to their republication): Wendy Duff, Evelyn Groenink, Sello Hatang, Peter Liberman, Christopher Merrett, and Rolf Sorenson. Shared passion is what brought us together. I am grateful also to the many readers who waded through first drafts of pieces being prepared for initial publication, notably Terry Cook and Kerry Harris, who consistently have been sounding boards and mentors.

## HOSPITALITIES

I have typified the work collected in this book as an expression of resistance to insularities. Such resistance is predicated on, and calls forth, a hospitality to what is outside the boundary, to what is "other." As I have already intimated, my own insistence on hospitality's primacy probably flows out of my experience of living apartheid insularities and fighting for release from them. Notwithstanding this necessary imprint of the subjective, through the last decade I have reached for a hospitality located beyond the bounds of the particular. I like to think that this is the strongest thread running through the work collected in *Archives and Justice*.

The "Archives" of the book's title risks obscuring my hospitality to ways of knowing "archive" that are "other" to the dominant discourses in Western English-language archivy. This "otherness" has come to me over the last decade most insistently from the work of Jacques Derrida (for focused engagement with it, see the essays comprising section 1) and what are called indigenous knowledges in my part of the world (see in particular "Archives, Identity and Place" in section 3). It has forced me to re-imagine who I am and what I do as an archivist. Indeed, I have coined the term "recordmaker" (and its derivatives) to suggest the complexity of the space I find myself in. To repeat a working definition offered in the essay "A World Whose Only Horizon Can Be Justice" (section 3): in this space archivists—together with the creators of records, the managers of records, the users of records, and a host of other players—narrate the meanings and significances of "the record" in an open-ended and contested process. The record, then, is always in the process of being made. And all of us who narrate its meanings and significances, whether we do so in a togetherness of hospitality or in a separateness of insularity, are recordmakers. The work of the archivist in this schema is as far removed from the traditional custodial role as is homemaking from housekeeping. The first published articulation of this concept by me is recorded in the essay "Stories and Names," co-authored with Wendy Duff. My use of the unhyphenated "recordmaker," as opposed to the hyphenated "record-keeper," should be noted. It marks my belief that recordmaking, like homemaking, is an archetypal activity flowing in its deepest reaches from the human soul. Record-keeping, on the other hand, like house-keeping, reaches most deeply into the realms of functional imperative and the pragmatic deployment of resources.

The harsh reality is that the shape (and the shaping) of recordmaking is determined by relations of power. My energies have been focused on understanding this in the shifting contexts of South Africa, but always I have looked for the structural dynamics to be found wherever recordmaking happens. The "Justice" of this book's title expresses my belief that the contexts of power in which recordmakers find themselves, and their unavoidable participation (their complicity) in the exercise of power, makes the call of justice the most important call of all. The essays in sections 1 to 3 could be read as an attempt to make this argument, while those in sections 3 to 5 could be read as an attempt to heed the call in specific contexts. The difference, if you like, between speaking of power and speaking to power. For me, any attempt to heed the call of justice is fundamentally about hospitality. It is, at once, to reach for what is not known (for what is, possibly, unknowable), and to reach out to those excluded or marginalized by prevailing relations of power.

Here I follow Derrida and Levinas, who argue that justice, if there be such a thing, is best understood as a relation to "the other."

Of course, hospitality—as a yardstick, as an ethic (see, in particular, the essays in section 3)—is impossible. How many of us, for example, would even aspire to an opening of the door to every stranger? How many of us care about, less wish to invite in, "the enemy"? But the point is that we human beings have been given a capacity to yearn for the impossible. Our calling, in my view, is to reach beyond learning to be good at doing the possible.

## CRACKS

"There is a crack," according to Leonard Cohen, "in everything." Those who fought against apartheid in South Africa found the crack in the system and ultimately forced it open. Speaking to power in any context is predicated on belief in a crack that can be forced open. It remains the belief of those in postapartheid South Africa who engage in continuing struggles for justice. Much of my work can be positioned in this space.

A hard lesson to learn for those of us (for everyone) whose daily tools are words, concepts, and discourses is that language invites light in through its cracks. Meaning and significance dance beyond the stable containers defined in dictionaries, models, and systems. In the same way, the meanings and significances of a record are located in the shifting, infinite reaches of context around it. Opening the crack to this impossible richness is the work of the archivist.

I speak here of at least three orders of "crack" (and each is implicated in the others). Understanding their connectedness, for me, is the fundamental insight of what is called "deconstruction." Of course, it is one thing to see the crack. That is the role assigned to deconstruction by those who have not offered it the basic courtesy of engagement. It is another thing to call the light in by forcing the crack. That is the role taken on by deconstruction in heeding the call of justice. That is hospitality.

VERNE HARRIS

# SECTION I

# DISCOURSES

# CHAPTER 1

## Claiming Less, Delivering More: A Critique of Positivist Formulations on Archives in South Africa[1]

### INTRODUCTION

The struggle against apartheid and the building of democracy has worked, and continues to work, fundamental changes in the sphere of social memory. And, increasingly, the manifold repositories and dynamics of memory in South Africa are being reshaped by technological revolution, international engagement, and exposure to the conditions of postmodernity.[2] This is the shifting ground on which archives—as discipline, profession, repository of memory, public service—finds itself. The 1990s have seen the supplanting of a sterile, outmoded archival discourse by what I call a transformation discourse—one informed by the assumption that archives require reinvention for a democratic South Africa.[3] This discourse connects assuredly with the country's new societal dynamics and underpins endeavors to transform South Africa's archives system.[4] And yet, as I shall argue in this article, in the same way that apartheid patterns in society are proving extremely resilient, in archives many of our core ideas resist new realities, at most entertaining re-formation (rather than trans-formation). These ideas, or formulations, are still embedded

9

in a paradigm I would describe as pre-postmodern or, more precisely, as Positivist. They continue to shape fundamentally how archivists conceptualize themselves and their endeavors.[5] They also raise significant questions about the nature of transformation in South African archives.

## POSITIVIST FORMULATIONS

By "Positivist" I refer to ideas stemming from the Positivism first given coherent expression by Auguste Comte in the first half of the nineteenth century and developed along various strands of Western philosophy into this century. Positivism posits a universe governed by natural laws, and a reality that is knowable. This knowledge is attainable through the exercise of reason and the application of empirical methods. The one who knows, the subject, stands apart from the natural world, the object. Science, and scientific inquiry, hold pre-eminent intellectual authority and carry the key to an inevitable human progress toward peace, prosperity, wisdom, and dominion over nature. This is the crucible of ideas out of which modern archives—"archival science"—emerged in the nineteenth century. We have traveled a long road since then, but, it is my contention, many of the route markers continue to bear a Positivist imprint.

At the outset, I wish to record several disclaimers. Firstly, I am not suggesting the existence of a coherent Positivist position or school of thought. Secondly, I am not suggesting that there is any one individual who would align (him)herself with all the formulations that I outline below. Thirdly, I am not denying the impact on South African archival discourse of later manifestations of modernism in Western philosophy. And fourthly, I am not disputing the fact that meaningful transformation is taking place in South African archives. What I am suggesting is that archival discourse in this country is dominated by a Positivist paradigm that has been dominant for a very long time and that cries out for interrogation.

Let me offer an outline of what I regard as the core Positivist formulations:

1. The meaning of the word *archives* is simple, stable, and uncontested. Archives are documents or records, in whatever medium, identified for preservation in archival custody; an

archives is the place where such records are preserved, or an institution providing such places.[6] The same attributes apply to a host of related words—*archive, archivist, record, document, copy, original, unique,* and so on.

2. Archives, in the sense of archival records, are the organic and innocent product of processes exterior to archivists and reflect, provide an image of, are evidence of, those processes.[7] Stated more crudely, the idea is that archives reflect reality.

3. While it is true that transformation discourse has substituted the notion of archivists as *impartial* custodians with the view of them as active shapers of social memory,[8] this discourse
   • still defines archival endeavor in terms of custodianship and conceptualizes archives in terms of physical things and places of custody;
   • proposes a (narrower) shaping of the record as the carrier of memory rather than a (broader) participation in the processes of memory formation; and
   • posits the primary archival challenge as being the preservation of a wider and richer reflection of reality.

4. Archives are South Africa's central memory institutions, preserving (holding, keeping) the collective memory of the nation.[9]

5. South Africa's transformation project in archives is interpreted in triumphalist terms.[10] Particular emphasis is placed on
   • the emergence of numerous new archival institutions in the last decade;
   • the formulation of national policies on heritage, archives, and related fields through broadly participative processes;
   • the passing of the National Archives of South Africa Act as the first of several interlinking pieces of legislation that will form the framework within which a new national archives system will develop;
   • the considerable support given by public archives to the Truth and Reconciliation Commission, the Commission

for the Restitution of Land Rights, the Investigation Task Unit, and other public bodies;
- the growing number and range of archives users;
- the expansion of oral history projects; and
- the National Archives' new mandates to fill gaps in its collections and to reach out to less privileged sectors of society.

# A CRITIQUE

## Words

I would now like to take each of the formulations in turn, beginning with the word *archives,* and offer a critique from what could be called a postmodernist (certainly a post-Positivist) perspective. The French philosopher Jacques Derrida regards the word *archive* as the least reliable, least clear of any today.[11] It was Freud, with his unfolding of the unconscious and repression (that instinct of forgetfulness at the very heart of memorization), who made possible the idea of an "archive" without "archives."[12] Michel Foucault defined "the archive" as the assemblage of all discursive formations existing in a given society.[13] Derrida himself, with his insistence on sign rather than image, questions any simple notion of archives as the documentation of process, let alone as a reflection of reality.[14] Within archival discourse narrowly defined, on the international stage there are a growing number of theorists indebted to postmodernism who are reconceptualizing the word *archives.* Much of their endeavor involves finding meaning for the word in the electronic environment. This is a complex tapestry, but let me pull out a few threads to illustrate what is involved:
- "…The structure, content, and context of electronic records exist in virtual or conceptual rather than in physical reality … there is information scattered in many places which the software and operating system stitch together at a particular moment in time to form that logical or virtual document."[15]
- With technologies like geographical information systems, relational databases, and hypertext formats, where users are presented with a series of constantly changing data "views," it is difficult to "detain" or "fix" a record.

- What constitutes "the record" in a database environment? The whole database? "Views" of the database, in electronic or hard copy form? The trace of a transaction between a user and the database?
- Electronic record-keeping renders the words *original* and *unique* meaning-less, and invests others—such as *archive, copy,* and *file*—with extraordinary complexity.

My point, simply, is this: the words and concepts that are archivists' basic tools are anything but simple, stable, and uncontested. The ground is shifting.

## A Reflection of Reality

And it slides away precipitously beneath notions of the archival record as a reflection of reality. Of course, the assumption that there is "a reality" capable of reflection in records is debatable from a number of perspectives. This full frontal attack I shall forego, offering instead three outflanking maneuvers. Firstly, even if there is "a reality," ultimately it is unknowable. The event, the process, the origin, in its *uniqueness,* is irrecoverable, unfindable. As Derrida points out: "The possibility of the archiving trace, this simple *possibility,* can only divide the uniqueness."[16] Secondly, while it is self-evident that the record is a product of process, it must be acknowledged that process is shaped fundamentally by the record or, more precisely, by the act of recording. Compare, for instance, someone penning a letter to a friend with the same person sending an e-mail communication to the friend. Not only are the experiences vastly different—in terms of duration, susceptibility to response, use of materials, use of the human body, and so on—but each medium stimulates particular thought patterns, encourages particular tones, or registers and fosters particular uses of language. Essentially, e-mail communication is a combination of conversation and correspondence; it is both, and it is neither. And thirdly, if archival records reflect reality, they do so complicitly, and in a deeply fractured and shifting way. They do not speak by themselves. They speak through many voices, including those of archivists. Far from enjoying an exteriority in relation to the record, archivists participate in the complex processes through which the record feeds into social memory. Let me illustrate these various points with the example of a researcher consulting a correspondence file originating from a government office:

- There are the voices of the documents' authors, formal and informal. Who are they? What functional-structural context animates and shapes them? What are their purposes, explicit and implicit? What are they hiding? What do they fail to see?

- There are the voices (usually silent) of the bureaucrats who used and managed the file. Did they place all relevant documentation on the file? It could be that related documents were placed on other files. It could be that material was never filed officially, but rather kept informally by officials and subsequently disposed of. Documents, even whole files, may have been destroyed to protect the interests of individuals or the office. So the researcher might be, and in most cases will be, looking at a partial, deliberately constructed representation of process. And the representation, as Foucault has demonstrated in various contexts, will bear indelibly the markings of the bureaucratic systems which spawned it.

- There are the voices of archivists. Why did they choose to preserve the file? What related records did they choose not to preserve? What policies, strategies, and methodologies informed the decision? How have they arranged and described the file? What descriptive connections to other records have they provided? How are they making the file available? And in all of this, what narratives, what sectors of the state, what societal processes, what categories of record, what user groups are archivists privileging?

(This interrogation of the file is about *context*—context to the text that the researcher reads in the file. Any reading of the text without this accompanying peeling back of layers of intervention and interpretation will be deeply flawed. And here, precisely, is the heart of archival endeavor—disclosure of context. The primary archival challenge, I would argue, is not the preservation of a wider and richer reflection of reality—although I would concede that a wider and richer documentation of *realities* is a major challenge—but rather the provision of a richer contextualization of what is preserved.)

- But to return one last time to the government correspondence file, there are the voices of the researchers who use the file. Each one brings to the reading a unique perspective, and each one adds his/her own voice to the many others through which the file speaks. So there can be no closing of the file, no closing of the archive. Each new user voice, indeed merely the *possibility* of a new user voice, will keep it open, as, of course, will the constantly changing archival context. Over time the file will be joined in archival custody by other records, its description will be expanded or revised, and it will be made available in different ways and contexts. And, if the file were an electronic record, it would continually be renewed (and reshaped) as it is migrated forward to new generations of technology. The archive, as Derrida puts it, "opens out of the future."[17]

## Defining the Role of Custody and Custodianship

The ground is also shifting under the notion that custody and custodianship define the archive. The electronic age is moving archivists inexorably into what has been called a postcustodial era.[18] One of the more tangible indications of this is the growing practice by national archives of requiring archival electronic records to be managed in environments other than archives repositories.[19] But there are many other indicators. Electronic record-keeping is forcing archivists into active involvement in the processes of record creation. There they are confronted by complex and fluid organizational structures and systems, information in vast quantities, records not visible to the human eye, and virtual rather than physical records. These realities are reshaping profoundly core archival functions. We are having to shift our focus from archives to archiving, from physical things to processes. Success in this new world hinges to a large extent on our willingness, in the words of Terry Cook, to "… stop being custodians of things and start being purveyors of concepts."[20]

## Archives as Memory of the Nation

The notion that custody and custodianship define the archives underpins, of course, the view of South African archives as holding the collective memory of the nation. Setting aside the question of whether the term *collective memory* means anything at all, this view dismisses the role of libraries, museums, art galleries, and other repositories of memory, not least the memories of individuals. It also suggests a glibness about the complex processes through which archives record and feed into social memory. I have already addressed several aspects of this. At this point I wish simply to focus briefly on the *extent* of the archiving trace offered by archives. I shall not revisit my argument on the irrecoverability of the event, except to assert that the record provides just a sliver of a window into the event. Even if we were to preserve every record generated throughout South Africa, and conceding the remarkably comprehensive and detailed documentation of process offered by the computer, we would still only have a sliver of a window into South African experience. But of course in practice this record universum is substantially reduced through deliberate and inadvertent destruction by records creators and managers, leaving a sliver of a sliver from which archivists select what they will preserve. And they do not preserve much—for instance, at present the National Archives aims to preserve 5 percent of all public records. Moreover, no record, no matter how well protected and cared for by archivists, enjoys an unlimited lifespan. Preservation strategies can, at best, aim to save *versions* of *most* archival records.[21] So archives offer researchers a sliver of a sliver of a sliver.[22] If the repositories of archives are South Africa's central memory institutions, then we are in deep, amnesic trouble.

Let me at once insist that I am not counseling despair, nor am I portraying the archival endeavor as a Sisyphus-like act of heroic futility. A Rationalist, or worse, a Positivist reading of the "sliver of a sliver of a sliver" would lead to this conclusion. An *imaginative* reading would emphasize the preciousness of the complex fragment that we preserve and feed into social memory. Moreover, the fragment plays a fundamental role in the documentation of citizens' enduring civic, legal, property, and other rights. And archivists with records management responsibilities promote corporate efficiency, accountability, and transparency. The archival endeavor, I would argue, is of critical importance to any society. But Positivist notions prevent us from unfolding the full richness of archives and, ultimately, undermine the archival endeavor.

## Triumphalism

Finally, I turn to the triumphalist interpretation of our archival transformation project. All the tangible indications of change and development that I recounted earlier in this article constitute a sound foundation on which to build. Indeed, I would go further and say that what has been achieved in a very short space of time is remarkable. Nevertheless, the sounding of a strong cautionary note is appropriate. Much of my critique up to this point has attempted to do so indirectly. Let me complete the note by making two final direct points:

1. Derrida has argued compellingly that control over the recording of memory—what he calls "consignation"—is at the heart of political power.[23] It follows that if archives were indeed so central to social memory, then archival institutions would be powerful, well resourced, and controlled tightly by the state. The contrary, of course, is true. Even in the public sector, archives enjoy substantial professional autonomy. And with very few exceptions South African archives, in both public and private sectors, are struggling to keep the ship afloat as budget cuts and staff reductions take their toll. The same can be said of libraries, museums, and art galleries. Indeed, it could be argued that archives receive an inordinately high proportion of funding relative to their impact on society in comparison with these institutions.[24] My point, simply, is this: none of these institutions is as central to social memory as professional practitioners like to believe.

2. Transformation discourse places particular emphasis on the need for archives to reach out to society[25]—to *create* rather than merely *serve* users—and to document societal processes more fully, with special emphasis on endeavors to give voice to the voiceless.[26] These are laudable objectives, and they are generating many innovative initiatives in archives. But let me flag issues that highlight the need for caution:
    - On the one hand, archives are reaching a fraction of the audience being reached by libraries, museums, art galleries, and other repositories of memory.[27] On the other, in press-

ing to reach out more effectively, too frequently archives are opting for the neatly packaged information product rather than the rich contextualization of text. And in doing so we are contributing to what Jean-Francois Lyotard has called the "commodification of knowledge."[28] Moreover, much of our outreach provides little or no space for competing narratives. We adopt the language of metanarrative too easily, using our exhibitions, posters, pamphlets, and so on to tell the story of, for instance, the struggle against apartheid, or of nation building, or of transformation. The counternarratives, even the subnarratives, too frequently are excluded, and so we deny our audience the very space in which democracy thrives.

- South Africa has a wealth of experience with oral history and tradition, and extensive resources in these fields.[29] However, both in the work that has been done and in the planning of future projects, there is a worrying tendency to underestimate, or simply not to grasp, the problematic of converting orality into material custody. There are two aspects to this. The first is a determination to view and to utilize recorded oral history as "source" rather than as "history" in its own right.[30] This is to privilege certain forms of history, particularly academic history, over other forms. The second is a failure to understand the extent to which oral history, in the words of Isabel Hofmeyr, "live(s) by its fluidity."[31] As Lyotard has argued, "a collectivity that takes narrative as its key form of competence … finds the raw material for its social bond not only in the meaning of the narratives it recounts, but also in the act of reciting them."[32] The act of recitation *carries* the meaning. This fluid context to the "text" is inextricably linked to *inter alia* social situation, space, landscape, physical landmarks, and items of material culture,[33] and it sustains (and validates) a collectivity's re-telling, re-vision, re-interpretation of its narratives. The recording of narrative, the archiving of orality, can so easily destroy the fluidity, destroy the contextual links, alienate the speaker from the word. And the attempt to give voice to the voiceless ironically becomes a reinforcement of voicelessness.

# CONCLUSION

South African archivists, I have argued, are on shifting ground. While we are coming to terms with postapartheid societal realities, we have been less successful in coming to terms with technological revolution and the conditions of postmodernity. We cling to outmoded Positivist ideas that underpin inappropriate strategies, distorted notions of our role, and inflated accounts of our accomplishments. In doing so, we invite the kind of criticism offered by Richard Tarnas of contemporary Western culture: "In the absence of any viable, embracing cultural vision, old assumptions remain blunderingly in force, providing an increasingly unworkable and dangerous blueprint for human thought and activity."[34] Instead, we need to rediscover ourselves as contextualizers in an age where context is more complex and more fluid than ever before. We need to broaden our concept of context to accommodate our own intervention, the interdependence of the many fields and institutions making up the arena of social memory, and the importance of disclosing what is absent from the archival sliver. We need to embrace *process* rather than *product*. And we need to foster the contestation of social memory, seeing ourselves, conducting ourselves, not as referees but as contestants. Some would regard all this as a sure way of handicapping ourselves terminally—of subverting our capacity to provide services through excessive philosophizing, contextualizing, self-reflection, self-disclosure, self-deconstruction, and engagement in processes not strictly "archival." I see it as a way of opening up space for imagination, for connection, for soul. And I see it as a way toward providing a more profound and enriched transformation of South African archives.

# Endnotes

1   This article was first published in *Archivaria* 44 (1997). I must record my grateful-ness and indebtedness to Terry Cook (National Archives of Canada) and Tim Nuttall (University of Natal) for commenting on a first draft of this article. I remain, of course, fully responsible for the final text. On 24 September 1997, I presented it as a paper at the seminar *The Role Records Play in Revealing the Past*, hosted by the Alan Paton Centre and the South African Society of Archivists in Pietermaritzburg.

2   The word *postmodernity* means different things to different people. In this paper I use it in the sense employed by Jean-Francois Lyotard in his *The Postmodern Condition: A Report on Knowledge* (Minneapolis: University of Minnesota Press, 1984). He uses the word *postmodern* to describe "... the condition of knowledge in the most highly developed societies ... it designates the state of our culture following the transformations which, since the end of the nineteenth century, have altered the game rules for science, literature, and the arts" (p. xxiii). Richard Tarnas employs it similarly, positing an intellectual sensibility "increasingly bereft of established cer-tainties, yet also fundamentally open in ways it had never been before. *The Passion of the Western Mind: Understanding the Ideas that Have Shaped our World View* (New York: Ballantine Books, 1991), 394.

3   For an extended account and contextualization of this discourse, see my "Redefining Archives in South Africa: Public Archives and Society in Transition, 1990–1996," *Archivaria* 42 (Fall 1996).

4   The extent to which this discourse informed the National Archives of South Africa Act (1996) is explored in my "Transforming Discourse and Legislation: A Perspective on South Africa's New National Archives Act," *ACARM Newsletter* 18 (1996).

5   These Positivist ideas also, of course, shape what archivists understand by "the past," what archivists understand by "revealing the past," and how archivists go about "revealing the past."

6   This understanding of the word *archives* is pervasive in South African archival discourse. A good example appears in the South African Society of Archivists' *Professional Code for South African Archivists* (Pretoria: Society of Archivists, 1993), section one.

7   Numerous examples of this type of formulation could be cited. One appears in the 1995 Annual Report of the Director of Archives: *Annual Reports of the Directorate State Archives and Heraldic Services*, RP41/1996, p. 1. Another appears in the "Report on Archives in South Africa by Luli Callinicos and André Odendaal, Convenors of the Archives Sub-committee of the Arts and Culture Task Group (ACTAG)," *South African Archives Journal* 38 (1996): 35 (par. 3.1).

8   See Harris, "Redefining Archives in South Africa," 16.

9   The 1995 Annual Report of the Director of Archives, for instance, asserts that "the State Archives Service is responsible for preserving a national archival heritage ... In a sense this heritage is the collective memory of the government and the people," 1.

10   While it is true that this note is sounded loudest from political platforms, it is also heard in institutional annual reports, publicity materials, conference floors, and in the professional literature.

11   Jacques Derrida, *Archive Fever: A Freudian Impression* (Chicago and London: University of Chicago Press, 1996), 90.

12   Derrida, *Archive Fever,* 66, 91, 92.

13　Michel Foucault, *The Archaeology of Knowledge and the Discourse on Language* (New York: Pantheon, 1992), 128–30.

14　Barbara Belyea, "Images of Power: Derrida/Foucault/Harley," *Cartographica* 29, no. 2 (1992): 4, 5, 7.

15　Terry Cook, "Keeping Our Electronic Memory: Approaches for Securing Computer-Generated Records," *South African Archives Journal* 37 (1995): 89.

16　Derrida, *Archive Fever,* 100.

17　Derrida, *Archive Fever,* 68.

18　For a powerful articulation of this argument, see Terry Cook, "Electronic Records, Paper Minds: The Revolution in Information Management and Archives in the Post-custodial and Post-modernist Era," *Archives and Manuscripts* 22, no. 2 (1994). See in particular page 307 of this article.

19　The National Archives of South Africa utilizes a state computer bureau (Bureau Nucleus) for the management of its archival electronic records. It also has a policy identifying categories of electronic records that are best preserved by the creating body. See also Terry Cook, "Leaving Archival Electronic Records in Institutions: Policy and Monitoring Arrangements at the National Archives of Canada," *Archives and Museum Informatics* 9, no. 2 (1995).

20　Cook, "Electronic Records, Paper Minds," 304.

21　See the section on preservation in David Bearman's *Archival Methods*, *Archives and Museum Informatics Technical Report 9* (Pittsburgh: Archives and Museum Informatics Technical Report 9, 1989).

22　And this sliver of a sliver of a sliver is seldom more than partially described.

23　Derrida, *Archive Fever,* 4, 5.

24　Of course, the role played by archives, particularly public archives, in documenting rights and supporting records management, needs to be built into the equation.

25　See Harris, "Redefining Archives in South Africa," 18.

26　Harris, "Redefining Archives in South Africa," 17–18.

27　A comparison of visitor statistics at four Pietermaritzburg institutions illustrates the point. In 1996, the Pietermaritzburg Archives Repository received 2,096 visitors, the Tatham Art Gallery approximately 40,000, and the Natal Museum received 48,633. The Natal Society Library averaged over 2,000 a day. Of course these statistics demand interrogation. A two-hour visit to the library by someone wanting to read national newspapers has a weight very different to that of a day-long visit to the archives by a historian researching a textbook that will impact thousands of students. By the same token, a family of three's morning at the museum or art gallery has a different weight to a day at the archives by three Land Commission researchers investigating a land claim that might affect the lives of a large community. Nevertheless, the statistics do tell a story.

28　Lyotard, *The Postmodern Condition,* 5, 45, 51.

29　See Andor Skotnes, "People's Archives and Oral History in South Africa: A Traveller's Account," *South African Archives Journal* 37 (1995).

30　Carolyn Hamilton explores this aspect in her " 'Living by Fluidity': Oral Histories, Material Custodies and the Politics of Preservation," paper presented at the conference Words and Voices: Critical Practices of Orality in Africa and African Studies, Bellagio, Italy, February 1997.

31　Quoted by Hamilton, " 'Living by Fluidity'," 17.

32 Lyotard, *The Postmodern Condition, 22.*

33 See Hamilton, "'Living by Fluidity'," 27.

34 Richard Tarnas, *The Passion of the Western Mind,* 409.

# CHAPTER 2

## On (Archival) Odyssey(s)[1]

The truth likes to hide
out in the open…
*Anne Michaels[2]*

The truth is why words fail
We can only reveal by outline,
by circling absence.
*Anne Michaels[3]*

Meaningful introduction to Canada occurred for me a long time ago through the work of Margaret Atwood and Leonard Cohen. "Introduction to Canada" and so much more, a "more" I think of now in terms of a revealing through the circling of absence. Much later came exposure to Canadian archival discourse—revelatory for me at the time, and still today for me the richest, most diverse national discourse in archives. Through that exposure came connection with Terry Cook, who visited South Africa in 1994 and 1997 and who enabled me to visit Canada for the first time in 1995. Intense professional collaboration and friendship transformed my thinking on archives, societal memory construction, and a host of other things—from bureaucracy to rock 'n roll, from "postmodernist" literature to motorbiking. Terry pre-eminently, but Canadian archival discourse generally, taught me that archives is a terrain for philosophy and poetry, as well as one for politi-cal struggle, community endeavor, and hard professional work. So many major voices made this call to me—Hugh Taylor, Brien Brothman, Tom Nesmith, Rick Brown, Joan Schwartz. Their impact on me personally and on South African archival discourse generally came at a historically significant moment. As in all South Africa's societal spaces, we were busy re-imagining the country's national archival system in a context of fierce debate and political maneuvering. It is no accident that the 1996 National Archives of South Africa Act demonstrates a patterning rooted in the drafters' decision to use the Canadian federal legislation as their point of departure; no accident that our new national system implicitly embraces the concept of "total archives"; and no accident that in 1996 the National Archives adopted a macroappraisal approach for its appraisal program. (Almost a hundred years after the South African War of 1899–1902, Canada was again having a significant impact on South African nation-building.)

So, a bright Canadian thread in the story of South Africa's transi-tion to democracy. And in my own life journey, or life story. (As I say this, cautionary words from a Leonard Cohen song vibrate in my head, as they did when I drafted these sentences: "Raise a tent of shelter now though every thread is torn…"[4]) To tell story, to make story, is argu-ably one of the most fundamental human instincts. We take the chaotic jumble of experience, the clutter of elusive meanings, and we weave them into the healing shape of story. There *is* a beginning, a middle, and an ending. There *is* a plot and a coherent patterning of characters. There *is*, in Cohen's words, "a tent of shelter." Shape, then, as Hayden White has argued, determining content in fundamental ways; shape becoming content. Invariably we cast story in terms of "odyssey"—a heroic engagement with the vicissitudes and trials of life, a meeting of challenges, a suffering emblazoned by a final tying of the last loose thread. In the end we come home; we come to the home which has been waiting for us; we find the "tent of shelter."

"Odyssey." "The Archival Odyssey." When this conference title arrived formally by e-mail, chance or the gods found me at my desk listening to Leonard Cohen with two texts before me—Jacques Derrida's "Ulysses Gramophone"[5] and James Joyce's *Ulysses*. (Let me footnote that "Ulysses" is the Roman version of the Greek "Odysseus.") Joyce's, of course, is one of myriad interpretations, readings, reworkings and re-imaginings of Homer's "original" story, *The Odyssey*. Most recently we've been offered the movie *Oh Brother, Where Art Thou?* Thirty-three years ago, Stanley Kubrick and Arthur C. Clarke gave us their seminal *2001: A Space Odyssey*. No accident, then, that here in 2001 we are being bombarded by gatherings and projects associated with the word *odyssey*—for example, the ARMA Odyssey, an Ice Odyssey, a Sleep Odyssey, even a Slut Odyssey. Reading further back we find works by Wallace Stevens, Tennyson, Shakespeare, Chaucer, Dante, and Virgil, among others. From Homer to George Clooney, then, a rich vein of image and metaphor in the Western tradition. Scholarship, we must note, tells us that the "beginning" marked by the proper name Homer is resonant with uncertainty. John Wheatcroft, for instance, says the following: "We know that the poet for whom we use the name Homer… inherited stories, from an oral tradition almost surely, about an event from centuries before…"[6] Here we are firmly in archival territory, addressing "the archival 'Odyssey,' or 'The Odyssey' as archive." Before us is a text that we cannot read without reading "through" all these and numerous other contextual layerings. And in time to come readers will have to negotiate many more layerings. Homer's *The Odyssey*, as with every text, as with all archives, can never close. It opens to both its antecedents and its descendents, which in turn are always opening to expanding contexts. *The Odyssey* is positioned within what Chris Hurley calls "ambience,"[7] an ambience that is ever changing because it has no determinable beginning and no determinable ending. Hurley's ambience explodes narrow definitions of provenance; releases "the record" from the confines of "life cycle" or "odyssey" into the wide open spaces of "journeying."

Over a period of months after receiving that e-mail, I posed to archival colleagues the question: "What does the word *odyssey* say to you?" The core ideas, or movements, which I outlined above, emerged from these discussions: a journey, multiple challenges, heroic endeavor, a final coming home. My South African colleagues, with few exceptions, perceived no etymological or mythological significance in the word. Most made no connection with Homer's text, nor to Homer's hero Odysseus. In contrast, international colleagues—predominantly from Canada and the United States—without exception moved straight to Homer. (A number of questions arise, but I want to move on.) And of all the many voices I listened to in that period, only one proffered a literary reference other than Homer, namely the movie *2001: A Space Odyssey*. An extraordinary thought. All these archivists for whom millennia of imprints on Homer's epic have left no conscious trace. So much for my claim about intertextuality! In pondering this extraordinary thought, I found it connecting to another equally extraordinary one—the degree to which the users of archives at worst ignore, at best pay cursory attention to, the contextual documentation prepared painstakingly by archivists. At the heart of archival theory is the assumption that the meanings and significances of a record are located in the contextual circumstances of its creation and subsequent custody and use. In Chris Hurley's terms, there is no understanding of the record without an understanding of its ambience. Yet how many users, even renowned scholars, interrogate the record through an interrogation of the documentation of that ambience—the guides and inventories, the records system in which the record was created, surviving related records, relevant appraisals, documentation of previous research use, and so on? In my experience, very few. Which poses profound questions to archival endeavor, and to archivists. Without buying into pragmatism, utilitarianism, or user-driven delivery, I find myself asking what is the purpose of all this rich contextualization that we attempt to provide? Do we do it in hope of one day educating users to respect it? Do we believe in a future generation free of information junkies searching for their next information hit? Or do we do it as a noble end in itself, as some kind of badge of professional identity? Something, perhaps, for which the gods will reward us? These questions haunt me. As does that giant specter looming behind every claim to archives being the memory of a nation, a society, or a community. Truth be told, archives narrowly defined, these "memory institutions" holding the treasure of records with archival value, contribute relatively little to social memory. In my country, the vast majority of citizens have not even heard of such archives. Their rights to citizenship, property, and so on might be protected by archives; their access to public services might be supported by the use of archives; some of their knowledge might be shaped by popular work drawing on archival research; but the tapestry of their memories, their stories, their myths, and their traditions, this tapestry is woven from other societal resources. The anti-apartheid rallying call of "take archives to the people!" has been quelled in face of the huge systemic barriers to its meaningful implementation. Another uniquely postapartheid South African problem? I think not. *All* archivists must engage this specter.

But enough on this interesting tangent. To return to *odyssey:* my researches suggest that semantically the word, connected or not to Homer by its users, still carries a powerful classical frame for archivists. What I want to do now is hold that frame to a deconstructive reading of the title "The Archival Odyssey." In other words, I will attempt to lay bare the assumptions informing the title as construction and invite in the specters, the ghosts, either held at bay or excluded by these assumptions. To invite these specters in will require me to name them, an extremely tricky business. For there are always more than any naming exercise can accommodate. I extend the invitation only to those I can see, rather sense, now. And every specter once named, seems to reveal a doppelganger, so that this naming becomes a process with infinite reach. Now, you might be muttering under your breath, "What is he going on about?" Let me quickly conclude this ground preparation by quoting three others who have marked the spectral space better than I can. First, Anne Michaels, whose words are quoted at the beginning of this article and provide just such a marking: a hiding out in the open; a circling of absence. But listen also to this line from her novel *Fugitive Pieces*: "What is the true value of knowledge? That it makes our ignorance more precise."[8] Second, Jacques Derrida, who wrote a book titled *Specters of Marx* in which, among other things, he traces the degree to which our post-Marxist, postsocialist world is still haunted by Marx.[9] Jacques Derrida, who wrote a book on archive in which he disclosed the spectral structure of the archive and concluded that "nothing is less clear today than the word 'archive.'"[10] Jacques Derrida, whose writings on literature are numerous but who confesses that "nothing to this day remains as new and incomprehensible to me, at once very near and very alien, as the thing called literature."[11] And third, 1960s student activist Jerry Rubin, who confessed in 1976 that "As I grow older I am learning how much I do not know about life… I will still be growing (up) on my death bed. The moment I think I know all about life, I find out I know nothing."[12] The more Anne Michaels, Jacques Derrida, and

Jerry Rubin throw light on their world, the more shadow they cast. Every specter named reveals a specter yet to be named.

So, to the specters I discern moving through the title "The Archival Odyssey." Notice first the use of the definite article *The* and the word *Odyssey* in the singular: "*The* Archival Odyssey." What is posited is a single archival odyssey. Not one among many, but the only one. The *one* archival odyssey. Let us assume for the moment that the words are denotative. Then we are considering a categorization of archival endeavor: however diverse our ideas and our interests, our nationalities and our professional positioning, we are all embarked on this single odyssey, many journeys becoming collectively one. And, to bring in the dimension of time, through the ages all the diverse archival thinkers and practitioners, however unorthodox or extraordinary, have been similarly embarked. An inspiring thought, an epic tent of shelter. But what of the specters? I sense at least two. One is pointing at the tent's threads, inviting us to feel the many tears. The other is mumbling about numbering exercises. Can we ever be sure of "one"? One odyssey, one goal, one meaning, one truth. Can we ever be sure of "two"? Two values in archives (primary and secondary), two disposition options (retain or destroy), two sexes, two genders. Can we be sure of any finite number? The possibility of "the other," the shadow of otherness, brings to all numbering the possibility of another, of one more. So that beyond any consideration of whether there is indeed an archival unity in diversity, in what we might call an epistemological beyond, there is a question mark behind the very notion of such unity.

But what if the title is not denotative? Perhaps it carries an implicit verb, a verb in the subjunctive mood. So that rather than describing a single odyssey, it is enjoining us to strive for the realization of such an odyssey. Would this not be a noble objective? For me, the question mark behind the notion of unity remains troubling. And this mark is joined by other spectral question markings: is the aspiration to odyssey, whether in the singular or the plural, a noble one? Is the desire for "one" not a totalizing one, a gesture carrying within it the marginalization of certain voices? Can we assume an essence, some pure archival essence, which clearly is preconditional to any striving for a single odyssey? What do we mean by "archival"?

To address this last specter first (although one is being addressed as much as one is addressing): the concept of "archive" today is a site of wide-ranging and sometimes fierce contestation. Eric Ketelaar's finely nuanced and increasingly postmodernist (his own label) formulations on archive, for instance, are a world apart from those to be found in formal ICA documents. The notion of archive driving activists in South Africa intent on documenting the experiences of the marginalized is a world apart from that driving the definers of standards for corporate record-keeping in a number of countries. A final example: In 1998, David Bearman visited the National Archives of South Africa, and horrified us by responding to our painstakingly secured snapshot of a government-wide human resources management database with the words: "But it isn't a record. It shouldn't even be here."

In recent years, numerous disciplines have been taking an "archival turn"—from philosophy to anthropology, from psychology to sociology, increasingly we hear voices exploring the meanings and significances of this thing we call "archive." Whether we ignore these voices—as most archivists and record-keepers do—or dismiss them, or engage them, a reality is that they are stretching traditional discipline- and profession-bound understandings of the concept. Derrida is right, I would argue, in claiming that "nothing is less clear today than the word 'archive.'" When Sir Hilary Jenkinson addressed a gathering of archivists in the 1930s and spoke of the archival mission, his audience could legitimately assume that they knew exactly what he meant by "archival" and that everyone present more or less shared his understanding. Today, a similar gathering listening to an Eric Ketelaar or a Terry Cook, or more scary, to a Jacques Derrida or a Gerda Lerner, would be foolish to make such assumptions.

So, the *archival* odyssey. Implied here is the assumption that there is *archival* odyssey; and there are other forms of odyssey. The form of odyssey that is archival is separable from these other forms. Do you hear a specter behind this assumption, whispering questions? For instance, even if we adopt the narrowest traditional definition of archives, does not every odyssey have an archival dimension? (Odyssey *as archive;* odyssey *in archives.*) Does this assumption of separability not at best downplay commonalities with other disciplines in, or approaches to, knowledge and memory construction? Is the assumption not expressing a process of identity formation that is exclusive rather than inclusive; that is about defensiveness and insecurity rather than about hospitality; that is about defending turf rather than tending turf? And does the assumption not resist broader understandings of "archive"? I want to avoid providing an inventory of these understandings, so let me mention but one, that of Jacques Derrida. Woven through many of his works is a depiction of archive as a kind of hyperwriting back of all human activity. This writing before writing, what he calls "archi-text," mediates all experience. So that odyssey, if there be such a thing, before being recorded, or archived, is an expression of archive. The archive is its very possibility. And thus the qualification of odyssey by the adjective *archival* becomes tautological. Every odyssey must be archival.

I want now to shift focus back to the word *odyssey,* before stepping away one final time to view the conference title as a whole.

*Odyssey* describes journey. But not any journey. In its shape and its modalities, it carries very particular attributes. This is not an open-ended journey, one from A to wherever whim or vicissitude will take the traveler. It is a journey with determinable beginning and ending. There is an itinerary, an A to B. And yet this is no linear journey, and the B is not B but A. For odyssey, in its classical form, is circular. Odysseus journeys *from* home and returns *to* home. He closes a circle. So that he represents, or initiates, notions of reappropriation and totalization. Is this the archetype, or the model, we envisage for archival endeavor? I want to suggest that this was precisely the archetype informing the work of our predecessors who sought to close a circle using the blueprint provided by the notions of provenance and original order. A finite and knowable provenance. An arrangement and presentation of the archive in its "original" order. The archetype is also embodied, ironically, in the work of James Joyce scholars. I say ironically, for in his *Ulysses,* Joyce holds open the circle that he institutes after Homer. Listen to Jacques Derrida on Joycean scholarship:

> Joyce experts are the representatives as well as the effects of the most powerful project for programming over the centuries the totality of research in the onto-logico-encyclopedic field... A Joyce scholar has the right to dispose of the totality of competence in the encyclopedic field... He [*sic*] has at his command the computer of all memory, he plays with the entire archive of culture—at least of what is called Western culture, and, in it, of that which returns to itself according to the Ulyssean circle of the encyclopedia....[13]

Within the conference title, then, we can discern the movement of the Ulyssean circle, which draws us to dream at once of a determinable ending and a gathering in, a corralling, of knowledge. But there is another movement, a spectral movement, that invites us to consider otherness, the eccentric (the outside of circle), the breach that is always already in every circle, and the circling of absence (a corralling of ignorance). Do we have the courage to allow deconstructive energies into our construction of odyssey?

Let me illustrate what I mean by this question, through the naming of at least three specters. I invite the first one in by returning to Derrida on Joyce. He said of the Joycean scholar that "he plays with the entire archive of culture—at least of what is called Western culture, and, in it, of that which returns to itself according to the Ulyssean circle of the encyclopedia." Now, listen to how Derrida continues:

> and this is why one can always at least dream of writing *on* Joyce and not *in* Joyce from the fantasy of some far Eastern capital, without, in my case, having too many illusions about it.[14]

In conventional Western wisdom Homer marks the beginning of the literary canon, the beginning of Western civilization. From him our odyssey has proceeded and continuously returns for succor. Kept outside the circle are non-Western ways of knowing, ways emanating from outside the West and from indigenous peoples within the West. Our metanarratives either appropriate or exclude the stories of the marginalized. A phenomenon from which archival discourse (narrowly defined) is not immune. Does not the dominant discourse in archives internationally evince a powerful Western frame of reference? Do non-Western and indigenous voices participate only to the extent that they adopt this frame? In South Africa, despite dramatic processes of transformation, we agonize over the continued dominance in archival discourse of white voices and Western modes of knowledge construction.[15] Entrenched patterns of power are not easily dislodged. The question remains, how committed are we to the venture of dislodging? Or, to phrase it differently, do we have the courage to allow deconstructive energies into our construction of odyssey? To risk stating the obvious, the question rang in my head as I gazed around the conference floor on the first morning of the ACA 2001 conference.

My gaze, unlike that of Anne Michaels, was a literal circling of absence, more precisely of absentees—First Nations people and visible minorities—in this most diverse of nations.

But the marginalized are, of course, legion. Naming them all is an impossible task. I restrict myself now to the possible by naming but two other specters at play in the word *odyssey*. The first moves behind the heroic register of Homer's tale, in particular behind Odysseus's triumphal return home. This specter invites us to consider the journeys and the stories of those who do not return home, who fail, who fall short. And those who are devastated by the return home. Consider, for instance, the unhappy suitors of Odysseus's wife, Penelope, brutally murdered, literally torn apart, by the returned Odysseus. Do we have place—meaningful place—in our storytelling for these unhappy souls? Does our Sunday school storytelling give space to the unhappy, ravaged Philistines? Do we have the courage to interrogate our heroes? Or do we retreat before the danger of our metanarratives unraveling? And what, says another specter, of the configuration of hero and heroine within the pattern of odyssey? Does this pattern not speak the terms of patriarchy? The man out venturing and conquering, the woman at home, bound by taboo and tending hearth. Is this the archetype, I ask again, we wish for archival endeavor? Few, I suspect, would venture "yes" to this question. But many might be tempted to point to the powerful presence of women in the archival profession and conclude that patriarchy (more accurately, patriarchies) are hardly a "problem." A conclusion inviting spectral questions: does "presence" equate with "power"? Does *a* woman in charge translate necessarily into a challenge to patriarchal modalities? Does the empowerment of women in itself release us from gender entrapment—the trap of moving only within the binary opposition man-woman? (Again a numbering exercise halting determinedly at "two.")

For me this path is extremely inviting, a path splitting exponentially into tributaries up ahead. But I want to retreat now, not into safety, for there is no safety in deconstruction, but back to a broader viewpoint. "The Archival Odyssey." Let us view all the title's elements in one movement. Or at least attempt to. In all its possible forms, moods, and tenses, it seems to hold this big question: What is "the archival odyssey"? A legitimate question? A useful question? Possibly, but do we discern the looming assumption behind it, namely, that there is a thing-in-itself, an essence, named "archival odyssey," transcending time and place. The impossible dream. Listen to Derek Attridge on this dream in philosophy:

> …what philosophy attempts, in its most fundamental mission, is a writing without a date, a writing that transcends the here-and-now of its coming-into-existence, and the heres-and-nows of the acts which confirm, extend, and renew that existence…. But all writing is a dating…, every text has a provenance, and the date, like the signature, exhibits the counter-logic of iterability….[16]

So that from the outset I have carefully avoided the question "What is 'the archival odyssey'?" Instead, I have been probing a more modest question: "What meanings do we attach, here-and-now, to the words *the archival odyssey?*" (As a footnote, I wish to pick up on a word used by Attridge—*provenance*. I have not come across an archivist who does not claim the "principle of provenance" as the cornerstone of archival theory. At the same time, I have not come across a conceptualization of the principle in the mainstream of current discourse which does not diverge fundamentally from its earliest formulations in the 1800s. And yet we continue to use the term, as if we mean the same thing as those archivists and bureaucrats in nineteenth-century Europe. Could this be an expression of our dreaming transcendence? Though everything is shifting, here is a thing-in-itself, a tent of shelter, a home. But it is a dating. It is dated.)

By now, I imagine, you are growing weary with my questions. Just one more before moving to a conclusion. The question "What is the archival odyssey?" has a companion question—"Who decides?" I want to suggest that I have been addressing this question implicitly from the outset. As with all questions on archives, answers are determined by those who hold power in the discourse: the macro-actors, the ones who have resources, who set agendas, receive the research and publication grants, enjoy access to the data necessary for the sustenance of intellectual endeavor. The ones, in short, who control record-keeping. Listen to Bruno Latour on this:

> [The] role of the bureaucrat qua scientist qua writer and reader, is always misunderstood because we take for granted that there

exist, somewhere in society, macro-actors that naturally dominate the scene.... Once accepted, these large entities are then used to explain (or to not explain) "cognitive" aspects of science and technology. The problem is that these entities could not exist at all without the construction of long networks in which numerous faithful records circulate in both directions, records which are, in turn, summarized and displayed to convince.[17]

Latour is worth listening to closely. I want to quote him again, this time applying his argument to a specific case:

The "'rationalisation" granted to bureaucracy since Hegel and Weber has been attributed by mistake to the "mind" of (Prussian) bureaucrats. It is all in the files themselves.... Economics, politics, sociology, hard sciences, do not come into contact through the grandiose entrance of "interdisciplinarity" but through the back door of the *file*. The "cracy" of bureaucracy is mysterious and hard to study, but the "bureau" is something that can be empirically studied, and which explains, because of its structure, why some power is given to an average mind just by looking at files: domains which are far apart become literally inches apart; domains which are convoluted and hidden, become flat; thousands of occurrences can be looked at synoptically.... In our culture's "paper shuffling" is the source of an essential power, that constantly escapes attention since its materiality is ignored.[18]

So, "the mind" and "the files." I wouldn't go as far as Latour—"it is all in the files." But he poses serious questions to those of us who emphasize the constructedness of the record. He does so by foregrounding the capacity of the record to structure cognition. The domination of any scene by macro-actors is never natural; it is constructed. And a key role in that construction—*the* key role according to Latour—is played by records. A question worth considering is the impact on the minds of macro-actors in the archival scene of the record-keeping environment under their control—the neat rows of carefully arranged and labeled files, photographs, maps, sound recordings, and other records categories; the pristine, closely managed stackrooms; the ordered and interlinked contextual documentation; the rational and heavily documented configuration of archival spaces; and so on.

A frequent criticism of deconstruction is that it deconstructs only to lay waste. It never builds; it never says "yes!" Always it says "no!" I would want to question the binary opposition within this view—"yes!" opposed to "no!" In my view there is no "yes!" without an implied "no!," and vice versa. But I let that rest. I want to conclude now by unfolding the "yes!" in all that I've been saying.

Yes, telling story is an unavoidable dimension of the human condition. Individuals and collectivities make sense of experience through narrative. Instinctively we raise tents of shelter. Yes, this is "good." But let us know the reality of torn threads. And let us know the tendency of narrative to slip into metanarrative, the slippage a totalizing movement stealing from us the pain and complexity we need to engage if we are to find healings and integrations.

Yes, in negotiating the darkened landscapes of life, we must deploy every light source life gives us. Reason, research, analysis, and so on, the gifts we usually associate with light in the Western world, are spurned at our peril. But let us know that all shining of light casts shadow. Or, to mix metaphors, let us recognize the spectral spaces within every circle of knowledge. And let us find the courage to offer the specters hospitality though they trouble us horribly. This recognizing and this courage draw on gifts usually associated with the shadow realms—imagination, poetry, intuition, emotion, passion, faith.

Yes, we need archetypes. Arguably, we function as human beings archetypally. But should we choose or allow Odysseus? What about Tiresias, the blind seer finding light in darkness? Or Margaret Atwood's Marian, determinedly ordinary but embarked on a noble struggle against patriarchies?[19] Or Bowman, the only human survivor of *2001: A Space Odyssey,* for whom survival is an impenetrable mystery? Whoever we choose, or allow, let it not be a case of one, or two, or three. The demand of hospitality is that that we remain open to the advent of "another," even if this other be a shadowy Odysseus.

To the notion of *odyssey* I say "no!" I have argued that we must embrace adventuring, but not with the false comfort of an itinerary and a determinable end. (Is not *adventure* a mysterious word? Beyond the limitations of etymology, it suggests a going forth, an openness to what is outside. And yet within it, nestling in its heart, is the word *advent*—the coming in, the arrival, beyond our control, of something or someone important. *Adventure*, then, as going out in response to what is coming in, a going out that brings comings in, a state of becoming in which coming and going are not binary opposites. Blessed is the one who does not know whether she is coming or going, but who lives a coming which is always already a going.) So, for archival endeavor, I am advocating a "yes!" to adventuring, but one informed by the unpredictability of *advent*. I am advocating a receiving of every advent with respect for otherness and passion for justice. *Otherness* and *justice*: each assuming the other, requiring the other; each equally beyond our understanding, and beyond assurance of a final coming. I respect, I yearn for, what I (precisely) do not know. The true value of knowledge, in Anne Michaels's terms, is that it makes our ignorance more precise. I am advocating, in other words, a destiny without destination. It is for the gods, not human beings, to write odyssey into adventure.

# Endnotes

1   This article was published in *Archivaria* 51 (2001). It is based on a paper presented as the keynote address to the Association of Canadian Archivists' conference in Winnipeg in June 2001. The conference was titled "The Archival Odyssey." Early drafts of the paper were read by Terry Cook, Wendy Duff, Kerry Harris, Ethel Kriger, Vicki Lemieux, and Sheila Powell. I am grateful to all of them for their patience and insight.

2   Anne Michaels, *Poems* (New York: Alfred A Knopf, 2000), 163.

3   Michaels, *Poems,* 129.

4   From "Dance Me to the End of Love," *Various Positions* (Columbia, 1984).

5   Derek Attridge, ed., *Acts of Literature* (New York and London: Routledge, 1992).

6   John Wheatcroft, *Transforming Texts: Classical Images in New Contexts,* ed. Robert Metzger (London and Toronto: Bucknell University Press, 1993), 93.

7   Chris Hurley, "Ambient Functions—Abandoned Children to Zoos," *Archivaria* 40 (1995).

8   Anne Michaels, *Fugitive Pieces* (Toronto: M and S, 1996), 210.

9   Jacques Derrida, *Specters of Marx: The State of the Debt, the Work of Mourning, and the New International* (New York and London: Routledge, 1994).

10  Jacques Derrida, *Archive Fever: A Freudian Impression* (Chicago: University of Chicago Press, 1996), 90.

11  Jacques Derrida, *Demeure: Fiction and Testimony* (Palo Alto, Calif.: Stanford University Press, 2000), 20.

12  Jerry Rubin, *Growing (Up) at 37* (New York: M. Evans and Company, 1976), 189.

13  Jacques Derrida, "Ulysses Gramophone," *Acts of Literature,* ed. Derek Attridge (New York and London: Routledge, 1992), 281.

14  Derrida, "Ulysses Gramophone."

15  See, for instance, Verne Harris and Sello Hatang, "Archives, Identity and Place: A Dialogue On What It (Might) Mean(s) to be an African Archivist," *ESARBICA Journal* 19 (2000).

16  Attridge, *Acts of Literature,* 371.

17  Bruno Latour, "Visualization and Cognition: Thinking with Eyes and Hands," *Knowledge and Society* 6 (1986): 28–29.

18  Latour, "Visualization and Cognition," 28.

19  See Margaret Atwood, *The Edible Woman* (London: Virago, 1990).

# CHAPTER 3

## A Shaft of Darkness: Derrida in the Archive[1]

## CONCLUSIONS

This essay is not an account of Jacques Derrida's *position* on, or *delineation* of, the archive. That would be to repeat the mistake of those who attempt to define postmodernism or deconstruction or Derridean thinking. Ultimately it is impossible to say *what* these things are. They are what they are becoming. They open out of the future. We can, at best, mark their movements and engage their energies. So the essay offers a shaft of darkness in all the harsh light of positivist discourse, a shaft aimed at Derrida in the archive. And in taking aim I strive to be as open as possible to Derrida aiming at me.

In a sense, all Derrida's work is about the archive. He converses with it, mines it, interrogates it, plays in it, extends it, creates it, imagines it, is imagined by it. It is impossible to speak of Derrida without also speaking of the archive. It is impossible to speak—now, at the turn of the century—of the archive without also speaking of Derrida. Of course, all these assertions assume a concept associated with this word, this noun, *archive*. An assumption Derrida questions. Not only are there numerous competing concepts associated with the word, but from within the word itself—coming from behind linguistics or semantics or etymology, coming from the very processes of archiving—there is a troubling of meaning. But however we understand the word *archive*, it remains true to say that all Derrida's work, in a sense, is about the archive. In a sense. And in sense and sensing, for his work—the sense of Derrida, the non-sense of Derrida—insistently, searingly, joyously, embraces the dimensions of reason, emotion and instinct contained in the word *sense*.

Derrida's work can be typified as an extended reading, or rewriting, of what others have written. Always the canon of Western philosophy and literature, the tradition, the archive, is his point of departure.[2] In the archive he generates archive, opening the future in the past. He reads, and reads again, the canonical texts:

> I think we have to read them again and again and I feel that, however old I am, I am on the threshold of reading Plato and Aristotle. I love them and I feel I have to start again and again and again. It is a task which is in front of me, before me.[3]

Out of his reading comes new text, which is old in its newness. He discloses—for himself and for all readers of text, readers of archive—that we are always and already embedded in archi-text.[4] There is nothing outside of the archive.[5]

And yet, at the same time, in what could be called an aporetics of being, or of becoming, everything is outside of the archive. In every(thing) known is the unknown, the unknowable, the unarchivable, the other. And every other is wholly other. This is not so much—though it is this—a marking of reason's limits. It is more a disclosing of structural resistance to closure. Every circle of human knowing and experience is always already breached—breached by the unnamable, by an (un)certain divine particularity, by a coming that must always be coming. In his more recent work, Derrida has opened (more fully) what could be called religious and autobiographical dimensions to his explorations.[6] These dimensions coalesce in an ever-closer heeding to the call of the other, more precisely of otherness. In heeding closely, he has been drawn, in one movement, to the otherness outside and the otherness inside—the otherness of the self, or of the selves, an otherness marking and marked by, but never found, in the personal archive.

So the quest for Derrida in the archive is one without (delimitable) horizon. In this essay I limit myself—for editors *do* have horizons—to consideration of two specific works by Derrida—*Archive Fever:A Freudian Impression* (1996), his most direct engagement with the archive as concept, and *Memoirs of the Blind: The Self-Portrait and Other Ruins* (1993), in which he posits explicit connections between archiving and ways of knowing, of being, of becoming. A bifurcated shaft of darkness, then. In a double sense. For with *Archive Fever* I strain to hold the shaft steadily on Derrida; with *Memoirs* I gather the shattered reflections projected back at me.

## ARCHIVE FEVER

Derrida's engagement with the archive in *Archive Fever* is more a lingering embrace than an engagement. His stated objective with this work is the positing of theses that define the "impression" left by the Freudian signature. He arrives there via an extended foreplay. His moves are at once heavy and light, focused and multilayered; they are always deliberately and self-reflectively complex. No word or term is safe from the passion of Derrida's embrace. And no Derridean gesture is without a flourish of new terms. He demands of the reader a reciprocal commitment—consummation is inconceivable without a willingness to play and replay Derrida's moves. (Which makes one wonder how it must have been for the audience that first heard the text as a lecture on 5 June 1994.)

Derrida's moves in epistemological space offer nothing new to deconstructionist discourse, but his focus on the archive brings a freshness to his fundamental assertions. I want to signpost four:

1. The event, the origin, the *arkhé*, in its uniqueness, is irrecoverable, unfindable. "The possibility of the archiving trace, this simple *possibility*, can only divide the uniqueness."[7]

2. The archiving trace, the archive, is not simply a recording, a reflection, an image of the event. It shapes the event. "The archivization produces as much as it records the event."[8]

3. The object does not speak for itself. In interrogating and interpreting the object, the archive, scholars inscribe their own interpretation into it. The interpretation has no meta-textual authority. There is no meta-archive. There is no closing of the archive. "It opens out of the future."[9]

4. Scholars are not, can never be, exterior to their objects. They are marked before they interrogate the markings and this pre-impression shapes their interrogation.

This last assertion Derrida buttresses through analysis of Yosef Yerushalmi's book *Freud's Moses: Judaism Terminable and Interminable* (1991). Yerushalmi concludes with a thirty-page fictional address to Freud—the "Monologue with Freud." Up to the "Monologue," Derrida points out, Yerushalmi presents himself as a historian "exterior to his object."[10] He is neither Jew nor psychoanalyst as such. But in the "Monologue" he demonstrates this exteriority to be a chimera—he is Jewish and his discourse bears a Freudian pre-impression. Ironically, one of Yerushalmi's intentions in the "Monologue" is to posit the pre-impression of Jewishness on Freud. He asks the question, "Is psychoanalysis a Jewish science?" and seeks to demonstrate that Freud believed that it was, but secretly—he never allowed this belief to become a part of the "public archive."[11] Derrida uses this as a platform for probing at Freud's discomfort with the influence of his own marking on his work. And in doing so, Derrida is, I think, marking the shadow of another related question: "Is *deconstruction* a Jewish science?"[12]

"Nothing is less reliable, nothing is less clear today than the word 'archive'... Nothing is thus more troubled and more troubling today than the concept archived in this word 'archive.'"[13] In fact, Derrida argues, we do not have a concept for the word; all we have is a notion, an impression, associated with the word. And the very process of archiving, the structure of archivization, will not allow it to be otherwise. Derrida's positing of the notion begins with a lexicon, an archive of the word *archive*. He demonstrates how in the "original" Greek usage it is inseparable from the idea of consignation—the marking on a substrate (through impression on paper, through circumcision on the human body) implies both process (the power of consignation) and place (the place of consignation). Control of consignation, the exercise of a topo-nomological "archontic power" is at the heart of political power. For South Africans it takes only a slight jiggling of memory to recall the obsessive guarding, patrolling, and manipulating of consignation by apartheid's *archons*—apartheid's memory institutions, for instance, legitimized apartheid rule by their silences and their narratives of power; the media were controlled by an oppressive censorship regime; official secrets were protected by the Protection of Information Act and numerous other pieces of interlinking legislation; and so on.

Unfortunately, Derrida's lexicon is restricted to the Greeks and the Romans. He offers no analysis of developments over more than two millennia; he declines to acknowledge archives as a discipline, one with its own discourses and histories;[14] and, while he describes the impact of the computer on archivization as an "archival earthquake," he does not explore how virtual electronic records have dizzied the *archons* and transformed how we conceptualize the place of consignation. What he does explore, drawing heavily, and explicitly, on Freud, is the "anarchontic" "instinct of destruction" at work within consignation. Aside from deliberate destruction, there is an instinct of forgetfulness, a death drive indissociable from memorization: "… the archives takes place at the place of originary and structural breakdown of … memory."[15] The archive, in other words, always works against itself. This is the "archive fever" of the book's title. Moreover, Derrida points out, Freud made possible the idea of a substrate that cannot be reduced to memory (that is, memory as conscious reserve or as act of recalling). Freud gave us the tools to expose repressed or suppressed (or super-repressed) texts, attested to by symptoms, signs, figures, metaphors, and metonymies. We must, Derrida concludes, reconceptualize the archive to accommodate this "archive of the virtual."[16]

This conjuring of virtual space, of spectrality, within the archive, together with the idea of the death drive in archiving, establish what Derrida calls a Freudian theory of the archive. A theory that we must take account of, and account for. Not that psychoanalysis offers us a concept of the archive, or even a means of resolving the contradiction, the unreliability, the lack of clarity inherent in the concept. Indeed, Derrida argues, in analyzing the *trouble de l' archive,* psychoanalysis succeeds only in heightening it, for "it repeats the very thing it resists or which it makes its object."[17] In the theses, the culmination of *Archive*

*Fever*'s foreplay, Derrida unfolds the internal division in Freud's discourse on the archive.

Interpreting Freud on the archive is but one thread in the tapestry of *Archive Fever*. The central thrust of Derrida's argument is that the archive, as concept, is cleft, contradictory, always dislocating itself because it is never one with itself; but that, far from being reason for despair, this is the very strength, the future, of the archive. One need not share Derrida's particular presuppositions and perspectives to recognize the accuracy of the diagnosis. Intrinsically unstable (rather, dynamic), the archive is being turned inside out by postmodernist epistemologies and technological revolution. And in South Africa it awaits, it needs urgently, a turning inside out by epistemologies that we might label "African" or "indigenous." But there is convincing evidence—none more so than in the work of Terry Cook and other heralds of a post-custodial era—that it is keeping its head above the troubled waters. Derrida's own exposition of the *trouble de l'archive*, in my view, demands serious consideration. Let me rephrase that. One doesn't respond to a playful seduction, nor a feverish coming on, by considering it seriously. It demands a hot, or a heated, response. Of course, braving the *trouble du Derrida* is no easy ride, and consummation is not guaranteed.

Pleasures are. For me, as an archivist, three stand out. Firstly, a compelling demonstration that we are in need of archives. To quote John Caputo on *Archive Fever*:

> The living past cannot rise up from the dead and speak to us like dead stones.... We must pick our way among the remains, wrestle with and conjure the ghosts of the past, ply them with patient importunity in order to reconstruct the best story we can.[18]

Secondly, an equally compelling demonstration that this need for archives should be embraced with passion. "Archive fever" should not render us cynical and arid; on the contrary, it is invitation to enchantment, to the play of ecstasy and pain, as we exercise that immemorial passion for the impossible. A passion that plays out in a waiting for a coming, more precisely in the inciting of a coming to come. A passion that is both response to and unfolding of the archive's messianic dimension. And, thirdly, a devastating rebuttal of the notion long cherished by archivists that in contextualizing text they are revealing meaning, resolving mystery, closing the archive. Derrida demonstrates that at best, archival contextualization reveals the multiple layers of construction in text, and in doing so adds yet another layer. Properly conceived, archival contextualization—archival endeavor as a whole—should be about the releasing of meanings, the tending of mystery, the disclosing of the archive's openness.

## MEMOIRS OF THE BLIND

In 1990, Derrida inaugurated a new series of exhibitions at the Louvre Museum in Paris with his *Memoirs of the Blind,* a selection of drawings from the Louvre's collections with an accompanying text. The exhibition became a book, first published in English in 1993,[19] with more fulsome text and a wider selection of drawings. A book—about vision, of vision, if ever there was one—that explores a congeries of ideas around ways of seeing and knowing: perception as originating always in recollection; the gaze of psychic interiority (eyes turned inward); the blindness of so much seeing; the profound seeing in blindness; the blind as the archivists of vision; the blindness of tears; eyes given for weeping as much as for seeing. I first read *Memoirs of the Blind* in 1998 during a stay in Budapest for an International Council on Archives meeting. The book's energies threw into grubby relief the passionless proceedings of the meeting. It also connected powerfully with South Africa's just-released Truth and Reconciliation Commission Final Report—that image of Archbishop Tutu in tears, the myriad stories of weeping, the sense of the report's writers with tear-stained cheeks—providing at the same time a way of understanding Hungary's very different approach to dealing with its past. And it resonated with a great lesson of my youth, the memory of it shafting in with Derrida, like ancient darkness.

As always, Derrida conjures with the general in the particular, the particular in the general. So while at a certain level he is moving in epistemological space, and at another he is probing the blindness cohering in the very structure of archivization, at the most obvious level—insistently at the reader's eye level—he is simply deconstructing the process of drawing, demonstrating that in or by drawing, the drafts(wo)man does not see. For in observing the subject (the object) of the drawing, the drafts(wo)man "sees" out of memory, out of the pre-impression of archi-text. She or he is preshaped to see certain things and not to see others. Moreover, there is always a delay—even if only for a second—between observation and the inscription of image on a substrate. In that pause memory plays. The drafts(wo)man is always confronted by the blankness, the blindness, of the substrate. Which "reflects" his or her own blindness.

Here is the resonance in my own memory, a resonance humming with the convergence between drawing and photographing. Throughout my youth, my father was an avid photographer. He specialized in shots of people captured at what he called "the significant moment," usually unaware of his camera, they and their surroundings transposed into the gorgeous hues of black and white. I remember him explaining to me his technique, closely modeled on that of his idol, the French photographer Henri Cartier-Bresson. "You have to absorb the atmosphere of a place and the people in it," he said. "Feel its rhythms, its energy, allow yourself in turn to become absorbed by it, until you and your camera are invisible. Only then will you be able to sense a significant moment developing, and position yourself to capture it in an absolute unity of observer, observed, and instrument of observation."

A lesson in vision. In a way of seeing. But more fundamentally, a lesson in blindness. In seeing with/through blindness. To even begin to close with the significant moment, the photographer must learn to become invisible. People are blind to his or her presence. And the closing, the moving into position, is in response to far more than visual perception. The crucial energies happen beyond vision, in the realm of feelings and instincts. What the photographer "sees" most people do not see, precisely because they are seeing only with their eyes. In the moment of capture, of course, the photographer is literally blinded. The release button is pressed by a finger wired to a complex of energies, the shutter closes, and for an instant—the critical moment, the critical five-hundredth of a second perhaps—the photographer is in darkness. He or she only "sees" the image when it emerges later in the darkroom. The moment and its image have been anticipated. The image is not the product of sight, but of prescience, prevision, that vision that "sees" into the future. A seeing in blindness. The soul's gaze. The photographer figured, or prefigured, by Tiresius, the blind seer. And the photograph as the archive of the invisible.

If my father were still alive, this extrapolating from his simple lesson would give him a good laugh. "Intellectual bullshit," he'd say, "you can't explain inspiration. You can't even describe it. It kills me how it's always people who patently haven't got it who can't stop talking about it." But his seeing in blindness, his archiving of the invisible, speaks directly to the "intellectual bullshit" of epistemological debates. In Western thinking—still in thrall to the "Age of Reason" despite the inroads made by romanticism, existentialism, and postmodernism—knowledge is linked to sight and ignorance to blindness in a binary opposition. As Derrida argues in *Memoirs of the Blind:* "...the whole history, the whole semantics of the European *idea*, in its Greek genealogy, as we know—as we see—relates seeing to knowing."[20] Light is opposed to darkness, reason to passion. And these oppositions spawn a plethora of others. One of which is that of remembering and forgetting. What we remember we keep in the light; what we forget is consigned to darkness. To remember is to archive. To archive is to preserve memory. In this conceptual framework the archive is a beacon of light, a place—or idea, or psychic space, or societal space—of and for sight. Its hallways ring with the cries of the initiated: "once I was blind, but now I see."

This notion of the archive, as Derrida has shown in *Archive Fever*—but using now my father's semantic bluntness, is bullshit. There is no remembering without forgetting. There is no remembering that cannot become forgetting. Forgetting can become a deferred remembering. Forgetting can be a way of remembering. They open out of each other, light becoming darkness, darkness becoming light. Between consciousness and the unconscious there are no stable boundaries. And dancing between remembering and forgetting, at once spanning them and within each, is imagining. No trace in memory, not even the image transposed onto film by a camera lens, is a simple reflection of event. In the moment of its recording, the event—in its completeness, its uniqueness—is lost. The dance of imagination, moving effortlessly through both conscious and unconscious spaces, shapes what is remembered and what is forgotten, and how the trace is configured. And each time the trace is revisited, this dance is busy with its work of shaping and reshaping. The archive, then, is a trilectic, an open-ended process of remembering, forgetting, and imagining. Here—whether "here" be understood as the archival record, as individual memory, as collective memory, or as the assemblage of society's discourses—here the cry of the initiated should be in the words of that great twentieth-century poet Leonard Cohen: "I am blind, but you can see, please don't pass me by."[21] Or, as another Canadian poet, Anne Michaels, expressed it in reflection rather than invocation: "I did not witness the most important events of my life. My deepest story must be told by a blind man…"[22]

In positing a blindness in the archive, and in delineating a seeing in blindness, Derrida neither dismisses reason nor abandons realities outside of human subjectivity. This blindness has no essential quarrel with reason. It insists only that the knowing of reason, the seeing of the eye—in light, by light, knower and known separated—be always joined to the knowing of passion, the seeing in blindness—in darkness, in the immediacy of feeling and touching. This I would call a knowing of soul.

At this point I imagine the frantic squawking of the *archons* of light: "Go on then, play your ridiculous games of blind man's buff! Follow the throbbings of your heart. Obey the voices that speak to you in the night. See where that takes you. Maybe into a mystical space all of your own, disengaged from the world around you. Or worse, into the spells of the great myth-makers, and of their foot-soldiers—the creators of apartheid hit-squads, the builders of the holocaust ovens." Derrida's response to such squawking is to talk of tears, and the blindness of tears: "Deep down, deep down inside, the eye would be destined not to see but to weep."[23] It is ordinary that when we weep, it is our eyes that fill with tears. But is this not an extraordinary thought—that we weep not from any other organ, but only from the organ of sight, and that we do so in a way that blinds us? It is precisely this blindness and its seeing—the seeing of tears—that captivates Derrida. He ends *Memoirs of the Blind* with a poem by Andrew Marvell that includes these lines:

> Thus let your streams o'erflow your springs,
> Till eyes and tears be the same things:
> And each the other's difference bears;
> These weeping eyes, those seeing tears.[24]

If seeing in blindness provides an image of knowing in passion, then the seeing of tears is an image of knowing in com-passion. I care for what I know; I weep at its suffering. I weep for those parts of myself struggling with alienation. I weep at the suffering of those I love, my neighborhood, my community. But I care also for what I do not know, the other. I weep at its suffering. For I know that in loving and tending my child I sacrifice the thousands of children around the world who have no love, no tending. I know that in buying a new pair of running shoes I sacrifice the workers in a sweatshop in some godforsaken part of the world.[25] I weep for the world. For the soul of the world. All my weeping originates in this, takes me to this. I plead for suffering to end. For justice to come. For God to appear. As another great twentieth-century poet, Allen Ginsberg, has wept:

> I'm crying all the time now.
> I cried all over the street when I left the Seattle Wobbly Hall.
> I cried listening to Bach.
> I cried looking at the happy flowers in my backyard, I cried at
>     the sadness of the middle-aged trees.
>
> Happiness exists I feel it.
> I cried for my soul, I cried for the world's soul.
> The world has a beautiful soul.
> God appearing to be seen and cried over …[26]

As a student I took up photography, modeling my approach on that of my father and of Cartier-Bresson. For nearly a decade I searched for "significant moments" with my camera. Later, career obligations and other pursuits squeezed photography out of my life, but my experience with it had marked me in fundamental ways. Crucially, it had sensitized me to and exercised me in ways of seeing and knowing beyond the boundaries of sight. Ways that appear subversive, and that can be subversive. I carried with me into archival work—as a metaphor, as a pre-impression—the irony of the camera's eye being positioned by the seeing of blindness, of it "seeing" in the moment of literal blindness. I was, then, predisposed to question notions of the archive as a reflection of reality and as necessarily an instrument of power. Without realizing it at first, the archive's seductiveness for me lay in its dance of remembering, forgetting, and imagining, a dance that ultimately can only be danced in blindness, and the dancing of which unravels the archontic strappings designed to bind archives and archivists into the work of subjugation.

## BEGINNINGS

Derrida in the archive is as Derrida is wherever he chooses to be—relentlessly, radically subversive. Nothing, except the right to question, is sacrosanct. No rhythm is left undisturbed by his determination to always, in one movement, get behind and in front of the pace. So as to disclose, and hold, the tension, the aporia, the unknowable, that is always already there. Bob Dylan expressed it well in his *Ballad of a Thin Man:*

> You're very well read, it's well known;
> But something is happening here and you don't know what it is,
> Do you, Mr. Jones?[27]

Derrida's deconstructing, contrary to the superficial reckoning of his many critics, is not designed to lay waste. He is not the herald of an arid relativism. On the contrary, with pounding heart, feverishly, he invites us always to re-spect, look again. The archive is not simply a resource to be plundered. It can never be closed, not by the exercise of reason, not by any work, even of the most impeccable scholarship. Always, always, an unknowable "something is happening here," which Derrida will not allow us to ignore. Nor does he allow himself to escape its reach—he acknowledges that he is, as we all are, another Mr. Jones.

Many of those who attended Derrida's seminar at the University of the Witwatersrand in August 1998 were surprised to discover not the dry, arrogant, cynical, almost incomprehensible deconstructionist that the popular caricature had led them to anticipate. Instead they discovered a person combining profound humility with the passion of an Old Testament prophet, speaking a language at once simple and poetic. (Although he claims difficulty with English, his use of it is masterful.) His principal concern was to disturb positivist notions of the archive, particularly in relation to South Africa's Truth and Reconciliation Commission. The archive, he argued, draws us forward in taking us back. Every beginning gathers energies from and carries pre-impressions from antecedent endings. All perception begins in recollection. But all recollecting, all remembering, is also forgetting. (So that forgetting in the commission's work is not to be found only in its exclusions—forgetting works within its inclusions.) All forgetting of the past is also a forgetting of the future. Always, always, the energy of the archive draws us forward, not to an end but to a coming that must always be deferred, to a beginning that will always be about to begin. "Something is happening here and you don't know what it is." The challenge is not to detain the "something happening," to find out what it is, but rather to affirm the unknowable (embrace, with a "yes!," otherness) as the very core of our humanity. In this psychic space, "beginning" and "ending" lose meaning, and initiates cry with infinite meaning: "I am blind, but I can see!"

# Endnotes

1 This essay has its origin—to the extent that anything has *an origin*—in a paper entitled "Jacques Derrida's *Archive Fever*: A Critique," presented at a seminar in the "Refiguring the Archive" series, University of the Witwatersrand, August 1998. The essay draws heavily on that paper and a later one, entitled "Blindness and the Archive: An Exergue," presented at the conference "Listen to Their Voices," University of Natal, Pietermaritzburg, June 1999. At the aforementioned seminar, intimidated by Derrida's presence and concerned for my own archivability, I offered several warning signals, including the following:

"I have read far more writings *about* Derrida than *by* him.
I have read considerably more writings by *archivists* than writings by *philosophers*. It was only on my third reading of *Archive Fever* that I began to dispense with dictionaries and to discern the enchanting coherence of Derrida's argument."

Since then I have read several more of Derrida's works and have overcome my feelings of complete inadequacy, but the disclaimers remain worthy of repetition. The essay was published in Carolyn Hamilton, et al., eds., *Refiguring the Archive* (Cape Town: David Philip, 2002).

2 In *Edmund Husserl's Origin of Geometry* (1978), for instance, Derrida engages Husserl and Joyce. In *Glas* (1986) he engages Hegel and Genet. *The Gift of Death* (1995) is a conversation with Kierkegaard and Jan Patocka. In *Politics of Friendship* (1997) he tackles the Western canonical discourse on friendship.

3 Jacques Derrida in *Deconstruction in a Nutshell: A Conversation with Jacques Derrida,* ed. John Caputo (New York: Fordham University Press, 1997), 9.

4 John Caputo describes "archi-text" as "various *networks*—social, historical, linguistic, political, sexual networks (the list goes on nowadays to include electronic networks, worldwide webs)—various horizons or presuppositions. . ." Caputo, *Deconstruction in a Nutshell,* 79–80.

5 This is a reading, a rewriting, of possibly Derrida's most misunderstood, most abused statement: "There is nothing outside of the text," *Of Grammatology* (Baltimore: Johns Hopkins University Press, 1974), 158.

6 See, for instance, *Memoirs of the Blind* (1993), *Circumfession* (1993), *Passions* (1993), *The Gift of Death* (1995), "Foi et Savoir: Les deux sources de la 'religion' aux limites de la simple raison" (1996), and *Monolingualism of the Other* (1998).

7 Jacques Derrida, *Archive Fever: A Freudian Impression* (Chicago: University of Chicago Press, 1996), 100.

8 Derrida, *Archive Fever,* 17.

9 Derrida, *Archive Fever,* 68.

10 Derrida, *Archive Fever,* 53.

11 Derrida, *Archive Fever,* 47.

12 John Caputo offers an extended exploration of this question in his *The Prayers and Tears of Jacques Derrida: Religion Without Religion* (Bloomington: Indiana University Press, 1997).

13 Derrida, *Archive Fever,* 90.

14 Was this move, I wonder, archontic or anarchontic?

15 Derrida, *Archive Fever,* 11.

16 Derrida, *Archive Fever,* 66.

17 Derrida, *Archive Fever,* 91.

18 Caputo, *Prayers and Tears,* 274.

19 Derrida, *Memoirs of the Blind.*

20 Derrida, *Memoirs of the Blind,* 12.

21 From the song "Please Don't Pass Me By (A Disgrace)," on the album *Live Songs* (Columbia, 1972).

22 Anne Michaels, *Fugitive Pieces* (Toronto: M and S, 1996), 17.

23 Derrida, *Memoirs of the Blind,* 126.

24 Quoted in Derrida, *Memoirs of the Blind,* 128.

25 In sacrifice there is a double blindness. The blindness that enables sacrifice (see 98–100 of *Memoirs of the Blind*), and the blindness (of tears) accompanies comprehension of sacrifice. For an exhaustive account of sacrifice, see Derrida's *The Gift of Death.*

26 Allen Ginsberg, *Collected Poems 1947–1980* (New York: Harper and Row, 1984), 151.

27 From the album *Highway 61 Revisited* (Columbia, 1965).

# CHAPTER 4

## Concerned with the Writings of Others: Archival Canons, Discourses, and Voices[1]

### ON CANONS AND HISTORICAL TURNS

When I first received the four books that form the fulcrum of this review essay, one of my professional colleagues expressed surprise: "Why are you wasting your time on these books?—besides boring you to tears, these are the voices of old or dead white men which are irrelevant to what you're doing now." My immediate response, I think, still bears repeating: "My voice is also that of an old white man, regarded by many as irrelevant."

Beneath such more or less facetious repartee are serious questions: Should the rereading of classic texts inform present archival discourses? To what extent have such texts shaped our discourses? Is the canonizing that such rereading contributes to desirable? From the early 1990s, Terry Cook has been advocating a historical turn in archival discourses, pressing archivists to historicize the concepts and views that shape their thinking. In his own work he has exemplified an approach that at once positions "archival" ideas within broader contexts and connects them to the pasts out of which they have come. It is no accident that

Cook is a co-editor of the Hugh Taylor collection *Imagining Archives*. It is also no accident that Jacques Derrida, whose work Cook has returned to increasingly in recent years, is another exemplar of this approach. Derrida's point of departure is always the canon of Western philosophy and literature, the tradition, the archive. He reads, and reads again, the canonical texts: "I think we have to read them again and again and I feel that, however old I am, I am on the threshold of reading Plato and Aristotle. I love them and I feel I have to start again and again and again. It is a task which is in front of me, before me."[2]

This reading (to and of) return, this reading "again and again," this repeated return of "old writing," is not without a problematic of its own. On the one hand, it can be read as—and can become—the loading of a weight from which we need release. In discourses already weighted by modes of patriarchy, do we really want to re-authorize the voices of old or dead white men? On the other hand, reading "again and again" raises the specter of a certain sterility. As Samuel Weber has written of deconstruction—and therefore, indirectly, of Derrida— "deconstruction concerns itself more with 'the opinions,' or more accurately, with the writings 'of others,' than with ideas of its own."[3] At this point I wish merely to flag rather than engage these questions. I will return to them in the final section of this essay, having first disclosed my reading (and rereading) of the old or dead white men.

Suffice it to note here that, problematic aside, powerful players in the English-language archival world have an interest in reproducing and promoting the work of venerated voices ("the masters"). The four books in question foreground the work of the Dutch trio Muller, Feith, and Fruin (their *Manual* was published in 1898 and first translated into English in 1940), Sir Hilary Jenkinson (essays spanning the period 1915–1960, and first published in collected form in 1980), Hugh Taylor (essays spanning the period 1969–1997), and Michael Cook (who has published from the 1960s to the present). Three of the four bear a Society of American Archivists' imprint (the *Essays in Honour of Michael Cook* is the odd one out), the first two being part of the Society's Archival Classics Series. The Cook volume is the odd one out in two further respects—rather than being a reproduction of previously published work by him, it is a *festschrift,* a collection of essays in honor of Cook; and while the Dutch trio and Jenkinson are indisputably part of the archival canon, and Taylor well on the way to incorporation, Cook's position remains uncertain.[4]

No canon constructs itself. A canon is always in the process of being constructed, and the process expresses prevailing relations of power. Veneration of voices past, or near-past, inevitably becomes an instrument in the shaping (even controlling) of current discourses. These four books, together with other classics that have already been published or are in the pipeline, provide us with a window into the process.

## AN INADEQUATE TURN

The appearance of these four books can, and should, be read as an expression of the historical turn in archival discourses. This turn, in my view, is to be welcomed, both as an idea and as a mode of discourse. Terry Cook got it just right. However, as I have already warned, the turn carries dangers. At this point I want to begin assessing the extent to which these four books avoid the dangers.

Each of them carries an implicit invitation—together with the explicit invitations of the books' editors—to read and reread "the masters." Each one also offers (in the interventions of the editors) a first new (or postpublication) reading.[5] This first reading, I would argue, is critical to the signaling of the historical turn, and to the nature and extent of the turn being invited. To return to my typification in the previous section, does the first reading critique "the masters" in relation to current discourses, position them within broader contexts, and connect them to the pasts out of which they have come? If it does these things, then it historicizes, it releases fresh energies, and (ultimately) it invites deconstruction in. If it does not, then it flings the door open to dangers.

In the preface to the 1898 edition of their *Manual,* the Dutch trio of Muller, Feith, and Fruin mark an important space when they say, "We ask of the critics much criticism."[6] That request, of course, is always being addressed to every reader of the *Manual,* but it was addressed with special force to the editors of the 2003 edition. Their response is disappointing. Certainly there is some criticism, but not the fulsome, wide-ranging critique that I for one anticipated. For instance, the editors offer accounts of the *Manual*'s reception in countries outside the Netherlands. They even include an article by Marjorie Barritt on its reception in the United States. But nowhere are the key questions addressed—what were the conditions in a specific country making it receptive to the *Manual;* and what has the impact on archival discourse in that country been? In South Africa, where the *Manual* has been hugely influential, one would have to look, at least, at the imprint of Dutch colonialism, the Eurocentric framing of South African elites, and the apartheid obsessions with "system," "science," the "organic," and the imposition of rules.[7]

In terms of the broader contexts to "the masters" under scrutiny, the editors of the *Manual,* the Jenkinson collection, and the Cook *festschrift* have drawn tight boundaries around the lives, careers, and writings of their subjects. Their concern is with what we could call immediate contexts. Here all three books offer generous and insightful accounts. But even within this narrow space the reader is offered very little critique. And as for the broader historical, intellectual, social, and political currents informing and engaging their subjects, the editors offer the reader, at best, a few markers. Here, for instance, are three from the editors of the *Manual,* each one left hanging tantalizingly unexplored: 1) "Certainly in the light of the nineteenth century's scientific propositions—in particular Darwinism from the biological perspective and historicism from a historical perspective—section 2 seems to follow naturally from the previous definition of archive."[8] 2) "The paradigm of descriptive archival science may then, in retrospect, have been codified for the first time in the Netherlands, but actually the whole of post-Napoleonic Europe was its intellectual cradle."[9] 3) "If we search for the roots of these concepts, then the first names we encounter are not those of archivists like Nijhoff, but rather those of Darwin and Stuart Mill."[10] I am suggesting that the *Manual*'s editors have sidestepped the dual imperative to re-spect (look again at) these markers and to read them from the text they are re-inscribing.

Hugh Taylor's editors do considerably better. Critique and contextualization are woven through an introduction as well as full-length articles by each of the editors, Terry Cook and Gordon Dodds. Moreover, in a delightful move (admittedly not available to the editors of the *Manual* and of Jenkinson), Taylor comments on each of the pieces published in the collection and offers a reflection on the collection as a whole. Nevertheless, I would have liked more on Taylor's "Christianity,"[11] the British intellectual crucible out of which he emerged in 1965, and the Canadian contexts that he entered in the same year. Of course, contexts are infinite, so that the desire for "more" is structurally determined. And Taylor's editors in large measure avoid the linked pitfalls of the closed context and the temptation to hagiography.

## PERSONAL SIGNIFICANCES

My introduction to the world of archives occurred in 1981, when I spent a year in South Africa's State Archives Service. At that time the intellectual training of state archivists consisted of a copy of the Dutch trio's *Manual* being handed to the novice with the instruction, "study this from cover to cover." No context, no engagement, no elaboration. But as I struggled through the turgid text, I found shafts of light that sustained me. Indeed, the first sentence of the authors' preface was a shaft I returned to over and over again: "This is a tedious and meticulous book. The reader is warned."[12] I loved this unexpected honesty and self-reflection. Much later, in the late 1980s, I came to appreciate the book's significance to archival discourses and its interconnections with strands of Western thinking. I still have that first copy of the *Manual* given to me, now in leather covers, and frequently used in the postgraduate course I teach at the University of the Witwatersrand.

I came to Sir Hilary Jenkinson later, when I was studying for the State Archives Service's National Diploma in Archival Science. I had taken to heart the editors' injunction in the 1980 edition of the *Selected Writings* to regard his *Manual of Archive Administration* as "basic reading for all archivists."[13] Today I regard it as enriching reading rather than basic reading. At the time I found his hyperbolic style refreshing—like moving from a string quartet to an opera—and will never forget the thrill unleashed by this statement: "Let it be said at once that the title to these notes is not to be taken ... as suggesting that any qualities of scholarship or experience will make it possible for anyone to 'choose' with certainty out of a mass of records those which future historians will find most useful."[14] This found a powerful resonance with my own resistance to the State Archives Service's arrogantly positivist approach to appraisal, and with my earliest venturing into "postmodernist" writing.

The first book-length account of the challenges posed by electronic records I read (in the early 1990s) was Michael Cook's *Archives and the Computer*. Although the conceptual frame in which he operated found little resonance with my own, his work played a key role in my own teeth-cutting processes. I was fortunate to meet him in 1999 and again in 2003, instinctively responding to his humility and enjoying highly productive professional engagement. The primary lesson I've taken away from him, reinforcing the influences of the Dutch trio and Jenkinson, is the importance of ideas connecting to the sweat and tears of work at the (to take a term from Jenkinson) archival coalface.

Terry Cook introduced me to the work of Hugh Taylor in the mid-1990s. Before that, international isolation, and Taylor's preference for article-length writing, had kept him on the periphery of my vision. My initial engagements with him flowed effortlessly into the stream of my reading on narrative, imagination, power, and poetry. At first I felt undone by his apparent anticipation of every move I planned to make in archival spaces, but gradually I came to see more clearly what Terry Cook calls his "blind spots," as well as the avenues opened up by the eclectic and unsystematic nature of his own reading and contemplation. He remains a huge inspiration, and in my view, together with Terry Cook, the most compelling tender of soul in archives.

## SIGNIFICANCES TO DISCOURSES 1

### Introduction

I have disclosed some of the significances of these "masters" to me. Part of me would like to end it right there. But discourse always beckons toward a broader engagement. So, how significant are these "masters" to current English-language archival discourses? My view, of course, is obscured by personal and other loves, familiarities, and experiences, and by my reading of the filters inserted by editors and interpreters of the "masters." In addition, it is obscured by what I "see" as the extraordinary messiness of these discourses. They heave and weave all over the place (an expression of the conditions of postmodernity?), making the clear and widely understood statement nigh impossible. Let me justify this disclaimer by identifying what I see as four spaces of confusion in these discourses. In each case I outline merely what I regard to be the more obvious examples of dysfunction.

## Inaccurate Deployment of Terms

Wherever I go (literally and virtually) in the archival world, I find the ubiquitous use of the term *principle of provenance*. For many, possibly most, this principle remains the cornerstone of archival theorizing. And yet its current readings are far removed from its initial readings in the nineteenth century. As they should be. But why insist on using the same term for these more or less dislocated readings? When one asserts, for example, that the meanings and significances of a record are located in the contextual circumstances of its creation and subsequent use, one is in a ballpark different from the Dutch *Manual*. Marking the ballparks, I would suggest, has become essential.

Another ubiquitous term, used sometimes pejoratively, sometimes approvingly, is *postmodernism* (together with the adjective *postmodernist*). In archival discourses, only Terry Cook and Joan Schwartz begin to suggest the problematic surrounding its usage.[15] So wide and indiscriminate has its application been, that its meaning has lost all coherence. My own work has been labeled "postmodernist," something I resist. A similar labeling of Jacques Derrida (the coiner of the term *deconstruction*) ignores his insistent deconstruction of labels, including that of "postmodernism," and his searing critiques of those who adopt the label willingly. Hugh Taylor himself conflates *deconstruction* and *postmodernism*—a move of considerable naivety given the fissures and disjunctures I am suggesting.[16] In most disciplines, scholars are either eschewing the term *postmodernism* entirely or are insisting on the plural *postmodernisms*. (How else to connect Fukuyama with Lyotard?)

But the worst case of misidentification (in this case a form of self-identification) I've come across is Sue McKemmish's attempt to claim a "post-modern philosophical" authority for the Australian records continuum model.[17] Her move is in a ballpark different from those I cite above. It is a co-opting—or colonizing—move designed to have us believe that what is a wild tiger is only a domestic cat. It ignores the fact that postmodernisms seek relentlessly to disturb every totalizing conceptual container. And the continuum model, whatever else its articulators attempt to do with it, is a totalizing conceptual container—in the words of McKemmish, the model issues from a "worldview" providing a framework that is "inclusive" and "unifying."[18]

To my ear the readers of the continuum are constructing a metanarrative at the same time as denying its "meta" attributes. I would suggest that a truly "postmodern" analysis would want to rip the continuum model to shreds.

## Misreadings

Here again I cite two examples. The grossest misreading I was exposed to by South Africa's State Archives Service was the caricature of Schellenbergian appraisal it both articulated and practiced.[19] Schellenberg's theoretical and methodological moves around what he called the "evidential values" in records were almost entirely ignored. The result was an appraisal program geared to identifying records with "informational values" through piecemeal interventions. Later I was to discover that a similar misreading informed appraisal thinking in many countries. One result is that the conceptual links between Schellenbergian appraisal and macroappraisal have been underplayed or overlooked.[20]

The other example draws me into a measure of culpability. Many of us deploy terms such as *recordkeeping discourse, recordkeeping paradigm,* and *recordkeeping approach* with a certain lack of rigor, thus inviting misreadings.[21] I discovered the consequences in the aftermath to my paper at the 2000 Seville ICA congress,[22] when my critique of what I called the "recordkeeping paradigm" (an approach to archives informed by the dissolving of thresholds between "archives" and "records," a defining of "the record" in terms of functional (or work process) requirements, a privileging of the evidential attributes of records, and an emphasis on accountability) elicited strong condemnation from Australian archivists who had read the critique as an attack on the continuum model.[23] Plainly I had failed to define the term clearly enough; failed to demonstrate the term's applicability to strands of thought as diverse as David Bearman, Luciana Duranti, and the emerging dominant archival discourse in postapartheid South Africa; and failed to acknowledge adequately the paradigm's influence on all of us engaged in archival discourses.[24] In my defense, I would suggest that in addition to my own lack of rigor, the sight of the Australians in this instance was somewhat clouded by their imperial aspirations for the continuum model.

## Reifications

Archival discourses are characterized (more accurately, blighted) by what is almost an instinct to reify. By this I mean the shifting into transcendent space of ideas, principles, and models. This shift wants there to be a "thing-itself," a thing that hangs pristine above the messiness of human construction. So, archival appraisers look for records with "archival value" rather than stooping to create and re-create such value as they select records for preservation. Theorists argue about what *provenance* means, rather than accepting that they are always in the process of according the concept meaning. Articulators of the records continuum model strive to reach into and disclose the richness of the model itself, rather than acknowledging that there are only, and will only ever be, readings of the model.

This links into the broader epistemological challenge posed by our reliance as human beings on language and narrative to connect with the realities we experience. We become the emperor without clothes when we reveal others' constructions of reality to be merely metanarratives and claim for our own constructions a faithful reflection of reality. If we are to open the door to a discourse that is liberatory and concerned not with winning intellectual skirmishes but with enriching life, then we must realize that the notion of a "reflection of reality" is a chimera; we cannot avoid constructing "metanarrative"; and the best we can do is to open our metanarratives to deconstruction. This insight, I would suggest, is what Hugh Taylor expressed (more or less instinctively) in his writing, and what Terry Cook, pre-eminently among the giants of current archival discourses, expresses (more or less in scholarly mode) in his work.

## Resistances to Theory

There are strong currents in the flow of archival discourses which I would describe as anti-intellectual. It is in these currents that we find accusations that theorizing is "much ado about shelving."[25] It is here that we find resistances to approaches that could be called variously multi-disciplinary, interdisciplinary, cross-disciplinary, or nondisciplinary. It is here that we find dismissals of broader intellectual inquiry by archivists as irrelevant, indulgent, or distracting. (How much longer do we have to put up with intellectual recluses dismissing Derrida, or Foucault, or Giddens as offering archivists nothing of value?) And it is here that we find engagement with sociopolitical contexts as outside the legitimate terrain of archivy. An extensive critique could be mounted in response. Suffice it to make two observations here. Firstly, it is ironic that archivists, the very people who claim special expertise in "contexts," choose to insulate themselves from the great weight of significant "contexts." And, secondly, the choice by many archivists to avoid the languages and idioms and formulations and discourses that frame and interpret the spaces that they inhabit (unavoidably) makes the reach of their discourses—and their capacity to connect with those having more generous understandings of significant "context"—extraordinarily narrow.

## SIGNIFICANCES TO DISCOURSES 2

My intention in the previous section was to demonstrate how difficult it is to answer clearly and meaningfully the question "How significant are these 'masters' to current English-language archival discourses?" It presupposes an identification of these discourses, in circumstances of extreme complexity. Of course, such attempts at identification are problematic in any circumstances. But enough of disclaimers.

International English-language archival discourses, in my reading, are patterned around three major streams. Each is characterized by numerous subcurrents, and each is more or less permeable to the others. I know of not a single archival thinker, or "school of thought," that I could position comfortably within a single stream.

The first (an arbitrary selection, although its historical roots arguably are the longest) resists higher level theorizing and is most comfortable with methodologies and practices. Here "the record" is not something to be problematized; what it means, what it signifies, and what its values are, are self-explanatory. Archivists are workers with the record. This stream draws its intellectual energies primarily from forms of Western positivism. Muller, Feith, and Fruin were founding fathers and remain influential. The work of Michael Cook, in my view, flows, and has influence, mainly within this stream.

The second stream embraces broader and higher layers of theorizing, and is more comfortable with disclosing its assumptions and presuppositions. Here "the record" is something to be defined against rationally determined frames and measures. Archivists are keepers of the record. I see this stream flowing out of the Enlightenment, its core energies those of a vigorous modernism. In my reading, its most powerful subcurrent is the continuum thinking being elaborated in Australia and elsewhere (although, as I intimated earlier, continuum thinkers are engaging the work of "postmodernists" and others outside the recognized bounds of the stream). The work of Muller, Feith, and Fruin is not completely out of the picture here, but it is Jenkinson of the "masters" who is most strongly evident.

The third stream flows strongly and widely in spaces defined by respect for narrative, comfort with multiple shifting meanings, acknowledgment of contingencies in knowledge construction, and an intense awareness of the dimensions of power. Here "the record" is something always in the process of being made. Archivists are narrators of the record. This stream is commonly labeled "postmodernist"—a label I resist for reasons articulated earlier—but it clearly draws on a range of energies variously labeled "postmodernist," "poststructuralist," and "deconstructionist." Of all the streams, it is the one most open to "the other," the voices and the knowledges marginalized by a Western-dominated global mainstream. It is in this stream that the work of Hugh Taylor flows luxuriously. Indeed, it would not be entirely unreasonable to see him as a progenitor—in the words of Terry Cook, there is a case to be made for regarding Taylor as "the first philosopher of archives."[26]

## MORE ON CANONS

Like metanarrative, "the canon" is not something we can avoid—indeed, every canon *is* a metanarrative—unless, of course, we choose to ignore our pasts and to dehistoricize the conceptual tools we work with. That, I have argued following Terry Cook, is impoverishing. In engaging our (professional, or disciplinary, or institutional) pasts, inevitably we foreground certain voices and marginalize or exclude others. And this is the stuff of canonization.

Earlier I flagged the dangers of this process. Now, in conclusion, I wish to revisit the question of how to avoid them. The starting point, in my view, is always to read our own motives in recalling those who have gone before us. We need to be extremely wary of the instinct to legitimize our own views, to find an authoritative stamp—ultimately, perhaps, a stamp of identity—for what we are saying. We can do this by adulation, rejection, or the full gamut of positionings in between. Legitimization is not something we can avoid, but we should be wary.

Beyond such wariness, we need to trouble the ideas of those we regard as authoritative. We do this by contextualizing (generously) the venerated voices, looking for their "blind spots," seeking spaces for "the other" inevitably dancing outside the circle of their knowing. In short, we need to find within every impulse to canonization what is a counterimperative. As I have tried to demonstrate (though not without qualification), the editors of the Hugh Taylor collection serve us well in this regard. The editors of the other three publications do less well.

In the opening paragraph of this review essay I marked an indisputable fact about the English-speaking canon in archives—it is dominated by the voices of white men. We could go further by observing that these dominant voices are those of straight white men shaped by the values and fantasies of Western traditions. If we are to break out of what constitutes an exclusive (and "exclusivizing") conceptual straitjacket, then we are going to have to find ways of creating a hospitality to "other" voices. The "easy" part (and it is extremely difficult) has been demonstrated by Jacques Derrida (whether we know it or like it)—deconstruct the canon tirelessly and respectfully, open it up to the "other" it excludes and to its own "otherness." (Derrida's demonstration is also a demonstration of the flaw in Samuel Weber's comment on deconstruction, which I quoted in the opening section of this essay. Deconstruction's concern with "otherness" is, precisely, the most powerful idea of its own.) The hard part is to engage the voices "outside," and to foster their empowering to speak to the "inside" and (the most difficult) to speak "inside."

How hard it can be is exemplified very simply by the four books under review. Consider their editors (eight in number) in relation to my typification of the dominant voices in English-language archival discourse—all eight are positioned within a Western intellectual tradition, all are white, and six of them are men.[27] They are, in short, an exclusive group mediating the work of an exclusive group.

# Endnotes

1    This review essay's first draft was commented on by Terry Cook (University of Manitoba) and Wendy Duff (University of Toronto). Both are friends, and are vigorous, but generous, critics of my work. I trust that their comments have seen the removal of that first draft's crudest excesses. It was published in the *Journal of the Society of Archivists* 25, no. 2 (2004). The books reviewed in the essay are Terry Cook and Gordon Dodds, eds., *Imagining Archives: Essays and Reflections by Hugh A. Taylor* (Lanham and Oxford: Society of American Archivists and Association of Canadian Archivists in association with Scarecrow Press, 2003); Roger H. Ellis and Pete Walne, eds., *Selected Writings of Sir Hilary Jenkinson* (Chicago: Society of American Archivists, 2003); S. Muller, J. A. Feith, and R. Fruin, *Manual for the Arrangement and Description of Archives* (Chicago: Society of American Archivists, 2004); and Margaret Proctor and Caroline Williams, eds., *Essays in Honour of Michael Cook* (Liverpool: Liverpool University, 2004).

2    Jacques Derrida, in *Deconstruction in a Nutshell: A Conversation with Jacques Derrida*, ed. John Caputo (New York: Fordham University Press, 1997), 9.

3    Samuel Weber, "In the Name of the Law," in *Deconstruction and the Possibility of Justice*, ed. Drucilla Cornell, et al. (New York and London: Routledge, 1992), 238.

4    I restrict myself to the most obvious differences, as difference always draws one into an infinite space. For example, the *Manual* is the odd one out in that, unlike the other three, it is not a collection of essays. Also, it is the only one of the four books in which the honored "master" is not of English origin. The Cook volume is more "odd" than I have indicated in that it is edited by women. Also, it is the only one of the four that represents voices that are not white or male. And so we could go on ...

5    Here and elsewhere I am, of course, stretching the analysis a bit far when including the Cook volume in my general comments. As a rule, the *festschrift*, as a genre, as an idiom, is allowed more latitude in indulging the temptation to adulation and hyperbole. (I say this with the weight of personal experience, having received a *festschrift* from my former colleagues at the National Archives of South Africa, and having been invited to participate in the compilation of a *festschrift* for Kent Haworth.) So that in the case of the Cook volume, the "invitation" I identify here is cast (structurally) in a very different way.

6    Muller, et al., *Manual for the Arrangement and Description of Archives* (2003 reprint of second edition), 10.

7    The *Manual* is a book of rules and promotes a rules-based approach. It is only in the last two decades that the archival profession internationally has begun to create spaces for other approaches.

8    Muller, et al., *Manual*, xx.

9    Muller, et al., *Manual*, xxxii.

10   Muller, et al., *Manual*, xxxiii.

11   I assume that his engagement with Christianity informed his almost religious conceptualization of the archival endeavor.

12   Muller, et al., *Manual*, 9.

13   Ellis and Walne, eds., *Selected Writings*, 11.

14   Ellis and Walne, eds., *Selected Writings*, xvi.

15   See, for example, their editorial contributions to *Archival Science* 2, nos. 1–2 (2002) and 2, nos. 3–4 (2002).

16  Cook and Dodds, eds., *Imagining Archives,* 247 and 250.

17  See Sue McKemmish, "Placing Records Continuum Theory and Practice," *Archival Science* 1, no. 4 (2001): 333–59.

18  McKemmish, "Placing Records Continuum Theory," 352.

19  See my "Exploratory Thoughts on Current State Archives Service Appraisal Policy and the Conceptual Foundations of Macro-appraisal," *Archives News* 37, no. 8 (1995).

20  Even Terry Cook has been culpable here. Although Schellenberg links "evidential values" to "government" rather than "governance," and fails to draw his account of "value" into a coherent conceptual and methodological frame, he offers an early articulation of several attributes of macro-appraisal—the appraisal analysis getting in "behind" records, value being located in processes rather than records, an awareness of records documenting function and structure, and the need for a methodology built on top-down analysis.

21  Note that I use here the Australian "recordkeeping" rather than the more grammatically correct "record-keeping." This is to follow dominant usage, despite its implicit naturalization of a construct (with all the power moves that expresses).

22  "Law, Evidence and Electronic Records: A Strategic Perspective from the Global Periphery," presented at the International Council on Archives quadrennial congress, Seville, Spain, September 2000. It was subsequently published in the *South African Archives Journal* 41 (1999/2000) and *Comma* (2001) nos. 1-2.

23  The debate raged on the Australian listserv during the last quarter of 2000.

24  Terry Cook was saying the same thing on a visit to Australia in 2000, but judging from his reception there he succeeded in avoiding the pitfalls I walked into. See his "Beyond the Screen: The Records Continuum and Archival Cultural Heritage," at http://www.archivists.org.au/sem/conf2000/terrycook.pdf.

25  J. W. Roberts coined this phrase. See his "Archival Theory: Much Ado About Shelving," *American Archivist* 50, no. 1 (1987), and "Practice Makes Perfect, Theory Makes Theorists," *Archivaria* 37 (1994).

26  Cook and Dodds, eds., *Imagining Archives,* 18.

27  I decline here, for obvious reasons, to measure degrees of "straightness."

# CHAPTER 5

## "Something Is Happening Here and You Don't Know What It Is": Jacques Derrida Unplugged[1]

## MOURNING

I heard of Jacques Derrida's death on the morning of 10 October 2004, standing at the reception desk of an Amsterdam hotel. Before me was the hotel manager, reading a phone message left for me by my partner in South Africa: "Derrida has died." He absorbed my blank expression for a few seconds, then said softly, "I'm very sorry for your loss." I knew that Derrida had not been well and, of course, I knew that he could not keep going forever. But instantly I seemed to be within the abyss that had yawned beneath me. And in the days thereafter I realized that the mourning that started long before his death would stay with me forever. It shouldn't have taken "an event" to bring this realization—in 1998 I had heard Derrida making the argument that "the work of the archivist ... is the work of mourning."[2]

It is not for me to mark Derrida's position in the pantheon of twentieth-century thinkers, nor to suggest his significance to intellectual endeavor in the broadest sense. Suffice it to note that he was one of the most prominent public intellectuals of his era; he had a profound influence on a wide range of disciplines and professions; in the last decade of his life he spoke insistently to what we name archival discourses;[3] and he is widely regarded as a key mover in what has been recognized by many as an archival turn in intellectual work.[4] My aim in this essay is a more modest, dual one: to offer a personal appreciation of his work and its significance to that terrain we call archival.

## MY BACK PAGES 1

My journey with Jacques Derrida began in 1995, in Terry Cook's basement study.[5] For some years, Terry and I, independently, had been exploring those streams of thinking commonly labeled "postmodernist." Both of us accepted the view of "experts" that Derrida was an important postmodernist (so, like all journeys, this one had begun before the first step), and during that 1995 visit Terry shared with me Derrida's essay "Sendoffs."[6] I read it without understanding a word, but was intrigued by the writing's rhythms, registers, and patterns. That took me to a more focused reading of texts about Derrida, and to the discovery that he had been associated with the anti-apartheid movement in Europe and had edited a book in honor of Nelson Mandela.[7] These constituted serious credentials in my eyes, and when his book *Archive Fever* was published in 1996, I devoured it, reading the text three times in the space of twelve months. It felt like finding the Song of Solomon in the Old Testament—after a decade of reading archival literature, here at last was a text on archive that was dancing with imagination and libido.[8] I was quickly seduced.

Ever since, I have been attempting what still proves to be an impossible reading project—to stay abreast of the new work pouring from his pen while at the same time catching up with his prolific output from the mid-sixties to the mid-nineties. As of now I have read as many of his pre-1995 texts as I have "current" texts, but from the outset I have felt drawn to the latter. This preference, in all honesty, has something to do with the groupie's need to have heard the idol's latest word. And that set a stern test—by my count he published fourteen books in English in the period from his seventieth birthday in 2000 until his death. But there are other (I hope more important) factors. In the last decade of his life he developed a style and an approach (arguably an idiom) that was far more accessible than that which characterized his intimidating—and occasionally impenetrable—earlier work, he opened himself more to the autobiographical, and he engaged increasingly in collaborative endeavor.[9] And he returned, over and over again, to themes that have been labeled (clumsily, but more or less accurately) "ethics" and "religion." All of this meant that, for me, the later Derrida was more engaging and more inspirational.

I met Derrida only once. That was in 1998 on his visit to South Africa, when he spoke at a seminar at the University of the Witwatersrand.[10] This seminar was part of a series entitled "Refiguring the Archive," and Derrida had agreed with the university's Professor Carolyn Hamilton at very short notice to speak to his book *Archive Fever*. The event remains the most terrifying moment of my professional career. Sue van Zyl and I shared the platform with Derrida, the two of us commissioned to offer critiques of *Archive Fever* before a response from him. In attendance was a huge audience spilling into an adjacent venue fitted with a movie screen. Later I was to remember that the audience was "surprised to discover not the dry, arrogant, cynical, almost incomprehensible deconstructionist that popular caricature had led them to anticipate. Instead they discovered a person combining profound humility with the passion of an Old Testament prophet, speaking a language at once simple and poetic."[11] What I did not recount was the patient and thoughtful manner in which he dealt with often crude questions from the floor. Nor the gracious informal feedback he gave to Carolyn, Sue, and me afterward; his readiness to listen to our accounts of the South African Truth and Reconciliation Commission and related processes; and his almost impish sense of humor. In short, Derrida in the flesh offered us a memorable experience of charm. We were not surprised a year later when he readily agreed to a transcript of the seminar being included in the book *Refiguring the Archive,* nor at the absence of fuss during the editing process.

## YOU DON'T KNOW WHAT IT IS

I have hinted at the widespread (and sometimes cynically ignorant) misreading (this isn't really the right word, for most of his critics don't take the trouble to read his work) of Derrida. One consequence is that those who rely on others' readings of Derrida rather than their own are in danger of being plugged into an archive of prejudice characterized by fundamental misconceptions about him and his work. Here I pause to address what appear to me to be the most common misconceptions, especially in archival discourses. Let me say at once that I myself have been guilty, at one time or another, of carrying each one of them.

*Derrida wrote a book about archives titled* Archive Fever. Statements like these, at one level, are not untrue. But, firstly, that book was about far more than what archivists call "archives." In it he concentrated—in a sustained interrogation, for the first time—the fruits of three decades of re-imagining "archive." For, secondly, as I have written elsewhere, "in a sense all Derrida's work is about the archive. He converses with it, mines it, interrogates it, plays in it, extends it, creates it, imagines it and is imagined by it. It is impossible to speak of Derrida without also speaking of the archive. It is impossible to speak—now, at the turn of the century—of the archive without also speaking of Derrida."[12] And thirdly, beginning with *Spurs: Nietzsche's Styles* in 1978, and increasingly after the publication of *Archive Fever*, in book after book Derrida returned explicitly to the concept of archive. Far from being evidence of a philosopher flirting with the world of archives before skipping off on other pursuits,[13] *Archive Fever* arguably offers us the richest window into Derrida's corpus.

*Jacques Derrida is (was) a French philosopher.* To call him a philosopher without qualification is to miss an extraordinary richness and to reduce him to something he perhaps only was in the very early years of his career. To name but three strands: he consistently troubled the concept archived in the word *philosopher* (he philosophized philosophy, so to speak); he worked comfortably in many disciplines other than philosophy; and he demonstrated the porosity of every disciplinary boundary. To call him French ignores his own discomfort with and interrogation of his "Frenchness."[14] He was born in North Africa of Jewish parents, lost his French citizenship during the Second World War, first arrived in France at the age of nineteen, and for a large part of his adult life had homes in both France and the United States. If anything, it was in the figure of the Marrano that he found the most satisfying markers for this order of identity.[15]

*Derrida is difficult.*[16] Of course Derrida is difficult. But we need to qualify the statement. Firstly, we live in an age of commodification, sound bites, and quick delivery, an age impatient with complexity. That says as much about us (we readers, we consumers) as it does about those who produce "difficult" work. Secondly, it is imperative that we distinguish between different orders of difficulty. There is a difference between a difficulty that works and one that does not. (In the realm of the novel, one could compare, for instance, work by Joyce or Calvino with that by many self-proclaimed "postmodernists" of fiction.) There is a difference between a difficulty that is intentional and one that is not. There is a difference between a difficulty embraced as a matter of principle (as with Theodor Adorno, for instance) and a difficulty that flows necessarily out of particular engagements, inquiries, and interrogations. And thirdly, as I have already noted, his later work was considerably less difficult. The difficulty of Derrida, I would argue, always works, expressing a determination not to slip the laws of language, which at once confine meaning and open it to deconstruction. Derrida discloses the complexities and contradictions (the difficulties) in using (in having to use) what is an oppressive tool in order to find liberation. And, let it be said, the translation of his work from French into English adds new layers of difficulty.

*Derrida is a postmodernist.* Derrida himself resisted this label and seldom, in any context, used the terms *postmodernist, postmodernism,* and *postmodernity.* It is not difficult to understand the association of Derrida with "the postmodern," nor to identify the threads that cross the work of Derrida and Lyotard, who first popularized the term *postmodern.* However, it is also clear that this and related terms have lost their significatory usefulness as a result of reckless and indiscriminate use. It is common, for instance (and it is certainly common in archival discourses) for thinkers as diverse as Foucault, Derrida, Lyotard, Baudrillard, Levinas, and Fukuyama to be thrown together in the hold-all "postmodernism." This is to invite in not only obfuscation, but also (at least) two reactionary agendas—on the one hand, by throwing together "good" and "bad," "reasonable" and "unreasonable," one can more readily dismiss them all; on the other, by privileging the "good" and the "reasonable" within the hold-all it is relatively easy to co-opt the hold-all. But I leave this line of argument to rest for another occasion. Here, I want to insist that the core attributes of any form of what is (or can be) called (legitimately) postmodernism cannot be attached meaningfully to Derrida. All postmodernisms (and it is, now, necessary to use the term in the plural) proclaim, explicitly or implicitly, in the words of Christopher Norris, "a break with the philosophic discourse of modernity."[17] This is most often identified with a positioning that is anti-Enlightenment or counter-Enlightenment, from which flows a skepticism in relation to all metanarratives, a hostility toward "the rational," and an embrace of relativism. Derrida, on the other hand, throughout forty years of rigorous intellectual inquiry, remained committed to a "working within" (again Norris's words) the "discourse of modernity."[18] He respected the Enlightenment project, and returned to, looked again at (respected), repeatedly, the canonical voices in that discourse. While deconstructing its every metanarrative, he was intensely, and openly, aware that metanarrative cannot be avoided. To state it crudely, within deconstruction, always, there are the energies of metanarrative construction. Far from rejecting "the rational," Derrida passionately took it as far as it could take him, and then reached beyond. And in that reaching, a reaching for the impossible, he moved outside, at once, discourses of rationalism and relativism. Indeed, I would argue, he moved into a space he himself called "religion without religion." There we find what I call the faith of Jacques Derrida, a belief in the impossible, a passion for a justice that must always be coming. There we find Jacques Derrida blinded by tears. Hardly, I would suggest, the figure or emblem or image of anyone's postmodernism.

*Deconstruction is a way of reading texts*. I am more comfortable with Derrida being labeled a "deconstructionist." After all, he coined the term *deconstruction* and used it frequently. However, he never defined it, and resisted those who would turn it into a theory or a methodology. For Derrida, deconstruction is something always already at work within texts. Whatever it is—and he only ever identified its attributes and invited in its energies—it disturbs meaning and troubles pattern in a cascade of multiplyings, splittings, and deferrals. The appearance of stability and seamlessness is always merely appearance. Now, it is true that engagement with deconstruction involves what Norris calls "textual close-reading."[19] But to reduce deconstruction to an activity of reading is to miss the Derridean "always already at work." And this form of reductionism usually ignores Derrida's insistence that readers and readings are embedded in "archi-text"[20]—so that "to read" can never be separated from "to be read."

# SOMETHING IS HAPPENING HERE

Derrida's direct impact on the archival terrain,[21] in my view, remains slight. My sense is that a significant number of archivists have read *Archive Fever*, but that very few have moved beyond it. It is true that in the period since its publication, Derrida's name and work have become more familiar to readers of archival literature, with a growing number of voices citing him and acknowledging his importance. However, in my reading very little of this expresses a serious study of Derrida's work. Indeed, much of it can be interpreted as a superficial opportunism, even as a form of co-option. The seminal archival voice heralding serious study was that of Brien Brothman,[22] but only a handful have followed Brothman's lead.[23] Nevertheless, Derrida's indirect impact has been substantial. Western intellectual discourses since the 1960s bear powerful Derridean imprints, and, as I have already suggested, his role in the "archival turn" has been central. He looms large in the wider intellectual environments in which mainstream archival discourses are embedded, so that archivists are influenced by his thinking without necessarily knowing it. An assessment of his influence on archivists would require a study beyond the bounds of this essay. The more manageable question, and arguably the more important, is what Derrida *offers* archival discourses. Not surprisingly, I believe that he offers a myriad of gifts. For me the ones with the greatest potential to enrich, enchant, and galvanize us are to be found, ironically perhaps, *outside* his more focused interrogation of "archive."[24] These are the ones I wish to consider briefly now.

As I have pointed out, while Derrida worked within the discourse of modernity and had huge respect for Enlightenment values, at the same time he developed a mode of knowing, a mode of knowledge construction, which at once challenged fundamentally and reached beyond what we could call an Enlightenment mode. Here I single out four of his moves that for me define the challenge he mounted. Firstly, he problematized the notion of a simple, direct relation between signifier and signified. He showed the dangers we court when we assume that the meanings of words are self-evident and that they represent (rather than construct) what we call "the real world" or "reality." Secondly, he demonstrated the degree to which we rely on binary oppositions in a hierarchy of value—for instance, good-bad, truth-lie, white-black,

West-East, light-dark, known-unknown, man-woman, straight-gay, life-death, and so on. He unfolded the processes of every such opposition's construction and revealed its unsustainability. Thirdly, he challenged every hard boundary, demonstrating its artificiality (or constructedness) and its porosity. Consider the boundaries we assume or draw between the concepts archived in the following word pairs, all of them woven into the tapestry of archival discourses: text-context, form-content, event-record, fact-fiction, remembering-forgetting, writing-reading, speaking-writing, author-addressee, and public-private. Consider the degree to which the ground shifts beneath our feet with this Derridean move. Fourthly, he showed us how wedded we are to the metaphor of sight for knowledge (with its binary opposite blindness representing ignorance) and to the concomitant privileging of reason. Working, as always, within these metaphors and the opposition that binds them together, Derrida posits a seeing in blindness, a seeing in the blindness of tears. In doing so, "Derrida neither dismisses reason nor abandons realities outside human subjectivity. This blindness has no essential quarrel with reason. It insists only that the knowing of reason, the seeing of the eye—in light, by light, knower and known separated—be always joined to the knowing of passion, the seeing in blindness—in darkness, in the immediacy of feeling and touching."[25] Derrida, in tears, calls for a knower weeping at injustice and importuning justice to come.

The Enlightenment bequeaths us an instinct to close every circle of knowledge. Postmodernisms are contemptuous of the instinct and dismissive of the circles. Derrida, in contrast, painstakingly, with respect, holds the logic of the circle and discloses the breach that is always already threatening to unravel it. This is, in the first instance, the work of deconstruction. But Derrida never stops there. Deconstruction never ends there. It poses, insistently, the relation to what is outside the circle, to what is at the same time inside. (For the inside-outside opposition is not sustainable.) The question that will not go away, and that Derrida listens for with his every move, is "What should that relation be?" What should our relation be to what is not known, to what is unknowable, to the stranger, to "the other"? The question, of course, is not simply an intellectual one, and Derrida was always at pains to point this out. It draws us immediately into the way we live in the world, our ethics, our politics. For Derrida, the question defines—if such a thing can be defined—the call of justice. A call that demands a relation of hospitality to the other. Ethics, to put it bluntly, *is* hospitality.[26]

This, I would suggest, is the central challenge that Derrida poses to archivists. How do we make our work a work of justice? How do we practice a hospitality to otherness, a hospitality to every other? (For every other is equally worthy of our hospitality.) The challenge, clearly, is an impossible one. We can close our ears to the call of justice, set ourselves manageable yardsticks, busy ourselves with standards and methodologies and procedures. Or we can reach for the impossible, in doing so understanding why the work of the archivist is mourning.

## (UN)PLUGGED 1

I wish to resist the temptation to attempt a summary—an "in a nut-shell"—account of Derrida's extraordinarily rich direct engagement with "archive." It is too rich for treatment in a section of a short essay. Instead, I want to offer, with a minimum of comment, a window into that engagement (and it is simultaneously a window into Derrida's "live per-formances," a window into Derrida more or less unplugged) by quoting at length from his 1998 seminar at the University of the Witwatersrand. Let me point out that he was speaking to an audience that he knew had been exposed to nearly three years of widely publicized and debated work by the Truth and Reconciliation Commission, South Africa's mech-anism for dealing with its traumatic apartheid past. The fragment below is extracted from the final moments of his formal address, as he comes to the work of the archivist as a work of mourning:

> Even in the case of let's say—by hypothesis—a successful archive—even if you really succeed in gathering everything you need in reference to the past, and that you interpret it in a way which is totally satisfactory (then we'll have here a full archive, correctly interpreted and no one would disagree on the truth and the fidelity of this archive, everything is now kept safe and everyone agrees on that …). Now, because of that, because of this very fullness, the hypothetical fullness, of this archive, what will have been granted is not memory, is not a true memory. It will be forgetting. That is, the archive—

the good one—produces memory, but produces forgetting at the same time. [Here Derrida 1) works within the opposition remembering-forgetting in order to subvert it; 2) eschews the forgetting associated with incompleteness, loss, selection, and destruction; and 3) signals a forgetting in all remembering, a forgetting that works precisely within a fullness of memory.] And when we write, when we archive, when we trace, when we leave a trace behind us—and that's what we do each time we trace something, even each time we speak, that is we leave a trace which becomes independent of its origin, of the movement of its utterance [Note Derrida marking the quality or attribute that distinguishes—not neatly, not without overlap— "archive" from "memory," namely, exteriority—archive as trace on an exterior surface. So that, *inter alia:* 1) shared memories, collective memories, orality, all are forms of archive; 2) traces in the unconscious—the outside (the exterior) inside—are also archive; and 3) the notion of a "private" archive, one that is protected from outside, is troubled.]—the trace is at the same time the memory, the archive, and the erasure, the repression, the forgetting of what it is supposed to keep safe. That's why, for all these reasons, the work of the archivist is not simply a work of memory. It's a work of mourning. [A mourning stimulated by the harsh reality that what ensures remembering at the same time provokes forgetting, that what promises safety at the same time exposes to danger. Here, for me, Derrida misses a move. Mourning also flows from a yearning for an impossible fullness, and from the injustice expressed in every archive, and from the unavoidable exclusions and marginalizations inherent to any process of selection.] And a work of mourning, as everyone knows, is a work of memory but also the best way just to forget the other, to keep the other in oneself, to keep it safe, in a safe—but when you put something in a safe it's just in order to be able to forget it, okay? When I handwrite something on a piece of paper, I put it in my pocket or in the safe, it's just in order to forget it, to know that I can find it again while in the meantime having forgotten it. If there is pure forgetting, it's because the archive, in order to be safe, in a safe, should be external to me, okay? [To reiterate, exteriority protects against forgetting, but at the same time exposes to other forms of forgetting—for example, accidental or deliberate destruction—and to other dangers—for example, the personal diary read by an unauthorized reader.] So, suppose that one day South Africa would have accomplished a perfect, full archive of its whole history—not simply apartheid, but what came before apartheid, and before before, and so on and so forth, and a full history—suppose that such a thing might be possible—of course it is impossible—let us suppose it's possible—everyone in this country, who is interested in this country, would be eager to put this in such a safe that everyone could just forget it, okay? And perhaps, perhaps, this is the unconfessed desire of the Truth and Reconciliation Commission. [In *Archive Fever,* Derrida, using the concept of "death drive"—drawn from psychoanalysis—posits an instinct of forgetting, of destruction, within memorization. The archive, in other words, always works against itself. And what we call "memory institutions" could just as easily be called houses of forgetting.] That as soon as possible the future generation may have simply forgotten it...."[27]

## MY BACK PAGES 2

Not long before Derrida died, my teenage son asked me, "Why do you love Derrida so much?" I might have questioned his assumption that reason has anything to do with love, but instead answered more or less facetiously: "For the same reasons I love Bob Dylan." He knew what I was getting at, having lived longer with my passion for Dylan than with my passion for Derrida. But aside from the idiosyncrasies of my personal passions, the case could be made that Derrida was to public intellectual life what Bob Dylan is to popular culture. After all, how many late–twentieth-century "philosophers" had sex appeal, played the media cleverly, produced a string of "live recordings,"[28] wrote "fiction" and "autobiography,"[29] stirred the academy into conducting rows over him in the newspapers,[30] was the subject of an award-winning movie while still alive,[31] and provoked what I would call iconic gestures?[32]

Like Dylan, Derrida made his entrance dramatically in the 1960s. He too was ambivalent about the street protests of that decade, and throughout his career attracted the ire of the left (and the scorn of the right) at a politics that refused to settle within any orthodoxy. Indeed, he refused to settle anywhere, his resistance to labeling seeming to increase the determination of commentators to pigeonhole him. His public performances were Dylanesque in their unpredictability. In 1998 at the University of the Witwatersrand, he held his seminar audience riveted for about an hour. The next day I watched him at the University of South Africa steadily lose a dwindling audience through over two hours of dense analysis. And, like Dylan, his work was woven through with playfulness. He specialized in wordplays, reveling especially in puns, semantic accident, and the vagaries of translation. But any play was fair game. At the 1998 seminar on *Archive Fever,* he teased his hosts in the opening moments: "I won't tell you how pleased I am, because I am not pleased—I am absolutely paralyzed by the situation ... I've totally forgotten the book!"[33] In a scene from the 2002 documentary movie *Derrida,* he is filmed in his substantial library. The interviewer asks him if he's read all the books in it, and he replies: "No, I've read four of them—but I read them very well." In *Without Alibi* (2002), he uses an account by Rousseau of a dying woman farting to make a serious point about "the last word."[34]

Both Derrida and Dylan have made an impact that is revolutionary and enduring. They both drew on long traditions to introduce new languages, idioms, and genres. Both were still bashing it out (and turning it on) in the first years of the twenty-first century, literally still on the road, vagrants not looking for a home.[35]

Derrida has never failed to move me. This has fundamentally to do with the fact that no matter where he traveled; which boundary he bounded across; what concept he chose to interrogate, tend, and play with; what text or fragment of a text he read and re-read, Derrida himself, always, was moved. John Caputo expressed this well in the title of his book *The Prayers and Tears of Jacques Derrida: Religion without Religion.*[36] Always, Derrida was passionately searching out the call of justice and raging against injustice. He wondered and mourned at the reality that justice calls us to hospitality (the impossible) when life seems only to have given us a capacity for community (the possible). He found this same aporia in the distances between gift and economies of exchange, and between forgiveness and (re)conciliation. He pondered the unspeakable possibility that justice is unjust.[37] Always he strove for understanding while disclosing his ignorance. He turned on himself (and this is something very few of his critics got), so to speak, Bob Dylan's scorching critique of Mr. Jones:

> You're very well read, it's well known;
> But something is happening here and you don't know what it is . . .[38]

And this, precisely, spurred him to reach for the impossible.

## (UN)PLUGGED 2

I have offered here yet another reading of Jacques Derrida. It is, as every reading must be, a partial (in the double sense of the word) reading. I would caution those who have read this far, and have never read Derrida themselves, against simply plugging into my reading. They should insist on Derrida unplugged. (It is not difficult to hear Derrida laughing at this notion. For if he has taught us anything, it is that we are always already plugged into an archive—archi-text—that at once precedes us and follows us. There is no Derrida unplugged. But, as I have attempted to show in this essay, he also taught us to reach for the impossible.)

# Endnotes

1    This essay was commissioned by the *Journal of the Society of Archivists* shortly after the death of Jacques Derrida. It appeared in volume 26, no. 1 (2005) of that journal. A Norwegian translation was published in the Norwegian publication *Bok Og Bibliotek* 1 (2005). I thank Terry Cook (University of Manitoba), Wendy Duff (University of Toronto), Sam Jacob (South African History Archive), Ethel Kriger (South African History Archive), John Samuel (Nelson Mandela Foundation), Kurt Shillinger (University of the Witwatersrand), and David Wallace (Catholic University) for their comments on the first draft. Whether they tempered and bounded my enthusiasm enough is for the reader to decide.

2    Carolyn Hamilton, et al., eds., *Refiguring the Archive* (Cape Town: David Philip, 2002), 54. In its Derridean usage, "mourning" is not in opposition to, or antithetical to, "celebrating." Derrida celebrated a celebrating that unfolds from within mourning.

3    What we—we who call ourselves archivists—name archival discourse is but part of a bigger family of discourses that can validly be named "archival." Most archivists don't realize this. Increasingly, scholars and practitioners from a wide range of other disciplines are stretching the boundaries of archival discourse by interrogating the concept of archive and applying it within their own disciplinary spaces. Nevertheless, we can still speak meaningfully of an archival discourse and an archival terrain narrowly defined—that space occupied by and defined by those of us who call ourselves archivists.

4    For evidence of this turn, see E. S. Burt and J. Vanpee, *Reading the Archive* (New Haven: Yale University Press, 1990); the special issues of *History of the Human Sciences,* 11, no. 4 (1998) and 12, no. 2 (1999); Hamilton, et al., *Refiguring the Archive;* and Rebecca Comay, ed., *Lost in the Archives* (Toronto: Alphabet City Media, 2002).

5    Brien Brothman had sounded the alert two years earlier (see below), but I had not paid heed.

6    In Burt and Vanpee, *Reading the Archive.* All dates of texts cited by me refer to versions published in English.

7    Jacques Derrida and Mustapha Tlili, eds., *For Nelson Mandela* (New York: Seaver Books, 1987).

8    Pre-1996 archival literature has to be one of the dullest bodies of written work imaginable. Obviously there are exceptions to this generalization, but they tend to prove the depressing rule. For me, the great exceptions are Hugh Taylor and Terry Cook. Happily, the last decade has seen the emergence of a new generation of archivists—some of them influenced directly by Derrida, Taylor, and Cook—willing to allow imagination space.

9    To cite seven collaborative works: *Chora L Works* (with Peter Eisenman) (New York: The Monacelli Press, 1997); *Religion* (with Gianni Vattimo and others) (Cambridge, U.K.: Polity Press, 1998); *Of Hospitality* (with Anne Dufourmantelle) (Stanford: Stanford University Press, 2000); *A Taste for the Secret* (with Maurizio Ferraris) (Cambridge, U.K.: Polity Press, 2001); *Veils* (with Helene Cixous) (Stanford: Stanford University Press, 2001); *Echographies of Television* (with Bernard Stiegler) (Cambridge, U.K.: Polity Press, 2002); and *Counterpath: Travelling with Jacques Derrida* (with Catherine Malabou) (Stanford: Stanford University Press, 2004).

10   The seminar proceedings are reproduced in Hamilton, et al., *Refiguring the Archive.*

11   Verne Harris, "A Shaft of Darkness: Derrida in the Archive," in *Refiguring the Archive,* 81.

12 Harris, "A Shaft of Darkness," 61.

13 I have heard many archivists and historians depicting *Archive Fever* dismissively along these lines.

14 Read especially "Circumfession," in *Jacques Derrida,* ed. Geoffrey Bennington and Jacques Derrida (Chicago: The University of Chicago Press, 1993) and *Monolingualism of the Other, or The Prosthesis of Origin* (Stanford: Stanford University Press, 1998).

15 See, for example, Derrida and Malabou, *Counterpath,* 90. (Marranos were Iberian Jews who—formally—converted to Christianity to escape the Inquisition.)

16 In this paragraph I draw heavily from a letter to the editor of *Scrutiny2* vol. 5, no. 1 (2000), which I co-authored with Sello Hatang.

17 Christopher Norris and Andrew Benjamin, *What Is Deconstruction?* (London: St. Martin's Press, 1988), 27.

18 Norris and Benjamin, *What Is Deconstruction?*

19 Norris and Benjamin, *What Is Deconstruction?* 10.

20 John Caputo describes "archi-text" as "various networks—social, historical, linguistic, political, sexual networks (the list goes on nowadays to include electronic networks, worldwide webs)—various horizons or presuppositions ..." John Caputo, *Deconstruction in a Nutshell: A Conversation with Jacques Derrida* (New York: Fordham University Press, 1997), 79–80.

21 I use the term in its narrow sense. See endnote 3.

22 See, for instance, his "The Limit of Limits: Derridean Deconstruction and the Archival Institution," *Archivaria* 36 (1993) and "Declining Derrida: Integrity, Tensegrity, and the Preservation of Archives from Deconstruction," *Archivaria* 48 (1999).

23 In fact, I would only name five (these have all published work on their study): Terry Cook, Eric Ketelaar, Sello Hatang, Tom Nesmith, and myself.

24 Brien Brothman and I have made this point before, independently, in the texts cited above.

25 Harris, "A Shaft of Darkness," 77.

26 Derrida makes the argument for this assertion most directly in *Of Hospitality* and *On Cosmopolitanism and Forgiveness* (London: Routledge, 2001).

27 Hamilton, et al., *Refiguring the Archive,* 54.

28 An extraordinary number of Derrida's books were lightly edited versions of papers presented by him or transcripts of seminar proceedings.

29 It would not be stretching things unduly to describe as fictional his *The Post Card: From Socrates to Freud and Beyond* (Chicago: University of Chicago Press, 1987). The strongest autobiographical threads are to be found in "Circumfession" and *Counterpath.* I cite these works in relation to Bob Dylan's novel and first volume of autobiography.

30 This happened most notably when the University of Cambridge decided to award him an honorary doctorate in 1992, and again in the weeks after his death.

31 *Derrida* (released by Zeitgeist Films, produced by Amy Ziering Kofman, directed by Kofman and Kirby Dick, 2002). The movie was an official selection for numerous film festivals and won the Golden Gate Award at the San Francisco International Film Festival.

32 I would describe the movie just cited, for example, as an iconic gesture.

33 Hamilton, et al., *Refiguring the Archive,* 38.

34  Jacques Derrida, *Without Alibi* (Stanford: Stanford University Press, 2002), 95–96.

35  In the last book he published before his death, *Counterpath,* he interrogated his need to keep traveling and explored the elusiveness of "home."

36  Bloomington and Indianapolis: Indiana University Press, 1997.

37  See, for example, *Adieu to Emmanuel Levinas* (Stanford: Stanford University Press, 1999) and *Without Alibi,* 125.

38  From the album *Highway 61 Revisited* (Columbia, 1965).

# SECTION II

# NARRATIVES

# CHAPTER 6

## Exploratory Thoughts on Current State Archives Service Appraisal Policy and the Conceptual Foundations of Macro-Appraisal[1]

## INTRODUCTION

Not all State Archives Service appraisers are comfortable with the service's appraisal policy.[2] In recent years concern has been expressed about the following aspects:

- Our approach is neither planned nor built on a strategic foundation.
- Individual appraisals are seldom located within the broader functional-organizational-records systems context.
- Our assumption that archival value is determined primarily by actual or anticipated research use is deeply problematic.
- The high proportion of support function records (particularly housekeeping records) that we preserve is difficult to justify.
- Given our limited resources and perennial space problems, we simply cannot persevere with an approach that secures the permanent preservation of an estimated 15 percent of the records generated by our client offices. Already we are close to being overwhelmed by our holdings.

These concerns were given greater weight and focus by the visit to South Africa of Canadian archivist Dr. Terry Cook in November 1994.[3] His analysis of "traditional" approaches to appraisal and exposition of the macro-appraisal approach employed by the National Archives of Canada posed two questions that demand our urgent attention:

1. Is State Archives Service appraisal policy sound?

2. Does macro-appraisal offer us a better alternative?

This article attempts to explore these questions at an elementary level as a first step toward a more comprehensive analysis. The focus shifts from Schellenbergian appraisal—the paradigm on which State Archives Service policy is based—to the Service's appraisal policy, and finally to macro-appraisal. In the conclusion, an attempt is made to draw the threads together and propose a way forward.

## BASIC TOOLS AND CONCEPTS

Before embarking on the exploration itself, a brief account of the assumptions that inform it. Appraisal policies/approaches can be evaluated in a number of ways; the perspective adopted in this article employs two fundamental criteria:

1. How sound are the theoretical and methodological underpinnings? "Soundness" in this context is measured against two yardsticks: validity in a philosophical sense; and "appropriateness" in a given set of circumstances.

2. How good is the result? In other words, what is the quality of the permanent records secured through appraisal?

By theory ("theoretical underpinnings") is meant the exposition of abstract appraisal principles.[4] Appraisal theory explains the value of records in the context of their creation and subsequent use, and in doing so defines "archival value" and the related concept of the "permanently valuable record." By appraisal methodology, on the other hand, is meant the system of methods and rules applicable to appraisal work.[5] Whereas appraisal theory addresses the question "What constitutes a permanently valuable record?," appraisal methodology addresses the question "How are permanently valuable records identified?"

## SCHELLENBERG ON APPRAISAL

Schellenberg comes under consideration first because of his huge influence on appraisers worldwide after World War II and, specifically, because his thinking was (and still is) the most important shaper of State Archives Service appraisal policy. At the outset it is vital to distinguish between Schellenberg's thinking on appraisal and the caricature of his thinking that underlies much appraisal practice today.[6] The primary elements of the caricature are as follows:

- Archival value is determined principally by actual or anticipated research use.
- The functional-organizational-records systems context is extrapolated from the records themselves.
- Records, records systems, and lists of records are appraised piecemeal as and when appraisers receive them.

Schellenberg, in fact, argued that archival value is a composite of what he called "evidential and informational values."[7] The latter are determined by records' usefulness to researchers "in all kind of disciplines."[8] Records are evaluated for these values *without reference* to the functional-organizational-records systems milieu out of which they come: in Schellenberg's words, "We are not concerned with the source of the records—what agency created them, or what activities resulted in their creation."[9] Consequently "informational values can … be appraised piecemeal…."[10] Two comments at this point: firstly, the notion that "usefulness to researchers" can be gauged without mediating between text and context is deeply flawed; and secondly, Schellenberg's account of "informational values" is clearly the source of the caricature outlined above. But this is only part of Schellenbergian appraisal; "evidential values" must also be taken into account. Records with these values are those containing "… all significant facts on how the agency was created, how it developed, how it is organized, what functions it performs, and what are the consequences of its activities."[11] Such records have value to public administrators, archivists, and researchers, but they "… should be preserved regardless of whether there is an immediate or even a foreseeable specific use for them."[12] They are preserved not for their potential usefulness, but because they provide an accurate and appropriate documentary reflection of the organization and functioning of the body that created them.[13] To identify "evidential values," Schellenberg proposes a methodology diametrically opposed to the one he links to "informational values." Here context is indispensable; and systematic, top-down analysis is the key. To quote him (at some length):

> To judge the evidential value of records an archivist should know in general terms (1) the position of each office in the administrative hierarchy of an agency, (2) the functions performed by each office, and (3) the activities carried on by each office in executing a given function. He should know the organization, functions, policies, procedures and operations of every agency with which he deals. He should also know in general terms the broad social, economic, or other conditions with which they are concerned. He should view an agency's records in their entirety to determine their interrelations and the significance of any given group of records to the entire system of documentation. He should not make his evaluations on a piece-meal basis or on the basis of individual organizational units within an agency.[14]

So Schellenberg offers us two measures of archival value without attempting to draw them within a single frame of reference.[15] Points of disjuncture are left unexplored. And he offers us two distinct and, arguably, conflicting methodologies without attempting to weld them into a system that will work at the appraisal coalface. Given these unresolved dichotomies in Schellenberg's thinking, it is perhaps not surprising that he spawned adherents who embrace the caricature rather than the substance of his exposition.

# STATE ARCHIVES SERVICE APPRAISAL POLICY

State Archives Service appraisal policy has its roots in the 1950s, when thes Service inherited the public records appraisal function from the Archives Commission. Schellenberg's writings constituted the first major influence on the fledgling policy, and they have continued to dominate developments ever since. The policy's foundation is elaborated in the service's *Handbook:*[16] terminological idiosyncrasies aside, the *Handbook*'s treatment of general appraisal theory and methodology is effectively a summary of Schellenberg's thinking. However, it is not my intention to focus on this narrow formal statement of policy. The analysis that follows draws on the shifting web of policy documentation[17] and gives significant weight to how policy is translated into practice.

Following Schellenberg, State Archives Service policy recognizes two categories of archival value: evidential (or functional) and informational (or research). They are conceived in precisely the same terms as Schellenberg uses, but in each case their application is characterized by an important deviation:

- Evidential values are not identified without relation to their usefulness. They are measured in terms of research value to the state (including archivists) and other users.
- We have not "bought" Schellenberg's denial of the importance of context in gauging informational values. Mediation between text and context is regarded to be as vital an ingredient here as it is with regard to evidential values.

In practice, then, the distinctions between evidential and informational values have become blurred. And, at the coalface, our appraisers tend not even to make the distinction—all considerations are subsumed by one dominant, all-embracing question, "Does this record possess actual or anticipated research value?"

State Archives Service policy on methodology delineates a strange, mongrel creature possessing elements of both Schellenbergian methodologies and of macro-appraisal. In principle, the policy requires individual appraisals to be placed within the broader functional-organizational-records systems context, and it advocates an approach almost identical to the one proposed by Schellenberg for identifying records with evidential values. In some respects, the policy takes the top-down paradigm further, moving into the realm of macro-appraisal:

- Most general and standing disposal authorities are issued not on records per se but on functionally based systems of records classification.[18]
- In certain areas, appraisal occurs at the supra-organizational level. All general disposal authorities encompass more than one client office, but consider, for example, the supra-organizational functional analyses that underlie Appraisal Instruction 19 (support functions in government offices) and general authorities PAA5 and PAL1 (filing systems and lists of other archives in local authorities).

On the other hand, however, top-down analysis is diluted, even subverted, by the following factors:

- In the main, contextual analysis for State Archives Service appraisals are hopelessly superficial.
- The emphasis of these analyses is on function. Structures, processes, and information/records systems get short shrift. Investigation of an organization's entire information management network is seldom attempted.
- In intensive appraisal little attempt is made to mediate between text and context. Usually the approach adopted is indistinguishable from the one proposed by Schellenberg for identifying records with informational values.
- With isolated exceptions, appraisal is done reactively rather than proactively. Records, records systems, and lists of records are appraised piecemeal as and when we receive them. We do not possess a broad-based appraisal strategy, and our endeavor is not planned.

And what of the results—the quality of the permanent records preserved in terms of State Archives Service appraisal policy? This is a big question, requiring extensive investigation to sustain a comprehensive answer, something beyond the scope of this article. My sense is that, in general terms, our documentary reflection of the functions and functioning of government is good, but that in three key areas this reflection is defective. Firstly, it is plain that we are preserving too much. Our shelves are filling too fast—not only are we faced by a space crisis, but the level of control we exercise over our holdings and our capacity to make them available effectively are being seriously eroded. Obviously the continuing explosion of paper-based and other records is the underlying factor. But this problem, I would argue, is compounded by our appraisal policy:

- Our unfocused endeavor to identify all records possessing potential research value results in a high proportion of appraised records being preserved.
- The inadequacy of our contextual analyses and our reactive approach result in (1) frequent failure to identify the best, most succinct record, and (2) high levels of duplication. We need look no further than our own filing system to illustrate the point. The appraisal on it takes no account of the variety of offices using it—for example, an A30[19] file description is A30 in the director's office, in regional chief's offices, and in depots, committing, for example, the Central Archives Depot to high levels of duplication between files of the director, the Transvaal regional chief, the Central and Transvaal Archives Depots; and the National Film, Video and Sound Archives.

The second key area of concern relates to our determination to focus on "government" rather than "governance," and our inability to link appraisal processes to collecting processes. On the one hand, then, we are satisfied to replicate in appraisal prevailing relations of power expressed in the records of state agencies. In the records we preserve, too often the voices of the governed, especially the underclasses, are either filtered through the voices of bureaucrats or are absent. On the other, the resultant gaps are not made the basis for focused collecting activities.

And then there is the challenge posed by electronic records. Unlike in the paper environment, timely appraisal and disposition arrangements are essential in the electronic environment if the loss of permanently valuable records is to be avoided. Paper records no longer of functional use are moved to strongrooms, empty offices, basements, and attics. Electronic records no longer of functional use are deleted or stored in formats that render them unintelligible when new technologies are introduced. Clearly proactive identification and archival analysis of electronic applications in client offices is essential. But our reactive approach to appraisal, and the inadequacy of our contextual analyses, condemn us to touching only the tip of the electronic record iceberg.[20] This does not mean, as in a paper environment, that the iceberg will descend on us eventually in a chaos of myriad pieces. It means that the iceberg will never reach us.

## MACRO-APPRAISAL

The concept of macro-appraisal has not leapt from nowhere. It has deep roots in the "evidential half" of Schellenbergian appraisal, and it has been articulated by Hans Booms, Helen Samuels, Terry Cook (who coined the term), and others. The account that follows is based on the practice of macro-appraisal by the Canadian National Archives.[21]

The macro-appraisal paradigm rejects actual or anticipated research use as a criterion for determining archival value. It is argued that research use fails the tests of reliability, workability, and validity. Instead, appraisers should revisit the principle of provenance—records have meaning within the "...contextual circumstances of creation and contemporary use...."[22] Records are the products of processes involving complex interactions between creators of records (structures, agencies, people), sociohistorical trends and patterns (functions, activities, programs), and clients/customers/citizens. All these elements constitute the dynamic contextual milieu in which records are created.[23] The purpose of appraisal is to secure an appropriate documentary reflection of this milieu. Records that provide the best, most succinct, most focused *evidence* of this milieu have archival value.[24] Plainly there are powerful resonances between macro-appraisal's theoretical underpinnings and Schellenberg's exposition of evidential values. The crucial difference lies in macro-appraisal's emphasis on the role of context in determining archival value. Macro-appraisal contends that archival value is located, in the first instance, not in records but in the processes that underlie their creation. First the archivist must identify the key elements of the contextual milieu (appraisal of processes), and then seek to document it (appraisal of records). In the words of Terry Cook:

…macro-appraisal has a "top-down" focus on assessing (or "appraising") the likelihood of particular records creators and records-creation processes to generate records of archival value. Macro-appraisal is not merely strategic. Archival value per se is often determined during macro-appraisal, because it eliminates some large bodies or media or creators of records from further appraisal at all, in the traditional sense.[25]

In appraising processes before records, macro-appraisal not only targets the records with archival potential, it also identifies processes, or aspects of processes, that are poorly documented by the records and that need to be supplemented by collecting activities (accessions, publications, oral history, etc).

The key to macro-appraisal methodology, as with Schellenberg's "evidential value methodology," is systematic top-down analysis. "Macro-appraisal moves in a top-down fashion from the purpose or broad societal function of the records creator, through various structures and processes designed to implement that function … to information systems created to produce and organize records that permit those processes to work, and finally to the records themselves which document all the foregoing as well as the impact of functions and structures on the citizen and, equally important, that of the citizen on the functions and structures."[26]

The core characteristics of this procedure accord with those of Schellenberg. What distinguishes the macro-appraisal approach is its broader top end ("societal function" as against Schellenberg's creating agency) and more rigorous analytical procedure. The approach is illustrated by what Terry Cook has called the Canadian National Archives' "…research-based, functionally-driven, strategically planned, and negotiated approach to archival appraisal…."[27] It operates at four levels:

1. **Supra-agency.** The main functions (or "conceptual sites of records creation") of government are identified, differentiated, and weighted. Government institutions are then ranked in priority order using various criteria designed to focus attention on "the most central, senior, complex and powerful in implementing the main functions or mandates or responsibilities of the Canadian federal government." At the same

time, functional overlapping between institutions is identified so as to circumvent appraisal and acquisition duplication. This endeavor issues in a "Government Wide Plan," according to which institutions are approached in priority order to negotiate appraisal/disposition plans.

2. **Agency.** Each institution (or "records creating entity") is subjected to a functional-structural analysis to assess the relative importance of internal branches and divisions. The "Institutional Profile" that emerges from this analysis is used to identify appraisal targets that are then placed in a "Multi-Year Disposition Plan."

3. **Subagency.** The functional-structural/organizational-records systems context of each appraisal target is analyzed. Here, strictly speaking, there are two levels of analysis: subfunction/subagency and information system. The focus is on the functional-structural matrix, the appraiser being required to formulate a hypothesis of where archival records are likely to be located—in which divisions, sections, registries, or systems.

4. **Records.** Having illuminated the entire context of the records to be appraised, the appraiser turns his or her attention to the records themselves. The initial focus is on testing the appraisal hypothesis (and modifying it if necessary); the ultimate goal is to identify those records that most sharply and succinctly mirror the functional-structural matrix. At this stage, macro-appraisal has been replaced by "micro-appraisal," and the "traditional" criteria are applied—the age, uniqueness, time span, authenticity, completeness, extent, manipulability, fragility, and so on of the records are assessed.

## CONCLUSION

To return to the questions posed in the introduction: 1) State Archives Service appraisal policy, both in its foundations and its superstructure, has serious flaws; and 2) macro-appraisal offers solutions to the problems identified in this article.

The arguments against actual or anticipated research use as a criterion for determining archival value are compelling:

- The shifting winds of research trends do not provide a reliable measure. In the past, for example, before the blossoming of "radical" historiography and social history, the State Archives Service's shaping of appraisal into a tool for academic researchers, particularly historians, resulted in the experiences of "ordinary people," and especially the experiences of the underclasses, being poorly reflected in the records we chose to preserve.
- Attempting to anticipate research trends is an exercise in futility.
- Archivists can never be properly equipped to meet the requirements of every research discipline.
- If the requirements of every research discipline *are* taken into account, the great majority of records have potential research value. Clearly an approach built on this definition of archival value is unworkable. And if the target is narrowed to encompass only "important" research, how does one begin to define such a concept?

On the other hand, macro-appraisal theory provides an explanation of archival value that is rooted in the theoretical bedrock of provenance; provides a *workable* yardstick; and meshes with a methodology appropriate to modern records environments. At the end of the twentieth century, we are confronted by overwhelming volumes of records; an explosion of new information-bearing media; new technologies that challenge our definition of "the record" and pose daunting challenges for archival preservation; functions and records systems that transcend institutional boundaries, even national boundaries; institutions that transcend national boundaries and institutions of great organizational complexity. As Terry Cook says, "THE ALARM BELL IS RINGING."[28] A strategically planned, top-down approach in these circumstances is not merely an attractive option. It is a necessity. Building on our Schellenbergian roots and our experience in the last forty years, we in the State Archives Service need to look long and hard at the options macro-appraisal methodology offers us. In particular, we need to examine the Canadian National Archives' translation of this methodology into practice. It is, I am convinced, the way to go. But we must not lose sight of the prerequisites for macro-appraisal success:

- Adequate legislative and administrative muscle.
- Adequate human and other resources.
- Possession of, or ready access to, expertise in functional-structural analysis, information management, and information technology.
- The will to make it work—support from both management and staff is indispensable.
- It must be sold, as a concept, both to our political leadership and to stakeholders.

Any analysis of macro-appraisal by the State Archives Service, if it is to be meaningful, must address these factors as well as evaluate macro-appraisal's conceptual foundations and implementation in Canada.

# Endnotes

1 This essay was published in the State Archives Service journal *Archives News* 37, no. 8 (1995). It became the basis for a review of State Archives Service appraisal policy, and in 1996 the service formally adopted a version of macro-appraisal as the foundation of its new approach to appraisal.

2 To the extent that the service can be said to have a coherent, overarching appraisal policy.

3 See my article "One Hell of a Pair: Personal Reflections on the Visit to South Africa by Terry and Sharon Cook, November 1994," *Archives News* 37, no. 7 (1995).

4 See the definition of *theory* in *Chambers Twentieth Century Dictionary* (1972).

5 See the definition of *methodology* in *Chambers Twentieth Century Dictionary* (1972).

6 I have frequently been guilty of confusing the caricature with the genuine article. In mitigation, even Terry Cook fails to make the distinction forcefully enough.

7 T. R. Schellenberg, *Modern Archives: Principles and Techniques* (Melbourne: F. W. Cheshire, 1956), 139–60. See also Schellenberg's "Principles of Archival Appraisal," reprinted from *Proceedings of the First Caribbean Archives Conference, Jamaica, 1965,* in *Modern Archives Administration and Records Management: A RAMP Reader,* comp. Peter Walne (Paris: UNESCO, 1985).

8 Schellenberg, *Modern Archives*, 149.

9 Schellenberg, *Modern Archives,* 148.

10 Schellenberg, *Modern Archives,* 148.

11 Schellenberg, *Modern Archives,* 140.

12 Schellenberg, *Modern Archives,* 140.

13 Schellenberg, *Modern Archives,* 140.

14 Schellenberg, *Modern Archives,* 142.

15 Although he suggests a hierarchy of values with assertions like the following: "… the chief reason why public records are preserved in an archival institution is because of their value for scholarly research." Schellenberg, "Principles of Archival Appraisal," 270.

16 State Archives Service, *Handbook* (Pretoria: State Archives Service, 1991), 6:46–6:58.

17 Among others, the *Handbook,* the *Appraisal Manual,* the "books of words" (notebooks in which appraisers note patterns and precedents), disposal authority precedents, and policy files.

18 Terry Cook has defined "macro-appraisal" as "appraisal that occurs before records per se are investigated or appraised." Lecture during workshop entitled "Macro-appraisal Theory and Methodology, Electronic Records (Especially), and Case-file Records," Pretoria, 15–18 November 1994.

19 "A30" is a disposal instruction signifying "permanently valuable, transfer to Archives when 30 years of age."

20 For statistics on this phenomenon, see Clive Kirkwood, "Records Management in the Public Sector and the Archival Challenges Posed by Electronic Records," *SA Archives Journal* 36 (1994): 12.

21 Macro-appraisal was formally adopted by the Canadian National Archives as the basis for its appraisal policy in 1990. The State Archives of the Netherlands, in terms of its PIVOT project, is pursuing a similar course, as are the national archives of Australia and Switzerland, and a number of state archives in the United States.

22 Terry Cook, "Negotiating Scheduling: A Step Towards Reinventing Archives," paper delivered to Working Meeting on Electronic Records Management, Pittsburgh, Penn., 9 April 1994, 12. For fuller, more philosophical explorations of the concept by Terry Cook, see his "Mind over Matter: Towards a New Theory of Archival Appraisal," in *The Canadian Archival Imagination: Essays in Honour of Hugh Taylor*, ed. Barbara Craig (Ottawa: Association of Canadian Archivists, 1992) and "Electronic Records, Paper Minds: The Revolution in Information Management and Archives in the Post-custodial and Post-modernist Era," *Archives and Manuscripts* 22, no. 2 (1994).

23 National Archives of Canada, *An Appraisal Methodology: Guidelines for Performing an Archival Appraisal* (Ottawa: National Archives of Canada, 1991), 11.

24 Cook, "Negotiating Scheduling," 7.

25 Cook, "Negotiating Scheduling," 10.

26 National Archives of Canada, *Appraisal Methodology*, 4.

27 Cook, "Negotiating Scheduling," 2. The account that follows is based on Cook's exposition in "'Negotiating Scheduling.'"

28 Cook, "Negotiating Scheduling," 9.

to a record finite in its reach? Does the making of a record, ultimately, have a beginning and an ending? Do archivists participate actively in the construction of a record's meanings and significances? Is the notion of the archivist maintaining an exteriority from both processes of records creation and broader societal processes a chimera? Do power relations, with their myriad privilegings and exclusions, find expression in archival intervention? Does the archivist have a moral obligation to engage the marginalized and excluded voices in records? Is the archivist a storyteller? How do the contingencies of language and narrative shape the work of archival description? Is archival description simply a form of narration? Should archivists disclose their complicity in the processes of recordmaking? And, in light of all the preceding questions, can there be a meaningful standardization of archival description?

Until very recently, the three streams in discourse outlined above have tended to flow past one another. It is our contention that they need to be encouraged to flow in the same channel. They need to churn against one another, find articulations, carve out a new channel. This, precisely, has been our intention with this essay. To the collaborative effort we have brought significant differences, one of us shaped primarily by the traditional stream, the other by that labeled "postmodernist."[3] One of us has devoted much effort to the development of descriptive standards both nationally and internationally, while the other has suggested that these standards have "no resonance in South Africa" and has consistently resisted standardization in archival practice.[4] In the process we have found a mode of exploration at once hospitable to difference and committed to what we would call an "integrative instinct." We believe that by respecting our differences we have found a commonality having to do with a shared conviction that records are always in the process of being made, that "their" stories are never ending, and that the stories of what are conventionally called records creators, records managers, archivists, users, and so on are (shifting, intermingling) parts of bigger stories understandable only in the ever-changing broader contexts of society. Records, in short, open into (and out of) the future.[5] And archivists are members of a big family of recordmakers. This shared conviction has enabled us to find acknowledgment of the importance of archival descriptive standards, re-imagined as instruments for calling the future in through a challenging of the instinct merely to replicate existing power relations.

We begin our exploration by addressing the traditional and ever-valid questions of the what and the why of archival description. Thereafter we engage the tumble of "postmodernist" questions. In these first two sections, our concern is with descriptive architecture, the analysis covering a number of specific architectures and including only oblique references to descriptive standardization. The concluding section attempts to draw out the implications of our analysis for endeavors—irrespective of the architecture(s) being used—to both define and justify descriptive standards.

## DESCRIPTIVE ARCHITECTURE AND ARCHITECTURES

There is much to represent in any archives, and much representing takes place. Abstracts, calendars, inventories, repository guides, accession records, biographical sketches, authority records, and a host of other descriptive tools describe the context, structure, and content of records, and provide access to archival material. Over the last twenty years, many individuals and teams have expended immense professional effort discussing archival description and related principles as well as promulgating standards and guidelines to codify this process. Recent literature on archival description suggests that archivists agree on the importance of documenting and preserving both information about creation and use of the records, and their documentary structures, but they disagree on the best method for doing so. Disagreement has issued in the emergence of two dominant approaches—and concomitant descriptive architectures—to capturing and presenting information about records.[6]

Traditionally archivists sought to preserve both the internal and external structure of a group of records by following the archival precept of *respect des fonds*. According to the Canadian *Rules for Archival Description,* the principle of *respect des fonds* directs that "the records of a person, family, or corporate body must be kept together in their original order, if it exists or has been maintained, and not be mixed or combined with the records of another individual or corporate body."[7] The principle incorporates two subprinciples: provenance and original order. The principle of provenance requires the identification of the whole of the records created and/or accumulated and used by one individual, family, or organization. Provenance protects the evidential value of records and makes visible the acts and deeds from which the records emanate. Original order refers to the internal or documentary structure of records. Maintaining "the documents as they were organized by the agent accumulating them"[8] fixes the relationships among records and preserves evidence of their use. The focus of arrangement and description is on intellectual ordering rather than the physical order at the time of accessioning. Terry Eastwood points out that arranging records by their accession unit, "fails altogether to solve the problem of identifying records with the grouping to which they belong." Furthermore, he suggests, "all contemporary authors agree on this matter."[9] There is, however, less agreement on how to preserve and represent the provenance of records or on what constitutes the fonds.

In modern bureaucracies, it is common for records to be created, accumulated, and used by numerous different agencies. Records emanate from business activities and in turn are used to support and carry out other business activities. Moreover, series of records move from the control and/or custody of one organization to another. Terry Cook explains that modern organizations "composed of tens of thousands of employees, subdivided into a thousand administrative units or offices, encompassing hundreds of functions and involving scores of record-keeping systems, all with a disturbing tendency to appear, disappear, merge, or migrate at a moment's notice to other agencies, offices systems or function,...makes it very difficult to identify the creator and thus to draw reasonably consistent boundaries around the resultant fonds."[10] This reality has led numerous archivists to suggest that the multifaceted aspects of provenance are eroded when archival practice dictates the creation of fonds-level description and credits the creation of the records to one, and only one, individual or organization.[11] For example, advocates of the series system challenge the notion that archivists require fonds-level descriptions to preserve the evidential value of records.[12]

The series system came out of the record-keeping culture of the Australian National Archives. The system as described in Peter Scott's article, "The Record Group Concept: A Case for Abandonment," bases the "arrangement of archives on the record series as an independent element not bound to the administrative context. The series is the primary level of classification, and the item the secondary level."[13] The original order of items within the series is maintained, and the administrative context of the series is documented by linking the description of the records series to the description of the agency or person who created them, and identifying relationships between the record entity and the context entity. Furthermore, the agency descriptions are linked to descriptions of organizations that controlled them, and descriptions of families are linked to descriptions of persons who make up the family. The system rejects the custodial approach, describing active, inactive, and archival records. It seeks to describe records series in their totality and links descriptions of records to all the contextual entities that created, accumulated, used, controlled, owned, or transferred the records in the series. This system emphasizes the importance of linking a record entity to its various contextual entities and stresses the importance of inter-relationships, thereby representing the multiprovenancial nature of records. Since the system's inception almost fifty years ago, archivists have made many refinements to it. Today it describes various units of records, including fonds, series, transfer sets, consignments, accessions, items, folios, and so on, as well as creators, functions, and record-keeping systems. Many North American archivists, especially those dealing with the records of large bureaucracies or electronic records, have suggested that this system deals with the complexity of modern records in a more meaningful and holistic manner. For example, Terry Cook and David Bearman have both been influenced by the series system and have, in turn, influenced Australian archivists' thinking about it.

The system is more than just a method of description. It is grounded in the belief that records creation is only one aspect of provenance and that "contextual entities" may be of very many different kinds. The scope of contextual information encompasses many different dimensions. Hurley admits, "[w]e are still thinking through (and in many ways only just beginning to realize) how much further ideas about context and provenance must go beyond mere records creation."[14] Sue McKemmish and her colleagues have developed a model that focuses on the role that functions, activities, and record-keeping systems play in the creation of records. They are also delineating the various types of relationships among creators, functions, record-keeping systems, and records entities.[15] In summary, the series system is based on the notion that records are multiprovenancial in nature and that "creation is only one aspect of provenance."[16]

Many advocates of fonds-based approaches agree that creating entities should be described in archival authority records that are separate, but linked to, descriptions of records. However, there is still disagreement over the practicality and wisdom of creating a single multilevel description to represent all the records of a modern bureaucracy. For example, Cook suggests that the fonds should be seen as "an intellectual construct" rather than a "physical entity."[17] For followers of the series system, the series, not the fonds, provides the level of physical arrangement that should be linked to related record series, creators, functions, and so on to give the clearest picture of the creation, accumulation, and use of the records. Supporters of this system suggest that a focus on the fonds constrains description and obfuscates important relationships. Describing only the fonds is too limiting. Sue McKemmish posits that "the physical reconstruction of the fonds in a record group, while providing one view of what is a multiple reality, obscures or obliterates other views."[18] One-dimensional, multilevel descriptions foreground one interpretation while obscuring others.

Some advocates of fonds-based approaches agree that the fonds is multiprovenancial but reject the notion that the fonds is merely an intellectual construct. Terry Eastwood, a strong defender of the principle of *respect des fonds,* agrees that the fonds should be conceived as "divorced from the sense that records can be seen in one and only one context and documented only in that way."[19] However, he rejects the notion that provenance goes beyond records creation and states that a record "has only one provenance, that of the office that generated it. All the records generated by the office constitute its fonds within, if you like, the hierarchy of fonds."[20] However, he admits that the transfer of records to other offices that take over some or all of the competences of an office make it difficult "to characterize precisely which records belong to which agency and / or office." He concludes that "such so-called multiple-provenance series virtually every authority agrees, need to be attributed to all their successive creators."[21] However, Eastwood still casts doubts on the series system's ability to reconstruct an appropriate view of the fonds.[22] These doubts are fostered by the views of other fonds-based advocates. Duchein, for example, continues to stress the importance of always reconstructing the fonds through finding aids.[23]

Heather MacNeil prefers a fonds-based approach to description. She states, "The reason why records must remain in the fonds from which they originate and, within the fonds, in their place of origin, is to ensure that the records being preserved provide authentic and adequate documentation of the functions and associated activities of their creator.... The records being described should represent a distinct and coherent whole, one that will illuminate, and not obscure, the context of activities out of which the records were created and maintained during their active life."[24] For MacNeil and other supporters of the fonds concept, arranging and describing the fonds provide the clearest articulation of the context of records creation.

Both the series system and fonds-based approaches appear to pursue the same goals, namely the illumination of the context to records and the preservation of the evidential value of records. Yet the differences between them are significant. Eastwood suggests that the fundamental difference is in their definitions of agency. However, they also differ in how they conceptualize records creation, provenance, the nature of archival records, and the purpose of description. Eastwood posits that the provenance of a record is the office that generated it, while supporters of the series system argue that the provenance includes the office that generated it, as well as the agencies that controlled, used, and had custody of it. Each new use adds to the provenance and changes the record. All actors are part of its creation, and therefore, need to be documented. Relationships are complex, multifaceted, and multidimensional. Information about record-keeping systems, functions, and activities also plays an essential role in understanding the meaning of records.

Many North Americans have contributed to our understanding of context and its various facets. As we have argued, their insights have informed the writings of Australian archivists and they, in turn, have been influenced by Australian archival theory. For example, Terry Cook suggests that, "the mere act of creating records alone does not necessarily define a fonds. The administrative context in which the creation occurred, the nature of the function performed which caused the records to be created and the control exercised over the record-keeping systems are other relevant factors."[25] Bearman goes further to suggest that archivists and archival systems also affect their evidential value. "The facts of processing, exhibiting, citing, publishing and otherwise managing records become significant to their meaning as records."[26] Moreover, Nesmith points out that the act of describing the record changes the record's meaning. He states that "[a]rchivists help make and remake the records through representation made when putting the record on the archival pedestal, realigning the context in which they may be understood through arrangement by centralized storage (which makes it easier to explore new contextual linkages between them than if they were scattered), by describing them in a different way at different times."[27] The power to describe is the power to make and remake records and to determine how they will be used and remade in the future. Each story we tell about our records, each description we compile, changes the meaning of the records and re-creates them. These different views of provenance significantly affect the type of descriptive architecture proposed by their advocates. Equally influential are their assumptions about what archival description is, when description takes place, and its purpose.

Much of the work of developing fonds-based descriptive rules in Canada has been guided by the assumption that archival description is comparable to bibliographic description[28] and produces information objects, or finding aids that are predominantly static objects that describe a pre-existing order with a predominant provenance. These objects represent equally static objects, for example, the unit being described, the fonds, the series, or the collection.[29] Descriptions lead to objects of study, such as fonds, series, or collections, but are not in themselves objects of study.[30] They provide "information about the structure, functions and content of records."[31] These descriptive objects are created by archivists and represent archival material that has crossed the archival threshold and is under the physical control of an archives. New accruals may be added to the unit on a piecemeal basis, but the archival unit—the fonds—is, for the most part, fixed and static. Description helps situate the material by providing information about its provenance and revealing the relationships between the records. Respecting and describing the fonds protects its provenance.

Adherents of the series system, on the other hand, believe that records series are dynamic and constantly changing and description must represent multiple horizontal as well as vertical poly-hierarchical relationships. This system is postcustodial and describes records across the entire records continuum. Its roots, as we have already suggested, lie with the Australian National Archives, an institution that dealt predominantly with records from still-current records systems. "For obvious practical reasons, therefore, it was necessary to classify and describe records in a manner which allowed for continuing and sometimes frequent changes in status (whether of location, arrangement and recordkeeping system, or provenance or control). There simply were no archives in the old-fashioned sense (a stable, finite, physical body of records held outside the continuum) to be described."[32] The series system requires and facilitates the establishment of multiple relationships between records and context entities, "to represent complex and dynamic realities"[33] because it describes dynamic, not static entities. Cook's main critique of fonds-based approaches is their inability to deal with dynamic fonds and series.[34] Working within a postcustodial milieu, archivists describe active government records in the same manner as records transferred to the archives, because archival control does not depend on physical custody. In the fonds-based approach common in Canada, description takes place after archives have physical custody of the records and after the records are arranged.

Debate also arises over the reasons for describing archival material. For example, MacNeil suggests that the purpose of description "is to preserve, perpetuate, and authenticate meaning over time so that it is available and comprehensible to all users—present and potential."[35] Hurley disagrees and suggests that "the primary purpose of documentation and finding aids is not repository control or the facilitation of access, but as an indispensable component in the making and keeping of records."[36] Bearman highlights the importance of documenting over describing and depicts documenting as "focused on activity in the records-generating institution or the creator of the records in the case of manuscripts.... It seeks to capture data about the relationship between the activity and the document created or received in that activity which is necessary in order for the document to serve as evidence."[37] He suggests that the development of standards must consider use and users. However, he states, "that content and data representation requirements ought to be derived from analysis of the uses to which such systems must be put and should satisfy the day-to-day information requirements of archivists who are the primary users of archives, and of researchers using archives for their primary evidential purposes."[38]

Users of the system must be considered, but for Bearman, the concerns of certain users, for example those seeking evidence, take priority. McKemmish acknowledges that the concerns of users have not played a role in the development of the series system; and Hurley admits, "researchers complain that the volume and complexity of contextual documentation raises barriers to getting at the records."[39] Users' opinions of the series system are not known.[40] Eastwood criticizes the series system developed at the Archives of Ontario for its complexity and suggests researchers "may find Krawczyk's 'cross-reference heaven' to be a nightmare."[41] Archivists have not invested much effort in seeking to understand the needs of records users. The few user studies that have investigated fonds-based approaches to description have found that finding aids based on the Canadian Rules for Archival Description are also confusing to researchers.[42] Research is needed to develop a user-friendly descriptive architecture that eloquently represents relationships and contextual information.

Our own view is that archival descriptive architectures should not dictate only one way of describing. Both the series system and fonds-based approaches are opening up avenues for exploration as they engage each other and broader discourses on description and classification. We need to investigate differences with a desire for inclusivity, rather than exclusivity. Acknowledging one type of provenance, one act of creation, or one method of describing will fail to capture the rich complexities of the records in our care. We need to move the debate beyond discussions of what provenance *really* is by problematizing the word *provenance* and the concepts archived in it, and by accepting that there always have been and always will be many provenances, multiple voices, hundreds of relationships needing to be documented, and multiple layers of context. Furthermore, we need to incorporate into our descriptive architectures a far greater receptivity to the views and activities of records users. In the following section we attempt to open further the approaches we have been discussing. No approach to archival description, no descriptive system or architecture, can escape the reality that it is a way of constructing knowledge through processes of inscription, mediation, and narration. No architecture can escape the biases of its developers. Disclosing the lines of construction is critical both to professional integrity and to meeting the demands of accountability to the users of records.

# DECONSTRUCTING DESCRIPTION

Our decisions to document, to describe, to make visible, to remember, or to forget are "positioned within and are shaped by larger forces which contest the terrain of social memory."[43] Personal histories, institutional cultures, gender dynamics, class relations, and many other dimensions of meaning construction are always already at play in processes of records description. Every representation, every model of description, is biased because it reflects a particular worldview and is constructed to meet specific purposes.[44] No representation can be complete. The representer's value system, shaped by and expressing a configuration of the forces mentioned above, is the final arbitrator on the content of a representation. Each archivist must decide what information about which records to highlight; what transitory data to capture and make visible. When describing records archivists will remember certain aspects and hide or forget others. They will highlight some relationships and ignore others. As Michael Buckland points out, "Every representation can be expected to be more or less incomplete in some regard. A photograph does not indicate movement and may not depict color.... A written narrative will reflect the viewpoint of the writer and the limitations of the language." Something in the event being represented is always lost. There is always some distortion even if only through incompleteness.[45] What we choose to stress and what we choose to ignore is subjective, and the value judgments that archivists make affect in turn how our researchers find and use records. Cook reminds us that "the traditional notion of the impartiality of the archivist is no longer acceptable—if it ever was. Archivists inevitably will inject their own values into all such activities, as indeed they will by their very choice, in eras of limited resources and overwhelming volumes of records, of which creators, which systems, which functions, which transactions, which descriptive and diffusion mechanism, indeed which records, will get full, partial, or no archival attention."[46] Archivists cannot describe records in an unbiased, neutral, or objective way. "There is no representation without intention and interpretation."[47] Description tells a story. Description is always storytelling—intertwining facts with narratives, observation with interpretation.

In describing records, archivists are working with context, continually locating it, constructing it, figuring and refiguring it. Context, in principle, is infinite. The describer selects certain layers for inclusion and decides which of those to foreground. In this process there is analysis, listing, reproduction, and so on, but its primary medium is narrative. The telling of a story. In archival description archivists tell stories about stories; they tell stories with stories. Whether they employ a fonds-based approach, or the series system, or a more eclectic approach, they cannot escape this reality. They are in the realm of "narrativity." And narrativity—as Jacques Derrida, Michel Foucault, Paul Ricoeur, Hayden White, and others have demonstrated—as much as it might strive to work with actual events, processes, structures, and characters (the "facts"), in its form—structurally—brings a certain fictionalization of what Ricoeur calls "these immediate referents."[48] For the form of narrativity—like all forms—is not merely a neutral container. It shapes, even determines, the narrative content in significant ways. Every narrative construction of the past is by definition creative, a work of the imagination—it recalls referents that in all their particularity, their uniqueness, are irrecoverable and flow in a chaotic open-endedness. The construction gives to them a shape, a pattern, a closure.

Archivists, then, should come to terms with the reality of story-telling in their descriptive work. Attempting to deny it, by insisting that they merely marshal facts rather than construct a narrative with a selection of facts, or by insisting that they are merely a conduit for a story that tells itself, leads to sterility and makes them vulnerable to story's dangers. For story invites—some would say cannot avoid—moralizing judgments and lends itself to becoming an instrument for social control. This is seen most starkly in the metanarrative, the big story. Hayden White argues compellingly that the big story steals from history and from the world their confusion, their lack of "a meaning." It imposes meaning on them, and therefore on people. In doing so, it steals from individuals what they need—space, confusion, a sense of meaninglessness—to construct their own meanings.[49] Arguably, metanarrative has dominated the realm of archival description for nearly two centuries—in the form of big stories such as the impartial custodian, *respect des fonds,* the principle of provenance, original order, the series, and records as evidence—expressed in the last few decades most powerfully in a range of thinking and activity concerning descriptive standards.

What we are marking here are the dangers of story; the power of the metanarrative; and the capacities to privilege or to marginalize, to construct knowledge, to exercise control. Pulsing insistently beneath these formulations is the reality of power. Many archivists, perhaps most, naively imagine that they can stand outside the exercise of power—even when they use records to hold power to account. And those of us who concede that there can be no "standing outside," hold to the notion that the power we wield as archivists is a constructive, as opposed to an oppressive, power. Our own view is that archivists are, from the beginning and always, political players; that they are active participants in the dynamics of power relations; and that the boundary between constructive and oppressive power is always shifting and porous. This is not an original view. It is one that has been made from different perspectives and in different disciplines by numerous commentators, from Michel Foucault to Bruno Latour, from Jacques Derrida to Ann Stoler.[50]

So archival description is a fraught terrain. How should archivists respond to it? Can they resist the systemic imperatives to privilege, to exclude, to control? The first step, as we have already intimated, is to acknowledge the nature of the terrain. Such acknowledgment breaches a circle of knowledge, allows in, invites in fresh and disturbing energies. As archival descriptions reflect the values of the archivists who create them, it is imperative that we document and make visible these biases. Users should have access to information about the worldviews of the archivists who acquired, arranged, and described archival records. Archivists need to state upfront from where they are coming and what they are doing. They need to disclose their assumptions, their biases, and their interpretations. Just as archivists document the background and biases of record creators, they need also to highlight their own preconceptions that influence and shape the descriptions and consequently the meanings of the records they represent.

Descriptions inevitably privilege some views and diminish others. When archivists describe records, they can only represent a slice, or a slice of a slice, or a slice of a slice of a slice, of a record's reality. Therefore it is imperative that we expose our biases and investigate how they shape and obscure the meaning of records. We need to move beyond the debate over whether to adopt a fonds-based approach or the series system, because both obscure the fraught terrain we have delineated and both tie us into the strictures of metanarrative. Both privilege the evidential value of records and foreground corporate and legal perspectives. The debate should move beyond its present narrow discourse and begin to investigate the aspects of records that are not being described and the voices that are not being heard. What values are we systematically ignoring, and therefore obscuring, in our descriptions? How can we resist continuing our present ways of describing that privilege certain ways of knowing but ignore others? Since our biases will always shape and distort the records, archivists need to discuss which attributes in records require greater emphasis and which can be diminished. Some voices have been silenced in archives, but our descriptions should strive to respect the rights of all voices. However, if we try to give voice to the marginalized, will we misrepresent, will we negatively bias the interpretation of the records, and will our own biases do more damage than good? Can the mainstream ever accurately represent the marginal? How can we invite in what is always beyond our limits of understanding? How can we avoid the danger of speaking *for* these voices? How can we avoid reinforcing marginalization by naming "the marginalized"? How can we invite in what we wish to resist—the voices, for instance, of white supremacists, or of hard drug dealers, pedophiles, rapists, pimps, and so on, and on and on? In the memorable words of Gayatri Chakravorty Spivak: "Let us, then, for the moment at least, arrest the understandable need to fix and diagnose the identity of the most deserving marginal. Let us also suspend the mood of self-congratulation as saviors of marginality."[51] It is imperative that we not romanticize "otherness." We need to fear it even as we respect it. We need to understand that it is as much "inside" as it is "outside." We need to engage it, without blueprint, without solution, without answers.

Our call, in a word, is for hospitality. We should be exploring new ways to open up archival description to other ways of representing records or naming the information in the records. We need descriptive architectures that open up our archives to other forms of representing. For instance, we need to resist the temptation to privilege text and to describe all records uniformly. The cry for uniformity and consistency has imposed a textual bias on other media and has underplayed the powers and attributes of visual materials, sound recordings, and other "nontextual" records.[52] We need to understand the limits of both fonds-based and series approaches and explore new ways of describing.

We need to create descriptive systems that are permeable. In doing so archivists will have to relinquish some of their power to control access to and interpretation of their records with which the current descriptive approaches invest them. Hope Olson reminds us that giving up the sole power to name or represent is risky to information professionals who are steeped "in the tradition of the presumption of universality of naming. The reason for this disease is that making space for the voice of the other means that we must relinquish some of our power to the other—power of voice, construction and definition. Instead of possessing this power exclusively, we who are on the inside of the information structures must create holes in our structures through which the power can leak."[53]

We need to create holes that allow in the voices of our users. We need descriptive architectures that allow our users to speak to and in them. Architectures, for instance, that invite genealogists, historians, students, and other users to annotate the finding aids or to add their own descriptions would encourage the leaking of power. Unfortunately, we have failed to investigate seriously the degree to which descriptive systems meet our users' needs. We need to understand better the users of our records. We need to identify all the different types of existing and potential users of archives. Our present descriptive systems facilitate the needs of certain types of users but give short shrift to others. To date, archivists have created systems based on their view of record values and their use of records. When studying users they will need to examine each group separately because the needs of genealogists will not be met by creating descriptive systems that meet the needs of historians. Tools designed to meet the needs of archivists will probably not help novice or casual users of archives. Doctoral students require systems different to those required by high school students. What other users require different descriptive systems? Do we have an obligation to meet first the needs of our resource allocators, or the creators of the records? What do the media specialists, lawyers, children, geographers, and so forth need? How do we understand what these users want? Can we afford to try to give them what they want, or does the archivist become the final arbitrator of what they need? What are our obligations to them? How accountable to them do we need to be? If we study the needs of academic researchers, are we simply studying the elite? We cannot meet the needs of all users so we must decide which users get preferential treatment, which users do we serve first and foremost. We can develop a number of interfaces to our descriptive systems but we cannot afford to develop a different system for each type of user. So we will need to decide who we serve first, who we study, and to whom we are accountable. We will also need to consider the importance of future researchers. If we meet the needs of present users, how will we disadvantage users not yet born? If we emphasize the voices of today's marginalized, will we create barriers to future researchers?

What our descriptions mean and what the records mean will not remain inviolate over time. They will change, because their inter-pretation is dependent upon the social worlds of their interpreters. Archives, ultimately, are not about the past but about the future. But can we anticipate the future? Can we meet all the needs of all the users across time? No! But we can respect the future, precisely by respecting "the present." To re-spect, look again, at the complex, messy present, we would argue, is to open it to the future. We heed a profound call when we engage what is "other"; when we strive to hear voices that are marginalized or silent; when we confront our own storytelling and seek ways of telling better, more inclusive stories; when we face our own complicity in the exercise of power; when we refuse to squeeze the concept of accountability to users into a neat, manageable box or descriptive template.

What we have been attempting above is a tentative outline of a deconstructive approach to archival description; an approach that posits an architecture that will resist adopting only what is manageable, that will resist neat boxing exercises. Is such an architecture amenable to any form of standardization? What does it say to descriptive standards? These are the questions we address in the final section of this essay.


## UNMASKING THE TITULAR

The last two decades of the twentieth century saw a proliferation of standards for archival description. Most of them were the products of initiatives emanating from Europe and North America, the sites also of their increasingly widespread implementation. The standardization of archival description, we would argue, must be seen as part of a more generalized push for standardization—in the view of some analysts, a late modernist endeavor to find order and sanity in increasingly chaotic tumblings of reality. Beyond the scope of this essay is an examination of linkages between this phenomenon and the broader conditions of modernity, bureaucratization, and globalization. Suffice it to say that the linkages are undeniable and that standardization cannot be understood outside of historical and political processes.

In this essay, we have sought insistently to name the dangers inherent to any process of archival description. These dangers are especially concentrated in moves to standardize. As Bowker and Star have argued: "Each standard and each category valorizes some point of view and silences another. This is not inherently a bad thing—indeed it is inescapable. But it *is* an ethical choice, and as such it is dangerous—not bad, but dangerous."[54] With standardization, then, archivists are clearly in a realm where power is exercised and where the dangerous processes of valorization and silencing are unavoidable. When does an approach to description, a system of classification, become a standard? Following Bowker and Star,[55] we would identify two key characteristics: a set of agreed-upon rules spanning more than one community of practice or site of activity and enduring over time; and the deployment of these rules to make things work together over distance and heterogeneous modes of measurement and description. The wider the span, the greater the distance, the more heterogeneous the modes, the greater the violence done to the local, the individual, the eccentric, the small, the weak, the unusual, the other, the case that does not fit the conceptual boxes unavoidable in standardization. Here we are dealing with degrees of violence. In other words, there can never be an absence of violence. Any approach to, or model of, standardization that claims such an absence is seeking to fool all of the people all of the time. By the same token, the positing of orthodoxy in descriptive standardization, whether based on the fonds or the series, marks a considerable presence of violence.

In many of his works, Jacques Derrida has addressed the question of "the name," seeking always to open up its closed spaces by deconstructing the processes of naming. What we name we declare knowable and controllable. In naming we bring order to chaos. We tame the wilderness, place everything in boxes, whether standard physical containers or standardized intellectual ones. In the realm of descriptive standardization, using big boxes such as fonds or series, or small boxes such as dates of creation or acquisition, we bring order to wild realities. Derrida's ideas do not sustain a marginal, esoteric exercise. Indeed, they reach into our daily lives, for arguably all use of language is about naming. Brien Brothman argues this point brilliantly in a recent essay,[56] drawing in technology's infinite expansion of naming spaces: "The world we speak and write, this world upon which we speak and write and name, is not flat. Nor is it round. It is a curved web of endless threads of meaning becoming. With information technology, as Derrida has explained, language has been dislocated from the territorial and the national. Language is a final frontier without boundaries, without edge, without finality."[57] Naming, then, is always pertinent. But it is particularly pertinent to descriptive standards. As Hope Olson has said to information professionals: "Naming nature is the business of science. Applied in our role as 'neutral' intermediaries between users and information, our theories, methods, models, and descriptions are as presumptuous and controlling as scientists' construction and containment of nature."[58] With "the standard" we pronounce the titular names, the metanames, the ones that will empower us to use the rest of our words to describe all in our purview.

Of course, metanames come in varying sizes. And the choices that inform their "sizing" are laden by value judgment. For example, a standard's grouping of various elements and the degree of descriptive specificity accorded each grouping expresses a particular view of reality. Some standards strive for simplicity, identifying relatively few distinct groupings. They group similar concepts under the rubric of a broader concept. These standards obscure difference and foreground sameness. Other standards focus on the finer grain by accentuating and reinforcing the distinctiveness of similar concepts. The sharper the focus, the plainer difference becomes. As Bowker and Star explain: "Blurring categories means that existing differences are covered up, merged, or removed altogether; while distinction constructs new partitions or reinforcement of differences. This mutual process of constructing and shaping differences through classification systems is crucial in anyone's reality."[59] A simple example: the *General International Standard Archival Description (ISAD(G))* (2nd edition) provides rules for recording dates of records creation and dates of accumulation in the same descriptive element. It makes no reference to dates of reproduction, receipt, or transmission, though it does give space for "other dates." However, this space is focused on levels of description (for example, fonds, series, file, or item), thus marginalizing the dating of other processes not tied to these recorded products.

For some, the critique of standardization that we have offered thus far might constitute grounds for dismissing descriptive standards as tools of oppression to be avoided at all costs. However, with Bowker and Star, we would argue that their dangers should not be equated with badness. Of course, there are bad standards. And even a good standard can be used badly. Before proceeding to attempt a depiction of what a good standard might look like, let us make the case for not dismissing descriptive standards out of hand. Our case rests on three arguments. Firstly, purism in this realm invites paralysis. The deconstructionist who eschews naming, or labeling, for the reasons outlined above, but who at the same time argues that all language is about naming, that every word is a sign, and that therefore all writing and all speech is a form of labeling, is bound to silence. Like Derrida, the archetypal deconstructionist, who writes and speaks in volumes unimaginable to most of his detractors, we would choose to engage the messy business of naming rather than to be silent. The silent archivist is an archivist with no story to tell. Surely the imperative driving all of us who call ourselves archivists is precisely that we must tell stories with our records? And like Derrida, while being suspicious of every metanarrative, we would acknowledge the impossibility of ever transcending metanarrative. For of course the deconstructive suspicion—and concomitant determination to create space for multiple stories—itself becomes a big story. Secondly, early twenty-first–century realities make it impossible to build a complex collective project without standards.[60] For example, every e-mail message relies on over two hundred Internet standards for its successful transmission. Thirdly, whatever our view of descriptive standards might be, the dangerous work of naming, of building and applying descriptive architectures, proceeds in a myriad archival sites and localities. More often than not, this work is characterized by an unquestioning replication of the power relations within which these sites and localities are embedded. In our view, the descriptive standard is one of the few direct means available to us for troubling and perhaps challenging this replication. It can be a means of questioning orthodoxies such as the fonds, the series, corporate record-keeping, and the pre-eminent focus on the evidential value of records. To classify is human. And to respect the metaname, the standard, is also human. Ironically, and dangerously, this provides us with an opportunity to unmask the titular.

But how to unmask the titular using what is by definition a titular tool? Let us confess upfront that we are not sure that it is possible. We have no blueprint, no final answer. We are cast in the realm of what is (im)possible. Our dream is of a descriptive standard that liberates rather than oppresses, one that works as a touchstone for creativity rather than as a straitjacket. What would the attributes of such a standard be?[61]

A liberatory standard would not seek to hide the movements of its construction. In particular, it would not obscure the dimensions of power that it reflects and expresses. In the words of Bowker and Star, it would resist the temptation to pose as a "naturalized object," one desituated and stripped of the contingencies of its creation.[62] The traces of its construction would be made explicit. In other words, it would, as far as possible, make known the biases of its creators. It would, in short, be hospitable to deconstruction.

A liberatory standard cannot emerge from a process that is exclusive, opaque, and beyond the demands of accountability. Enormous as the hurdles might be, as resilient the resistances, standards writers need to seek inclusivity and transparency. The process is as important as the product. The more boundaries—geographical, cultural, class, gender, disciplinary, institutional, and other—crossed by the process, the more liberatory its product is likely to be.

A liberatory standard would not position archives and records within the numbing strictures of record-keeping. These strictures posit "the record" as cocooned in a timebound layering of meaning and reduce description to the work of capturing and polishing the cocoon. The work, to shift metaphors, of housekeeping. In contrast, a liberatory standard would embrace the work of homemaking. It would posit the record as always in the process of being made, the record opening out of the future. Such a standard would not seek to affirm the keeping of something already made. It would seek to affirm a process of open-ended making. This would mean, *inter alia,* encouraging the documentation of continuing archival intervention. It would mean finding ways of documenting the continuing use of records. It might mean providing space for researchers to embed their own stories of use within the descriptive layerings. Such a standard would, in other words, be permeable to the naming work of users.

A liberatory standard would take the needs of records users seriously. Without this attribute a descriptive standard courts the danger of being oppressive or irrelevant. A standard *with* this attribute would acknowledge that different categories of user deploy different semantics and require different paths into the record. It would seek to allow different ways of searching, different ways of interrogating records, different ways of organizing and manipulating representations. It would, in short, place a premium on flexibility.

A liberatory standard would encourage archivists to get in under the dominant voices in the processes of recordmaking. Without falling for reductionist formulations, and mindful of the dangers attendant on any attempt to know "otherness," it would require engagement with the marginalized and the silenced. Space would be given to the subnarratives and the counternarratives.

A liberatory standard would seek ways of troubling its own status and its *de facto* function as a medium of metanarrative. It would push the capacity of description to accommodate partial or multiple closure. It would strive for an openness to other tellings of story, to retellings, and to the holding of competing stories. It would, in the words of Bowker and Star, embrace "a politics of ambiguity and multiplicity."[63] Things that don't fit the boxes would not be either discarded or manipulated to size. Rather, cross-box and multiple-box positioning would be encouraged. And, as has already been suggested, the boxes would be given optimal flexibility and permeability. Holes would be created to allow the power to pour out. For, again as Bowker and Star have argued, "The toughest problems in information systems design are increasingly those concerned with modelling cooperation across heterogeneous worlds, of modelling articulation work and multiplicity. If we do not learn to do so, we face the risk of a franchised, dully standardized infrastructure … or of an Orwellian nightmare of surveillance."[64]

Archivists, we have argued, exercise power. They certainly have the power to choose a better fate for archival description than Bowker and Star's two-headed monster. Do they have the will?

# Endnotes

1 The authors wish to thank David Bearman, Terry Cook, Catherine Johnson, Thea Miller, and Joan Schwartz, whose comments and ideas have greatly improved the essay. It was first published in *Archival Science 2*, nos. 3–4 (2002).

2 S.Muller, J.A.Feith, and R.Fruin, *Manual for the Arrangement and Description of Archives* (1898). For an insightful assessment of the *Manual*'s position in the history of archival discourse, see Terry Cook, "What Is Past Is Prologue: A History of Archival Ideas since 1898, and the Future Paradigm Shift," *Archivaria* 43 (1997): 20–22.

3 Of course, we brought to the exercise a host of other differences, including gender, global positioning, and culture. Some we are aware of, others we are not. Some seem significant, others do not. While we have worked hard at fashioning a coherent "voice" for the essay, we determined not to hide the tensions generated by these differences. It is our hope that the tensions are creative ones. For the record, Verne produced the first drafts of the introductory and concluding sections; Wendy the middle two sections.

4 Verne Harris, *Exploring Archives: An Introduction to Archival Ideas and Practice in South Africa,* 2nd ed. (Pretoria: National Archives of South Africa, 2000), 57.

5 In finding this commonality we note our indebtedness to articulators of so-called postmodernist ideas, as well as to the records continuum thinking that dominates Australian archival discourse. But it was Jacques Derrida who coined the phrase "the archive opens out of the future." Jacques Derrida, *Archive Fever: A Freudian Impression* (Chicago: University of Chicago Press, 1996), 68.

6 This essay presents two different points of view on description: one based on the principle of *respect des fonds,* and the other focused on series. It presents these approaches as opposites to tease out and explain the different perspectives that underlie and influence much of the debate. In reality, many archival descriptive systems contain some elements of, and are influenced by, the perspectives of both.

7 *Rules of Archival Description,* D-5.

8 Terry Eastwood, ed., *The Archival Fonds: From Theory to Practice* (Ottawa: Bureau of Canadian Archivists, Planning Committee on Descriptive Standards, 1992), 4.

9 Terry Eastwood, "Putting the Parts of the Whole Together: Systematic Arrangement of Archives," *Archivaria* 50 (Fall 2000): 997.

10 Terry Cook, "The Concept of the Archival Fonds: Theory, Description, and Provenance in the Post-Custodial Era," in *The Archival Fonds,* 42–43.

11 For some of the writing on this topic, see Peter J. Scott, "The Record Group Concept: A Case for Abandonment," *American Archivist* 29 (October 1966): 493–504; C. Hurley, "The Australian Series System: An Exposition," in *The Records Continuum: Ian MacLean and Australian Archives First Fifty Years,* ed. Sue McKemmish and Michael Piggot (Clayton: Ancora Press, 1994), 50–172; Cook, "The Concept of the Archival Fonds, 42–43; David Bearman, "Item Level Control and Electronic Recordkeeping," *Archives and Museum Informatics* 10, no. 3 (1996): 207–45; David Bearman, "Documenting Documentation" *Archivaria* 34 (Summer 1992): 33–49; Bob Krawczyk, "Cross Reference Heaven: The Abandonment of the Fonds as the Primary Level of Arrangement for Ontario Government Records," *Archivaria* 48 (Fall 1999): 131–53.

12 We chose not to label the series system the "Australian" system for two reasons: it is not applied universally in Australia; and many non-Australians are supportive of the series system, have written about it, and have influenced its development.

Of course, "series system" is also inadequate as a label, for as it is being elaborated today by people like Sue McKemmish and Chris Hurley it embraces far more than the idea of the series.

13   Scott, "The Record Group Concept," 496.

14   Hurley, "The Australian Series System," 155.

15   Sue McKemmish, Glenda Acland, Nigel Ward, and Barbara Reed, "Describing Records in Context in the Continuum: The Australian Recordkeeping Metadata Schema," *Archivaria* 48 (Fall 1999).

16   Hurley, "The Australian Series System," 155.

17   Cook, "The Concept of the Archival Fonds," 73.

18   Sue McKemmish, "Are Records Ever Actual?" in *The Records Continuum*, 192.

19   Eastwood, "Putting the Parts of the Whole Together," 108.

20   Eastwood, "Putting the Parts of the Whole Together," 113.

21   Eastwood, "Putting the Parts of the Whole Together," 144.

22   Eastwood, "Putting the Parts of the Whole Together," 105.

23   Michel Duchein, "Theoretical Principles and Practical Problems of Respect des Fonds in Archival Science," *Archivaria* 16 (Summer 1983): 64–82.

24   Heather MacNeil, "The Context Is All: Describing a Fonds and Its Parts in Accordance with the Rules for Archival Description," in *The Archival Fonds,* ed. Eastwood, 202.

25   Cook, "The Concept of the Archival Fonds," 42.

26   Bearman, "Documenting Documentation," 237.

27   Tom Nesmith, "What Is a Postmodern Archivist?: Can Douglas Brymner, an Unmuzzled Ox, and Star Trek Tell Us?" paper delivered at Association of Canadian Archivists Annual Conference, Halifax, 29 May 1998.

28   Canadian Working Group on Archival Descriptive Standards, *Toward Descriptive Standards* (Ottawa: Bureau of Canadian Archivists, 1985), 10.

29   The Canadian *Rules of Archival Description* uses the term for the level of unit being described (e.g., *fonds, series, file, item*) while the American *Archives, Personal Papers, and Manuscripts* uses the term *collection* to denote the object of description. In both standards, the assumption is that the rules relate to the description of static, previously arranged groupings of records.

30   EAD Design Guidelines (adopted July 1995), http://lcweb.loc.gov/ead/tglib/tlprinc.html, accessed 2 July 2001.

31   *RAD,* Glossary, definition of *Description.*

32   Hurley, "The Australian Series System," 151.

33   Sue McKemmish, "Is the Record Ever Actual?" 195.

34   Cook, "The Concept of the Archival Fonds."

35   Heather MacNeil, "Metadata Strategies and Archival Description: Comparing Apples to Oranges," *Archivaria* 39 (Spring 1995): 30.

36   Chris Hurley, "The Making and the Keeping of Records (2): The Tyranny of Listing," *Archives and Manuscripts* 28, no. 1 (2000): 8–23.

37   Bearman, "Documenting Documentation," 34.

38   Bearman, "Documenting Documentation," 237.

39   C. Hurley, "The Australian Series System," 154.

40 This statement is not to suggest that all supporters of the series system are opposed to studying users. Many supporters of this system, including Terry Cook, Adrian Cunningham, and David Bearman, have promoted the importance of understanding how users seek information and how they use descriptive tools.

41 Eastwood, "Putting the Parts of the Whole Together," 105.

42 Wendy Duff and Penka Stoyanova, "Transforming the Crazy Quilt: Archival Displays from a User's Point of View," *Archivaria* 45 (Spring 1998): 44–79.

43 Verne Harris, "Redefining Archives in South Africa: Public Archives and Society in Transition, 1900–1996," *Archivaria* 42 (Fall 1996): 7.

44 Godfrey Rust, "Metadata: The Right Approach, An Integrated Model for Descriptive and Rights Metadata in E-commerce," *Dlib magazine* (1998), at http://www.dlib.org/dlib/july98/rust/07rust.html.

45 Michael K. Buckland, "Information as Thing," *Journal of the American Society for Information Science* 42, no. 2 (1991): 358.

46 Cook, "What Is Past Is Prologue," 46.

47 David R. Olson, *The World on Paper* (Cambridge: Cambridge University Press, 1994), 197. In this paragraph we are consciously deploying the word *represent* with the "postmodern" resonances it now carries. We see archival description as a form, or mode, of re-presentation.

48 Quoted in Hayden White, *The Content of the Form: Narrative Discourse and Historical Representation* (Baltimore and London: Johns Hopkins University Press, 1987).

49 White, *The Content of the Form*, 72.

50 See, for instance, Michel Foucault, *The Archaeology of Knowledge and the Discourse on Language* (New York: Pantheon, 1992); Bruno Latour, "Visualization and Cognition: Thinking with Eyes and Hands," *Knowledge and Society* 6 (1986); Derrida, *Archive Fever;* and Ann Stoler, "Colonial Archives and the Arts of Governance: On the Content in the Form," in *Refiguring the Archive,* ed. Carolyn Hamilton, et al. (Cape Town: David Philip, forthcoming). These commentators have influenced, and are influencing, a growing number of "postmodern" archivists. In terms of discourse, the most prolific of the latter are the Canadians Terry Cook, Brien Brothman, Joan Schwartz, Tom Nesmith, and Richard Brown.

51 Gayatri Chakravorty Spivak, *Outside in the Teaching Machine* (New York and London: Routledge, 1993), 61.

52 For a fascinating discussion on archival practice and photographs see Joan Schwartz, "We Make Our Tools and Our Tools Make Us: Lessons from Photographs for the Practice, Politics and Poetics of Diplomatics," *Archivaria* 40 (Fall 1995): 40–74.

53 Hope A. Olson, "The Power to Name: Representation in Library Catalogs," *Signs: Journal of Women in Culture and Society* 26 (Spring 2001): 659.

54 Geoffrey Bowker and Susan Leigh Star, *Sorting Things Out: Classification and its Consequences* (Cambridge, Mass.: The MIT Press, 1999), 5–6.

55 Bowker and Star, *Sorting Things Out,* 13–14.

56 Brien Brothman, "In the Name of the Name: Keeping Archives in the Late Modern Age," in *Wresting the Archon from the Arkheion: A Question of Right(s) and a Call for Justice to Always Come?* ed. Ethel Kriger (Pretoria: National Archives, 2001).

57 Brothman, "In the Name of the Name," 158.

58 Olson, "The Power to Name," 640.

59 Bowker and Star, *Sorting Things Out,* 230.

60  Bowker and Star, *Sorting Things Out,* 14.

61  We do not claim originality in the outline of a liberatory standard that follows. Bowker and Star, explicitly, have influenced our thinking. But a number of "archival" thinkers, notably Terry Cook, have also influenced us. Cook's groundbreaking ideas are spread through numerous texts, but are concentrated in a text that appeared after we began work on this essay: "Fashionable Nonsense or Professional Rebirth: Postmodernism and the Practice of Archives," *Archivaria* 51 (2001).

62  Bowker and Star, *Sorting Things Out,* 299.

63  Bowker and Star, *Sorting Things Out,* 305.

64  Bowker and Star, *Sorting Things Out,* 308.

# CHAPTER 10

## The Record, the Archive, and Electronic Technologies in South Africa[1]

## INTRODUCTION: OF TERMS, CONCEPTS, AND PLOTS

When we use (or address) concepts connected to the words *record* and *archive* we are, whether we realize it or not, standing above a semantic abyss. Space constraints, and concern for the reader's tolerance, do not allow me to explore this abyss. Suffice it to make a few preliminary observations, as a first movement, on my use of key words. Firstly, my conceptualizations of "record" and "archive" are most heavily influenced by the interrogations and uses of the words by Jacques Derrida and Michel Foucault.[2] So that, for instance, I would happily regard as "archive" the shared narratives of a collectivity. Secondly, by "recordmaking" I understand that huge and messy realm in which what are conventionally called records creators, records managers, archivists, users, and so on, negotiate, contest, and narrate the meanings and significances of what are called "records."[3] In this understanding, records are always in the process of being made, they open into (and out of) the future.[4] And by "politics" I understand an equally huge and messy realm, reaching across orders of the individual and the collective, the personal and the public, in which the dynamics of power and authority engage with issues of principle. In this essay, for the most part, I have focused my inquiry in terms of narrower categories—on "records," particularly "archival records," more particularly "electronic archival records"; and on the dynamics of power and authority in the public domain, particularly as exercised by structures of the state and of government. The patterns that emerge, I would argue (though space constraints do not allow it), are to be found as well in societal sectors we call "civil" or "private." Clearly, each of these categories also demands semantic subinquiry, but to go there would be to risk losing the plot before it's begun.[5]

A further (de)limitation of my inquiry is constituted by the name "South Africa." Rather than attempt to mount my arguments within the impossible reach of the "in general," I do so out of that geographical space we call "South Africa." The analysis perforce embraces the particular, but in drawing conclusions I look always for what we could call the universal. I am not offering a case study; rather, in the specificities of South Africa I look for the play of structural dynamics. The conceptual site for my search is the nexus of recordmaking (specifically electronic recordmaking), archives, and the exercise of power. The search reaches from the late apartheid era to the present era of postapartheid democratization in South Africa. While it unfolds certain significant discontinuities, it also confronts a number of worrying continuities. As Jacques Derrida has intimated, diagnoses of totalitarian practices can be "extended to certain current practices of so-called democracies in the age of a certain capitalistico-techno-mediatic hegemony."[6] The central argument that I mount is that electronic recordmaking—in South Africa; in any country—must always be understood within broader organizational and societal contexts, and that endeavors to promote sound electronic recordmaking are doomed to failure unless they, at least, engage these contexts. I go further, and suggest that these endeavors, ultimately, are political, and that getting the politics right matters more than anything else. What "getting the politics right" means is, in the end, and in the beginning, a question of ethics.

# HISTORICAL CONTEXTS[7]

We know very little about the apartheid state's deployment of electronic technologies for the purposes of recordmaking. Between 1997 and 1998, the Truth and Reconciliation Commission (TRC) conducted a focused investigation into apartheid-era state recordmaking, with special emphasis on the systematic destruction of records undertaken by the security establishment.[8] It revealed only a broad outline of electronic recordmaking, namely, that deployment of electronic technologies became significant in the 1970s, that it gathered momentum in the 1980s driven primarily by the security establishment, and that by the early 1990s in many institutions electronic systems were becoming the primary sites of recordmaking. But three details unearthed by the investigation point to significant underlying dynamics:

1. Despite the large-scale destruction exercise mentioned above, the TRC team located substantial accumulations of paper-based apartheid-era records. In contrast, the surviving electronic record was sparse. This speaks to two dimensions of electronic recordmaking: the relative ease of erasure and the relative ease of concealment.

2. Certain electronic records located by the TRC team were discovered to be unreadable. This speaks to the special challenges posed by the longer term preservation of electronic records.

3. While the National Archives was able to provide the TRC team with a fund of information on apartheid-era recordmaking and opened its doors to a vast collection of paper-based records, it knew very little about electronic recordmaking and had negligible accumulations of archival electronic records.

I want to dwell briefly on this last point. Under apartheid the State Archives Service (the predecessor to the postapartheid National Archives) enjoyed wide-ranging powers over state recordmaking.[9] It was also an early user of electronic recordmaking technologies, having introduced automated information retrieval systems in 1974.[10] It would not, then, be unreasonable to anticipate its having secured a handle on state electronic recordmaking by the early 1990s. But for several reasons this was not the case:

- State archivists regarded electronic media as unsuitable for archival preservation—they were acceptable for applications such as finding aids (and for bringing efficiencies to process), but not as the bearers of information with archival value. Cut off from international discourse and practice by sanctions, and concentrating expertise in a single division of the organization, the State Archives Service would not accept records for archival preservation in electronic media until 1991.
- In terms of positioning, state archivists under apartheid were subordinate functionaries and bureaucrats within the cultural sector. So that despite their legal powers, they had neither the resources nor the status to challenge powerful agents and agencies. Among the former were IT managers and specialists, who thrived in organizational cultures that privileged "science," efficiency, and technology. Among the latter were those making up the security establishment. Until 1990, both electronic records and the security establishment effectively were placed outside the ambit of the State Archives Service.

The combination of neglect, ignorance, lack of resources, marginalization, and deliberate erasure has had dire consequences for South Africa. Two decades of widespread electronic recordmaking by the apartheid state have left almost no residue in archival repositories. And this pattern is replicated outside the state. Researchers intent on engaging our electronic memory resources for the pre-1994 period will find the cupboard almost bare. Extensive databanks documenting natural and human observation, monitoring and surveillance have evaporated. The traces of early word processing, document management, and electronic communication systems have gone.

## REGIME CHANGE

If the loss of electronic memory from the 1970s and 1980s has had a severe impact, then a similar loss of memory from the 1990s and 2000s would be disastrous. For the growth in deployment of electronic technologies in the latter period has been exponential. The introduction of PC-based applications in the late 1980s, followed by the Internet and integrated office management systems, finally revolutionized record-making in offices of the state. While paper and its surrogates will never disappear, today the shape of recordmaking, its heart and its core, are electronic.

While State Archives Service records management archivists did not anticipate this revolution, it was in response to its early rumblings in the late 1980s that they had been pushing for a review of archival policy.[11] That the policy shift on electronic records finally occurred shortly after the state's 1990 unbanning of the ANC and other liberation movements is no accident. The shift was part of a broader process in which the organization's leadership began to acknowledge new realities, accept that fundamental change (whether technological, social, or political) was inevitable, and give space to a younger generation of archivists keen to engage international discourses and try fresh approaches to old problems.

The new policy was predicated on a three-pronged strategy:[12] archival involvement in the design and maintenance of electronic records systems; the earliest possible transfer into archival custody of electronic records with enduring value; and the identification of electronic records that should remain in the custody of creating agencies under the supervision of archival authority. Archival involvement was effected through the building of in-house expertise and the development of appropriate legal instruments. Staff were trained in electronic recordmaking, a dedicated unit within the records management division was established, and when the new National Archives of South Africa Act was passed in 1996 it contained significant and explicit provisions relating to electronic records.[13] Soon after the policy shift an agreement was reached with Bureau Nucleus (a substructure of the state central computer service, later named the State Information Technology Agency) whereby the latter would house electronic records transferred into archival custody and provide technical support for their maintenance. By 1994, two electronic records acquisitions had been effected.

In the last ten years the National Archives has focused considerable energy on regulation and standards setting. At the legislative level it has overseen the drafting of provincial archival legislation with provisions for electronic recordmaking, and contributed to the drafting of the Promotion of Access to Information Act (2000) and the Electronic Communications and Transactions Act (2002). In 1999 it published a *Guide to the Management of Electronic Records in Governmental Bodies,* which included a standard for electronic records management systems. In 2002 it published as a discussion document a *Minimum Mandatory Metadata Set*.

The scenario I have just sketched would have sounded like some kind of Eden to those of us who found ourselves in the State Archives Service records management division in the late 1980s. And yet the attributes of Eden end at the list of things that have and are being done. For if we measure the *impact* of these interventions, then we find ourselves in a depressing exercise.[14] Compliance with statutory and other regulatory requirements by state agencies is almost nonexistent. National Archives attempts to educate, monitor, and regulate these agencies is reaching only the tip of the iceberg. Its power to approve electronic records systems deployed by the state is almost never exercised. The two electronic records acquisitions mentioned above have not been added to in ten years.[15] In short, despite the postapartheid shifts I have outlined, we are looking at a continuing large-scale loss of electronic memory.

Let me illustrate the dynamics at play by pausing briefly at the archives of the Truth and Reconciliation Commission.[16] I must stress at once that the TRC archives is not representative of state agency archives in general. It was and is a special case. We are looking at a best-case scenario. The National Archives was involved in its recordmaking from the outset. It assisted the TRC with the design of both electronic and paper-based filing systems. It trained its documentation officers and conducted regular records management inspections. It participated in the planning for the archiving of records as the TRC wound down its operations. The paper-based records went straight into the custody of the National Archives. The stage was set, then, for a smooth transfer of the electronic records from a functional to an archival domain. However, the reality has proved to be messy and worrying:

- The databases are reportedly still fully functional, under the auspices of the President's Fund for continuing reparations work.[17]
- The Web site is being hosted by the Department of Justice. Anyone who has tried to use it knows that it experiences persistent problems, with down-times and failures in functionality.

- But it is the rest of the TRC's electronic applications where the real problems lie. Here I refer to word processing, spreadsheets, electronic communications, and other office management systems. These, I would argue, are the sites of recordmaking where the richest evidence of organizational process is to be found. The plan initially was for all records generated by these systems to be classified and stored on office file servers in terms of the National Archives–approved classification system. In practice, use of the system was extremely uneven. The usual attrition associated with anarchic hard drives and a cavalier approach to e-mail occurred. But it was at the point of close-down that the real damage occurred. In a short space of time, and under severe pressure, the contents of file servers, hard drives, and floppy disks were simply downloaded onto tapes. It is unclear what the results of this process were, but clearly metadata loss and jumbling must have taken place. Later some of the tapes were downloaded onto CD-ROMs. Already at that stage difficulties were experienced in reading some of the data. Today, four years on, the tapes and CDs are in the custody of the Department of Justice receiving preliminary archival intervention. According to the project leader, it will take extensive consultation with the people who created the records to begin making sense of what is a maze.[18]

So much for the TRC electronic archive, a crucial part of arguably the most important postapartheid archives generated thus far. In comparison, what is taking place in further reaches of the state is a wild West. Why is this? What has gone wrong? I am naming the need for a diagnosis. But before moving into this space, we must pause to examine one further symptom, namely, restriction on public access. And here I begin with one last mention of the TRC archives. Needless to say, with the exception of the Web site, the electronic records of the TRC are not accessible to the public. At least three dimensions are at play here—the lost records are forever inaccessible; those awaiting archival intervention are at best potentially accessible; and those that are technically accessible now remain under wraps as sensitivities around access to the TRC archives are negotiated.

South Africa's 1996 constitution enshrines the right of access to information—uniquely the right applies not only to information held by the state.[19] The Promotion of Access to Information Act (PAIA) was passed in 2000 to give effect to this right, which came into operation in 2001. PAIA has its flaws, but overall it is an excellent piece of freedom of information legislation. The rub lies in its implementation. Because it provides specifically for access to information held in records, it is predicated on sound recordmaking. Agencies with poor records systems, agencies that do not maintain electronic records effectively over time, agencies that do not deploy resources to deal with access requests undermine the intent of the law. And both incapacity and a lack of will to implement the law are rampant in South Africa. Another (related) factor is constituted by pervasive cultures of secrecy inherited from the past. Too many information officers reflexively adopt the role of gatekeeper, relying on the prohibitive costs of court action to avoid being held accountable for unreasonable denials of access. It is difficult to determine trends specifically in the electronic records arena. What is clear is that the systemic barriers outlined above are supplemented by other dynamics: very often requests are dealt with by people who don't even consider what relevant information might be contained in electronic records; older electronic records are often not accessible for technical reasons; and in a country where a relatively small elite has expertise in and access to electronic recordmaking, the medium itself constitutes a significant barrier to access for most people.

## A DIAGNOSIS

Analysis of the electronic record in postapartheid South Africa reveals sometimes startling continuities in relation to apartheid-era realities. Electronic memory is still evaporating. While no longer paralyzed, the National Archives remains ineffectual. Levels of surveillance by the state remain high. Public access to records is blocked by systemic barriers. The production of public knowledge is skewed by difficulty (sometimes it is an impossibility) in accessing, on the one hand, databanks documenting natural and human observation, monitoring, and surveillance, and on the other, evidence of organizational processes. To repeat my questions: Why is this? What has gone wrong?

For some, the answer is a simple one at certain levels of analysis—this is further evidence of the fact that democratization in South Africa has not yet effected fundamental, structural change. I am tempted by this answer, but to stop with it would be to avoid complexity. For the symptoms we discern in South Africa have global dimensions. The disease, if you like, is far bigger than South Africa:

- Despite notable exceptions (national and institutional), and despite continued progress with legislation, standards-setting, software development, and so on, on a global scale the reality is that on the one hand just a sliver of electronic memory is being archived, and on the other, just a sliver of archival memory originates in electronic form.[20]
- Again, despite notable exceptions, national archives around the world remain ineffectual.
- One of the distinctive features of the twenty-first–century state—and globalization is rapidly creating a universal pattern—is its massive accumulation of information, particularly about its own citizens. It does this through both programs with a service provision rationale and the activities of bodies charged with various surveillance mandates. The "new" information technologies—the pace of their development means that they are always new—provide the state with a capacity for this massive accumulation, which is growing exponentially.
- Although it is not unreasonable to characterize our age as the information age, even as the age of freedom of information, the struggle for public access to information continues around the world.[21]

So, South Africa is not unique. To return to the terminology of Jacques Derrida, South Africa is part of "a certain [global] capitalistico-techno-mediatic hegemony." I will return to this theme in my conclusion.

There *are* South African specificities, and they demand attention. Of course, they are complex enough to require at least an essay-length inquiry. But space is not on my side, so let me offer just an outline of a window into process by focusing on five dimensions informing electronic recordmaking by the state:

1. The key auditors of state recordmaking (the National Archives and provincial archives services) are desperately under-resourced. This has to do with questions of status, positioning, and strategy (dealt with below), but beneath all of them is the harsh reality

that in a country prioritizing redress of past injustice and confronted by challenges such as poverty, drought, and HIV/AIDS, archival concerns are simply not high on the agenda.

2. IT managers and specialists (now often dressed in flashy new names like "knowledge managers"[22]) remain influential in a country intent on lifting itself into the global mainstream. On the one hand, these players as a rule remain unconcerned about long-term memory, and, on the other, archivists have been singularly unsuccessful in either harnessing or co-opting the leverage that such players enjoy.

3. An attribute shared by most national archives enjoying success in meeting the challenges of electronic recordmaking is the degree to which they have been able to imagine and position themselves as more or less autonomous recordmaking auditors. During South Africa's transition to democracy (specifically, during the debates that informed the transformation of South Africa's national archival system), advocates of this approach proved unsuccessful in effecting a meaningful shift.[23] The main obstacle proved to be concern at giving autonomy to institutions still in the early stages of transformation. The result is that—at both national and provincial levels—state archivists remain subordinate functionaries and bureaucrats within the cultural sector.[24]

4. South African archivists seeking to address the challenges of electronic recordmaking have too often uncritically adopted strategies that have worked elsewhere. So, for example, they have spent enormous energy in developing standards and regulating the terrain, but have paid little attention either to the political contexts or to the recordmaking cultures they are dealing with.

5. South Africa has inherited powerful cultures of secrecy and intolerance for dissent. These cultures flow out of the old apartheid state milieus, the exile experience, and the underground. Moreover, South Africa did not experience a revolution. In

transitions from oppressive regimes to democracy, the nature of the transition is critical in determining subsequent access environments. A quick overthrow is the best-case scenario (e.g., East Germany). Protracted negotiated settlements give the oppressive regime time to destroy records and provide the space for more or less secret deals that stimulate sensitivity to later disclosures.[25] Which in turn stimulate concern about the "danger" of giving state archives their heads.

## CONCLUSION: UNDERSTANDING POWER

Conventional wisdom suggests that the loss of electronic memory has to do—at its profoundest levels of causality—with the absence of appropriate recordmaking cultures. To use the terminology of Terry Cook, "paper minds" addressing "electronic records" is a recipe for disaster.[26] Now, I don't wish to dismiss this analysis out of hand. There is an element of truth in it, and it would be foolish to underestimate the importance of changing "paper minds." But I wish to conclude by suggesting an even profounder level of causality.

It is relatively easy (and therefore frequently done) to make the argument that the very structure of archiving, that the process that is recordmaking, both invites politics in and generates a politics of its own wherever "archive" happens. Ultimately there is no understanding of the archive without understanding of politics. But, as I have argued elsewhere, politics is archival, and the archive is the very possibility of politics. I submit that the elites that oversee Derrida's "capitalistico-techno-mediatic hegemony"—and this could easily be true of all elites—draw their power primarily from their control of contexts. They are the ultimate purveyors of context. They create contexts, destroy them, promote or discourage them, co-opt or discredit them. And they are primarily interested in recordmaking as an instrument in the exercise of power. Concern for good records systems has to do with immediate functional imperatives. Concern for long-term memory and all the concepts, values, and processes associated with it—history, heritage, archives, legacy, freedom of information, and so on—does not stretch far beyond the imperative to control contexts. Elites are never interested in what actually happened—it is too complex, messy, and potentially explosive—or in creating space for people to contest the past; that leads to dominant metanarratives being challenged. They are interested in shaping the past and containing contestation. We saw this play out in almost exemplary fashion during the build-up to the war on Iraq (2002–2003).

This analysis invites archivists to contemplate certain uncomfortable conclusions:

- The most powerful imperative to ensure good recordmaking is constituted by the desire to exercise control. (It is no accident that oppressors are the best recordmakers.) So that recordmakers who extol the value of recordmaking to good governance, to accountability, to transparency, and so on, are probably undermining rather than promoting their cause.

- It is common cause that long-term memory in paper-based records is still better and more comprehensive than that in electronic records. But it would be a mistake to assume that this has to do primarily with the relative absence of archival cultures in the electronic domain. A more obvious explanation is that archival cultures are weak across the board, and that the nature of electronic media simply makes it more difficult for archivists to rescue an enduring record.

- Changing "paper minds" is but the first step in what has to be a long and comprehensive agenda for struggle. Ultimately our struggle is a political one. Polities that care about good governance, that care about justice, also care about history, heritage, archives, and so on. Get the policies, standards, techniques, and so on right, but ignore the politics, and we are wasting our time. Get the politics right, and all the other elements will want to fall into place.

For archivists and others who care about electronic memory it is time—and it has always been time—to wise up. Good recordmaking seems to thrive in what we could call extreme environments: oppressive environments, on the one hand, and environments shaped by the call of justice on the other. Unless we understand the political dimensions and conceptualize our struggle as a struggle for justice, we condemn ourselves to rearranging deckchairs on a sinking *Titanic*.

# Endnotes

1 This essay was prepared initially as a paper for presentation at the annual Society for the History of Technology conference in Amsterdam, October 2004. An edited version was published under the title "Ethics and Electronic Recordmaking," in *Managing Electronic Records,* ed. Catherine Hare and Julie McLeod (London: Facet Publishing, 2005). The version reproduced here is closely modeled on the latter, but with several additions and excisions. It benefited from comments on early drafts by Brad Abbott and Heiko Roehl, and from decisive interventions by the editors of *Managing Electronic Records*. Nevertheless, I take full responsibility for the "final" text.

2 See, in particular, Michel Foucault, *The Archaeology of Knowledge and the Discourse on Language* (New York: Pantheon, 1992), and Jacques Derrida, *Archive Fever: A Freudian Impression* (Chicago: University of Chicago Press, 1996).

3 For an extended making of the argument, see Wendy Duff and Verne Harris, "Stories and Names: Archival Description as Narrating Records and Constructing Meanings," *Archival Science* 2, nos. 3–4 (2002).

4 It was Jacques Derrida who coined the phrase "the archive opens out of the future." Derrida, *Archive Fever,* 68.

5 I have explored the semantic nuances archived in these words in numerous other texts, especially *Exploring Archives: An Introduction to Archival Ideas and Practice in South Africa,* 2nd ed. (Pretoria: National Archives, 2000).

6 Jacques Derrida, *Without Alibi* (Stanford: Stanford University Press, 2002), 59.

7 For a detailed analysis of recordmaking by the apartheid state, see my "The Archival Sliver: Power, Memory and Archives in South Africa," *Archival Science* 2, nos. 1–2 (2002).

8 Harris, "The Archival Sliver."

9 See my "Redefining Archives in South Africa: Public Archives and Society in Transition, 1990–1996," *Archivaria* 42 (1996).

10 For the first two decades these systems were run off STAIRS software.

11 I was an archivist in the State Archives Service's records management division from 1988 to 1994.

12 Harris, *Exploring Archives,* 89–91.

13 See Harris, *Exploring Archives,* chapter 10.

14 This conclusion was drawn by Louisa Venter (assistant director, Electronic Records Management Programme, National Archives) during discussions at the conference Expectations and Realities in Managing Electronic Records, Johannesburg, June 2004. She confirmed it in written responses to me later in June 2004.

15 One of the acquisitions, a snapshot of the statewide personnel administration system PERSAL, has been supplemented by subsequent annual snapshots.

16 From 1996 to 2001, I was responsible for liaison between the National Archives and the TRC. In this position I became intimately acquainted with processes designed to ensure the effective archiving of TRC records.

17 Interview with Ruendree Govinder, 12 August 2004. Govinder is the project leader in an exercise designed to ensure the proper archiving of TRC electronic records.

18 Interview, Govinder, 12 August 2004.

19 See section 32 of the constitution.

20  I made this argument in the paper "The Challenges of Preserving Electronic Memory Over Time," at the conference Challenges and Best Practices in Electronic Records Management, convened by Long Sight, Sandton, South Africa, July 2003.

21  The work of the South African freedom of information nongovernmental organizations SAHA (South African History Archive) and ODAC (Open Democracy Advice Centre) attests to the access challenges facing people even when freedom of information legislation is in place.

22  In my view, organizations can manage information, records, people, business processes, etc. They cannot manage knowledge. What is called "knowledge management" is simply the coordinated management of resources and processes.

23  I document this in "Redefining Archives in South Africa." The Truth and Reconciliation Commission also recommended a fundamental repositioning of the National Archives. However, its recommendation lost its force through contradictory elaboration—at one and the same time it advocated independent agency status (the ideal) and positioning within either the office of the president or that of the deputy president.

24  In 2001, the National Archives of South Africa Act was amended by the Cultural Laws Amendment Act. One of the changes tied the National Archives more tightly into the state bureaucracy.

25  In 2003, the proceedings of the Hefer Commission provided a fascinating window into how this sensitivity is playing out in South Africa. See my "After the Hefer Circus," *Natal Witness,* 29 December 2003.

26  Terry Cook, "Electronic Records, Paper Minds: The Revolution in Information Management and Archives in the Post-custodial and Post-modernist Era," *Archives and Manuscripts* 22, no. 2 (1994).

# SECTION III

# POLITICS AND ETHICS

# CHAPTER 11

## Redefining Archives in South Africa: Public Archives and Society in Transition, 1990–1996[1]

### INTRODUCTION

"Archives hold the memory of a nation" is an assertion archivists are fond of making.[2] A stirring slogan, it dismisses the role of libraries, museums, and other repositories of information, not least the memories of individuals. It also suggests a glibness about the complex processes through which archives feed into social memory, and it is closely allied to the concept of archivists as impartial custodians who somehow remain insulated from institutional and societal dynamics.[3] Of course, in everything they do—the records they choose to preserve, how they arrange them, describe them, and make them available—archivists are active shapers of social memory, and they in turn are positioned within, and are shaped by, the larger forces that contest the terrain of social memory.

Under apartheid, this terrain, together with all social space, was a site of struggle, not only of narrative against narrative, but also, in the crudest sense, of remembering against forgetting.[4] In imposing apartheid ideology, the state sought to destroy all oppositional memory through censorship, confiscation, banning, incarceration, assassination, and a range of other oppressive tools. This was the context within which public archivists practiced under apartheid—struggle informed not only their institutional and social environments, it permeated the fabric of their daily professional work. Impartiality was patently a pipe-dream.[5]

South Africa's formal transition to democracy began in 1990 and culminated in 1994 with the adoption of a new interim constitution and the holding of the country's first democratic general election. Two years on, the Government of National Unity has successfully secured adoption of a final constitution and managed elections at the local government level.[6] But the monumental task of transforming apartheid South Africa, of building democracy, has just begun. In the sphere of archives, particularly public archives, the focus of this essay, the process has not gotten beyond foundational spade-work. This work has been energized by and positioned within two overlapping arenas of transformation: the public service and social memory.

My account[7] of transition begins with a brief analysis of public archives under apartheid. I then explore transformation discourse in South African archives, firstly from the perspective of process, secondly in terms of the core issues that occupy it. In the final section I assess the present position and offer some thoughts on the future.

## PUBLIC ARCHIVES AND APARTHEID

In addressing public archives under apartheid, it is not my intention to attempt a comprehensive historical analysis,[8] nor is it to engage debates around the professional quality of the work done by public archivists. My purpose is to locate public archives within the arenas of state bureaucracy and social memory in the period 1948 to 1990,[9] and to suggest in broad terms how public archives were shaped by the system of apartheid. In doing so, I focus deliberately on the State Archives Service; excluded from analysis are the South African Defence Force (SADF) Archives and the various homeland (or *bantustan*) archives services.[10] It should be noted, however, that the SADF Archives and the homeland archives services in both conception and administration reflected faithfully apartheid logic. Under a system according inordinate power and autonomy to the military, it is not surprising that the

SADF Archives, although legally subject to the professional supervision of the State Archives Service, in practice sustained an independent operation.[11] Nor is it surprising, in the context of apartheid homeland policy, in particular the inadequate professional and administrative assistance made available by central government, that the homelands either neglected public archives entirely or maintained only rudimentary services.[12]

The State Archives Service has its origins in the fledgling public archives facilities maintained by the pre-union Cape, Natal, Orange River, and Transvaal colonies.[13] In the decade after union, these facilities were fashioned into a national archives service positioned in the Department of the Interior. Empowered legislatively for the first time in 1922, it subsequently underwent a number of name changes and moved from the Interior Department to Union Education, then to the Education, Arts and Science Department, and finally to the National Education Department. From the outset, its custodial mandate embraced the archives of all central and provincial government offices; in 1962, this was extended to incorporate all local government offices.[14] Also from the outset, the service enjoyed a mandate to supplement its official holdings by collecting private records.[15] Its functions vis-à-vis public records still in the custody of government offices—its records management functions—remained modest and purely advisory until 1953. Thereafter, especially after the passing of the 1962 Archives Act, the service developed a significant records management capacity sustained by wide-ranging regulative powers.[16] By 1990, the service had facilities in seven cities across the country,[17] including six archives repositories and five intermediate repositories (or records centers).

Throughout the apartheid era, the State Archives Service, by virtue of its positioning within the state, was shackled by its identification with the apartheid system. Denied membership in the International Council on Archives (ICA) and shunned by most other countries, particularly during the cultural boycott of the 1980s, the service was largely excluded from the international exchange of professional ideas and resources. Individuals attempted to keep abreast of developments through the literature, but this was no substitute for active participation. Within the country, mutual suspicion erected barriers between the service and many institutions and individuals active in the arena of social memory. This impacted directly on the service's functions—for instance, the service found it difficult to secure donations of private records from other than establishment-aligned sources, and participation in the service's computerized national registers of manuscripts, photographs, and audiovisual material was constrained.[18] At a more profound level, however, isolation fostered a laager mentality resistant to new ideas and enthralled by an outmoded professional discourse.[19]

Apartheid realities and the service's status as an organ of the state combined to ensure that many of its services, whatever the intentions of the service or of individual archivists might have been, were fashioned into tools of the apartheid system. Three examples illustrate this. Firstly, despite the fact that user services were open to all and offered free of charge,[20] black South Africans made up only a small proportion of the service's users. Systemic barriers—low educational standards, high rates of illiteracy, physical isolation from city centers, competency in languages other than the official Afrikaans and English, and so on—ensured that most South Africans enjoyed only nominal access to public archives. Secondly, the service's records management functions—designed in the first instance to identify and safeguard public records with archival value, but also effective in promoting administrative efficiency—in effect oiled the wheels of apartheid bureaucracy.[21] Thirdly, in its relationship with homelands archives services the service was placed in a classic apartheid dilemma: cutting them loose professionally would have meant reinforcing homeland underdevelopment; providing comprehensive support would have meant buttressing grand apartheid policy. In practice, the service's approach fell uncomfortably between the two.

Another dilemma confronted the service in the form of powerful state organs obstructing its legitimate activities and flagrantly ignoring or defying its legal instruments. Given the apartheid system's disregard for accountability and transparency, and the service's junior status within government,[22] the service was poorly positioned to resist. Again, three examples serve to illustrate this dimension. Firstly, a number of government offices persistently refused to subject their records systems to design analysis and archival appraisal or to co-operate in the transfer of records into the service's custody.[23] Secondly, from the late 1980s numerous cases of unauthorized destruction of public records by government offices were documented and many more alleged.[24] They pointed to a systematic endeavor to secure a selective amnesia as the apartheid system crumbled. The service was singularly unsuccessful in opposing this or exposing the culprits. Thirdly, in the 1980s the service was forced by its political masters to withdraw open access to certain records in its custody—those less than fifty years old of six government offices, and all post-1910 records of a further four offices.[25] These restrictions were lifted in 1991 and in practice constituted only a minor infringement of public access to the records concerned.[26] Nevertheless, this incident contributed to a perception of the service as a willing collaborator in state-imposed public amnesia.

Not that willing collaboration with the apartheid system was not a powerful dynamic in the service. Indeed, I would argue, it was molded as an institution by apartheid and absorbed apartheid bureaucratic culture. Until the mid-1980s, public service legislation laid down that only whites could be appointed to professional and many administrative posts. By 1990, not a single professional post had been occupied by a black person.[27] As in the rest of the bureaucracy, senior positions were dominated by white, Afrikaans-speaking males.[28] The service's structure was rigidly hierarchical and its management ethos authoritarian. Transparency and broad participation in decision making were given short shrift. Official language policy was implemented, with Afrikaans dominant in the upper reaches of management. Much core policy documentation was produced only in Afrikaans. Language usage, needless to say, also impacted on the service's interface with users and the public generally, as did the service's provision of racially segregated reading room and toilet facilities until the 1970s.

The absorption of apartheid bureaucratic culture, and, at a deeper level, of apartheid ideology, shaped the service's functions and left indelible marks on its contribution to social memory. A close analysis of the service's archival appraisal function is beyond the scope of this article.[29] However, it is clear that until the blossoming of social history and revisionist historiography in the 1970s, the service's fashioning of appraisal into a tool for academic researchers, particularly historians, resulted in the experience of the underclasses being poorly reflected in the records chosen for preservation. The fact that most of the service's appraisers were taught as undergraduates by establishment-aligned Afrikaner historians was an important contributory factor. A more fundamental skewing of social memory is evident in the service's collections of private records. With the exception of the Boer resistance to British imperialism, they document poorly the struggles against colonialism, segregation, and apartheid. Black experience is also poorly documented, and in most cases is seen through white eyes. Similarly, the voices of women, the disabled, and other marginalized people are seldom heard. A number of practical difficulties, for instance inadequate budgets and the rareness of skills required to give the voiceless voice, must be considered in explaining this phenomenon. I have already mentioned the problems posed by the service being identified with the apartheid state. But the heart of the issue was a collecting policy that quite deliberately directed archivists away from grassroots experience toward society's pinnacles.[30] A more blatant ideological intervention was demonstrated by the service's official history project, which involved the production of a multi-volumed official history of one of the central events in Afrikaner history, the Anglo Boer War of 1899–1902.[31] "It was," according to historian Albert Grundlingh, "the Afrikaner's answer to the *British Official History of the War* and *The Times History of the War*."[32] Ideological considerations also informed the selection of theses for publication in the service's *Archives Year Book for South African History*. Introduced in 1938, the series became an important vehicle for Afrikaner nationalist historiography, with the legitimization of white rule and the exclusion of oppositional voices being key objectives in selection policy.[33]

Debate around the shaping of the State Archives Service by the apartheid system has produced two dominant (and conflicting) characterizations of the service. One portrays the service simply as an instrument of the system—as Jill Geber asserted in 1987: "Primarily the Government Archives Service is an important auxilliary [*sic*] administrative tool of the National Party used to further the efficient execution of apartheid policy throughout the administrative structure."[34] The other characterization posits an institution straitjacketed by the system but resilient enough to emerge largely unscathed. Neither is accurate. Both employ narratives without complexity or texture. My analysis offers an interpretation somewhere between these two extremes. Ultimately it delineates public archives in South Africa—whether positioned in the public service terrain or that of social memory—as bearing profoundly the imprint of apartheid and in urgent need of transformation.

# TRANSFORMATION DISCOURSE: PROCESSES

The unbanning of the African National Congress (ANC) and numerous other organizations in February 1990, and the subsequent initiation of formal negotiations on the dismantling of apartheid, marked the beginning of what many journalists and other commentators termed South Africa's period of "Pretoriastroika."[35] Terms such as *transparency, accountability, stakeholders, public participation, restructuring, reconstruction,* and *transformation* exploded into public discourse. The sphere of archives was no exception. A transformation discourse— one informed by the assumption that archives require redefinition, more precisely reinvention, for a democratic South Africa—quickly emerged. This despite the fact that participants in this discourse, unlike in many other spheres, had very little to build on. They were confronted by a paucity of revisionist thinking and debate.[36] A survey of pre-1990 South African archival literature, for instance, reveals a predominance of work positioned comfortably within the status quo.[37] The only significant exception was Jill Geber's 1987 master's dissertation, *The South African Government Archives Service: Past, Present and Future,* which attempted a historical analysis of the State Archives Service and offered a vision for public archives in a postapartheid South Africa.[38] This seminal work marked the birth of transformation discourse, but its immediate impact was slight.[39] From 1990, South African archival literature underwent a sustained rejuvenation as it exploited a blossoming of professional exploration and debate.[40] But in the early stages of transition, participants in transformation discourse were forced to rely on ideas from international archival literature and from more broadly based debates around social memory within the country.

Between 1990 and 1994, South Africa's formal transition period, in terms of process three main tributaries fed into the river of transformation discourse: the State Archives Service, the ANC, and the South African Society of Archivists (SASA).[41] Within months of February 1990, and thereafter with increasing urgency, "Pretoriastroika" dynamics fashioned change within the State Archives Service. Two conflicting imperatives competed for supremacy in this process: a conservative survival instinct located mainly at senior levels and focused on adapting to new realities; and, mainly at junior levels, a progressive determination to effect meaningful changes. The process was facilitated by a significant shift in the balance of power in the service's senior management—the six most senior officials in 1990 had all retired by 1994, and whereas all twelve of the most senior positions had been occupied by Afrikaners (only one a woman) in 1990, by 1994, four women and three English-speakers were placed in the top eleven positions.[42] Racial exclusivity broke down more slowly, with just five professional positions occupied by blacks in 1994, and the first such appointment at senior management level taking place in 1995.[43] Another significant impetus to progressive elements was provided by the ending of international isolation. The service was admitted to membership in the ICA in 1991 and quickly embraced participation in all its structures, notably the Eastern and Southern African Branch (ESARBICA).[44] The service hosted numerous visits by foreign archivists and, in turn, responded to invitations from other countries.[45] In 1992, the service's director appointed a Committee to Investigate the Impact of Social and Political Changes on Archives Services in Other Countries and reinforced it with the appointment of several issue-based committees and task teams. For the first time, albeit cautiously, management was encouraging internal debate and seeking engagement with debates in the archival profession and beyond. Participation in professional and other gatherings became more common. Management style was also changing, with broader participation in decision making and the faint glimmerings of transparency and accountability. All of this, needless to say, impacted on the service's coalface activities. A project to translate into English core policy documentation only available in Afrikaans was embarked on. The theoretical and methodological underpinnings of the service's archival appraisal program were revisited in the light of international developments, and an endeavor to document apartheid more fully through the appraisal program was initiated. Public programming was implemented systematically for the first time through, *inter alia,* open days, extended reading room hours, group visits, and formal consultation with users. An electronic records management program, long overdue, was established. These are examples of a far broader phenomenon, one which demonstrated the service's willingness and capacity to adapt to new realities. However, it would be misleading to suggest that this constituted a commitment to transformation. In 1994, the survival instinct, drawing on the inertia of the previous four decades, still held sway.

The ANC, on the other hand, occupied a position squarely within a transformation paradigm. Long traditions of oppositional discourse, policy formulation around the reconstruction of postapartheid South Africa, and the development of concepts such as people's education, people's history, and cultural liberation energized the ANC's voice on archives. In 1992, the organization's Department of Arts and Culture established a Commission on Museums, Monuments and Heraldry that convened an Archives Subcommittee with the following short-term mandate:

- To examine the state of management of archives in the country;
- To formulate a draft policy document regarding archives in a democratic South Africa;
- To formulate guidelines regarding interim measures; and
- To make recommendations regarding transformation, popularization, and democratization of current archives structures.[46]

The subcommittee produced its "Preliminary Report" in June 1992. Although it provided comprehensive and wide-ranging analysis—one of the objectives being to perform an educative function within the ANC—its policy formulations and specific recommendations focused on the State Archives Service. The thrust of its thinking is captured in the assertion that "the guiding principle must be the repositioning of the Archives Service within the structures necessary to liberate the minds and memories of the people, so that they can empower themselves as citizens of a democracy."[47] Its proposals were organized around several core ideas: institutional transformation; accountability and transparency; freedom of information; outreach; public participation; oral history as a mechanism for giving the voiceless voice; and the promotion of people's history. The only proposal that addressed directly the position of private archival institutions posited a "national, co-operative collections policy" managed by a "democratized State Archives Service."[48] The report made a considerable impact on archival discourse. Popularized by Graham Dominy in a 1993 *South African Archives Journal* article,[49] it injected fresh ideas and gave momentum to transformation discourse. Its influence within the ANC, however, was marginal. Absorbed into broader positions adopted by the Commission on Museums, Monuments and Heraldry, it emerged from the ANC's 1993 Culture and Development Conference as an arid collection of slogans that were neither acted on by leadership structures nor publicized.[50] The subcommittee continued promoting archives as an issue within the organization, but by the end of 1993 it had effectively ceased to exist.

SASA, South Africa's oldest and largest professional association of archivists,[51] was the other major contributor to transformation discourse. Until the 1980s, it was dominated by State Archives Service archivists and did little beyond producing the annual *South African Archives Journal*. During the 1980s, it established branches in all four provinces, which began to attract new members and create space for the exchange of ideas. However, given the State Archives Service's hegemony, in particular the National Committee's faithful reflection of the service's management hierarchy, it is not surprising that an outmoded professional discourse prevailed, dissident voices were muted, and SASA never adopted a critical stance vis-à-vis the state. From 1990, a sea change became evident.[52] "Pretoriastroika" in the State Archives Service reverberated through the SASA as well. Changes to SASA's constitution made it easier for non–State Archives Service members to secure election to the National Committee.[53] A new leadership infused energy, broader awareness and experience, and a determination to invigorate the association professionally while positioning it on the public stage. Internal procedures and processes were upgraded and made more transparent. A professional code was adopted.[54] Almost overnight the *South African Archives Journal* was transformed from a space for nuts and bolts musings into a forum for meaningful exploration and debate. Many of the key texts in transformation discourse appeared in its pages. New voices, including major players on the international archival stage, used it as a medium.[55] SASA-convened gatherings became more frequent and more relevant. In 1992, the National Committee, together with the Association of Archivists and Manuscript Librarians (AMLIB), convened South Africa's first international archival gathering, with the theme "Archives and Users in Changing Societies."[56] Another international gathering, entitled "Archives for the People: Securing an Archival Heritage," was convened in 1994.[57] For the first time SASA made formal interventions in public debates. Its 1993 "Position Paper on Information and Archives" was distributed to all organizations participating in South Africa's transitional negotiation process.[58] Subsequently it petitioned government structures concerning the Truth and Reconciliation Commission, the Arts and Culture Task Group, the National Archives of South Africa Bill, and South Africa's final constitution.[59] These interventions were not expressions of a coherent vision or paradigm. SASA's heterogeneous membership, internal tensions, and the baggage of its past militated against this. The focus was on specific issues; the imperative to articulate positions representative enough of members' views. But SASA's leadership was geared to the dynamics of change; it was comfortable with transformation discourse, and it was well positioned to participate fully in structures created by the new government after 1994.

The State Archives Service, the ANC, and SASA were not the only tributaries into transformation discourse during its formative 1990 to 1994 period. A host of smaller ones swelled and enriched it. Numerous individuals used conference platforms, journal pages, even the press, to contribute their ideas.[60] Broader debates, for instance around issues such as freedom of information, both absorbed and fed into archival debates. I have already noted the international dimension. Worth specific mention is the impact made during their visits to South Africa by Eric Ketelaar, Terry Cook, and Andor Skotnes. All three made forceful interventions, traveling widely in the country and bringing to bear their experience of archives in established democracies and participation in cutting-edge debates on the international stage.[61] Other significant local contributors included the Association of Archivists and Manuscript Librarians, the South African Historical Society, the South African History Archive, and the William Cullen Library (University of the Witwatersrand).

The general election of 27 April 1994 ushered in the new interim constitution and the formal transfer of power from the National Party to the ANC-led Government of National Unity. In terms of transformation processes in archives, it also marked a shifting of the initiative to government and various structures appointed by it. The interim constitution provided for the devolution of the state's responsibility for culture, and with it archives, from the central government to the country's nine new provinces. This implied the conversion of the State Archives Service into a national public archives service at the central level and the creation of nine more or less autonomous provincial public archives services.[62] During 1994, the State Archives Service was moved from the defunct Department of National Education to the central

Department of Arts, Culture, Science and Technology, and the various homeland archives services were allocated to the provinces in which they were situated. It was also accepted in principle that State Archives Service facilities located in the provinces would be allocated to them in due course. In November 1994, the minister of Arts, Culture, Science and Technology appointed the Arts and Culture Task Group (ACTAG) to advise him on a new arts and culture policy for South Africa. The group's Heritage Subcommittee was mandated to address the question of archives. Although it did not possess a representative from the archival profession, this subcommittee consulted widely, traveling the length and breadth of the country to ensure a process that was as inclusive as possible. ACTAG's final report, submitted to the minister in June 1995, positioned archives firmly in the heritage terrain and emphasized their importance as an agent of reconciliation and nation building. The records management functions of public archives services were totally ignored, as were widely expressed misgivings about the unqualified placement of public archives within structures of government for "culture." A complex network of heritage structures, embracing all three tiers of government, was proposed, and, in line with the government's Reconstruction and Development Programme, the report advised a shifting of public archives resources to programs designed to empower people and redress the imbalances of the past.[63] The report provided the conceptual framework intended to inform the drafting of new archival legislation.[64] In April 1995, the State Archives Service, acting on a mandate from the minister, convened a Consultative Forum for Archival Management and Legislation.[65] With representatives from a wide range of interest groups and consisting of over sixty delegates,[66] the forum brought together the diverse streams in South Africa's archival discourse. Over seven months, the forum hammered out a synthesis position and gave it expression in a unanimously adopted draft National Archives of South Africa Bill.[67] This was submitted to the minister in December 1995 and reached Parliament in February 1996.[68]

Progress at the provincial level has been slower. Provincial governments face a mammoth and complex restructuring process. There is keen awareness of the need for clarity to emerge at the national level before provinces formulate archival policy, and most provinces have little to work with in the way of archival infrastructure, expertise, and experience. A number have sustained debate through provincial task groups on arts and culture. Only KwaZulu-Natal and the Eastern Cape have task groups specifically for archives. The former, appointed in 1994 to advise the province's minister of Education and Culture on all matters related to archives and to draft archival legislation for the province, produced a "Position Paper on Archives and Public Records in KwaZulu-Natal" in 1995 and a draft Provincial Archives of KwaZulu-Natal Bill in 1996. The Eastern Cape task group was appointed in 1996 specifically to draft archival legislation for the province.[69] The indications are that the launching of provincial public archives services, and the establishment of a new archival "system" for South Africa, still has a long road to travel.

## TRANSFORMATION DISCOURSE: CORE ISSUES

What I have called transformation discourse focuses heavily on public archives, the main target for transformation. Nevertheless, it addresses a myriad issues spanning archival theory and practice, archival functions and structures, and the broader terrains of social memory and public service. Clearly any attempt at identifying the *core* issues is a highly subjective business. In this account, I restrict myself to areas of debate specific to archives, thus excluding, for instance, more general debates around public service transformation and government restructuring. Within these parameters, I explore the issues that in my view give the discourse its fundamental shape. In each instance, I would suggest, the ground being contested is the very identity of archives.

Considerable earlier post-1990 debate revolved around the nature of a public archives as an institution. There are proponents of the view that it is essentially a cultural, or more specifically, a heritage institution.[70] Others, and they have gained the ascendancy, argue that while its heritage function is indisputable, it cannot be understood properly without taking into account its roles in information management and public administration.[71] This position is predicated on the assumption that records management functions[72]—which draw public archives into advising, monitoring, controlling, and auditing government offices—are *archival* functions.[73] Public archives, both as an institution and as an idea, the argument is elaborated, straddles various disciplines and social arenas. Some go further and maintain that public archives must be conceptualized around processes rather than records in physical custody.[74]

Adherents of the heritage model advocate the positioning of public archives within government structures for culture. The thrust of their challenge to the apartheid status quo has consisted in critique of the tight control exercised over the State Archives Service by the apartheid bureaucracy,[75] and in promotion of greater bureaucratic status or professional autonomy for public archives.[76] In contrast, those who posit a broader conceptualization of public archives argue that positioning within structures for culture undermines the efficacy of public archives' records management functions and contributes to misconceptions about the nature of archives. While they have achieved no consensus on an ideal positioning—ideas range from a more central position within government to independent agency status[77]—they agree, for different reasons, that tight bureaucratic control is undesirable.[78] This debate was effectively pre-empted by central government's decision in 1994 to place the State Archives Service as a directorate within the Department of Arts, Culture, Science and Technology, and the subsequent assumption of responsibility for archives by provincial departments of education and culture. Prospects for a repositioning or for a significant change in status appear slim.[79]

Underpinning debate around control over and the relative independence of public archives has been a more fundamental one in which the notion of public archivists as impartial custodians has been swept off the stage by the view of archivists as active shapers of social memory and documenters of society.[80] This idea is arguably the defining characteristic, the leitmotif, of transformation discourse. Exploration of its implications has occupied center stage, developing several strands and generating fierce debate. Perhaps the least contested argument is that public archives, because of their role as active shapers and documenters, must be subject to high levels of transparency and accountability. The apartheid model for public archives—answerable only to the state and their operations largely opaque—has been firmly rejected. This, of course, fuses with the broader imperative to democratize South Africa's public service. Debate in archives has revolved around mechanisms for achieving transparency and accountability,[81] and the question of how an appropriate balance of accountability to the users of archives, to society, and to the state is to be achieved.[82] The achievement of a substantial consensus on the desirability of such a balance[83] has been accompanied by a decline in the view that the shaping power of archives should be harnessed by the state to promote particular narratives, for instance that of reconciliation and nation building.[84] The importance of this development for the future of public archives in South Africa can scarcely be overemphasized. History is littered with examples of states controlling their public archives to manipulate social memory.[85] In 1993, Albert Grundlingh warned against it in the context of a transitional South Africa by raising the specter of the State Archives Service being "… called upon to provide a legitimizing historical project for the new state. Will that," he went on to speculate, "involve the appointment of an official state historian … to narrate the anti-apartheid struggle in the same way that Breytenbach started some thirty years ago to chronicle the Afrikaner struggle against the British Empire?"[86]

Similar questions permeate discussion of those two core "shaping" functions of public archives: appraisal and collection.[87] With the former, the focus has been on appraisal as an institutional process: Who should be responsible for appraisal? To whom should appraisers be accountable? How transparent should the process be? How reliable are the appraisals done during the apartheid era? These questions are rooted in an intense distrust of State Archives Service appraisal practice, which is characterized by an unrelenting opacity.[88] Some have gone so far as to recommend that the appraisal function be taken from public archives and given to independent boards comprising academics and other "stakeholders." The intensity of this distrust was illustrated in November 1995, when South Africa's National Cabinet imposed a moratorium on the destruction of all public records—irrespective of whether or not they had been appraised by the State Archives Service—until the passing of new national archival legislation.[89] By 1995, however, debate had yielded substantial agreement on a number of issues. Appraisal is an archival function and archivists should be responsible for it. Nevertheless, democratic imperatives demand that levels of transparency be high, that public account be given of appraisal decisions, and that there should be some measure of public participation in the decision making. These positions were reflected in the draft National Archives of South Africa Bill prepared by the Consultative Forum for Archival Management and Legislation. The draft proposes that the National Archives be charged with the appraisal of public records, subject to the approval of its overarching appraisal policy and monitoring of the policy's implementation by a National Archives Commission appointed by the minister of Arts,

Culture, Science and Technology.[90] The commission, in other words, would be the minister's and society's watchdog.[91]

Debate around the theoretical and methodological underpinnings of appraisal practice has been less widespread but equally vigorous. Located mainly within State Archives Service structures, the debate has pitted defenders of the service's established practice against advocates of macro-appraisal.[92] The service's appraisal policy has its roots in the 1950s and demonstrates the powerful influence of T. R. Schellenberg. The policy is built on the assumption that archival value is a composite of Schellenberg's informational and evidential values. However, in practice the distinctions between these values have become blurred, and at the appraisal coalface one dominant question tends to subsume all others: Does this record possess actual or anticipated usefulness to researchers? The service's methodology is incoherent, with elements of both Schellenbergian methodologies[93] and of macro-appraisal.[94] Not surprisingly, the service's policy has proved an easy target for advocates of macro-appraisal, who question the validity of its intellectual foundation and its appropriateness to the realities of the 1990s. Macro-appraisal, they argue, provides an explanation of archival value that is rooted in the archival bedrock of provenance, which, unlike the idea of usefulness, secures a workable yardstick and meshes with a methodology appropriate to modern records environments. In 1996, the State Archives Service formally discarded its Schellenbergian appraisal underpinnings and embarked on a macro-appraisal–inspired overhaul of its appraisal program.[95]

The State Archives Service's collecting function—outlined in the second section of this article—has also proved to be an easy target. Apologists for it are nowhere to be found. Its critics have developed broad consensus on the defining characteristics of an alternative vision for collecting by public archives, one deeply influenced by the concept of "total archives."[96] Policy, it is asserted, should direct archivists not only to society's pinnacles, but also, firmly, to grassroots experience and the full gamut of experience in between. Policy should accommodate the complementing of official holdings but be directed primarily at the filling of its gaps. Collecting should be driven by the postapartheid imperative to give the voiceless voice. Public archives should not compete with the country's numerous private collecting institutions for material that would be more appropriately preserved by the latter. This vision is already reshaping public archives collecting policy, but two key questions remain unresolved. Firstly, to what extent, if at all, should the collecting function be subordinated to the management of official holdings?[97] Secondly, what should public archives' involvement be in the collection of oral tradition and history?[98] In South Africa, with its strong oral traditions and high rates of illiteracy, it is clear that giving voice to the voiceless will require a strong commitment to the collection of oral sources. As the ANC's Archives Subcommittee articulated it:

> People's History programmes, including oral documentation programmes, should be fostered as part of a programme of democratization and empowerment of the voiceless by the Archives Service in collaboration with other cultural and heritage organisations...[99]

Still being debated is whether public archives should collect oral tradition and history themselves, acquire oral sources collected by experts in the field, facilitate access to oral sources by means of the national registers,[100] coordinate and promote the collecting of oral testimony, or be invested with a combination of these functions.[101]

Debate around the use and making available of public records has followed numerous streams. Much attention, for instance, has been paid to the question of public rights of access, with substantial cross-fertilization taking place between the archival debate and the wider public debate on freedom of information.[102] However, the defining issues in transformation discourse, in my view, hinge on the assertion that it is not enough for public archives to ensure equal access to their holdings, even if they do so in terms of constitutionally entrenched rights of public access. They must go beyond being merely servers of records users. They must become *creators* of users; or, in the words of the popular slogan, they must "take archives to the people."[103] From the outset, this position formed one of the dominant streams in transformation discourse, and quickly secured hegemony, even within the State Archives Service.[104] Its proponents pointed to the array of systemic barriers to access raised by the apartheid system, the alienation from public archives of most South Africans, and the urgent need to utilize public resources in addressing the huge inequalities and imbalances inherited from apartheid. Public archives, in short, should be transformed from a domain of the elite into a community resource.[105] They also pointed to the State Archives Service's inertia, even indifference, in the face of systemic barriers under apartheid and to the dominance within the service during the apartheid era of the view that outreach is, at best, a luxury and, at worst, simply not a function of public archives. While there is broad agreement that outreach and other public programming activities *are* functions of public archives—crucial functions in the postapartheid era—cautionary voices point out that they constitute a severe drain on limited resources and that care should be taken to ensure that they do not undermine other archival functions.[106]

There are numerous manuscript collecting institutions outside the ambit of public archives in South Africa,[107] some of which have done innovative and extremely valuable work in filling the gaps in the official record.[108] But their role in a democratic South Africa and their relationship to public archives have received relatively little attention. Nevertheless, critique of the status quo has seen the emergence of the key elements to a new approach. The lack of interinstitutional cooperation, sharing of resources, and coordination have been identified as major problems.[109] The prevalence of overlapping collecting fields and consequent inter-institutional rivalry has been singled out in particular;[110] past attempts at collaboration in identifying and demarcating collecting fields did not have encouraging results.[111] Some institutions' overly restrictive access policies, and cases of collections being sold to foreign purchasers, have also drawn criticism, as has the State Archives Service's pre-1990 lack of engagement with other collecting institutions—with the obvious exception of its national automated registers of manuscripts, photographs, and audiovisual material. The new approach is built on two foundations: the transformation of public archives from ghetto-dwellers into effective members of a broader archival community; and the promotion of voluntary cooperative endeavor. Mechanisms for the exercise of state control over private institutions, with two exceptions, have attracted little support. The role of the state is seen as one of coordination, support, and advice rather than of control. The draft National Archives of South Africa Bill envisages just such a role for a new National Archives.[112] Other suggestions include the management of the national registers through a forum of participants, the promotion of coordinated archival policy formulation and planning at national and provincial levels by a National Archives Commission, and the provision of state grants to heritage—

including archival—institutions by a National Heritage Council. The two exceptions to this voluntary model relate to access provisions and the disposal of records. Some voices call for state regulation of access to records in private custody;[113] this has been rejected within archival debate, but is still on the table in the broader debate around freedom of information. In contrast, there is consensus on the need for state control over the disposal of records in private archival custody: the draft National Archives of South Africa Bill makes it an offense to destroy, export from South Africa, or otherwise dispose of records recorded on a national list by the National Archives Commission without the commission's approval.

## NOW AND THE FUTURE

For South African archivists, both as South Africans and as archivists, the last six years have been at once exciting, frightening, and enriching. A fledgling democracy, with all its growing pains, has supplanted the apartheid regime. At the same time a sterile, outmoded archival discourse has been vanquished by a tougher successor—sometimes cruder, sometimes more sophisticated—born of and connecting assuredly with the new societal dynamics. If nothing else, this experience demonstrates again that archivists are not, and can never be, insulated from larger forces.

What I have called transformation discourse in archives is open-ended. Its ideas are not accepted by all South African archivists. It accommodates sometimes intense debate. And yet it possesses a remarkable coherence and offers a fundamental redefinition of archives, particularly public archives, for a democratic South Africa. At the same time, it is characterized by many consensus positions arrived at by compromise, reflecting, I would argue, the contours of South Africa's political terrain. The discourse, then, is distinctively South African. Nevertheless, as I have suggested at various points in this essay, it has been influenced by and meshes with recent developments in international archival discourse,[114] which in turn reflects the post-1990 ending of South Africa's international isolation.

As public archives in South Africa take on the future, one big question will be asked of them: Can transformation discourse deliver at the archival coalface? Strong signs of renewal within the State Archives

Service are encouraging. But systematic transformation of existing programs and the launching of new ones will be expensive, as will the establishment of nine provincial archives services, nine provincial archives councils and heritage councils, a National Archives Commission, and a National Heritage Council, and the successful tackling of problems posed by electronic record-keeping, all in the context of ever-diminishing resources and an acute shortage of qualified and appropriately skilled archivists. The position of the provinces in this regard is of particular concern. Add to this the vulnerability of public archives to uncooperative professional staff—re-education programs are essential—and to political and bureaucratic manipulation, and the magnitude of the challenge is apparent.

To this big question I would add two subsidiary ones. Firstly, as public archives "take archives to the people," will they be able to resist what Jean-Francois Lyotard has called the mercantilization, or commodification, of knowledge?[115] We would do well to remember Terry Cook's eloquent reminder:

> ...the quest for knowledge rather than mere information is the crux of the study of archives and of the daily work of archivists.... Quite simply, archivists must transcend mere information ... if they wish to search for, and lead others to seek, "knowledge" and meaning among the records in their care.[116]

In nurturing new branches it is imperative that we provide sustenance to our roots. And secondly, in finding ourselves as active shapers of social memory, will we provide space—will we be *allowed* to provide space—for competing narratives? The extent to which we do so will be the primary measure of our contribution to the enrichment and democratization of the nation's memory.

# Endnotes

1   This essay is based on a paper of the same title that I presented at the University of the Western Cape Conference "The Future of the Past: The Production of History in a Changing South Africa," Cape Town, July 1996. I must record my indebtedness to Clive Kirkwood, Kerry Harris, Albert Grundlingh, Christopher Merrett, Michele Pickover, and Marie Olivier for commenting on an early draft of the paper. Nevertheless, the views expressed in the article are my own—they do not necessarily reflect the standpoints of these individuals nor of the State Archives Service. The essay was first published in *Archivaria* 42 (1996).

2   See, for example, the publicity brochure *National Archives of Canada Act* (Ottawa, 1992), 1. One of the mission objectives of the Canadian National Archives is "to preserve the collective memory of the nation and the government of Canada." Another example is to be found in the State Archives Service's *Annual Reports* for 1995: "…the State Archives Service is responsible for preserving a national archival heritage… In a sense this heritage is the collective memory of the government and the people." (Pretoria, 1996), 1.

3   The concept, derived primarily from the writings of Sir Hilary Jenkinson, had a strong presence in pre-1990 South African archivy, despite the pervasive influence of T. R. Schellenberg.

4   Novelist Milan Kundera explored the relations between power, memory, and forgetting in his *The Book of Laughter and Forgetting* (London: Penguin Books, 1983).

5   Readers of the article in draft form have understood me to imply here that public archivists collaborated in the destruction of oppositional memory; other readers have discerned an implication that public archivists engaged in struggle against such destruction. At this point in the article I imply neither. My point is that struggle informed the work of public archivists and that an impartial stance was impossible. For an account of censorship under apartheid, see Christopher Merrett, *A Culture of Censorship: Secrecy and Intellectual Repression in South Africa* (Cape Town and Pietermaritzburg: David Philip and University of Natal Press, 1994).

6   The paper on which this article is based was written in May and June of 1996. I prepared this article from it during July 1996.

7   While I have striven for scholarly distance, this remains an insider's account. I have been in the State Archives Service since 1985, as part of senior management since 1993; on the National Committee of the South African Society of Archivists since 1988; editor of the *South African Archives Journal* since 1988; a member of the KwaZulu-Natal Project Task Group: Archives Services since 1994; and I served on the African National Congress's Archives Subcommittee in 1992–1993. By virtue of these positions I have been a direct participant in most of the processes described in the article.

8   Such analysis cries out for attention. The only general texts that enter the terrain are State Archives Service, *Handbook* (Pretoria: State Archives Service, 1991), chapter 3; Jill Geber, "The South African Government Archives Service: Past, Present and Future," unpublished master's diss. (University College of London, 1987), chapters 1–4; and Razia Saleh, "A National Archival Policy for a Democratic South Africa," unpublished master's diss. (University College of London, 1993), chapter 4.

9   Strictly speaking, the apartheid era began in 1948, when the National Party assumed power, and ended in 1994 with the country's first democratic general election and the establishment of a Government of National Unity. My analysis

excludes the formal transition period of 1990 to 1994, as the State Archives Service underwent significant changes during it. These changes are addressed in the next section of the article. For useful introductory general histories of the apartheid era, see William Beinart, *Twentieth-Century South Africa* (Oxford: Oxford University Press, 1994) and Nigel Warden, *The Making of Modern South Africa: Conquest, Segregation and Apartheid* (Oxford: Oxford University Press, 1994).

10   The apartheid government allocated a homeland to each of South Africa's major black ethnic "groups." In terms of separate development policy, black South Africans were to exercise full political rights only in these homelands. The ultimate goal was to establish each homeland as an independent country—by 1994 four of them had taken "independence."

11   See Verne Harris, "Public Access to Official Records and the Record Management Function of the South African State Archives Service," *Innovation* 4 (1992): 15.

12   By 1995, eight of the ten homelands had archives services. KwaZulu boasted thirty-four staff members (all appointed after 1990), while the rest combined possessed twenty-nine. Unpublished report by the Arts and Culture Task Group's Archives Subcommittee, "Archives in South Africa," 1995, 6–7.

13   In 1910, the four British colonies joined to form the Union of South Africa.

14   Excluded from this mandate were the South African Defence Force, the homelands, and so-called offices of record; the latter were defined as offices "responsible for documents which require special treatment in order to ensure that the authenticity and legality of the contents cannot be questioned." State Archives Service, *Handbook*, 15:35.

15   In 1995, the State Archives Service had in its custody 7,292 linear meters of private records, 5.4 percent of its total holdings. Verne Harris and Clive Kirkwood, "The State Archives Service and Manuscript Collections: Some Thoughts on Policy and Practice," *Archives News* 37, no. 12 (1995): 16–17.

16   The 1962 act (as amended) charges the director of archives with general responsibility for records management in government offices. It also gives him or her the power to approve filing systems, microfilm projects, and the destruction of records.

17   Pretoria, Johannesburg, Bloemfontein, Durban, Pietermaritzburg, Port Elizabeth, and Cape Town.

18   Harris and Kirkwood, "The State Archives Service and Manuscript Collections," 12.

19   Almost every area of thinking and practice was dominated by a discourse cemented in the 1950s and 1960s. Primary influences were Muller, Feith, and Fruin (as late as the 1980s, new archivists were given a copy of the *Manual* as their fundamental training text), later Dutch literature (Afrikaans speakers are usually comfortable readers of Dutch), Jenkinson, and Schellenberg.

20   A nominal fee was charged for copies of documents.

21   This point has been made by Geber, "The South African Government Archives Service," 56. However, she overestimated the capacity of the service's records management components, which were severely under-resourced. Harris, "Public Access to Official Records," 15.

22   In the 1980s, the senior public servant in a government department held the rank of a director-general. As a director, the head of the State Archives Service was three levels lower.

23   Notable examples were the Department of Foreign Affairs and the National Intelligence Service.

24　Verne Harris and Christopher Merrett, "Toward a Culture of Transparency: Public Rights of Access to Official Records in South Africa," *American Archivist* 57 (Fall 1994): 684.

25　In terms of the Archives Act of 1962 (as amended), open access applies to records more than thirty years old, unless the minister (at the time, of National Education) withdraws it on the grounds of "public policy."

26　State Archives Service records indicate that between 1980 and 1990 requests for permission to consult 2,381 items in the archives of these offices were received, and access was denied to only nine items.

27　In 1990, the service's professional staff comprised seventy people. All of them were white, with thirty-nine women and thirty-one men.

28　In 1990, only one of the twelve most senior officials was not an Afrikaans-speaking male—she was an Afrikaans-speaking woman.

29　The most thorough analysis is in State Archives Service, "Report on Current State Archives Service Appraisal Policy and the Theory and Practice of Macro-appraisal," internal document (approved by the director of archives on 23 April 1996).

30　See Harris and Kirkwood, "The State Archives Service and Manuscript Collections," 5–8.

31　The project was initiated in 1959 and continued into the 1990s.

32　Albert Grundlingh, "Historical Writing and the State Archives in a Changing South Africa," *South African Archives Journal* 35 (1993): 81.

33　Albert Grundlingh, "Politics, Principles and Problems of a Profession: Afrikaner Historians and Their Discipline, c.1920–c.1965," *Perspectives in Education* 12, no. 1 (1990): 11–13. Theses were selected by the Archives Commission, on which the State Archives Service was represented by the director. See also note 87 below.

34　Geber, "The South African Government Archives Service," 56.

35　Useful accounts of the "Pretoriastroika" period are given by Beinart, *Twentieth-Century South Africa* and Allister Sparks, *Tomorrow Is Another Country: The Inside Story of South Africa's Negotiated Revolution* (Chicago: University of Chicago Press, 1996).

36　The reasons for revisionist thinking not being forthcoming from the State Archives Service are obvious. The inertia of the broader archival profession is addressed later in this article. Criticism from historians, genealogists, and other users tended to focus on specific problems—the denial of access to records, the destruction of specific categories of record, poor reading room service, etc. I am aware that this assessment might be seen as an endorsement of the powerful myth that before 1990, South African information and heritage practitioners were either passive fellow-travelers or active supporters of the apartheid system. In most disciplines, 1990 was not a watershed, with numerous individuals and organizations having fought courageously against the system for many years. But in archives, oppositional voices were rare before 1990, and in most cases they were severely hamstrung by their positioning within the State Archives Service.

37　There were a few notable exceptions, but in every case except the one addressed in note 38 below, the challenge was muted and narrowly focused.

38　Geber's historical analysis tends to be superficial. It offers no sense of the service's internal dynamics or coalface activity. The only service records consulted by her were annual reports—a notoriously unreliable source of information.

39  It did find a resonance in post-1990 debates, having a considerable influence on the African National Congress's Archives Subcommittee. See, for example, African National Congress, "Preliminary Report of the Archives Sub-committee," (internal document, 1992), 11 and 14.

40  The most important broadly focused revisionist pieces include the following: African National Congress, "Preliminary Report"; Eric Ketelaar, "Archives of the People, by the People, for the People," *South African Archives Journal* 34 (1992); Eric Ketelaar, "Unfolding South African Archives: A Candid Report on a Working Visit," *South African Archives Journal* 35 (1993); Verne Harris, "Report of the Committee to Investigate the Impact of Social and Political Changes on Archives Services in Other Countries," *Archives News* 35, no. 10 (1993); Saleh, "A National Archival Policy"; Grundlingh, "Historical Writing and the State Archives"; Graham Dominy, "Archives in a Democratic South Africa: The Proposals of the ANC: An Evaluation," *South African Archives Journal* 35 (1993); South African Society of Archivists, "Position Paper on Information and Archives," *South African Archives Journal* 36 (1994); Arts and Culture Task Group's Archives Subcommittee, "Archives in South Africa," Arts and Culture Task Group, *Final Report* (Pretoria: Department of Arts, Culture, Science and Technology, 1995), 50–114; KwaZulu-Natal Project Task Group: Archives Services, *Position Paper on Archives and Public Records in KwaZulu-Natal* (Ulundi: Archives Service, 1995); and Marie Olivier, "Continuity Amid Change: The Process of Establishing a New Archival Dispensation for South Africa," *South African Archives Journal* 37 (1995). Numerous more narrowly focused, issue-based articles and conference papers have also appeared.

41  My order of treatment should not be seen as indicative of my assessment of their relative importance. The order is arbitrary.

42  By 1996, another four Afrikaner males had retired from the top eleven positions. The service's old guard leadership had departed.

43  In 1996, the professional staff component consists of fifty-six people; 11 percent are black and 66 percent are women.

44  It is significant that Marie Olivier, director of the State Archives Service, was elected ESARBICA vice-chair in 1995.

45  The influence of Eric Ketelaar, Terry Cook, and Andor Skotnes was especially significant. See note 61 below.

46  African National Congress, "Preliminary Report," 2.

47  African National Congress, "Preliminary Report," 14.

48  African National Congress, "Preliminary Report," 10–11.

49  Dominy, "Archives in a Democratic South Africa." This article was awarded the South African Society of Archivists' SASA Prize for 1993.

50  The Culture and Development Conference took place in April–May 1993. No formal document of conference positions and recommendations emerged. One of the recommendations, that there should be a moratorium on the destruction of all public records, was implemented by the Government of National Unity two years later. This is dealt with elsewhere in the article. (See especially note 89 below.) In 1995, the ANC produced a collection of some of the documents presented at the conference as well as summaries of some of the conference recommendations. ANC Department of Arts and Culture, *Looking Forward, Looking Backwards: Culture and Development Conference, April–May 1993, Johannesburg* (Bellville: Mayibuye Books, 1995).

51 SASA was established in 1960. Largely in reaction to its inactivity, the smaller, less State Archives Service–influenced Association of Archivists and Manuscript Librarians (AMLIB) was established in 1978. Most of its members remained members of SASA.

52 For accounts of SASA in transition, see Clive Kirkwood, "The South African Society of Archivists and the Cultural Historian," *Archives News* 38, no. 3 (1996), and Verne Harris, "Archivists, Archives and Professionalism" *South African Historical Journal* 32 (1995).

53 By 1994, the eight-member National Committee included five members from outside the State Archives Service, four non-Afrikaans speakers, three women, two ANC members, and one black person.

54 South African Society of Archivists, *Professional Code for South African Archivists* (Pretoria: South African Society of Archivists, 1993). The *Code* was also published in *South African Archives Journal* 35 (1993): 106–9.

55 The four issues between 1992 and 1995 contained contributions by the following writers from outside the country: Eric Ketelaar (Holland), two articles; Masisi Lekaukau (Botswana); Samuel Njovana (Zimbabwe); Mark Mbewe (Zambia); Brigitte Lau (Namibia); Jacob Kufa (Botswana); Robert Egeter-van Kuyk (Holland); Terry Cook (Canada), two articles; Alan Bain (U.S.); Andor Skotnes (U.S.); Helen Harrison (U.K.), two articles; and Joseph Phiri (Zambia).

56 The symposium had five international and two South African speakers, and it brought together seven heads of national archives. The heads of most home-land archives services also attended. The keynote address was delivered by Eric Ketelaar, general state archivist of the Netherlands.

57 The symposium had six international and eleven South African speakers, with the keynote address delivered by Terry Cook of the Canadian National Archives.

58 South African Society of Archivists, "Position Paper."

59 The submission on the Truth and Reconciliation Commission was published in the *South African Archives Journal* 37 (1995). The others are planned for publication in the 1996 issue.

60 The State Archives Service seldom appeared in newspaper pages before 1990. After 1990, it was frequently in the news, often in the context of controversy.

61 Ketelaar, general state archivist of the Netherlands, visited in 1992. He subsequently published "Archives of the People" and "Unfolding South African Archives" in the *South African Archives Journal* and "Keuren en Kiezen," *Archives News* 35, no. 2 (1992). He received the 1992 SASA Prize for the former. Cook, director of the National Archives of Canada's Records Disposition Division, visited in 1994. He was awarded the 1994 SASA Prize for the two papers he presented at the Archives for the People Symposium. They were adapted for publication as articles in volume 37 (1995) of the *South African Archives Journal:* "From the Record to Its Context: The Theory and Practice of Archival Appraisal since Jenkinson" and "Keeping Our Electronic Memory: Approaches for Securing Computer-generated Records." He also published "The Canadian Archival Scene," *Archives News* 37, no. 11 (1995) and "Living with Your Conscience at the End of the Day: Ethical Issues and the Archivist," *Archives News* 37, no. 10 (1995). For a sense of the impact he made in South Africa, see Verne Harris, "One Hell of a Pair: Personal Reflections on the Visit to South Africa by Terry and Sharon Cook, November 1994," *Archives News* 37, no. 7 (1995). Skotnes, assistant professor of history at the Russell Sage College in New York, also visited in 1994. He subsequently published "People's

Archives and Oral History in South Africa: A Traveller's Account," *South African Archives Journal* 37 (1995).

62 Under the interim constitution, public archives was a "concurrent power" of central and provincial governments. This implied some form of central supervision over provincial archives services. The final constitution establishes public archives as an "exclusive power," which implies that provincial services will not be accountable in any way to a national archives.

63 For a critique of the ACTAG report, see Verne Harris, "Getting our ACTAG Together: Musings on the Challenges Facing South African Archivists, with special reference to the Arts and Culture Task Group's (ACTAG) Report on Heritage," *South African Archives Journal* 37 (1995).

64 Strictly speaking, the report should have formed the basis for a government white paper on arts and culture, which in turn should have informed the drafting of legislation. The Draft White Paper on Arts, Culture and Heritage was released on 4 June 1996—it simply does not address the question of archives.

65 It had a broader consultative mandate, but focused almost exclusively on the drafting of new archival legislation. For fuller accounts of the Consultative Forum's establishment and work, see Olivier, "Continuity Amid Change," 8–14; Clive Kirkwood, "Drafting New Archival Legislation for South Africa: A Consultative Process Paves the Way," *Archives News* 38, no. 1 (1995); and Clive Kirkwood, "Consultative Forum Gives Assent to South Africa's Draft National Archival Legislation," *Archives News* 38, no. 2 (1995).

66 The following bodies were represented on the forum: Bureau of Heraldry; State Archives Service; Public Service Commission; Arts and Culture Task Group; Association of Archivists and Manuscript Librarians; South African Society of Archivists; Genealogical Society of South Africa; South African Institute for Library and Information Science; South African Historical Society; South African Museum Association; KwaZulu-Natal Project Task Group: Archives Services; South African National Defence Force Archives; Department of Justice; South African Police Services; Historical Association of South Africa; Department of Education and Culture (Northern Cape Province); National Monuments Council; KwaZulu Archives Service; Lebowa Archives Service; South African Data Archive; Department of Arts, Culture, Science and Technology; Transkei Archives Service; Department of Arts and Culture (Mpumulanga Province); Department of Education and Culture (North West Province); QwaQwa Archives Service; Department of Education and Culture (Gauteng Province); Department of Education and Culture (Northern Province); Venda Archives Service; Bophutatswana Archives Service; Parliamentary Portfolio Committee on Arts, Culture and Languages; Science and Technology; Southern African Institute of Information Management; Committee of University Principals; Institute of Town Clerks; Library and Information Workers' Organization; South African Library; and Gazankulu Archives Service. The Union of Democratic University Staff Associations was invited but did not send a delegate.

67 The drafting was done by a Working Committee for the Drafting of Archival Legislation elected by the forum. In studying international archival legislation, the committee focused on the legislation of Australia, Canada, Malawi, Namibia, and Zimbabwe.

68 At the time of writing (May–July 1996), the bill was being debated by the Parliamentary Portfolio Committee for Arts, Culture and Language, Science, and Technology.

69    The Free State component of the State Archives Service has produced, with the concurrence of the Free State Branch of the South African Society of Archivists, a position paper for the Free State Province modeled closely on the KwaZulu-Natal document. Public archivists in both the Free State and Northern provinces are currently drafting provincial archival legislation.

70    Perhaps the clearest articulation of this view is to be found in Arts and Culture Task Group, *Final Report*.

71    This view has been most strongly advocated by the State Archives Service, but see also South African Society of Archivists, "Position Paper," 97 and KwaZulu-Natal Project Task Group: Archives Services, "Position Paper," 6.

72    These are functions related to records still in the custody of government offices and to records systems in use by government offices.

73    Both the draft National Archives of South Africa Bill and the draft Provincial Archives of KwaZulu-Natal Bill give expression to this view. It has also been adopted by the drafters of archival legislation in the Free State and Northern provinces.

74    See, for example, State Archives Service, "Report on Current State Archives Service Appraisal Policy." These voices have been strongly influenced by Terry Cook and other international heralds of a postcustodial era for archives.

75    The apartheid Department of National Education was responsible for formal state involvement in "culture." The director of archives reported to the department's chief director for culture.

76    The ANC's Archives Subcommittee elaborated on the difficulties created by the State Archives Service's "low bureaucratic status." "Preliminary Report," 7. The Arts and Culture Task Group proposed "framework autonomy" (without defining the term closely) for public archives in its *Final Report,* 65.

77    SASA has recommended that "South Africa's national archives service should be an independent agency directly answerable to the national legislature and advised by a board or commission representative of all archives users." SASA, "Position Paper," 97. The KwaZulu-Natal Project Task Group: Archives Services (PTG: AS) recommended that "... the provincial archives service ... should be positioned as centrally as possible and with the status required to audit public records management. Independent agency status similar to that of the province's Public Service Commission, is the ideal." PTG: AS, "Position Paper," 20.

78    They argue that effective monitoring, controlling, and auditing of government offices requires both relative autonomy within the bureaucracy and significant bureaucratic status.

79    Indeed, there is a danger of what autonomy the State Archives Service currently enjoys being further eroded. The delay in the passage of the National Archives of South Africa Bill through Parliament has been caused primarily by disagreement about the measure of control the minister is to exercise over the National Archives. There are those who wish to increase significantly the powers afforded the minister in the Consultative Forum's draft bill. See also notes 82 and 91 below.

80    I do not imply that all Jenkinsonians have been converted; merely that their views have no currency in transformation discourse.

81    One of these mechanisms, arguably the most important, is a statutory body with certain controlling powers over public archives. In transformation discourse there has been unanimous rejection of the present Archives Act's provision for

an Archives Commission with an almost purely advisory function and appointed without public participation.

82   Disagreement on this question, specifically on the respective powers and duties of the national archivist, the minister, and the National Archives Commission, is the cause of the troubled passage through Parliament of the National Archives of South Africa Bill. See also note 79 above and note 91 below.

83   Such a balance has been advocated by, *inter alia,* the Arts and Culture Task Group, the Consultative Forum on Archival Management and Legislation, and the KwaZulu-Natal Project Task Group: Archives Services.

84   Nevertheless, this view still has powerful advocates. Elsewhere in this paper I have indicated its qualified expression in the Arts and Culture Task Group's *Final Report* and the ANC's Archives Subcommittee's "Preliminary Report." Powerful voices in the broader terrains of culture and heritage give it unqualified support.

85   I have already elaborated on apartheid South Africa's record, but there are numerous other international examples. See Cook, "From the Record to Its Context," 37, 38, 44.

86   Grundlingh, "Historical Writing and the State Archives," 83.

87   There is no clear conceptual distinction, of course, between appraisal and collection. Active documenting is an integral part of appraisal, and collection pre-supposes appraisal decisions. But in South African archival discourse and practice, the distinction has been made firmly, with appraisal a function related to public records and collection to private records.

88   Between 1926 and 1953, the Archives Commission was responsible for the appraisal of official records. Thereafter the function was assumed by the State Archives Service, although the commission retained the power to authorize destruction until 1979. The commission had little credibility—it was not appointed by a democratic government, the appointment process was not democratic, and it was not broadly representative (it was dominated by white, Afrikaans-speaking, male academics in the apartheid period). Both before and after 1979, there has been no attempt to make appraisal a more transparent process, for instance by publishing policy documents or individual disposal authorities.

89   The idea of a moratorium was first mooted by the ANC's Commission on Museums, Monuments and Heraldry in March 1992. The commission's Archives Subcommittee subsequently called for "a moratorium on the destruction of records relating to the history of the struggle and to the organization of popular movements which may be in the hands of the security services." "Preliminary Report," 14. At the ANC's Conference on Culture and Development in 1993, it was resolved that "there should be an immediate cessation of the destruction of all State records regardless of existing policy." (I quote this from my own confer-ence notes.) The Arts and Culture Task Group (ACTAG) recommended that "a moratorium should be declared on the destruction of records in all security-related departments until the new National Archives Commission has undertaken a review…" ACTAG, *Final Report,* 96. ACTAG's Archives Subcommittee later called for a moratorium on the destruction of "records related to land transactions and of all records by the military, police, National Intelligence, State President's Office and Department of Justice subject to urgent review of disposal authorities." ACTAG Archives Subcommittee, "Archives in South Africa," 19.

90   The draft bill provides for the appointment of commission members through a process of public nomination. Nominees should be "knowledgeable and/or have an interest in archival matters." The minister is constrained to take provincial

interests into account and to ensure that the commission "reflects to a reasonable degree the demographic and gender realities of South Africa."

91    A similar role is envisaged for the KwaZulu-Natal Archives Council in draft provincial legislation prepared by the KwaZulu-Natal Project Task Group: Archives Services. Drafters of archival legislation in the Free State and Northern provinces are pursuing the same course. At the national level, debate around the National Archives of South Africa Bill has seen proposals that the commission should actually formulate appraisal policy and review individual appraisals. Another proposal is that the minister should approve individual appraisals. See also notes 79 and 82 above.

92    Macro-appraisal first became an issue in South African archival debate during Eric Ketelaar's visit to the country in 1992. His account of the Dutch PIVOT Project was received with skepticism within the State Archives Service. However, subsequently, the writing of Terry Cook on appraisal and the Canadian macro-appraisal approach raised considerable interest. This was the primary consideration behind the State Archives Service's invitation to him to visit the country in 1994. His explosive impact led directly to the service's establishment of an Appraisal Review Committee, which in 1996 recommended the adoption of macro-appraisal.

93    Schellenberg offers two distinct and, arguably, conflicting methodologies for the identification of records with informational values, on the one hand, and those with evidential values on the other.

94    Most general and standing disposal authorities are issued not on records *per se* but on functionally based systems of records classification. In certain areas of practice appraisal occurs at the supra-organizational level.

95    State Archives Service, "Report on Current State Archives Service Appraisal Policy." The report recommends a phased introduction of macro-appraisal. This development will have to receive the approval of the National Archives Commission.

96    For an account of this concept, see for example Jean-Pierre Wallot, "Free Trade in Archival Ideas: The Canadian Perspective on North American Archival Development," *American Archivist* 57, no. 2 (1994): 385.

97    The State Archives Service has subordinated the collecting function firmly—in 1995 private records made up 5.4 percent of the service's total holdings. See note 14 above. In contrast, in Canada, where the concept of "total archives" originated, private records make up roughly half of the National Archives' holdings. Harris and Kirkwood, "The State Archives Service and Manuscript Collections," 5–6.

98    With the exception of the National Film, Video, and Sound Archives, whose audiovisual holdings contain a significant quantity of oral testimony, and a single accession in the Central Archives Depot, the State Archives Service's repositories are devoid of oral sources.

99    Dominy, "Archives in a Democratic South Africa," 74.

100   Sandy Rowoldt has proposed that details of oral sources in South Africa should be included in the National Register of Audiovisual Material. Sandy Rowoldt, "Some Thoughts on the Processing of Oral History Recordings for Inclusion in the National Register of Audiovisual Materials (NAROM)," *AMLIB Newsletter* 56 (1994). The possibility of creating a national register specifically for oral sources is also being considered by the State Archives Service.

101   The lack of consensus on this issue also reflects uncertainty about the functions of the National Living Culture Commission proposed by the Arts and Culture Task Group. Clearly the functions of this commission and of the National Archives vis-à-vis oral sources will have to be integrated.

102 For exploration of the issues involved, see Harris, "Public Access to Official Records," and Harris and Merrett, "Toward a Culture of Transparency." South Africa's final constitution recognizes the right of public access to official information—the Open Democracy Bill, which is currently in a pre-Parliamentary debate phase, is designed *inter alia* to legislate this right.

103 See, for example, Arts and Culture Task Group's Archives Subcommittee, "Archives in South Africa," paragraph 5.6(ii).

104 This found expression in the State Archives Service embarking on public programming in the period 1990 to 1994, as I mention elsewhere in this article.

105 See Verne Harris, "Community Resource or Scholars' Domain? Archival Public Programming and the User as a Factor in Shaping Archival Theory and Practice," *South African Archives Journal* 35 (1993).

106 Harris, "Community Resource or Scholars' Domain?" 12.

107 The South African Library listed one hundred such institutions in 1985—*Directory of Manuscript Collections in Southern Africa* (Cape Town, 1985). Others have been established since then.

108 Worth special mention are the Cory Library (University of Rhodes), the William Cullen Library (University of the Witwatersrand), the South African History Archive, the Mayibuye Centre (University of the Western Cape), the Alan Paton Centre (University of Natal), the Killie Campbell Africana Library (University of Natal), and the ANC Archives (University of Fort Hare).

109 The one outstanding example of successful interinstitutional cooperation is the building of computerized national registers—over forty collecting institutions participate in the registers. Most of the credit for this must accrue to the State Archives Service. See Clive Kirkwood, "Inter-institutional Co-operation in the Computer Retrieval of Information on Private Archives: The South African National Register of Manuscripts (NAREM)," in *The National Register of Archives: An International Perspective. Essays in Celebration of the Fiftieth Anniversary of NRA,* ed. Dick Sargeant (London: University of London, 1995).

110 Harris and Kirkwood, "The State Archives Service and Manuscript Collections," 8–9 and fn 17.

111 Harris and Kirkwood, "The State Archives Service and Manuscript Collections," fn 18.

112 The draft Provincial Archives of KwaZulu-Natal Bill does the same for a KwaZulu-Natal provincial archives service.

113 The ANC's Culture and Development Conference, for example, recommended that "The Freedom of Information Act should also refer to private information. For example, multi-national corporations have vast amounts of information of public interest, and mechanisms such as the courts or tribunals must be set up to ensure access if the public interest overrides privacy provisions." (I quote this from my own conference notes.)

114 I was privileged to read a draft of Terry Cook's paper "Interaction of Archival Theory and Practice since the Publication of the Dutch Manual in 1898" for the 13th International Congress on Archives (Beijing, China, September 1996). This outstanding piece of scholarship demonstrates how South African discourse on archives connects with a wider international discourse.

115 J-F. Lyotard, *The Postmodern Condition: A Report on Knowledge* (Minneapolis: University of Minnesota Press, 1993), 5, 45, 51.

116 Terry Cook, "From Information to Knowledge: An Intellectual Paradigm for Archives," *Archivaria* 19 (Winter 1984–85): 49.

# CHAPTER 12

## Knowing Right from Wrong: The Archivist and the Protection of People's Rights[1]

Until the still relatively recent political and broader social changes in South Africa, the question of rights in relation to archives was largely restricted to discussion and debate around rights of public access and the preservation of essential records—those records documenting citizen's rights. South Africa's transition to democracy has seen archivists catapulted into a new era, with all their work, all their professional decisions, ultimately subject to the Bill of Rights now enshrined in the country's constitution. Moreover, re-admittance to the international community has exposed us to a growing worldwide emphasis on the value of appropriate record-keeping in protecting the rights of citizens. This emphasis is drawing considerable attention to the record as evidence of transaction, to the need for record-generating and record-keeping systems in the electronic environment, and to notions of transparency, accountability, freedom of information, and the protection of privacy. These realities are impacting fundamentally on the way archivists—in South Africa and in most other countries—perceive their role in society, and on the strategies they are devising for providing effective services.

The question of rights is complex in any context. Not only does each society define them in a particular way for a particular time, but rights operate at different levels simultaneously and are constantly being shaped in challenging ways by developing technology. The application of copyright to the Internet is just one example of the latter. And in practice archivists must apply this shifting rights framework to the often competing claims of records creators, users, colleagues, the archival profession, and society as a whole. In this essay I cannot hope to do justice either to the broad sweep or to the rocky detail of this terrain. I propose to focus on the ethical dimension, positioning the archivist in the terrain with that timeless struggle to know right from wrong.

In his inaugural address last year as chair of archivistics at the University of Amsterdam, Eric Ketelaar probed the heart of this struggle in these words:

> According to the Code of Ethics, laid down in 1996 by the International Council on Archives, archivists should protect the integrity of archives and should resist pressure from any source to manipulate evidence so as to conceal or distort facts. They also have to take into account the rights and interests of owners and data subjects and they must think of the user. The Code doesn't give a recipe how to balance these different interests. Do the interests of the living outweigh those of the dead?... Does the privacy of living persons override the importance of historical research and does the right of access give way to the right to forget? The official and legal discussion about these issues should get new impetus....[2]

In substantiating his point, Ketelaar offers just a few examples of myriad questions that could be posed, for instance: At what point does state security give way to public interest? Does the right of access give way to preservation imperatives? Do obligations to users outweigh those to an employer? Should personal conscience override the law? And Ketelaar's questions beg other questions: Do dead persons have legitimate interests? What are reasonable parameters to the right of privacy? Questions, questions, questions. As Ketelaar rightly points out, the heart of the uncertainty, of the ethical struggle, is that no professional code of ethics provides a recipe, or blueprint, for resolving competing rights and interests. I would go further, and argue simply that there is no such blueprint.

Ketelaar's professorial probing into ethics was stimulated by his reading of the American writer Martha Cooley's novel *The Archivist*, which was published in 1998.[3] The story's narrator, Matt Lane, is a university archivist responsible for the university's collection of literary archives and rare books. The plot revolves around Lane's relationship with an acquisition of T. S. Eliot letters and manuscript poems and his ultimate decision to destroy the letters. Ketelaar's assessment of Lane's action is perfunctory:

> I would consider the archivist in this novel to be guilty of a serious offence against the professional code of archivists.[4]

Later in his address, Ketelaar associates Lane's action with various infamous cases of records destruction. A cut and dried issue, then. Lane was wrong. But what of Ketelaar's own positing of complexity, of uncertainty and struggle, in the realm of ethics? Surely only a blueprint, which Ketelaar eschews, can sustain a quick, simple, unqualified condemnation? I must point out that the English translation of Ketelaar's text leaves out certain passages in the original Dutch, a fact brought to my attention by Ketelaar in an e-mail correspondence between us. The Dutch version gives a more nuanced account of Lane's action. Nevertheless, the condemnation remains decisive, untroubled by doubt.

Let us take a closer look at Lane's story. The Eliot letters and poems are the product of a correspondence over many years between the poet and Emily Hale. Their intimate relationship ultimately founders, but Hale keeps the documents in her possession and in old age decides to bequeath them to a renowned American university. She tries to persuade Eliot to do the same with the correspondence she had addressed to him. Eliot is outraged at the suggestion—he does not want the correspondence to enter the public domain. He requests her to destroy his letters, but remains silent about the manuscript poems. Hale, believing that she owes it to posterity, proceeds with the bequest, but out of respect for Eliot makes it conditional on public access being denied until the year 2020.

At this point several questions arise. Legally, Hale was within her rights to make the bequest. The documents were her property, with the law recognizing only Eliot's claim to copyright in their contents. But what of the moral dimension? Was Hale justified in placing the interests of posterity before those of Eliot? Does the right to remember outweigh the right to forget? Does Eliot have a right to privacy reaching beyond the grave? Given Eliot's wishes, should the university have accepted the bequest? Particularly as he had destroyed the part of the correspondence in his possession, thus severely decontextualizing the part in Hale's possession and undermining the integrity of what would be left to posterity. It is not my intention to answer these questions. I pose them merely to demonstrate that long before Lane comes into contact with the documents, the ethical issues around their archival status are far from cut and dried.

Lane joins the university soon after it receives the bequest. It falls to him to catalogue the documents. He is an admirer of Eliot's poetry and has expert knowledge of the poet's life and other writings. Eliot's troubled marriage to Vivienne Eliot, who died after years in an asylum, fascinates Lane. His own wife committed suicide while in an asylum. From the outset, Lane is uncomfortable about the bequest, and this turns to intense concern as he reads the letters while cataloguing them. They reveal a deeply flawed Eliot, a man who failed both his wife and Emily Hale in profound ways. Eliot's reasons for wanting the letters destroyed seem plain, and these reasons find a powerful resonance with Lane. After his wife's suicide, he had read her asylum journal, which documents her sense of abandonment, and ultimately of betrayal, by Lane.

Matters come to a head when Lane develops a relationship with Roberta, a poet and graduate student who tries to persuade him to give her access to the Eliot letters. Not only does Roberta provide warning of what Eliot will be exposed to when the letters become accessible, she also unlocks the barriers Lane has constructed around memories of his wife. His pain and Eliot's conflate, and he wrestles to a conclusion:

> An archivist serves the reader's desire. Yet what of the writer's—is it of no consequence? ... Eliot's letters to Emily were not ... his bequest. We were never meant to read them: only she was, and she relinquished them. Poetry was what he left us. It was all that mattered. *The rest is not our business.*[5]

Lane destroys the letters, leaving only the poems for his custodial successors to find in the locked cabinet in 2020. He gives Roberta photocopies of the poems.

Was he wrong? His action was certainly illegal. It transgressed provisions in most archival codes of conduct. It infringed on the rights of Emily Hale, the university, and researchers. But was it morally wrong? Was Lane not in fact profoundly *right* to respect Eliot's rights and to obey the call of his own conscience? On balance, was the destruction of this unhappy, contested, partial archive not justifiable? Notice I say *justifiable,* not *right.* These are two different concepts. I think their destruction can be justified. But judgment on whether Lane was right or wrong needs to take the following into account. Lane confides in no one. He subjects his thoughts, his feelings, his motives, to no external measuring. His action fits snugly into a pattern of control, of an almost dictatorial exercise of will. When his wife enters the asylum, he destroys her files against her wishes. After her death, he reads her journal despite her desire that it be read only by her psychiatrist and then destroyed. He reads Eliot's letters despite their being closed. He teases Roberta with the hope that he might give her privileged access to the letters. Ultimately he privileges her only with access to the manuscript poems. This is a pattern of playing memory god. In destroying the letters is he protecting Eliot's rights, serving the writer's desire, or merely playing god? Is he obeying his conscience, or is he, in a symbolic act, literalizing his struggle with the memory of another writer—his wife?

At this point, I want to leave Lane's story—with questions rather than answers. Which is where I believe its author would want us to leave it. Why, you might ask, have I devoted so much of this essay to it? Because it demonstrates so compellingly the absence of a blueprint for resolving competing rights and interests. It takes an instance of what most archivists would agree to be the cardinal archival sin—an archivist destroying material in his care that is of indisputable historical value—and shows that even here, where right should be discernable from wrong, the boundary between them is blurred.

Another reason for giving so much time to Lane's story is that it assumes what we so often forget—and what Ketelaar in his condemnation of Lane underestimates—the *archivist* has rights and interests. As human beings, as citizens, as professionals, as employees, we have rights and interests. We need to know them, and to learn to exercise them—

when necessary, to protect them—with confidence. They are at play in every moment of our professional lives, whether we are appraising a records series, assisting a researcher, attending a management meeting, or taking a tea break. For instance: You are alone on duty in the reading room one day when two researchers arrive simultaneously. Both require substantial assistance. How do you balance their legitimate demands against your limited and stressed resources? How do you balance their competing demands on your attention? Or you are assisting a client who has previously consulted with colleagues of yours. You become aware of the fact that your colleagues have misinformed the client. Do you cover for your colleagues, or expose them? Or you are advising a senior bureaucrat on records management issues. He is pompous, has friends in high places, and in the course of the meeting gratuitously expresses offensive views on unrelated matters. Do you hold your peace in the interests of a good working relationship, or do you express your distaste?

Merely knowing our rights and best interests is a challenge, intellectually and morally. Far more challenging though—and Lane's story also illustrates this so well—is knowing how to balance one's own rights against those of others, and knowing how to resolve the conflicting rights and competing interests of others. Knowing how. This, I would argue, is *the critical* question. But before addressing it directly, I wish to return to an observation I made at the outset and which Lane's story again illustrates—rights operate at different levels simultaneously.

There are what we call human rights, those fundamental rights that we believe to transcend time, place, law, and culture. And yet, as we know only too well, we humans disagree on what is and what isn't a human right; we interpret these rights in different ways; and we disagree on how to resolve conflicting rights—for instance, freedom of the press versus privacy, or the right to life versus a woman's right to control her own body. More precise and more specific, and therefore easier to work with, are rights defined by law—international, national, and at other levels. I say *easier,* not *easy*. For all law is subject to interpretation—many people make a living out of it—it is subject to the vicissitudes of political change, and even in democracies law can contradict both human rights and the tenets of religious and other ethical codes. In apartheid South Africa, for instance, what was *legal* and what was *just* seldom coincided. For those concerned with justice, with choosing right over wrong, breaking the law was a way of life.

Then there are rights defined by a web of social codes, the web's complexity correlating with the degree to which a particular society is open and heterogeneous. Such codes are informed by the dynamics of social memory, tradition, culture, religious belief, politics, and so on. It is here that I would position professional codes of conduct. As with the law, these social codes are dynamic and subject to interpretation. And clearly no two individuals configure their values in relation to these codes in precisely the same way. Of course, those of us who are practicing archivists are held accountable professionally to the ICA's *Code of Ethics* and to any other code that we subscribe to by professional association. I have already quoted Eric Ketelaar on the ICA code's provision of guidelines rather than a blueprint for resolving competing rights and interests. At this point I wish to go a step further in suggesting complexity by arguing that in many instances the guidelines framed in professional codes are far from helpful when applied in practice. They define tension rather than suggesting an appropriate way of resolving it. Let me quote two instances, one from France and one from South Africa, to illustrate this. In February 1999, French archivist Brigitte Laine testified in the defamation trial of Maurice Papon against the writer Jean-Luc Einadi.[6] The latter had accused Papon, a convicted war criminal, of wrongdoing while he was a police official in 1961 when police killed North African protestors. Papon sued him for libel. In her trial testimony, Brigitte Laine confirmed the existence of archival records substantiating Einadi's accusation. For doing this she was condemned for misconduct by both the French Archives Directorate and the French Association of Archivists on the grounds that she had defied legally defined restrictions on access to information. The association cited provisions of the ICA's *Code of Ethics* in taking this stance. In contrast, Eric Ketelaar, who drew the whole episode to my attention, has defended Laine's action, citing different provisions of the code.[7]

The other instance is from my own experience. In 1993, I was working as a records management archivist in South Africa's State Archives Service. During July of that year, I received reports from junior officials in several government departments that they had received instructions to destroy certain categories of classified record without authorization from the director of archives. My investigation revealed that these departments were acting on a governmentwide circular instruction issued by the state's security secretariat. This was a large-scale destruction of sensitive public records outside the operation of the Archives Act. I briefed the director accordingly and was assured that every effort would be made through official channels to halt the destruction exercise. As days went by and it became apparent that official action was achieving nothing, and that even if it eventually was successful it would be too late to prevent the loss of huge quantities of records, I was faced with a difficult decision. Should I allow the official process to take its course, or should I act outside official channels in an attempt to stop the destruction? In my struggle with right and wrong, I turned to the South African Society of Archivists' *Professional Code*. One of its provisions asserts that "the archivist has a moral duty to preserve information about the past and present for the future";[8] another that "the archivist must protect the integrity of archives/information against alteration, removal, damage and theft."[9] Surely a powerful mandate to break the rules, to break the law if necessary, in acting against what I believed to be the illegal destruction of public records with archival value? And yet the code also posits the following: "At all times the archivist must act within the parameters of the policy laid down by his/her employer";[10] and "the archivist respects the confidentiality of records in his/her care as determined in consultation with his/her employer."[11] My employer was the state. For me to disclose what was happening to the press and other outside agencies, especially by providing them with a copy of the circular instruction—which was itself a classified document—would involve defying state policy on confidentiality, breaking public service regulations on proper conduct, and committing an offense in terms of the Protection of Information Act—which at the time carried a maximum penalty of ten years imprisonment. I was confronted by contradictory imperatives and no guidance on how to resolve them.

Ultimately I did what was wrong in the eyes of the law, my employer, and the last-quoted tenets of the *Professional Code*. I disclosed what was happening to a journalist and to Lawyers for Human Rights, and provided them with copies of supporting documentation. My employer was subsequently taken to court and forced to acknowledge that the destruction exercise had ignored the operation of the Archives Act. I had become a whistleblower, someone who exposes wrongdoing, most commonly in the context of an employer-employee relationship. (As a footnote, it is perhaps worth noting that South Africa is in the process of passing legislation that will protect public servants who blow the whistle on wrongdoing within state structures.) In making my decision I had been forced to reach beyond articulations of right and wrong provided by law and professional ethics. I had scoured my own sense of right and wrong in an engagement with my understanding of human rights, my identification with a variety of relevant social values, and an assessment of risk to me and my family. In the end, my moment of decision was an intensely subjective one. Me and my conscience. And this, I want to argue, is where all of us find ourselves after we have exhausted the space provided by investigation, analysis, and discussion. There is no knowing of right without giving account to personal morality. For each of us has the right, and the obligation, to be true to ourselves.

Which brings us back to the question of *how* to resolve conflicting rights and interests, on which note I wish to draw to a conclusion. I have argued that the ethical dimension is always at play in archival work, not only at those extreme moments that secure the limelight in professional discourse. We need this awareness. I have also argued that the boundary between right and wrong is blurred. Very seldom is a choice clear-cut. In most instances we will be choosing the lesser of two evils, or choosing the most right option that circumstances will allow, or choosing the best of various options with equal claims to being right from different perspectives. Moreover, none of us is impartial. We can neither stand outside process nor avoid bringing to process a pre-impression shaped by our unique experiences as individuals. The most we can do is ensure that in taking difficult decisions we have done so in an appropriate way—in other words, we have got the *how* right. Getting the *how* right, I want to argue, always involves at least four elements. Firstly, an illumination of the web of rights as it applies to the interested parties at different levels. Secondly, an analysis aimed at weighing competing claims against one another in the specific circumstances confronting the archivist. Thirdly, a testing of one's views and feelings with respected colleagues and friends. And finally, paying heed to one's conscience. If we follow conscience without taking the first three steps, we abandon accountability and risk assuming godlike powers. If we ignore conscience and rely only on the exercise of reason, we deny our humanity and seek to avoid bearing the burden of choice. It is only when we embrace all four elements that we can feel confident about having fulfilled the responsibilities invested in us as professionals. And feel confident that when we "pull a fast one," bend the rules, even break the law, we do so with justification.

And that's the note I intended to end on. However, when my partner read the draft of this essay, she objected with the words, "But that's too neat—you're almost suggesting a blueprint." Fair comment, I think. So let me rather end by stressing that no matter how rigorous our commitment to proper process, there is no escaping subjectivity. Two archivists confronted by the same moral dilemma can embrace the four elements of process I've outlined and come to different conclusions. And both be *right*. More disturbing is the reality that these two archivists might come to the same conclusion, but one be right and the other wrong. For ultimately right and wrong are determined in a realm beyond the reach of any human observer—in the deeper spaces of the subject's psyche. And that's why, unlike Ketelaar, I cannot pronounce on Matt Lane's destruction of the Eliot letters. Who knows what was happening in the deeper spaces of Lane's psyche? Who knows what was happening for Brigitte Laine when she gave testimony in the trial of Jean-Luc Einadi? Who knows what was happening for me when I blew the whistle on South Africa's Security Secretariat? Who knows?

## Endnotes

1   This essay was presented as a paper at the 1999 ESARBICA Conference in Zanzibar and subsequently published in *Janus* 1999.1.

2   Eric Ketelaar, "Archivalization and Archiving," unpublished inaugural address as chair of archivistics, University of Amsterdam, 23 October 1998, 6.

3   Martha Cooley, *The Archivist* (London: Abacus, 1998).

4   Ketelaar, "Archivalization and Archiving," 6.

5   Cooley, *The Archivist*, 322–23.

6   http://listerv.muohio.edu, accessed 26 March 1999.

7   http://listserv.muohio.edu.

8   South African Society of Archivists, *Professional Code for South African Archivists* (Pretoria, 1993), 4.1.

9   South African Society of Archivists, *Professional Code,* 4.3.

10  South African Society of Archivists, *Professional Code,* 4.6.1.

11  South African Society of Archivists, *Professional Code,* 4.6.2.

# CHAPTER 13

## Archives, Identity, and Place: A Dialogue on What It (Might) Mean(s) to be an African Archivist[1]

*Verne Harris and Sello Hatang*

**Harris:**

Sello, I cannot remember now our initial discussions around the possibility of such a dialogue. Maybe your psychic archive—if we can use the term *archive* to describe something with an exteriority which to say the least is debatable—is more comprehensive than mine. But I do remember—and the remembering is intertwined with forgetting, like all archives—I do remember the thoughts that first pushed me toward suggesting a formal dialogue with you. These thoughts took shape in the weeks after I attended the ESARBICA Biennial Conference in Zanzibar during July 1999. The conference was conducted entirely in English, and although much of the deliberations addressed regional issues and conditions, in terms of discourse—the words, the concepts, the values, the conceptual connections, the forms of analysis, the ways of constructing knowledge—the conference was positioned comfortably within a Western modernist paradigm. In other words, the conference might have been taking place anywhere in the Western world. There was nothing distinctively "African" or regional about the discourse. And yet,

215

outside the conference hall was a rich "otherness," in language, in culture, in ways of knowing—indeed, by almost any measure one would care to use. My sense was of the living archive of Zanzibar—Zanzibar as archive—having no impact whatever on the conference. Now, I remembered feeling exactly the same at the 1997 ESARBICA Conference in South Africa, and at the 1995 conference in Namibia. Let us call this a feeling of disjuncture. And spreading the net more widely, in my general experience of archival discourse—and of archival practice—in this part of the world, it belongs snugly within a Western-dominated global mainstream. Again, it leaves me with a feeling of disjuncture.

The 1990s have seen the archival scene in South Africa transformed by sweeping societal changes that have moved the country from apartheid into an era of democratization. Yet even here, where a powerful opportunity has been presented for refiguring and re-imagining archival endeavor, I would argue that our discourse—and the practice shaped by it—has not questioned, less contested, what are essentially Western foundations.[2] We speak the same language, so to speak, as our colleagues on the international stage. What we could call indigenous ways of knowing have no currency in our discourse.

Now, myriad questions jostle for attention. But let me kick off by posing just a few of them to you. (Ignore them if you feel I'm setting an agenda for you.) If my analysis is sound, is the disjuncture I posit a problem? Or can it be seen rather as a strength, as an indication of the degree to which Africa is engaging in global realities? Is a distinctively African archival discourse desirable? Is such a thing feasible? And what do we mean by "African" in any case?

**Hatang:**

Verne, I also have a bit of a problem recalling precisely what led us to engage in this dialogue. But I would add to what you have said by suggesting that it all started with our debate around "Africanness" and "whiteness," specifically in relation to what South African journalist Max du Preez had to say on these issues in the media during 1999.[3] That debate extended into discussion about the extent to which our archival discourse is "African," and finally into discussion of what would have given the ESARBICA Conference a distinctively African identity. Before I respond to your difficult questions, let me pose a few of my own. What is it that you think might have broken down the Eurocentric nature of the conference's discourse and made it distinctively African? Is it a question of language? (Here I would argue that English serves as a vehicle for unity and common understanding among the diverse nations constituting ESARBICA.) And what do you mean by a "distinctively African discourse"? Do you suggest a shedding of Western influences and a return to our pristine past?

But let me address the "disjuncture" you posit. Is it a problem or a strength? I would say that it shouldn't be a case of either/or. It is both a strength and a problem. I think you should remember that rejecting Western philosophy—considering the influence it had and still has on archival discourse (indeed I would argue that the discourse is Western)—rejecting it without engaging it, connecting to it, finding points of commonality, would leave indigenous ways of knowing isolated from the global world. Engagement is a strength. The problem is that our form of engagement does not allow spaces for indigenous ways of knowing to operate effectively. And this is a shortcoming of the African intelligentsia in our part of the world. Archival discourse simply has to open itself to the "other."

But all of this begs a fundamental question, which you identified and which I pose back to you: What is an "African"?

**Harris:**

The quickness and directness with which you come to the point is unseemly! (Some might say "un-African.") Now, I don't want to ignore the questions you pose about the ESARBICA Conference, but your last question logically precedes them and demands a focused response.

Here in South Africa, of course, debates have raged in the last five or six years around this question. These debates have flowed out of our postapartheid nation-building endeavors, and have linked into a wider discourse on South Africa's position(ing) in Africa and dreams of an "African Renaissance." I don't want to even think of rehashing or summarizing these debates, which have been characterized by huge dollops of naiveté, ignorance, self-importance, and barely disguised racism. Instead, let me simply develop a few thoughts out of what I believe to be the seminal—and still the most valuable—contribution, the "I am an African" speech of then–deputy president Thabo Mbeki on 8 May 1996.[4]

In this speech, Mbeki posits an African identity built on three cornerstones. Firstly, an embrace of the land, its peoples, and its pasts. An African is one who is shaped by and draws sustenance from the natural world of Africa. An African is one who is shaped by and draws sustenance from all who have made Africa their home. Their pasts are the pasts of an African. Their stories are the stories of an African. Secondly, a commitment to justice for Africa. An African cares about the sufferings and the aspirations of Africa's peoples. An African joins the continent's struggles for justice, freedom, and peace. And thirdly, a dream of what is to come. An African wishes the blessings of the gods on Africa. An African is shaped by hope for a justice that is coming.

I find it really hard to analyze rationally this clarion call. It pulls my heartstrings, seduces me with its nobility. But let me try. I endorse unreservedly Mbeki's marriage of memory and dream, of past and future. I find compelling his call's inclusivity, celebration of diversity, and central positioning of justice. What defines an African in the final analysis is not birthplace, language, race, and other easily measurable attributes of personal history. Mbeki plumbs deeper into what sustains a person's soul, his or her values, self-identity, and commitment to justice.

But the call raises serious questions and begs others. I want to outline just the crucial ones for me. Firstly, we need to avoid notions of identity that underplay the degree to which it is always complex, multilayered, and shifting. Secondly, any notion of a hard boundary between "African" and "non-African" (or "un-African") should be resisted. Thirdly, we need to keep in our discourse awareness of the troubled history of the concept "Africa." The word itself comes from Europe and it was used as a totalizing tool in the colonial era. So we should always problematize our own use of the concept. And fourthly, any celebration of diversity must confront the challenge to unity posed by that diversity. Is a common African identity possible? What does a South African have in common with a Moroccan? How much does a professional from Lagos share with an illiterate farmer from rural Tanzania?

**Hatang:**

Verne, thank you for seeing my approach as being "un-African"! That's the whole point: to trouble your notions of "African" and "non-

African" (or "un-African"); to demonstrate that there are no clear-cut answers as to what these concepts mean.

Your response to President Mbeki's speech seems to be an exercise in fence-sitting—you go along with him, but not all the way. I must admit that I also found the speech compelling, seductive if you like. It is a speech against racism, and informed by a close and heartfelt knowledge of what our country has gone through, what our continent has gone through. He appeals to all South Africans to unite through an identification with the idea of a "rainbow nation." This idea demands a celebration of diversity together with a determination to unite in the endeavor to transform.

However, a cynic might remind us that President Mbeki is a politician and suggest that he was playing a political game with the concept "African." His readiness to embrace as his own the histories of both black and white South Africans might be seen as confirming his party's view that South Africa belongs to all who live in it. And this might be seen as a move to secure support from those who never identified with Africa's struggles for justice. I must add that essentially he offers a definition of a "South African." He just does not go far enough to establish a definition of "African"—as you said, he does not explore the commonalities between South Africans and other Africans.

Your comparison between a South African and a Moroccan simply assumes a common South African identity. I find this problematic. Let me pose a question to illustrate the problem I have. How much does a black rural-dweller in KwaZulu-Natal or the Northern Cape have in common with a black counterpart living in urban Pretoria? Would the latter not have more in common with a (white) urban Canadian? Think about the influences of globalization, access to the media, and exposure to Western notions of human rights, justice, feminism, and so on. Of course, the two South Africans in this example share their blackness and significant layers of cultural shaping. But we need to take into account the vastly different cultural environments offered by their divergent realities. What does the (probably) illiterate rural-dweller know of the world beyond the farm or village? What does the notion of a constitution mean to him or her? Or of "women's rights"? And so on.

Pinning down what we mean by an "African" is difficult, to say the least. Let me suggest that we should start by "undefining" the concept.[5] Do concepts such as these not fall into the trap of marking a boundary between "us" and "them," between "us" and the "other"? Does justice not demand that we always trouble such boundaries, that we invite the "other" in, that we make friends with the "otherness" within ourselves?

## Harris:

Yes! You make a point of fundamental significance. I think, by definition, all identity formation is a marking of boundaries. Would you agree that it is no coincidence that accompanying South Africa's drive to form a national identity is the shadow of xenophobia? Would you also agree that moves to find an "African" identity might trouble the boundaries patrolled by the xenophobes? And do you have hope that we can subvert community (protecting "us" against "them") with hospitality (welcoming strangers, "them," among "us")?[6]

## Hatang:

I hope you don't expect me to answer these questions. Exploring them would take us far from our course. So let me just add layers to them before inviting you to return to that course.

Isn't it interesting that the very country that champions "African Renaissance"—South Africa—is suffering from this xenophobia? Here we have a country experiencing opposing processes. On the one hand, we have South African business people entering the rest of Africa, apparently responding to a call for the development of Africa in the spirit of "African Renaissance." On the other hand, people on the ground, the impoverished, are rejecting their African brothers and sisters. Does this mark the divide between the elite—the rich, the powerful, the intelligentsia—and the impoverished masses? And do we not see a similar divide marking the discourse around "African Renaissance"? Consider this response by Philip Tabane, renowned South African musician, to the question, "Does the 'African renaissance' and the new millennium mean anything to you?" These are his words: "I don't understand these big names or concepts. Whatever they are, they mean nothing to me. I'm an ordinary person who does not understand these things and I wish someone can explain them to me. To me, they seem to be ideas that are based on other peoples' experiences. They seem to be far-fetched and have little reference to Africa."[7]

But let us return to our course. Can we find a working definition of what it means to be an "African," at the same time recognizing the need for a process of undefining?

## Harris:

Before responding to your insistent call to get to the point, just a few words on your "layering." Sello, I would caution against the simple divides you posit. I find it hard to imagine business interests motivated by the ideals of "African Renaissance." Surely the profit motive is paramount? Concerning xenophobia, I think it reaches beyond class and other boundaries. And I would venture to suggest that even within the intelligentsia in South Africa, "African Renaissance" still means little more than a collection of catchphrases.

However, to return to our course. I still think that Mbeki's "I am an African" speech offers us the most useful handle on these issues. Your point that he does not go much beyond defining a "South African" is well taken. But, paradoxically, this is arguably the key to a defining through undefining. As soon as we move beyond the search for national identity and into the realms of pan-Africanism, we quickly lose touch with local realities, the human and other diversities of our continent, and the fracturing impact of global capital. The securing of a common identity, I would argue, remains the stuff of hope and dream. Stuff not to be disregarded, for as Mbeki understands, it issues from the very soul of humanity. But it in turn must not be allowed to disregard the material and other specificities of particular human experience. However, can the terms of Mbeki's identity formation not be marshaled to argue that the degree to which one is an African is measurable by the degree to which one is a South African, or a Kenyan, or a Nigerian? As an illiterate worker of the land in an isolated African rural community, with maybe only the vaguest conception of "Africa," with little knowledge of the histories and the struggles of even neighboring countries, am I any less an "African"? Is what makes me an African not my shaping by the land—the land that sustains me—and its people, my commitment to these people, and my dream of a justice that is coming? And here, Sello, right here, Mbeki offers another thread of undefining. For justice ultimately is indivisible. A true yearning for justice cannot be restricted to "my people," to "us." It must embrace the stranger among us. Justice compels "community" to accommodate "hospitality." Without which there can be no hope for pan-Africanism.

So, I am positing a unity through a shattering. The search is not for an African way of knowing, an African episteme, an African discourse. It is for ways of knowing, epistemes, discourses, and idioms coming out of and nurtured by African realities (past and present). Such a shattering was envisaged by Cheikh Anta Diop in his 1948 essay on "African Renaissance." Having argued that every language has a "peculiar genius," he asserted that "the development of our indigenous languages is the prerequisite for a real African renaissance."[8] He was, if you like, positing a metalanguage through the medium of particular languages. Diop's view is supported by the Ghanaian professor Kwesi Kwaa Prah, although Prah argues that "language" should be more broadly defined so that in sub-Saharan Africa the focus would be on the development of ten core language groupings, or clusters.[9]

**Hatang:**

Yes, Verne, I think we have now found our course. Tsela modikologa ga e latse nageng.[10] But let me first respond briefly to your comments on simple divides. While you are correct to point out the danger here, you know me well enough to realize that I am not blind to it. Notice that I pose the divide—and there is an element of truth in even the most reductionist of divides—in the form of a question. I hoped that I had marked my awareness of complexity. On the other hand, I wonder if you haven't missed complexity even as you point out the need to recognize it. Take, for instance, the question of business interests. It might very well be that for these interests, the profit motive is paramount. However, behind them is the South African state, and I don't think that we can simply dismiss its role in terms of profit motive. Is it not possible that the state's promotion of "African Renaissance," its talk of sharing resources and expertise with the rest of Africa, of investing in other African economies, of contributing to building Africa's economic strength, is at least in part something other than power and greed? Is it not possible that we see something here of an African spirit of giving, of awareness that one cannot have a good night's sleep while one's neighbor is starving? Certainly, South Africa can neither enjoy its relative prosperity nor dream of an "African Renaissance" while its neighbors are caught up in poverty and conflict. And certainly any attempt to reach out to neighbors must involve business interests.

I am comfortable with what I would call your working (un)definition of an "African." Just one worry is that you seem to imply national identity as a prerequisite—measuring the degree to which one is an African by the degree to which one is a Kenyan, and so on. I would want a further "layering" here. Take that illiterate worker of the land of yours, without meaningful notions of "Africa" or of the realities of neighboring countries. Let me suggest that he or she does not even require a sense of national identity. Africanness within the framework we are proposing is established by connections to land and to people and to justice, not to nations. Whether or not that worker defines him- or herself in terms of national identity is immaterial. In fact, I would go further, and argue that Africanness can accommodate resistance to national identity.

But we must move on. This has been the easy part of our dialogue, Verne. Tse re di dirileng e sale mantlwantlwane, dikgolo di sa tla.[11] The real challenge lies ahead—to explore what distinctively African discourses on archives might look like. Now, Verne, I think that it's about time you responded to a question (now refigured in the light of our explorations) I posed at the outset: What would have given the 1999 ESARBICA Conference an identity establishing it as distinctively African?

### Harris:

Okay, time to grasp the nettle. (By now I have had enough time to pull on my glove!) Without suggesting a divide between form and content, I want to start with what would commonly be referred to as "form"—the shape, or patterning—of the conference. It conformed seamlessly to what could be called the international model for professional conferences: keynote address; scholarly papers delivered from a lectern; raised platform for dignitaries, chairpersons, and speakers; the audience seated in neat rows; sessions comprising formal presentations followed by short opportunities for discussion; diplomatically constructed session summaries and resolutions; and so on. You know the model. Now, I'm not in a position to even begin suggesting how engagement with Zanzibari realities might have challenged this pattern. I can go no further than asserting that such an engagement would have allowed difference in.

Sello, I know that you won't allow me to avoid addressing specifics, so let me attempt this by suggesting how an ESARBICA Conference held in South Africa might endeavor to allow difference in. I imagine a far less rigid conference program, with more space given to discussion and debate, and latitude provided for shifting boundaries in response to the dynamics of interaction. I imagine seating arrangements, the rhythms of formality and informality, attention to the clock, and so on shaped to some extent by the traditions of *indaba*. I imagine a willingness to at least contemplate a venue other than an upmarket hotel or conference center. I imagine strands of "living" archive—praise poets, storytellers, folk singers, traditional dancers, and so on—woven into proceedings. Focus groups, workshops, and the like providing the space for conference-goers to engage local issues, discourses, and communities. A process for the formulation of resolutions that encourages tough interrogation and bargaining. All of these elements—and they are obviously just a sample—are offered not to constitute an alternative to the "international model." I am proposing a fusion, or "jazzification," of local, regional, and international elements.

And then, of course, there is the question of language. (Here the form-content opposition blurs altogether.) I don't want to discount the advantages of a lingua franca, English in the case of the ESARBICA region. But ways have to be found of bringing the understandings of archive carried by/in indigenous languages into archival discourse. I want to invite you to explore this dimension, Sello. Suffice it for me to suggest here that this cause is not advanced by a conference in which only a handful of delegates ventures a phrase or two in an indigenous language, and in which the dominant English resists even the marking of any regional or local imprint.

The challenge I am flagging is, I think, of the same order as that confronting the National Archives of South Africa in its endeavor to transform a corporate ethos framed by a white, male, Afrikaans-dominated apartheid past. Yes, the staff is increasingly diverse, increasingly representative of South Africa's demographic profile, but is this diversity challenging established patterns, rhythms, and processes, or is it being managed to conform to an ethos not fundamentally different from the one we inherited? Has English not simply replaced Afrikaans in forcing other languages into informal spaces? Has rigid hierarchy been subverted? Has a white male voice—articulated by both men and women, black and white—been dislodged from that hierarchy's apex? Has bureaucratic red tape been unraveled? To what extent do you, Sello, have to shed your blackness at the front entrance to survive?

**Hatang:**

You pose many questions, all of them invitations hard to refuse. But let me respond to two of them, hoping that in my response I will be able to touch on others.

I venture to suggest that transformation at the National Archives has not allowed in the difference, the otherness, offered by black staff. This means leaving not only one's blackness at the front entrance, but one's Africanness (in the sense that we are using this term). You have covered enough of the constraints in formal spaces. Let me touch briefly on my experience outside those spaces. The ethos you speak of impacts on how black staff members relate to one another. Who you are and how you relate to others are haunted by the possibility of being found inappropriate. For instance, when you speak to a colleague who is a few meters from you, you run the risk of being accused of being "noisy" and of disturbing the peace in the passages. Casual conversation during office hours, even if related to work issues, is likely to be regarded as time wasting rather than as building the fabric of interrelationships. Discussion and negotiation around even the simplest things, such as a tea club or end-of-year party, is resisted as a bringing into the office of "street politics." Bringing a radio to work can be viewed as disturbing. You speak to black colleagues about archives in your own language, with confidence and in richness, but when you speak to white colleagues you must rely on a powerless translation into English. And, of course, this affects all conversation—when conversing with white staff, black staff must translate into English. So that black staff do not feel in the mainstream. This goes to say that my experience at the National Archives has been of me as the other, the one threatening to disturb the peace and tranquility that the institution has always experienced. And, given the realities of power, I do my best to conform. Is this not about the sacrificing of Africanness?

I must differ with your view that language carries meaning. I believe that meaning is woven into language, so that these concepts are not (meaningfully) separable. But every language, including English, is open to reshaping, including reshaping by what is other. So that here in Africa, English can be reshaped by meanings found in African realities. As Chinua Achebe has argued: "I feel that the English language will be able to carry the weight of my African experience. But it will have to be a new English, still in full communion with its ancestral home but altered to suit new African surroundings."[12] Now, I believe that just such an English is common in the township and downtown streets of South Africa. There, meanings are not bent to fit English—English is bent to fit meanings. So that my problem with the dominance of English in archival discourse in this part of the world is not a problem with English *per se*. It is a problem with a certain kind of English. An English that is unbent! And it is a problem with an unquestioning acceptance of English as the only language for professional discourse. As Ngugi wa Thiongo has argued in relation to "literature"—and he has critiqued Achebe accordingly—we abandon our indigenous languages at our peril.[13]

Verne, before you challenge me to suggest practical solutions, let me address the challenge. I think the starting point would be for archivists in the ESARBICA region to think archives in their own languages. In other words, they must resist the pressure to simply adopt the dominant English discourse. They should explore the richness their languages offer them in relation to the archive, engage their colleagues in those languages, write in those languages. This would empower them to bend English appropriately when they enter the dominant discourse. So, while English remains the lingua franca, and the connection to international archival discourse, space would be opened up for other languages. In terms of ESARBICA conferences, perhaps three or four core indigenous language groupings could be identified for accommodation. Participants could use any one of these groupings, with translation into English being provided. Of course, cost constraints would have to be taken into account. (But maybe organizers could sacrifice other expensive and unnecessary trappings ...)

From what I've said, you can see that I am in full agreement with Prah on language groupings. For South Africa he offers the basis for a language policy with far more promise than our current one—eleven official languages in theory, but effectively only one, namely English. With perhaps four—the Nguni grouping, the Sotho-Tswana grouping, English, and Afrikaans—receiving equal recognition, there would be hope of all South Africans being able to understand one another.

**Harris:**

I love your notion of bending, which, I think, as process, is precisely the same as the fusing, the jazzification, I was talking about earlier. And I take your point about language and meaning. Which paralyses me as I contemplate moving further into an exploration of how archival discourse might accommodate indigenous ways of knowing. The only "indigenous" language I speak is Afrikaans, which as you know, in the realm of archives is wholly colonized by its Dutch origins and contemporary obeisance to Muller, Feith, and Fruin. So, what meaningful thing can I say about indigenous ways of knowing the archive? (But are you not also paralyzed? Has the English you have used in this dialogue not been anything but bent?)

**Hatang:**

Verne, ke nnete ke sule bogatsu. Mme tota le fa nka swa bogatsu, ke sa ntse nka kgona go bina. Ke binela moribo o o tliswang ke thuto ya seeng. Bonnye ga bo lekane le bosilo.[14]

**Harris:**

You suggest, I think, a belief in the impossible. The paralyzed one dreaming of dance; bringing dance through the dream; finding in paralysis the divine capacity to dance. Is this ancient Tswana wisdom, or is it the religion (without religion) of Jacques Derrida?

**Hatang:**

Verne, you should know better than to ask either/or questions.

**Harris:**

Surely. I pose it only rhetorically, to express something of my excitement. In two sentences, you have captured the very heart of our dialogue. We are, in one movement, delineating the absence of dance in archival discourse, revealing our own paralysis, and dreaming the dance that must come.

But our dreaming, Sello, if it is to bring the dance, must be about more than verbal dueling and rhetoric. It must be a thing of passionate calling forth, of courageous step-taking with limbs that reason tells us are paralyzed. At the National Archives of South Africa, for instance, we need you and your black colleagues to refuse to shed anything at the front entrance. We need you to force parameters, create spaces, assert yourselves, pioneer a discourse in your own languages.

**Hatang:**

Verne, you understand, of course, my sense of paralysis as we embarked on this dialogue. In terms of language, of discourse, of positioning within that discourse, power rests with you. Passion and courage have brought me this far …

And what is the call of dream to you, and those like you who enjoy power in archival discourse? Is it perhaps to learn the languages that will open up other ways of knowing?

**Harris:**

The note you sound is a powerful one. The kind of note I think would be appropriate for concluding our dialogue. (So maybe you need to sound it again!) Thank you for the call to get up and walk out of my paralysis. Yes, I must learn at least one other language of this land. But while I am learning, there is dreamwork to be done. The dominant discourse must be engaged with determination to invite what is "other" in.

So, let me go back to the 1999 ESARBICA Conference and our exploration of how it might have been different. To be simplistic for a moment, we have addressed the conference's "form"—what about its "content"? What words, concepts, values, conceptual connections, forms of analysis, ways of constructing knowledge were excluded by what I called at the outset a Western modernist paradigm?

I begin—fumbling, fumbling in my paralysis—with a series of questions that I hope will tease out dimensions of our knowing archive in our region that were (remarkably) absent.

The conference theme was "Archives and the Protection of People's Rights." Is it not problematic that participants adopted uncritically a Western conceptual framework for "rights"? Take, for instance, the question of privacy. Is it not demonstrable that, at the very least, the boundaries between public and private spaces in this part of the world evince distinctive regional and local characteristics? Arguably there are traditions in our midst that call into question the public-private opposition.

Archival discourse internationally is informed by what I would call defining images, or metaphors. The archive as a mirror of "reality." The archivist as custodian. The record as progressing through a life cycle. And so on. Where, I ask, were images expressing local realities? Where was a troubling of the dominant images by African ways of knowing? Think, Sello, what African connections between "the archive" and "the storyteller" would mean for the notion of "the custodian." Think how a weaving with "the ancestors" might trouble the notion of life cycle.

Story, as mode of knowledge construction, as bearer of memory, is part of the fabric—arguably is the fabric—of public discourse in this part of the world. And it has ancient roots. Why was so little of this narrative richness evident at the conference?

Do African ways of knowing not resist Western modernism's weakness for the clear-cut conceptual divide and the binary opposition? Such resistance was conspicuous by its absence at the conference. Participants accepted unquestioningly, for instance, hard boundaries between right and wrong, the written and the spoken word, subject and object, humanity and nature. This informed every aspect of the conference's deliberations, but I give you one to illustrate the point. There was no space for the soul, the spirit, to be found in things and places. No space, therefore, for the dance of soul in archives (as "objects") and in the places of archival consignment.

Things and places. In the Western modernist paradigm, "the archive" is confined within a custodial conceptualization—the possession of, or control over, things. Has Africa not through the ages imagined and experienced "the archive" differently? Links to things and places are significant, but is the storyteller not central, configured always in relation to performance and to community (present and past)? And does this conceptualization not challenge the dominant Western notion of the archive as the stable carrier of evidence? Does it not posit the archive as characterized by its fluidity; the archivist as the tender of ever-shifting meanings and significances?

Sello, I pose these questions specifically in relation to the conference. But they are as pertinent to an interrogation of archival discourse generally in our region.

## Hatang:

I hoped that this time you would have answers rather than questions. Instead you present me with more questions than ever before in this dialogue. You will be disappointed to find that I am not going to attempt to answer them.

However, I cannot resist stating my views on orality, which you address so well without ever mentioning the term. As you suggest, orality underpins ways of knowing in this part of the world. (From what you say, the ESARBICA Conference ignored this reality.) I will raise just a few key issues here, not wanting to repeat myself unnecessarily—an account of orality and the archive is to be found in my article appearing elsewhere in this issue of the journal.[15]

Firstly, from what you have said to me about the conference, oral history was mentioned by several delegates, but always as a luxury for public archives. It is seen as something of secondary importance to their responsibilities in relation to public records and as something requiring expenses that public archives cannot afford. This position, even within the logic from which it emerges, is flawed. Given the high levels of illiteracy in Africa, orality is the medium, the archive, in which most people express themselves. To reduce the recording of orality to a luxury, then, is to exclude the majority of voices from public archives.

Secondly, it is problematic that archivists who do engage in oral history projects seem to focus their endeavors on capturing stories before they are lost. The objective is to record story—convert it into material custody; convert it into a record. This gives it "status" and "authenticity." But, of course, orality is fluid. Every telling of a story is different.

Awareness of this resistance to "freezing," and of its unsettling impact on notions of "meta-archive," is rare. As is awareness of the extent to which orality depends on performance and a rich context extremely difficult for archivists to "capture"—social situation, physical space and landmarks, items of material culture, and so on.

And thirdly, in our work with orality we have accepted the Western notion of exteriority and the related clear-cut distinction between memory and archive. This results in us believing that to archive orality, we must extract it from the people and consign it into the custody of archivists. Thus we give it the exteriority of the archive. Ideally, we must go further and convert orality into the written word through the practice of transcription. Verne, for me this is deeply problematic. Does our understanding of exteriority here in Africa not allow us to regard orality as already having an exteriority? Are the tracings in people's memories—shared in collective contexts, conveyed and performed by storytellers—not already archive? An archive without archive? Do we not trouble the boundaries between memory and archive? So that oral history projects are more complex than merely the capturing into archive of memory.

Verne, I wonder if we, in archival discourse, have got beyond merely accepting what the West has given us in terms of understanding orality. The time has come, I would argue, for us to empower our own ways of knowing in order to engage the dominant ideas from the West.

**Harris:**

You know that I am in fundamental agreement with your analysis of orality. Perhaps I should just stress one point. Your argument is with the dominant Western modernism. There are, of course, other epistemological strands prominent in the West that would welcome the perspective you offer. Indeed, it could be argued that your understanding of the archive is influenced deeply by deconstruction, and Jacques Derrida in particular.

**Hatang:**

Sure.[16] But I would want to argue that my understanding comes out of engagement with Derrida rather than colonization by him.

**Harris:**

Sure. Now let me return (through the door just opened by you) to my inventorying of exclusions (or absences) from the ESARBICA Conference. Again, I want to disclaim comprehensiveness—I only want to flag what were for me the most notable absences. Deconstruction was one of them. Feminism was another. As were gay and lesbian ways of knowing. (You know how much I hate labels, so understand that I use them now, with misgiving, for shorthand purposes.) In our region we have gay and lesbian archivists. We have archivists who call themselves feminists. We have (as you and I know only too well) archivists who are labeled deconstructionist or postmodernist. However, their voices are hardly heard in our archival discourse. They have not begun to challenge the dominance of the Western modernist paradigm.

**Hatang:**

We could argue about who exactly opened the door here! But we have both walked through it now. You realize, of course, how your marking of these "absences" will make you vulnerable to the accusation of colonization by Western values and influences. (Ironic, given that this is precisely your accusation against archival discourse in our region.) We have heard prominent and powerful voices in broader public discourse denouncing all these absences as "un-African."

**Harris:**

Sello, the temptation is either to ignore such denunciation as beneath contempt or to allow one's fury free reign. And sober analysis runs the risk of simply repeating arguments that have been made countless times before—the arguments some of the liberation movements in Africa have been forced to make in defense of democracy or socialism; the arguments millions of African Christians and Muslims have been forced to make in defense of their religious beliefs; and so on. Also, there is the risk of having to state the obvious—like asserting that soccer is now a game of Africa although it came from the streets and fields of England.

But I shall try to say something meaningful. Firstly, a few general points, then several observations on deconstruction specifically.

The position defined by the "un-African" denunciation assumes an "Africa" pristine and timeless before the wrecking by colonialism. We have already attempted to problematize the notion of "Africa." The point to stress here is that no episteme, no culture, no collectivity is pristine (in the sense of being impervious to outside influences) and timeless. The work of fusion continues relentlessly. These "things" live by their capacity to grow through fusion.

So that the position posits recovery of the irrecoverable. The pre-colonial past is past, knowable only through a present irrevocably changed and changing. The position also would deny us the powerful creative energies of fusion. And it is dismissive of the experiences and struggles of myriad (un-African) Africans deemed to be beyond the pale. Is it even necessary, for instance, to cite Africans who have fought, and continue to fight, for women's rights?

But what of deconstruction (if there is such a thing)? Is it just another colonizing Western import? Its Western figuring, I would argue, must be problematized. It is outside the epistemological main-stream of the West; it is framed precisely to subvert that mainstream. Many of its articulators are from the global periphery. Derrida, decon-struction's leading authority figure, disturbs his "French philosopher" appellation. He was born in Africa. He questions his "Frenchness" within a shifting Maghreb-France-Jewry constellation.[17] None of this, of course, refutes the denunciation. (An impossible task.) But we should observe that deconstruction importunes a justice that is always coming. The resonance with the President Mbeki speech we recounted at the outset is significant. We should also observe that deconstruction is defined by its respect for "the other"; its determina-tion to disclose the breach always already in every circle of knowing; its disclosure of the shifting ground beneath its own feet. So that it is hospitable to every "other" (including the "other" reverberating in its own deeper reaches) and responds to every hospitality. It embraces fusion(s).

Not surprising, then, that your own analysis of orality fuses what we could call, for convenience sake, "deconstructive" and "indigenous" ways of knowing.

**Hatang:**

Verne, habits die hard. It is interesting that although you are against the use of labels, you're still using them. Phiri e sola bowa fela, mokgwa ga e o latlhe.[18] (You cannot but use what society gives you to use—labels—though you vow not to use them because they close down meaning.)

**Harris:**

Yebo baba.[19] Maybe I cannot escape the influence—here comes another label—of the "Western modernism" I think I despise. You will have noted that I try as far as possible to mark my awareness of difficulty through the use of inverted commas whenever I cannot avoid using labels. But perhaps that's too easy an option. Of course, if we accept that words are signs, then in a sense all words are labels and discourse becomes a form of labeling . . .

**Hatang:**

Sure. All memory, all meaning is constructed. And what "modernism" wants to forget—or hide from—is this constructedness.

**Harris:**

And it forgets something else. In labeling "postmodernism" as lost in "constructedness" and "relativism," it forgets that the energies of deconstruction are generated by a passion for justice and shaped by the values—demanding, uncompromising—that flow from that passion. If it is anything at all, deconstruction is belief—and the way of living that such belief inspires—in the impossible. The (impossible) coming of justice. An (impossible) transcendent meaning. It believes with a "yes!" while insisting "no!" to all ways of knowing that exclude "otherness."

**Hatang:**

So that the archive—although removed irrevocably from the event by layers of constructedness, although a gathering of signs rather than images, of stories rather than reflections—is a resource of great richness to the human soul. (Many people make the mistake of seeing only the oral archive as being defined by constructedness, sign, and story. Our argument, Verne, is that these characteristics apply equally well to the written archive.) The archive, all archives, feed our yearning for this coming. It is not, in the end, about the past. It is about the future.[20] As Derrida puts it, the archive opens out of the future. Ga o sa utlwe thuto le botlhale ya bagolo otla utlwa ya manong. Thuto le botlhale ya bagolo, jaaka akhaefe, ga se ya maloba, ke ya gompieno, mme se se botlhokwa ke ya bokamoso.[21]

**Harris:**

Sure.

# Endnotes

1   We struggled to find an appropriate title for this "piece." Possibilities included: "Finding Fusion in Archival Discourse"; "Borakanelo jwa dikitso mo akhaefeng ya Afrika"; "Akhaefe, kitso ya seeng le thuto meonon le kitso ya Afrika"; "Jazzifying Ways of Knowing"; "Welcoming the Strangers In"; and "Making Space for Otherness." At one point we considered not having a title at all. For our struggle was more about the nature of titles than about a particular title. For titles always necessarily close rather than open, direct rather than invite, gather in rather than disseminate. As Derrida has interpreted Mallarme: "Mallarme prescribes a *suspension* of the title, which—like the head, or capital, or the oracle—carries its head high, speaks in too high a voice, both because it raises its voice and drowns out the ensuing text, and because it is found high up on the page becoming the eminent center, the beginning, the command station, the chief, the archon ... But the function of the title is not merely one of hierarchy. The title to suspend is also, by virtue of its place, suspended, in suspense or in suspension. Up above a text from which it expects and receives all—or nothing." Jacques Derrida, *Dissemination* (Chicago: University of Chicago Press, 1981), 178–79. This dialogue was first published in *ESARBICA Journal* 19 (2000): l, and later in *The Canadian Journal of Information and Library Science* 25, nos. 2–3 (2000).

2   I have argued this at some length in "Claiming Less, Delivering More: A Critique of Positivist Formulations on Archives in South Africa," *Archivaria* 44 (1997).

3   At the time, Max du Preez, former editor of *Vrye Weekblad*, was a freelance journalist. He was quoted or contributed to a number of newspapers, radio stations, and TV channels in South Africa.

4   I use the text of this speech appearing on the ANC Web site: www.anc.org.za/anc-docs/history/mbeki/1996/sp960508, accessed 23 October 1999.

5   I must acknowledge David William Cohen for the notion of "undefining." See his "The Undefining of Oral Tradition," *Ethnohistory* 36, no. 1 (1989).

6   This play of hospitality against community I draw from the writings of Jacques Derrida.

7   Quoted in the *Mail and Guardian,* 22–29 October 1999.

8   Cheikh Anta Dioph, *Towards the African Renaissance: Essays in African Culture and Development, 1946–1960* (London: Karnak House, 1996), 35.

9   Prah articulated this argument at an African Renaissance Colloquium hosted by the South African Department of Arts, Culture, Science and Technology outside Johannesburg on 7 February 2000. The paper on which his input was based is entitled "African Languages for the Mass Education of Africans."

10   Setswana: In taking a long route we were not misled.

11   Setswana: What we have done thus far is child's play. Bigger issues are still coming.

12   Chinua Achebe said this in a 1964 speech entitled "The African Writer and the English Language." Quoted in Ngugi wa Thiongo, *Decolonising the Mind: The Politics of Language in African Literature* (London: Heinemann, 1986).

13   See, for instance, Thiongo's *Decolonising the Mind*.

14   Setswana: Indeed, I am paralyzed. However, I can still dance. Dance to the tune of Western education. Being young is not equivalent to idiocy.

15   See the article "Converting Orality to Material Custody: Is It a Noble Act of Liberation or Is It an Act of Incarceration?", *ESARBICA Journal* 19 (2000).

16 "Sure" is South African township English for "Yes!"

17 Most directly perhaps in his *Monolingualism of the Other; or, The Prosthesis of Origin* (Stanford: Stanford University Press, 1998).

18 Setswana: A hyena will lick its wounds after a beating by a farmer. And it will return to try stealing again.

19 IsiZulu: Yes father or yes sir.

20 In my reading, this is the primary argument of his *Archive Fever: A Freudian Impression* (Chicago: University of Chicago Press, 1996).

21 Setswana: If you do not listen to the teaching of the elders you will be impoverished. You will end up eating the shit of your peers. The teaching and the wisdom of the elders, as with the archive, are not for the past. They are for the present and, most importantly, they are for the future.

# CHAPTER 14

## The Archive Is Politics[1]

### MARKING

In one of his better-known articles, Kent Haworth said the following in 1992:

> Archivists have developed rationales to justify their existence to users and sponsors of archives, without informing those constituencies of their purpose. Understanding purpose involves thinking about the "why" questions rather than the "what" questions.[2]

Of course he was very good at the "what" questions, but I think his passion and his commitment were fired by the "why" questions. I wish to dedicate this piece to his memory and to honor that memory by speaking to my own passion with an insistent respect for the bigger purposes informing what archivists do.

I have chosen two markers for what I will say, the first being the just-quoted passage; the other is a verse from a Bob Dylan song published just three years earlier:

We live in a political world
Turning and a'thrashing about,
As soon as you're awake, you're trained to take
What looks like the easy way out.[3]

## POLITICAL PRESSURE

A conference to be convened in Liverpool during July 2003 bears the title "Political Pressure and the Archival Record." Over many months, I read and re-read the explanation for this title offered by the conference organizers, and listened intently for uses of the term *political pressure* in the public domain. Two assumptions, it seems to me, inform most usage of the term. Firstly, that the pressure that is political tends to pull people, perhaps especially professional practitioners, away from principle, away from the ethical, away from the legitimate. So, for instance, you might have a senior bureaucrat in the public service shifting resources from an important public program in order to satisfy the demands of his political bosses; or political pressure being brought to bear on the work of an inquiry into corruption in order to protect certain persons. During the 1980s, the director of the South African State Archives Service withdrew access from a range of archival records under his control in response to political pressure from the cabinet member to whom he reported.[4] The second assumption is that political pressure is something that comes from "outside." As in the example just quoted, the person going about a legitimate activity, an activity duly mandated and prescribed, is intruded upon by a power outside the bounds of that activity.

Both these assumptions, I want to suggest, while clearly connected to the realities we all experience, exclude dimensions that are critical to an adequate problematization of "the political." On the one hand, political pressure need not be "bad." There are uses of it, deployments of it, that are constructive rather than oppressive; that are in the service of, rather than against, the principled, the ethical, and the legitimate. Two examples from South Africa: the pressure that anti-apartheid activists exerted on state archivists in the 1980s embraced the "political"; and during the post-1994 transformation of the apartheid archival system, it was necessary, and in the interests of democratization, for professional archivists to be pressured into change by political powers. In the early years of transformation, I was a senior manager in the South African National Archives and remember frequently lobbying political powers to clear obstacles being put in the way by archivists.

On the other hand, political pressure never only comes from "outside." It is always also at work from "inside." This is a more difficult argument to make, so let us dwell here for a moment. In what follows, I assume that archivists are part of a large and diverse family of "recordmakers," and that in mounting the argument in relation to recordmaking, I do so at the same time for archives.[5]

Many of us recordmakers naively imagine that we can stand outside the exercise of power even as we use "the record" to hold power to account. And those of us who concede that there can be no "standing outside," hold to the notion that the power we wield as record makers is a constructive, as opposed to an oppressive, power. My own view is that recordmakers are, from the beginning and always, political players; that they are active participants in the dynamics of power relations; and that the boundary between constructive and oppressive power is always shifting and porous. This is not an original view. It is one that has been made from different perspectives and in different disciplines by numerous commentators, from Michel Foucault to Bruno Latour, from Jacques Derrida to Ann Stoler.[6] All of them emphasize structural dimensions to the play of power in recordmaking. Records always already express relations of power and invite the exercise of power. In the memorable words of Latour:

> The "cracy" of bureaucracy is mysterious and hard to study, but the "bureau" is something that can be empirically studied, and which explains, because of its structure, why some power is given to an average mind just by looking at files.... In our cultures "paper shuffling" is the source of an essential power....[7]

Derrida's interrogation goes beyond "paper shuffling." He demonstrates that in all recording—the diarist making an entry, the rock painter at work, the person sending an e-mail message to a friend, the parent recounting a family story to his or her children[8]—what he calls "archontic power" is in play. Recordmakers cannot avoid deploying archontic power, for its pull is a structural one.

Very few recordmakers demonstrate awareness of this structural pull. For all kinds of reasons this is a pity, not least because they are best placed to tease out its complex dimensions. The Canadian archivists Terry Cook and Joan Schwartz are among the few who have interrogated recordmaking with this awareness. They are worth listening to:

> Records … are about imposing control and order on transactions, events, people, and societies through the legal, symbolic, structural, and operational power of recorded communication.[9]

Schwartz and Cook readily concede that recordmaking is not only about the exercise of power, that it is never only about imposing control and order; but, without naming it, they discern the structural pull of archontic power.

Political pressure, then, is always already at play *from within* processes of recordmaking. Archivists, whether they realize it or not, are at once the objects and the instruments of political pressure.

## INTERNATIONAL ARCHIVAL DISCOURSE

For at least two decades, it has been relatively commonplace for archivists to talk about and write about the politics of recordmaking. Until quite recently, the discourse has been dominated by voices speaking to the harsh realities of recordmaking by and within what can be called oppressive regimes—apartheid South Africa, the Soviet Union, Nazi Germany, Cambodia, and so on. These voices tended to adopt uncritically the two assumptions about political pressure that I outlined earlier—that it is a "bad thing," and that it comes from "outside." The 1990s saw the emergence of powerful new streams within the discourse that offered more nuanced accounts and critiques of the politics of recordmaking. These streams, sometimes implicitly, challenged the notion of political pressure as symptomatic of dysfunction in recordmaking and in society. In my reading, two of these streams have been most influential. On the one hand, voices more rather than less permeable to what has been called "postmodernist" thinking;[10] on the other, voices espousing the values and insights of the Australian record-keeping for accountability approach.[11] My own work could be, and has been, positioned among the former.

One of the most prolific, challenging, and insightful voices from the latter stream has been that of Chris Hurley.[12] As a way of at once honing my argument and suggesting some of the key tensions between the two streams, I wish now to engage briefly a particular text by Hurley—his 2001 Association of Canadian Archivists' Annual Conference paper "The Evolving Role of Government Archives in Democratic Societies." Drawing on his long experience as a government archivist in two established democracies, Hurley elegantly demonstrates that for archivists and other recordmakers, "the political" is unavoidable. Those who believe they can separate the "professional" from other spaces, who believe they can remain professionally impartial, fool themselves and condemn themselves to being the pawns of those who hold power. As he points out graphically: "We cannot comfortably design a better system for documenting the number of heads being processed through the gas chambers as if good recordkeeping (in a technical sense) can be divorced from the uses to which it is put."[13]

To the question of what one does with this reality and the concomitant question of how to find political direction, Hurley advocates support of democratic values, but with an important qualification:

> Like everybody else, recordkeepers are ultimately bound to the society in which they live (the context in which they operate).... Our professional standards are no longer value-free once they are applied into one society or another—once they are given a context. In application, they acquire a colour of the society in which they operate. It is because we live in a democracy, therefore, not because we are archivists, that our professional standards and practices support democratic values.[14]

This statement resonates strongly with me—I know only too well my own shaping by South African realities. For both of us, then, "the archive" never speaks as a thing in and of itself. It always speaks through specificities, including those of particular societal dynamics and relations of power.

The degree to which I concur with Hurley's analysis should be evident. Nevertheless, I am uneasy with aspects of it. Firstly, it borders on determinism. If democracy spawns democratic archivists, then how do we explain archivists fighting for democracy in oppressive regimes? Secondly, it underplays the extent to which "democracy" is contested. There are any number of forms to democracy, and arguably democracy only has meaning as long as people are contesting its meaning and fighting for it to come. And finally, it limits inordinately the space in which "democracy" can be contested. Take, for instance, this comment on debates over e-mail surveillance:

> If we are to uphold the integrity of the record in support of democratic accountability, we must have a mandate from society to do so. Similarly, having that mandate imposes limitations: we cannot afford the luxury of letting our own views on personal liberty subvert our professional duty to maintain the integrity of recordkeeping systems. No matter what our personal views on email snooping, if we accept that that corporate control is necessary to maintain and protect the integrity of the record (the matter is open to dispute, of course) then any promptings of private conscience must be resisted.[15]

Two things. Not even suggested by Hurley is that the terrain marked by the phrase "having a mandate from society" is a very troubled one. And Hurley comes perilously close to drawing a hard rather than a soft boundary between the "professional" and the "personal."

A determinist might explain the differences between Hurley and me in terms of one of us having lived in stable democracies all his life and the other living through a transition from an oppressive regime to a fledgling democracy. One of the aims of this essay is to demonstrate that other things are also at play here.

## POLITICS IS ARCHIVAL

Thus far I have concentrated my analysis around establishing that "the archive" is political. I have made the argument that the very structure of archiving, that the process that is recordmaking, both invites politics in and generates a politics of its own wherever "archive" happens. Ultimately, there is no understanding of the archive without understanding of politics. "We live," in the words of Bob Dylan quoted at the outset, "in a political world." I wish now to go a step further by arguing that politics is archival; that the archive is the very possibility of politics.

Let me acknowledge at once that this is not an original argument. Without drawing the conclusions that I do, many archivists have moved into this space, even implied the argument, by pointing out the strong correlation between oppression and thorough recordmaking. To quote Chris Hurley, for example:

> A respectable argument could be mounted that archivists had more to gain from employment by dictators and oppressors than by their democratic counterparts. Historically, tyrants have more regard for good recordkeeping than democrats. Totalitarians are notoriously good recordkeepers.[16]

In my reading of the literature, however, only Terry Cook—in scattered references throughout his more recent work—has suggested that politics is best understood in archival terms. It is no accident that a feature of Cook's work is its openness to discourses outside the narrowly "archival," in particular to the epistemological moves of the so-called postmodernists. It is from the latter, in particular Jacques Derrida and Michel Foucault, that I derive the argument.

Scholars and commentators from many disciplines and many countries, working with a range of theoretical and epistemological frameworks, have unfolded how the exercise of political power hinges on control of information. My own favorite is Noam Chomsky, whose searing critiques of democracy, in the United States especially, demonstrate how elites depend on sophisticated information systems, media control, surveillance, privileged research and development, dense documentation of process, censorship, propaganda, etc., etc. to maintain their positions.[17] But it is Derrida and Foucault who reach most deeply in exposing the logic, even the law, underlying these phenomena. In the words of Derrida: "There is no political power without control of the archive, if not of memory."[18] And Foucault, coming from a different direction but nailing the same law: "The archive is first the law of what can be said...."[19] And *when* it can be said, *how,* and *by whom.* Both of them insist on the archive as a construction, one that issues from and expresses relations of power. Listen to Derrida elaborating this insistence in relation to media apparatuses:

> Who today would think his time and who, above all, would speak about it ... without first paying some attention to a public space and therefore to a political present which is constantly transformed, in its structure and its content, by the teletechnology of what is so confusedly called information or communication?[20]

The confusion in this naming of "information" and "communication" stems from an underestimation—sometimes an ignoring—of what Derrida calls "fictional fashioning":

> No matter how singular, irreducible, stubborn, distressing or tragic the "reality" to which it refers, "actuality" comes to us by way of a fictional fashioning.[21]

"Information" is always fashioned, always constructed. Derrida clears away the confusion by deploying the term—the concept—"archive."

In its Derridean deployment, "the archive" is the law determining meanings and significances; the law, if you like, determining contexts. Here, beneath the surface whirl and clatter of information, is where the instruments of power are forged. Instruments that in their most fundamental of operations create and destroy, promote and discourage, co-opt and discredit, *contexts*. I need not stress—nor resort to citation in order to demonstrate—that archivists—from dyed-in-the-wool Jenkinsonians to so-called postmodernists, from Schellenbergians to records continuum advocates—have conceptualized what they do around their special expertise in context. But it is the politician—more precisely, the archon—who is the purveyor of context. The archon, then, is the archetypal archivist. And the archive, the archeion, is the place of the archon.

If this is a law informing even the most established of democracies, then how do we measure democracy? To this question Derrida responds decisively, and not surprisingly, in archival terms:

> Effective democratization can always be measured by this essential criterion: the participation in and the access to the archive, its constitution, and its interpretation.[22]

If power is exercised through the construction of archive, then the locus of participation in the exercise of power is precisely the processes of the archive's construction. And that implies contestation. For society is always an assemblage of competing interests and perspectives. As the British intellectual Richard Hoggart has reminded us: "A well-running democracy will constantly quarrel with itself, publicly, about the right things and in the right way."[23] The time for activism, in other words, is never past. When we give up on activism, we give up on democracy. This was an axiom that I think Kent Haworth lived.

Even in democracies, of course, there are limits—there must be limits—to contestation. These are pointed to by Hoggart with the notion of quarrelling "in the right way." Here he suggests the space for contract—social contract—sometimes, but not always, formalized in laws and constitutions. Activists need to be wary of the penchant of those who hold power in democracies to hold up *contract* as a substitute for *contest*. Sometimes the powerful even go so far as to suggest that contestation unravels the contract. These, I want to suggest, are subterfuges; strategies for entrenching power. It is to confuse law, and right, with justice. The notion of contract assumes potential contest, puts in place frameworks and mechanisms for managing contestation appropriately. Indeed, ensuring that the contract is respected, adapted to accommodate new realities and new needs, and kept open to the call of justice hinges on our capacity to foster contestation within and around it. So that the contestants—and at times they might be bitter foes—are at the same time *partners* in a noble endeavor—the endeavor to bring justice.

## CONCLUSION: ARCHIVES FOR JUSTICE

I would readily concede that the argument mounted in this paper is a dangerous one. Give up on the notion of the archivist as impartial custodian, as honest broker, and one opens the door to activist archivists pursuing any and every political agenda. While acknowledging the danger, I have argued that archivists are always already political players. They cannot be merely custodians and brokers. Recognizing this, I have insisted, is critical to avoiding the greater danger of archivists, while wearing the mantles of custodian and broker, becoming pawns in bigger power-plays. For, any attempt to be impartial, to stand above the power-plays, constitutes a choice, whether conscious or not, to replicate if not to reinforce prevailing relations of power. It is a choice, to return to the words of Bob Dylan, "to take what looks like the easy way out."

I have offered no blueprint for avoiding the dangers. I don't know, and I can't imagine, how the dangers can be avoided. What I do know is that the call of justice, the call for justice, is an insistent one that we ignore at our peril.

I would readily concede that my understanding of "archive," and this paper's particular argument, are shaped indelibly by my experience as a South African. A South African who cut his teeth as an archivist in the 1980s and developed his thinking in the cauldron of debates around "transitional justice." But I have insisted that there are dynamics and laws that transcend the specificities of any particular space-time nexus. I insist also that oppression happens in even the most mature of democracies; that every archivist is confronted by and must confront oppression; and that the call of justice comes to every archivist.

To the questions "Should recordmakers strain against the gradient of archontic power?"; "Should they strain against a 'power to control'?"; "Should they strain to deploy constructive rather than oppressive power?"; I say "yes!" Not because "the record" itself calls me to respond in this way. If anything, as Derrida, Latour, Foucault, Stoler, Schwartz, and Cook in different ways all suggest, "the record" encourages us to move with rather than against the gradient. I say "yes!" because I believe that the call of justice—which comes from outside of "the record," outside of any archival or recordmaking theory—is a calling more important than any archival calling. Those who believe they can keep these callings separate, who believe they can separate the "professional" from other spaces, who believe they can remain professionally impartial, fool themselves and condemn themselves to the role of pawn. And the role of pawn, even in a democracy, is closed to the call of justice and, in the end, is profoundly reactionary.

I offer no blueprint for identifying the call of justice. Following Derrida, I don't believe that justice, ultimately, can be knowable. Like democracy, it must always be coming. It is a phantom, at most "a relation to the unconditional that, once all the conditional givens have been taken into account, bears witness to that which will not allow itself to be enclosed within a context."[24] The call of justice resists the totalization of every such enclosure. It resists, if you like, what is traditionally regarded as the fundamental archival impulse—contextualization. It is open to the future and to every "other." It respects—gives space to, looks again at—"radical otherness."[25] In the powerful formulation of Levinas: "the relation to the other, i.e., justice."[26]

Recordmaking, I have suggested, is a messy business. The hands of recordmakers are always dirty. Neat theorizing denies this complexity and falls willy nilly into the untroubled exercise of archontic power. Its exponents, willingly or unwillingly, posit a knowledge that heroically promises an overcoming of ignorance. The record, they argue, or simply assume, can be located within a cocoon of meaning. They are training us, to return once again to the words of Bob Dylan, to take what looks like the easy way out. It would be naïve, of course, even bloody-minded, to ignore the degree to which this archontic discourse is informed by strategic positioning. To access resources, to secure the status we need to do what we have to do effectively, we are forced to adopt neat theorizing to a greater or lesser degree. I have done so at the recordmaking coalface and will continue to do so. The danger is that we are so susceptible to believing our own rhetoric, to allowing the means we adopt to overwhelm the ends we hold dear. My call is simply to remember this. To remember that our neat theorizing hides a profound raggedness haywiring just beneath the surface of our immaculate constructions.

"The record," "the archive," always dances outside any conceptual cocoon. We do not know, cannot know, ultimately, what "the record" is. The dynamics of power trouble all our doing and all our knowing. Knowledge is always contingent, always standing above an abyss. In the words of the Canadian writer Anne Michaels: "What is the true value of knowledge? That it makes our ignorance more precise."[27] A view echoed by the French writer Helene Cixous in commenting on what she calls the mysteries of sexual difference: "We could think over these mysteries but we don't. We are unable to inscribe or write them since we don't know who we are, something we never consider since we always take ourselves for ourselves.... I'll tell you frankly that I haven't the faintest idea who I am, but at least I know I don't know."[28] Strategic imperatives might demand that we foreground our knowledge. But justice, if there be such a thing, demands that we ac-knowledge our ignorance.

The theme of this session is "accountability." Archivists, as we all know, must give account to a range of people, processes, structures, and ideals. My argument is that in the end, and in the beginning, the most important accounting is the one geared to answering the call of justice. To return to Kent Haworth, we should never lose sight of our purpose. And, if our purpose is to bring justice, then this must involve a ceaseless importuning of our purpose not to lose sight of us.

# Endnotes

1 This essay started out as a paper delivered at a symposium in honor of Kent Haworth, Toronto, March 2003. It drew on work in progress for the conference "Political Pressure and the Archival Record," Liverpool, July 2003. It was published under the same title in Marion, Beyea, et al., eds. *The Power and Passion of Archives: A Festschrift in Honour of Kent Haworth* (Ottawa: Association of Canadian Archivists, 2005). The version published here retains the text of the previously published version, but includes a longer section titled "International Archival Discourse," drawn from the paper I presented at the Liverpool conference.

2 Kent Haworth, "The Principles Speak for Themselves: Articulating a Language of Purpose for Archives," in *The Archival Imagination: Essays in Honour of Hugh A. Taylor,* ed. Barbara Craig (Ottawa: Association of Canadian Archivists, 1992).

3 Bob Dylan, lyrics from "Political World," *Oh Mercy* (CBS Records, 1989).

4 See Verne Harris, "Redefining Archives in South Africa: Public Archives and Society in Transition, 1990–1996," *Archivaria* 42 (1996).

5 I made this point for the first time in published form together with Wendy Duff in our essay "Stories and Names: Archival Description as Narrating Records and Constructing Meanings," *Archival Science* 2, nos. 3–4 (2002).

6 Key works by Foucault, Derrida, and Latour are cited elsewhere in this essay. An outstanding example of Ann Stoler's work is her "Colonial Archives and the Arts of Governance: On the Content in the Form," in *Refiguring the Archive,* ed. Carolyn Hamilton, et al. (Cape Town: David Philip, 2002).

7 Bruno Latour, "Visualization and Cognition: Thinking with Eyes and Hands," *Knowledge and Society* 6 (1986): 28.

8 Even that most fluid of records, orality, that trace consigned to a dispersed substrate no one can "see," is shaped within the power relations of a collectivity. To be a record, to become a record, a story, a memory must have exteriority—it must be consigned to the psychic apparatuses of others—which implies a stamp of collective approval.

9 Joan Schwartz and Terry Cook, "Archives, Records and Power: The Making of Modern Memory," *Archival Science* 2, nos. 1–2 (2002): 13–14.

10 It must be said that the term *postmodernism* has been used extremely loosely in archival discourse—for instance, to label both Foucault and Derrida without qualification as "postmodernists" is to risk draining meaning from the term. Nevertheless, for a comprehensive listing of such voices, see footnote 17 of Schwartz and Cook, "Archives, Records, and Power."

11 In my view, the most vigorous voices in this stream are Chris Hurley, Sue McKemmish, Michael Piggott, and Frank Upward. For a recent articulation of the politics of recordmaking from this perspective, see Michael Piggott and Sue McKemmish, "Recordkeeping, Reconciliation and Political Reality," paper presented at the Australian Society of Archivists' annual conference, Sydney, August 2002.

12 Hurley is probably best known for his courageous interventions around the infamous "Heiner Affair."

13 Chris Hurley, "The Evolving Role of Government Archives in Democratic Societies," paper presented at the Association of Canadian Archivists' annual conference, Winnipeg, June 2001, 1–2.

14 Hurley, "The Evolving Role of Government Archives," 2.

15  Hurley, "The Evolving Role of Government Archives," 5.

16  Hurley, "The Evolving Role of Government Archives," 1.

17  See, for instance, Peter Mitchell and John Schoeffel, eds., *Understanding Power: The Indispensable Chomsky* (New York: The New Press, 2002).

18  Jacques Derrida, *Archive Fever: A Freudian Impression* (Chicago: University of Chicago Press, 1996), 4.

19  Michel Foucault, *The Archaeology of Knowledge and the Discourse on Language* (New York: Pantheon, 1992), 129.

20  Jacques Derrida and Bernard Stiegler, *Echographies of Television* (Cambridge, U.K.: Polity Press, 2002), 3.

21  Derrida and Stiegler, *Echographies*.

22  Derrida, *Archive Fever,* 4.

23  Quoted in Christopher Merrett, "A Tale of Two Paradoxes: Media Censorship in South Africa, Pre-Liberation and Post-Apartheid," *Critical Arts* 15, nos. 1–2 (2001): 64.

24  Jacques Derrida and Maurizio Ferraris, *A Taste for the Secret* (Cambridge, U.K.: Polity, 2001), 17.

25  Derrida and Ferraris, *A Taste for the Secret,* 21.

26  Quoted in Derrida and Ferraris, *A Taste for the Secret,* 56.

27  Anne Michaels, *Fugitive Pieces* (Toronto: McClelland and Stewart, 1996), 210.

28  Helene Cixous in *The Helene Cixous Reader,* ed. Susan Sellers (London and New York: Routledge, 1994), 200.

# CHAPTER 15

## "A World Whose Horizon Can Only Be Justice": Toward a Politics of Recordmaking[1]

### OF ORIGINS, TERMS, AND ASSUMPTIONS

This article has a provenance long in reach and, in principle, infinite in its contextual layerings. Indeed, an article about this article arguably is both necessary and desirable. What is certain is that such an article would be extremely tedious, and, for this and other reasons, will never be written. But I feel obliged to disclose certain elements of provenance, as the disclosure will enable me to avoid unnecessary repetition, establish the terms of my inquiry, and focus on the mounting of a more or less fresh argument.

In July 2003, I presented a paper in Liverpool at the conference "Political Pressure and the Archival Record."[2] That paper drew on and expressed my experience as an archivist through two decades of turbulence and fundamental social change in South Africa. (I am attempting here to name "beginnings," though of course there are always beginnings back of those we have the insights and the resources to name.) Over a year has passed since then, and the contexts have shifted, but this element of provenance still requires reading. In that paper I made three arguments which form the conceptual foundation for this article and which I want to pass over relatively quickly. Firstly, the very structure of recordmaking both invites politics in and generates a politics of its own. Ultimately, there is no understanding of the record, or of the archive, without understanding of politics. Secondly, and this argument flows directly from the first, political pressure never only comes from "outside." It is always also at work from "inside"; from within the processes of recordmaking. Recordmakers, including archivists, are, from the beginning and always, political players. Thirdly, not only is recordmaking ("the archive") woven through by the political; politics is woven through by the archival. In each instance so woven through that neither concept is imaginable, nor understandable, without the other. This is to go beyond a claim that the archive is political. It is to assert that the archive *is* politics. These are arguments that I must perforce assume need not be made all over again.

Admittedly, the semantic weave at play here is dense, but I hesitate to address it, as the threads are endless. But two words are critical to the argument of this essay and demand at least cursory definition. Firstly, by "politics" I understand that huge and messy realm, reaching across orders of the individual and the collective, the personal and the public, in which the dynamics of power and authority engage with issues of principle. The engagement is unavoidably messy, seeming to invite in, almost structurally, the maneuver, the jockeying for position, the strategic intervention, the half-truth, the lie.[3] And secondly, by "recordmaking" I understand an equally huge and messy realm in which what are conventionally called records creators, records managers, archivists, users, and so on, negotiate, contest, and narrate the meanings and significances of what are conventionally called "records."[4] In this understanding, records are always in the process of being made, they open into (and out of) the future,[5] and what we call "archivists" are, whether they like it or not, members of a big family of recordmakers.

As I do the rounds, disciplinary and geographical, the dominant question I hear addressed to "the political" by recordmakers is along the lines of "What are we to do with this intruder?" (At the 2003 Liverpool conference, for instance, paper after paper addressed this question, implicitly or explicitly.) And so they construct codes of conduct that define their core principles as a defense against the dynamics of power and authority, which is precisely why most professional codes of conduct are entirely useless. Think about prominent recent cases of recordmakers becoming embroiled in clashes with power and authority, and mark how professional colleagues have used codes of conduct both to support and to condemn them.[6] In my reading of these cases, the confusion for professionals lies in the fact that codes of conduct eschew political contexts, thus reducing themselves to lucky packets rather than clear guides for action. Politics is not the intruder. It is the stuff of daily professional work. And the test of principle, the making of principle, the defining of ethics, happens in the crucible where principle and power engage, fast and loose, low down and dirty, sublimely and ridiculously. What we need is not the codification of theory and principle; rather, we need articulations of praxis (to use another register of "articulation," the articulating of theory and practice). The dominant question, I would argue, should be along the lines of "What should our politics be?"

This is the question I propose addressing in this essay. Before doing so, let me return briefly to the question of provenance. This essay does not mark the beginning of the address. In a sense, the question has troubled me for two decades, shaping everything I have attempted as a recordmaker. But in a tighter mode of context, it should be recorded that in March of 2004, I mounted a direct response to the question in a keynote address at a conference in Oslo with the theme "Archives in Multicultural Societies."[7] There I framed my argument within the contingencies of the moment (of course, none of us can ever escape entirely the limitations of contingency), so that three subquestions drew my attention: What do recordmakers make of a society (and this is true of all societies) to be documented in the context of multiple cultures positioned and oriented by the exercise of power? What is the responsibility of recordmakers in face of a deeply cultured record? What do recordmakers do with their own agency as culturers? These are questions I will address only tangentially here. They illustrate the chasm above which we all stand when we entertain the question, "What should our politics be?"

In September 2004, I presented a paper with the same title as this essay in Glasgow at the Society of Archivists' (U.K.) annual conference. The paper drew heavily from the Liverpool and Oslo papers, but was framed in the contexts of the conference theme "Accountability,

Citizenship and Ethics" and a session devoted to building on the platform constituted by the Liverpool conference. This essay is a modest reworking of the Glasgow paper.[8]

## OF JUSTICE

"What should our politics be?" At the risk of oversimplification, I want to suggest that the question invites attention to at least two dimensions—direction and contour. (Others, like language and idiom and content, require inquiry beyond the limitations of an essay.) To frame these two dimensions in the form of questions: "Where should our politics be taking us?" and "What should our politics look like?"

The "where?" question moves us irrevocably outside conventional disciplinary or professional boundaries. We are talking about a call, or a calling, that must come (structurally, logically) from beyond any rational demarcation. So that necessarily we find ourselves in a terrain that is about belief rather than analysis. I believe—and no doubt my belief is inextricably interwoven with my experiences as a South African who has lived through long struggles against oppression and is living now the struggles to bring democracy to the oppressed—I believe that the call of justice, the call for justice, is the highest calling. Here I find myself in congregation with thinkers like Jacques Derrida and Emmanuel Levinas. Listen for a moment to Peggy Kamuf reading Derrida reading the work of literary theorists. In her reading, Derrida "ties this work to its political responsibilities in the world it is attempting to think, a world whose horizon can only be justice. I would even say that the notion of *oeuvre* being elaborated here must be understood as this work of making connections to a world that *could* still be more just, that is thereby being urged or called to more justice, more justice for all, for all the living and the dead, past and still to come. To put it still more boldly or baldly: the work of the *oeuvre* is justice and resistance to injustice."[9] In the last decade of his life, Derrida engaged more and more directly the question of "archive," and this engagement invites a direct transposition from Kamuf's reading—for Derrida, the work of the archive is justice and resistance to injustice.[10] And to transpose one more time—the work of recordmaking is justice and resistance to injustice.

But what is this call we name "justice," and where does it come from? As I have argued elsewhere, following Derrida, "I don't believe [and remember, we are unavoidably in a terrain of belief rather than analysis] that justice, ultimately, can be knowable. Like democracy, it must always be coming. It is a phantom, at most 'a relation to the unconditional that, once all the conditional givens have been taken into account, bears witness to that which will not allow itself to be enclosed within a context."[11] The call of justice resists the totalization of every such enclosure. It resists, if you like, what is traditionally regarded as the fundamental archival impulse—contextualization. It is open to the future and to every "other." It respects—gives space to, looks again at—"radical otherness."[12] In the powerful formulation of Levinas: "the relation to the other, i.e., justice."[13]

I am *not* suggesting that the call of justice undermines archival endeavor by destroying the conceptual foundations of contextualization. I *am* arguing that justice requires us to re-imagine archival contextualization. Conventionally understood, contextualization has to do with the disclosing of all relevant contextual layers. That is to pin down meaning and significance. But (and I elaborate on this later in the essay) context is infinite, ever-changing, and permeable to "text," so that contextualization can only ever be about a preliminary and highly selective intervention, in which pinning down is not a possibility. The most that we can aspire to is an opening of contextual richness, and concomitantly, an opening to richness in meaning and significance. An approach that is about opening, in my view, respects the call of justice.[14] Justice resists pinning down, totalizing, signing off; justice embraces openness, a welcoming of what is coming, hospitality to what is beyond the limits of understanding. In a word, we must engage context, but let us do so knowing (and acknowledging) its horizon of impossibility.

## OF ACCOUNTABILITY

If the work of recordmaking is justice and resistance to injustice, what should our politics (the politics of we who are recordmakers) look like? The beginning of an answer takes us into that space we name "accountability." For the call of justice demands a response. It demands, in the first instance, a "yes!" But it also demands a giving of account. We are all accountable to (and responsible for) the call of justice. Discourses of accountability, generally, tend to emphasize the *giving* of account. I believe that if we are to emphasize any particular dimension, then it should be the *listening* to a call. As Robert Gibbs argues in his compelling book *Why Ethics?*: "We begin in a conversation, where two people respond to each other.... Moreover, the listening is primary. My first responsibility arises in listening to another person, not in speaking to her."[15] Listening, in my view, is the beginning of ethics, and it should be the beginning of politics.

To whom, and to what, should we recordmakers be listening? The short answer (the answer that Derrida and Levinas and Gibbs would surely offer) is that we should be listening to *every* "other." For justice is the relation to "the other." So, the inventory is endless—colleagues, communities, users, potential users, employers, lawmakers, governments, funders, forebears, descendants, strangers (especially strangers), and so on, and on. How to begin listening to them all? How to begin dealing with their insistent demands, how to begin weighing their often contradictory imperatives, how to even begin finding them all? I have no easy answer, certainly no blueprint. But let me suggest a preliminary move toward an appropriate politics of recordmaking, that is to say, a *just* politics of recordmaking, by focusing on "the record." I am not saying that the record should enjoy priority. I am proposing that the record is something we need to learn to listen to, and that our responsibility for it separates us (not wholly, but meaningfully) from the plumbers and lawyers and footballers seeking an appropriate politics. And it gives us a readily usable window into a complexity that will always be impossible to contain.

So, what is the record saying to us? Surely, by now, after two centuries of disciplined historiographical and archival inquiry, we have begun to hear at least the fundamentals of a message? Well, right here, here at the outset of an answer, we are confronted by an intractable complexity spinning in numerous directions. Let me tease out just two threads. On the one hand, history has shown that recordmakers hear either what they want to hear or what they are (en)able(d) to hear. In other words, in aphoristic mode, recordmakers cannot transcend their contexts.[16] And who are we to think that we can change this pattern? On the other hand, the record never speaks for itself. It speaks through many intermediaries—the people who created it, the functionaries who managed it, the archivists who selected it for preservation and make it available for use, and the researchers who use it in constructing accounts of the past. Far from enjoying an exteriority in relation to the record, all these intermediaries participate in the complex processes through which the record feeds into social memory. These intermediaries, of course, are all recordmakers. So that the imperative is (to simplify things somewhat) to listen to ourselves, arguably the most difficult form of listening.

So, the simple line of inquiry is already appearing impossible. And I am thrown, as all of us must be if we are honest with ourselves, into an intensely subjective space. What do *I* hear the record (through its many intermediaries, including myself) saying? Many things, obviously, often contradictory, often confusing, always enriching. But three seem fundamental. The first I have already named. It wants us to know that it is always already being made. Its stories are never ending. The stories of what are conventionally called records creators, records managers, archivists, users, and so on are (shifting, intermingling) parts of bigger stories understandable only in the ever-changing, broader contexts of society.

Secondly, the record invites us to acknowledge that, far from being an innocent byproduct of activity, a reflection of reality, it is a construction of realities expressing dominant relations of power. It privileges certain voices and cultures, while marginalizing or excluding others. This was very clear to us in South Africa during the apartheid era. It didn't take a genius to see how the state recordmaking system faithfully reproduced oppressive relations of power. And for the oppositional archives, the archives of resistance to oppression, it was easy to justify a counterarchive privileging anti-apartheid voices and cultures. But we make a mistake—and many of us in South Africa are making this mistake—when we think that the dynamics of privileging, marginalizing, and excluding occur only in extreme conditions. Ten years after liberation in South Africa, these dynamics can still be discerned in the record—the state recordmaking system is now privileging the new metanarratives of postapartheid liberation, democratization, reconciliation, and African Renaissance; archives like the South African History Archive,[17] on the other hand, are privileging the stories of continuing struggles for justice. This is because the record is always already a construction of realities. And because recordmakers construct realities with constructions of realities. And because the cultures of the state (including its archival system) are different from the cultures of continuing struggle.

Thirdly, the record invites us to acknowledge that its meanings and significances are located in the circumstances of its creation and subsequent use. In other words, context rather than text is the determining factor and we recordmakers should be *the* experts in context. However, even if we believe this, we are faced with daunting problems. Context is always infinite, and ever changing. So that, in the words of Derrida: "No context is absolutely saturable or saturating. No context can determine meaning to the point of exhaustiveness."[18] So, what layers of context do we disclose? How do we disclose them? Here, without thinking very hard, we are deeply into the politics of archival description. Furthermore, the boundary between "text" and "context" is permeable.[19] When we think we are dealing with text, we find elements of context leaping out at us. When we are sure that we are dealing with contexts, we find texts all around us. I am *not* suggesting that the concept of the record as a connection of "text" and "context" should be discarded. Nor that the terms "text" and "context" are without coherent (or distinguishable) meanings. I *am* suggesting that these terms and the concepts they bear are complex and troubled; that the semantic boundaries between them are shifting and porous. And that in using them—for use them we must—we should remember these realities.

## OF RESPONSIBILITIES

I am still attempting to respond to the question, "What should our politics look like?" I have given a sliver of a (more or less subjective) reading of one of many voices (an insistently multivocal voice) to which we should be listening as we formulate a response. So, partially (in the double sense of the word), I ask what seems to me to be the key subsidiary question: What responsibilities does the record (just one of many voices) place upon us?

Of course, there are many responsibilities. A whole book could be written on the topic. And how one reads them is determined to a large extent by one's own contexts, by one's own culturing. The four I outline below are simply those that have pressed most strongly on me through twenty years of working as an archivist in South Africa.

The first is the responsibility to understand. This is a call to understand the extent to which both the recordmaker and the record are woven through with the indeterminate and are cultured in a space defined by the political. State archivists in apartheid South Africa who declared themselves to be merely impartial custodians, and thus not implicated in the state's mobilization of the archive as a tool of oppression, epitomize a refusal to understand. State archivists in the South Africa of today who declare themselves to be merely impartial custodians, and thus not implicated in the state's mobilization of the archive as a tool of consensus building, epitomize the same refusal. The essay up to this point could be characterized as an attempt to promote such understanding.

Secondly, there is the responsibility to disclose. This is a call to make plain to users the culturing (a culturing broad and complex in its reach, but patterned decisively by the political) of both the record and the recordmaker. In essays elsewhere in this collection I have suggested what this might mean in practice for archivists engaged in appraisal and description.[20]

Thirdly, there is the responsibility to be hospitable, specifically to be hospitable to "the other"—the other ways of knowing and of doing, the ways outside a society's mainstream. For me, this responsibility works at two levels. In the first instance, it works at the level of what constitutes the record. In my part of the world there are indigenous knowledges that understand the record primarily in terms of the storyteller—the storyteller, configured in relation to performance and to community (past and present). This understanding (and we can call it an expression of culture) challenges the dominant Western notion of the record as the stable carrier of evidence. It challenges privilegings of writing over orality. It posits the record as characterized by its fluidity and the recordmaker as the tender of ever-shifting meanings and significances. Now, in postapartheid South Africa, mainstream archives have responded to this call of the other by rushing out to capture stories with video cameras and tape recorders. That, in my view, is not an expression of hospitality. The call, instead, is to respect the other, and to engage it with a willingness to have one's own ways of knowing and doing changed in the process.[21]

But this responsibility works at another level as well. As I have already argued, in this essay and elsewhere,[22] records express power relations. The voices and experiences of the weak, the underprivileged, the disadvantaged, the marginalized will either be in the margins of the record, or simply absent. In every society, the dominant cultures will dominate the record. Should recordmakers seek to document this reality in their work, or should they work against it by actively documenting the marginalized and the absent? The answer to this question, I would argue, ultimately resides outside recordmaking theory. It has to do with choices in political, ethical, and epistemological realms. It has to do with choices in the exercise of power. We could say a lot about this. But let me just pose a few questions. If we try to document the marginalized, will we misrepresent, will we negatively bias the interpretation of the record, and will our own biases do more damage than good? Can the mainstream ever accurately represent the marginal? How can we invite in what is always beyond our limits of understanding? How can we avoid the danger of speaking *for* these voices? How can we avoid reinforcing marginalization by naming "the marginalized"? How can we invite in what we wish to resist—the voices and the cultures, for instance, of white supremacists, or of hard-drug dealers, pedophiles, rapists, pimps, and so on, and on and on? In the memorable words of Gayatri Chakravorty Spivak: "Let us, then, for the moment at least, arrest the understandable need to fix and diagnose the identity of the most deserving marginal. Let us also suspend the mood of self-congratulation as saviors of marginality."[23] It is imperative that we not romanticize "otherness." We need to fear it even as we respect it. We need to understand that it is as much "inside" as it is "outside." We need to engage it, without blueprint, without solution, without ready answers.

Fourthly, and lastly, there is the responsibility to be active. This is a call to engage openly the politics of the record; to engage it very specifically within a shaping offered by the call of justice. In my country there is a long tradition of recordmakers being involved in struggles for justice. Under apartheid, as I have already argued, it was easy to see that the establishment's record had to be challenged, its privilegings, marginalizings, and exclusions countered. Today, the dominant discourse in South African recordmaking suggests that the time for activism is past. Activism was necessary in extreme conditions, so the argument runs, but now, with the coming of democracy, recordmakers can resume traditional mantles and focus on service delivery. South African society has been "normalized," and recordmakers should follow suit—that is, offer a professional and impartial service outside the buffetings of "politics." But this is to misunderstand democracy, and to misunderstand the record. As I have argued elsewhere, "Society is always an assemblage of competing interests and perspectives. As the British intellectual Richard Hoggart has reminded us: 'A well-running democracy will constantly quarrel with itself, publicly, about the right things and in the right way.'[24] The time for activism, in other words, is never past. When we give up on activism, we give up on democracy. And, to repeat myself, every record has its privilegings, marginalizings, and exclusions. In postapartheid South Africa this reality is not as monolithic and as crude as that which obtained in the past. But it is there, and it needs to be contested.

## OF JUSTICE (ONE MORE TIME)

All of us who call ourselves recordmakers, who are recordmakers (whether we acknowledge it or not), practice politics (whether we acknowledge it or not). The only pertinent question is, "What politics do we practice?" In this essay, I have made the argument for a politics driven and shaped by the call of justice. I hope that at least two strands to the argument have been evident—on the one hand, the strand that insists on *a* politics (in other words, a more or less conscious, more or less coherent, politics); on the other hand, the strand that insists on a *just* politics. I hope that I have demonstrated that the call of justice (ultimately, at the extreme of concepts like hearing and responsibility) is impossible to hear. The responsibilities I have outlined (drawn, more or less arbitrarily, or, from other perspectives, imperialistically) are at once political, ethical, epistemological, and professional. They are, by any measure, in any conceptual frame, within the contexts of any culture, impossible to fulfill. But it is in reaching for the impossible—with passion and faith and humility—that we begin to make a just politics of recordmaking possible.

# Endnotes

1   This essay was presented as a paper at the conference "Accountability, Citizenship and Ethics," Society of Archivists (U.K.), Glasgow, September 2004.

2   The paper I originally prepared for the conference was entitled "The Archive Is Politics: Truths, Powers, Records and Contestation in South Africa." In the weeks leading up to the conference, I prepared a separate (but derivative) paper that I entitled "Archives, Politics and Justice." It was published in *Political Pressure and the Archival Record* (Chicago: Society of American Archivists, 2005). An essay, titled "The Archive Is Politics" and drawn from work in progress for the Liverpool paper, was published in Marion Beyea, et al. eds., *The Power and Passion of Archives: A Festschrift in Honour of Kent Haworth* (Ottawa: Association of Canadian Archivists, 2005).

3   Jacques Derrida has asserted, following Hannah Arendt, that "politics is a privileged space of lying...." Derrida, *Without Alibi* (Stanford: Stanford University Press, 2002), 39.

4   For an extended making of the argument, see Wendy Duff and Verne Harris, "Stories and Names: Archival Description as Narrating Records and Constructing Meanings," *Archival Science* 2, nos. 3–4 (2002).

5   It was Jacques Derrida who coined the phrase "the archive opens out of the future" in *Archive Fever: A Freudian Impression* (Chicago: University of Chicago Press, 1996), 68.

6   Here I refer to cases like Chris Hurley in Australia, Brigitte Laine in France, me in South Africa.

7   "The Cultured Archive: An Interrogation of the Nexus Between Archive and Culture from a South African Perspective," keynote address at the conference "Archives in Multicultural Societies," convened by the Norwegian Archive, Library and Museum Authority (ABM-Utvikling), Oslo, April 2004. The paper is due to be published in Norwegian by the ABM-Utvliking as part of a collection of texts within the series *ABM-skrift*.

8   In reworking the text I have drawn on comments offered by Eric Ketelaar and a number of people who attended the conference. I am grateful to all of them.

9   Peggy Kamuf in Derrida, *Without Alibi,* 21.

10  See my reading of Derrida on the archive in my essay "A Shaft of Darkness: Derrida in the Archive," in Carolyn Hamilton, et al., eds., *Refiguring the Archive* (Cape Town: David Philip, 2002).

11  Jacques Derrida and Maurizio Ferraris, *A Taste for the Secret* (Cambridge, U.K.: Polity, 2001), 17.

12  Derrida and Ferraris, *A Taste for the Secret,* 21.

13  Quoted in Derrida and Ferraris, *A Taste for the Secret,* 56.

14  A growing number of theorists and practitioners, using different terms and offering a variety of emphases, are exploring approaches to archival contextualization that are about opening. In my reading, the theoretical groundbreaking work was done by Terry Cook, Tom Nesmith, Eric Ketelaar, and continuum thinkers in Australia.

15  Robert Gibbs, *Why Ethics? Signs of Responsibilities* (Princeton, N.J.: Princeton University Press, 2000), 30.

16  Terry Cook has demonstrated this hard truth repeatedly, most powerfully in the following three essays: "Electronic Records, Paper Minds: The Revolution in Information Management and Archives in the Post-custodial and Post-

modernist Era," *Archives and Manuscripts, 22*, no. 2 (1994); "What Is Past Is Prologue: A History of Archival Ideas since 1898, and the Future Paradigm Shift," *Archivaria* 43 (1997); and "Fashionable Nonsense or Professional Rebirth: Postmodernism and the Practice of Archives," *Archivaria* 51 (2001).

17  The South African History Archive is a nonprofit, nongovernmental organization, first established in the 1980s to document the struggles against apartheid. Its mission now is to document and contribute to continuing struggles for justice.

18  Jacques Derrida, *Aporias* (Stanford: Stanford University Press, 1993), 9.

19  For an extended argument supporting this assertion, see my *Exploring Archives: An Introduction to Archival Ideas and Practice in South Africa,* 2nd ed. (Pretoria: National Archives, 2000), 81–88.

20  See "Postmodernism and Archival Appraisal: Seven Theses," *South African Archives Journal* 40 (1998) and "Stories and Names".

21  I first made this argument in Verne Harris and Sello Hatang, "Archives Identity and Place: A Dialogue on What it (Might) Mean(s) to be an African Archivist," *ESARBICA Journal* 19 (2000).

22  See Harris and Duff, "Stories and Names," 278–79.

23  Gayatri Chakravorty Spivak, *Outside in the Teaching Machine* (New York: Routledge, 1993), 61.

24  Quoted in Christopher Merrett, "A Tale of Two Paradoxes: Media Censorship in South Africa, Pre-Liberation and Post-Apartheid," *Critical Arts* 15, nos. 1–2 (2001): 64.

# SECTION IV

# PASTS AND SECRETS

# CHAPTER 16

## Toward a Culture of Transparency: Public Rights of Access to Official Records in South Africa[1]

*Verne Harris and Christopher Merrett*

"Open government is a contradiction in terms. You can have openness. Or you can have government. You can't have both."[2] This was the opinion of the archetypal British civil service mandarin, Sir Humphrey, in the British Broadcasting Corporation (BBC) TV comedy series *Yes Minister.*[3] One of that series' many virtues was the humor it created out of reality; and to show that it was well based in real events, one need go no further than a circular about greater openness distributed by British premier Margaret Thatcher's private secretary in 1979—which is classified and embargoed until 2010. Secrecy is fundamental to the British system of government, providing a model we believe to be antithetical to South Africa's requirements.

## BACKGROUND

If South Africa is ever to become a participative democracy it will require first, a large number of educated people, and second, information. Without background knowledge about issues and the way government has tackled and intends to tackle them, the ability of the electorate to make informed and intelligent decisions, especially in an increasingly technologically based society, is limited. Knowledge does not equal power, as the cliché would have it, but power cannot be exercised without it. Information is essential to efficient and thereby effective democracy, which is why the concept of the right to know is recognized as fundamental in democratic societies. Informed judgments and choices are attributes of a responsible citizenry.

Politicians and public servants are, understandably, not comfortable with the notion of transparency, preferring to operate beyond the glare of public scrutiny. In apartheid South Africa this was especially apparent, with government and the operations of its bureaucracies being cloaked in secrecy. Official secrecy (also known as "statutory censorship") was framed in legislation that controlled vast areas of public life and gravely inhibited the press from comprehensive reporting of national affairs. This is not to say that the restrictions on public access to official records were, and still are, exceptional. Indeed, in an international context, South Africa compares reasonably favorably. But it is to say that these restrictions were manipulated to secure an extraordinary degree of opacity in government and that South Africa's national information system became grossly distorted to the benefit of government propaganda in an attempt to preserve the power of a white elite and its allies. And it is to say that as we move toward a democracy, it is crucial to remember that the public's right of access to official records, and its right to place the processes of government under scrutiny, are defining characteristics of democracy. The more transparent government is, the more vigorous is democracy.

From the mid-1950s until the late 1980s, information on certain topics became difficult, and even dangerous, to acquire. Real debate on vital issues was hampered by both a dearth of information and punitive action by the government against dissenting opinion.[4] To varying degrees, information about the following was circumscribed:

- Business, foreign trade, and sanctions
- Capital punishment, especially racial bias in sentencing
- Conscientious objection to military service
- Corruption and cases of fraud
- Detention without trial and the treatment of detainees
- Liberation movements and their activities and policies

- Mental health institutions
- Military incursions into Angola and repression in Namibia
- Nuclear power and the development of nuclear weapons
- Oil supplies and reserves
- Police involvement in repression in South Africa
- Prisons and the treatment of prisoners
- Territorial consolidation of black homelands (*bantustans*)
- Weapons procurement and development

These are all topics about which voters and taxpayers have a right to be well informed. Current legislation restricting access to relevant information can be classified very broadly as follows:

- Acts that control official information (e.g., Archives Act, Protection of Information Act, Statistics Act)
- Acts that restrict information from all sources on specific topics (e.g., Nuclear Energy Act, Petroleum Products Act)
- Acts that regulate administrative and legal functions (e.g., Criminal Procedure Act, Disclosure of Foreign Funding Act, Inquests Act)
- Other acts extending government power (e.g., Indemnity Act, Internal Security Act, Publications Act)

Did South Africa explode a nuclear device in the southern Indian Ocean on 22 September 1979, and if so, who else was involved? Which countries have transferred technology to South Africa in the course of developing its arms and nuclear industries? Who lost the country $30 million in 1979 by paying twice for a stolen cargo of oil from the tanker *Salem?* Why did the plane of the president of Mozambique, Samora Machel, crash just inside South Africa in October 1986? Was the South African Airways plane *Helderberg* carrying volatile material for Armscor, South Africa's armaments corporation, in defiance of international air traffic regulations, when it crashed off Mauritius in 1987? Who was responsible for the deaths of numerous anti-apartheid activists?[5] These are all legitimate questions of public interest to which we have a right to expect comprehensive answers. In each case, our knowledge is deficient, hampered by official secrecy.

# OFFICIAL SECRECY AND THE "NEW" SOUTH AFRICA

The situation has improved slightly since 1990 without major changes to legislation. The exceptionally high level of secrecy began to break down as government confidence waned and investigative journalism flourished, reinforced by lessons learned by the democratic movement during the State of Emergency, 1985–1990. The *Weekly Mail, Vrye Weekblad,* and *New / Sunday Nation,* for instance, published exposés on certain aspects of prisons; psychiatric hospitals; the activities of hit squads and "special forces"; arms supplies to Rwanda, Iraq, and Israel; oil supplies; and the Inkathagate funding scandal.[6] The authorities have threatened legal action in some cases but seem less sure of themselves than they were a few years ago. From this, it is possible to draw the lesson that watertight control in the sphere of information requires confidence on the part of the authorities. During 1992, laws about the police and prisons were relaxed; and Reg Rumney, writing in the *Weekly Mail* about oil supplies, remarked that he was able to work, for the first time in years, without the fear of "the Special Branch paying visits to researchers who asked too many questions about the ... industry."[7]

However, Max du Preez, editor of *Vrye Weekblad,* was convicted and fined under the Protection of Information Act in 1990 for publishing news that an institute attached to Stellenbosch University acted as a conduit for information to the National Intelligence Service. The same act was invoked in a fraud case, which revealed the fact that the Civil Cooperation Bureau (CCB, a covert operations unit of the South African Defence Force) was interfering in the affairs of another state. No further evidence about this interference was allowed in court. In November 1990, the trial of a conscientious objector, Michael Graaf, was hurriedly adjourned when he revealed details about security force actions in Namibia as part of his evidence, thus infringing the Defence Act. As Mathew Blatchford remarked, "The armed forces operate in secret, a secrecy protected by a huge number of interlocking statutes.... Without this concealment the South African public might have been revolted by what the armed forces have done."[8]

Secrecy has been a worrying and prominent feature of the "new" South Africa. Commentary on the Conference for a Democratic

South Africa (CODESA) in 1992 and on the work of the Advisory Committee on Land Reform (ACLA)[9] has been especially critical of the secrecy involved. A particularly worrying current issue is that concerning South Africa's nuclear weapons. In 1991, South Africa signed the Nuclear Non-Proliferation Treaty, which opened up its stockpile to inspection by the International Atomic Energy Authority (IAEA). The IAEA fears that because the nuclear program was secret and unmonitored for so long, weapons-grade material is undocumented. U.S. government sources suggest that the South African authorities have shredded documents concerning the nuclear program and may have fabricated records showing how much enriched uranium it produced. There is a major worry that material unaccounted for may fall into the wrong hands. Hidden from the public was the fact that South Africa had developed battlefield nuclear weapons that could be launched from Armscor's G5 and G6 guns, capable of projecting a two-kiloton warhead forty-two kilometers. Another fact that was carefully concealed was the amount of international assistance given to this country. The image of a robust, defiant economy becoming self-sufficient in armaments was largely propaganda; enormous amounts of assistance were provided by Germany, the United States, France, Canada, and Israel.[10]

Perhaps the most blatant potential use of secrecy is found in the Further Indemnity Act of 1992, which provides for a National Indemnity Council to meet in secret to decide who should receive indemnity for political crimes. Evidence and documentation are strictly confidential (section 10 of the act). This measure was rejected even by South Africa's unrepresentative, pre-April 1994 Parliament and forced through via the appointed President's Council. Enforced amnesia about the past is no beginning for a society requiring openness.[11] Hilda Bernstein writes evocatively in a recent essay on South Africa's history as one of "torn and missing pages."[12] We need to complete some of those pages by finding out who did what to whom and why: reconciliation requires truth and justice. South African journalist Philip van Niekerk argues persuasively that "there are matters of honour, of setting the record straight, of making sense of the sad history of our country that still require the truth."[13]

Another tool (and, ultimately, the most effective) in securing enforced amnesia is the deliberate destruction of official records.

Numerous cases of such action have been documented and many more alleged since the late 1980s. They point to a widespread and systematic endeavor to eliminate incriminating material. Perhaps the most blatant example surfaced in 1993 when the National Intelligence Service (NIS) advised central government departments to destroy certain classified records, especially those concerning the work of the National Security Management System (NSMS). The action rested on a state-generated legal opinion that exempted classified records from the operation of the Archives Act. Lawyers for Human Rights contested the validity of the action in a Supreme Court application, which resulted in an out-of-court settlement effectively overturning the legal opinion. All the parties involved agreed that classified records qualify as archives in terms of the Archives Act and that their destruction can be authorized only by the director of archives.

The long-term survival of security police files is an issue that has been addressed frequently. At the Library and Information Workers (LIWO) Conference held in Cape Town in 1992, Albie Sachs—lawyer, former political detainee, and adviser to the African National Congress—pointed out that these files constitute the most comprehensive biographical dictionary in South Africa. Some would say, knowing the amount of inaccurate information they contain and something about the experience of revealing police files in East Germany,[14] that their continued confidentiality is perhaps a good thing. There is also the fear that documents seized from anti-apartheid organizations by the security police over the years have been destroyed.

There are thus two main reasons why South Africans should be concerned about freedom of information and its relation to a future democratic society. First, South Africans must reclaim their history. Any nation that has an incomplete understanding of its past rests on shaky foundations, and there are parallels here with the German experience after the Second World War. Second, government must be made accountable, especially in the light of the historically repressive role of the South African state. In view of this, South Africa needs to develop freedom of information rights, law, and practice concentrating not just on the relation between government and individual, as in some countries,[15] but on redressing socioeconomic inequities as well.

# TRANSPARENT GOVERNMENT: PRINCIPLES, METHODS, AND AN ARCHIVAL PERSPECTIVE[16]

It is widely accepted that governments have a legitimate right on behalf of the citizenry as a whole to restrict access to certain information. The parameters of this right need not be, however, as wide as most governments would like us to believe. Certainly, the South African government's systematic use of secrecy laws in the apartheid era is insupportable—a use meant to confuse the security of the state with the protection of party political and other sectional interests, and to cover up human rights abuses, corruption, and maladministration. In a real sense, the state became dedicated to secrecy, and dissent was equated with treason. Transforming official secrecy by both defining its legitimate parameters in a democracy and providing the instruments for testing its validity in specific instances will be one of the major challenges facing postapartheid South Africa.

The health of a nation depends upon a good measure of dissent and unfettered questioning. One of the speakers in the freedom of information debate in the British House of Commons in February 1993 described secrecy as a "corrosive disease." Philip van Niekerk has made the telling point that the litmus test of any political movement's commitment to society is its policy on freedom of speech and information;[17] and Tony Heard (a former editor of the *Cape Times)* quite correctly argues that "deceit, secrecy and obfuscation have been the norms for four decades" and points to the danger of "trip switching from one sterile era of conformity to another."[18]

Official secrecy will not be reduced to reasonable proportions by legislative reform alone: for instance, by repealing statutory censorship clauses embedded in a multiplicity of laws and loosening the Protection of Information Act. The right to information must be entrenched in a constitution or bill of rights guaranteed by an independent judiciary. A climate of greater openness can be assured in the long term only by changes in the attitudes of individuals and groups and by a radical alteration of the national ethos. South Africans must become less deferential to those with political and economic power, more cynical about their motives, and more ready to challenge them, if necessary, in imaginative ways.

This is embodied in calls for a strong and resilient civil society independent of government, in which trade unions, churches, the press, universities, professions, and librarians and information workers act as society's watchdogs in such matters. Certainly there can be no such freedom without a vigorous, pluralistic, free press with high standards of journalism, especially in the field of investigative reporting. This is a unifying issue, which should appeal also to conservative elements in society as it has potential for more efficient government, greater accountability, and a higher quality of decision making.

It is the authors' contention that archival law and practice hold the key to some of the issues raised above. The Archives Act, after all, lays down the legal framework for public rights of access to official records. Until recently, South African archivists, in both professional debate and practice, tended to identify the making available of records as just one of many archival functions.[19] At last, however, there appears to be consensus among archivists in South Africa that the use of archives is the goal of all their endeavor. In its *1993 Professional Code,* the South African Society of Archivists, for example, begins a definition of the archival mission as follows: "The archivist is responsible for ensuring the availability and use of permanently valuable archives by identification, acquisition, description and preservation."[20] This implies a powerful imperative to provide optimum access to archives, something elaborated elsewhere in the *Professional Code.*[21] However, in striving to meet this imperative, archivists are constrained by a range of often-conflicting rights and interests: as the *Professional Code* goes on to warn in the remainder of its mission statement, "Accountability to the archives creator, employer and user should shape the performance of these tasks."

Archivists clearly do not operate in a professional vacuum, as a hypothetical situation can illustrate. A student researching the social history of Soweto requests permission to consult a hundred files. Half of these files fall within the "closed period" as defined by the Archives Act, and they have to be withheld until the director of archives has cleared them for access on the basis of a thorough examination of their contents. Guidelines are applied, and three of the files, coincidentally all dated 1977, present difficulties. One is a South African Police file containing names and addresses of police informers: providing access to it could reasonably be expected to endanger the lives or physical safety of these people. The second file is that of a government Commission of Inquiry into violence, which contains evidence submitted to it by residents of Soweto on condition that their names not be made public. Would making the file available to the student constitute a breach of confidence and/or endanger the witnesses' physical safety? The third file documents Department of Manpower services to persons with disabilities in Soweto, and it contains intelligence tests, psychological profiles, and other confidential matter relating to individuals. Providing access to it would involve an infringement of these people's right to privacy. The recommendation, a hard but straightforward one, is that access to all three files be denied. But what if another researcher requests access to these files in twenty years' time, when they no longer fall within the closed period? Legally there will be no constraint on access, but, we would submit, it is unclear whether by then the balance of rights and interests will in reality have shifted in favor of the researcher.

Archivists have a professional obligation to ensure optimum access to the archives in their custody. This is especially true of public archivists, for most of their holdings are public records. As already suggested, one of the critical gauges of democracy is the degree to which the public's right of access to such records is recognized. Nevertheless, there are legitimate limitations on this right. The remainder of this article explores the current parameters of this right and ways in which those parameters might be revised.

## RIGHT OF ACCESS TO OFFICIAL RECORDS IN SOUTH AFRICA: THE PARAMETERS

Excluded from this discussion are South Africa's various "independent" and "self-governing" homelands, whose relevant legislation and administrative practices warrant a study of their own. Also excluded are the numerous public services that have been privatized in recent years. Suffice it to say that, while they are free to determine access provisions for records postdating privatization, their preprivatization records are subject to the measures described below.

Official records are kept either in the state office that has generated or inherited them or in a State Archives Service repository. The fundamental guideline for public access to records *in state offices* is laid down in the Archives Act:

Subject to provisions of any other law no person shall have access to any archives in a government office or an office of a local authority: provided that the head of such office may, in his discretion and on such conditions as he may determine, but subject to the directions of the Minister [of National Education] and the provisions of this Act and any other law, authorize any person to have access to such archives.[22]

Public access to the vast majority of official records in state offices, whatever the age of the records, is a *privilege* granted by senior administrative officials. Moreover, the power to grant this privilege is circumscribed by a range of legislation containing secrecy clauses, notably the Protection of Information Act (mentioned earlier). On the other hand, there is legislation that secures the right of access to specific categories of records in state offices—for instance, to deceased estate files in the custody of Masters of the Supreme Court—but the number of record categories covered by such legislation is insignificant.

Before turning to the position in State Archives Service repositories, two classes of state office deserve special mention. First, the so-called offices of record are defined as offices "responsible for documents which require special treatment in order to ensure that the authenticity and legality of the contents cannot be questioned."[23] These documents are exempt from the Archives Act and are in the custody of institutions such as Parliament, the Registrar of Deeds, and the Registrar of Births, Marriages, and Deaths. Some of them are governed by legislation providing for public access to their records, but others are not.

A second atypical class of state office is the South African Defence Force (SADF). Many countries recognize the particularly sensitive nature of military records and a need for longer-term confidentiality. In South Africa, the Archives Act allows for a separate SADF-controlled archives repository and makes access to SADF archives dependent upon approval from the minister of national education acting in consultation with the minister of defense.[24] In effect, the public enjoys no right of access whatever to military archives, no matter the age of those archives. A person wishing to consult records related to the First World War is as dependent upon the discretionary power of the two ministers' delegated officials as someone researching the 1975 invasion of Angola. Access to classified records depends on the successful negotiation of a security clearance process, which can take anywhere between six weeks and six months.[25]

The Archives Act requires that offices subject to it transfer their permanently valuable records to a repository of the State Archives Service when the records reach thirty years of age, unless the minister of national education authorizes extended retention.[26] Such extended retention has been authorized in numerous cases, always on the grounds that the records concerned have longer-term (sometimes indefinite) administrative value to the state office that has custody of them. Examples of this type of record are contracts, agreements, maps, and plans. While there is little doubt that the extended retention arrangement is appropriate in these cases, it does mean that, for as long as the records remain outside the custody of the State Archives Service, the public enjoys no right of access to them.

Public access to records older than thirty years in an Archives Service repository is unrestricted, unless the minister of national education withdraws access on the grounds of "public policy."[27] Given that the Archives Act does not define what is meant by "public policy" in this context, this provision affords the minister authority to restrict access arbitrarily. For example, in the 1980s it was used without public explanation to close access to records younger than fifty years of six offices (Governor-General, State President, Public Service Commission, Commissioner of Police, Inland Revenue, and Home Affairs) and to close access to the post-1910 records of a further four (Executive Council, Prime Minister, Foreign Affairs, and Information). These restrictions were lifted in 1991, and in practice constituted only a minor infringement of public access to the records concerned. Between 1980 and 1990, requests for permission to consult 2,381 items in the archives of these offices were received, and access was denied to only nine items. Moreover, it should be noted that this case was exceptional: extended closure is applied rarely and, as far as can be ascertained, in all other cases with due regard for the interests of all parties concerned. Nevertheless, it does illustrate that it is imperative for the grounds on which public policy restrictions can be applied to be established in law.

Not all records in repositories of the State Archives Service are older than thirty years. Offices subject to the Archives Act may place records in repositories before the obligatory transfer point is reached.

Public access to such records is restricted by the thirty-year closed period applicable to all official records in Archives Service repositories.[28] Access to them can be secured only with the special permission of the director of archives. As with the public policy restrictions mentioned above, in practice this restriction is far from severe: in the period 1980 to 1990, special permission was granted for access to 6,750 items, while permission was refused in the case of only 159 items, this despite the fact that before 1991 special access was denied to items loosely defined as "sensitive." Since 1991, the director has applied a comprehensive set of guidelines for closed period applications that identify information categories widely accepted as requiring prolonged confidentiality.[29] This is a significant improvement, but it still falls short of the need for publicly debated legislation that lays down the grounds on which "closed period" applications can be refused.

Lone voices in South Africa's archival profession have questioned the need for a closed period at all. They point to the examples of the United States and Canada, where a closed period has been dispensed with and rights to confidentiality are protected by statute, court decision, and, in the case of the United States, by presidential executive order.[30] It must be conceded that good government requires some measure of extended confidentiality and that a closed period is an easily administered means of affording it at the same time as providing effective protection of the range of rights to confidentiality, which archivists must respect. Provision for a closed period is common practice internationally, with most countries opting for a period of thirty years. A 1979 amendment to the Archives Act reduced the period in South Africa from fifty to thirty years, although the five-yearly opening of archives means that effectively the period fluctuates between thirty and thirty-five years. However, even if the need for a closed period is accepted in principle, the question of what constitutes a reasonable period must be addressed. It is worth noting in this regard that one southern African country, Zambia, applies a twenty-year closed period.

## REVISING THE PARAMETERS: PROPOSALS

In South Africa, as in most countries, the state's point of departure is that public access to official records in state offices and to records less than thirty years old in archives repositories is a privilege, not a right. With the exception of the few record categories for which legislation provides access, the public, whether academics, journalists, or casual researchers, are dependent on the discretionary powers of public servants. Academics and journalists have frequently expressed the view that this state of affairs (1) curtails access to official information unreasonably and (2) affords the state an inordinate degree of protection. More recently, support for this view has been expressed in other quarters. A South African Society of Archivists position paper, for example, argues that "access to information is a right rather than a privilege" and that "there should be free access to public information and any restrictions on this right should be defined in law." The architects of the country's new interim constitution have recognized freedom of information as one of the document's fundamental "constitutional principles": "Provision shall be made for freedom of information so that there can be open and accountable administration at all levels of government."[31] However, in its statement of "fundamental rights," the interim constitution severely circumscribes the scope of this freedom: "Every person shall have the right of access to all information held by the state or any of its organs at any level of government in so far as such information is required for the protection or exercise of any of his or her rights."[32] Further legislation is required to provide a finer definition of the limits to the right of access.

Clearly, archivists who take seriously the imperative to provide optimum access to information need to look closely at the possibilities provided by freedom of information legislation. In particular, they need to examine the implementation of such legislation in Sweden, the United States, Canada, Australia, and France. In Sweden, for example, freedom of information is recognized as a public right in the country's Freedom of the Press Act: "To further free interchange of opinions and enlightenment of the public every Swedish national shall have free access to official documents."[33] Interestingly, Sweden first legislated freedom of information in 1766, and the freedom has been in place continuously since 1809.[34] However, the right is not an absolute one, its limits being set as follows:

The right to have access to official documents may be restricted only if restrictions are necessary considering:

1. The security of the Realm or its relations to a foreign state or to an international organization.

2. The central financial policy, the monetary policy, or the foreign exchange policy of the Realm.

3. The activities of a public authority for the purpose of inspection, control, or other supervision.

4. The interest of prevention or prosecution of crime.

5. The economic interests of the State or the communities.

6. The protection of the personal integrity or the economic conditions of individuals.

7. The interests of preserving animal or plant species.[35]

These limits may seem imprecise for practical purposes, but a separate Secrecy Act, running to ninety pages of text, defines in great detail what is meant by each. Implementation of such legislation can be costly and problematic. The U.S. Freedom of Information Act initially spawned a huge body of litigation around such matters as its interpretation, requests for either access to or destruction of records, and requests for either the prevention of access or the prevention of destruction. In addition, there were fears that it inhibited both the documentation of decision making by officials and the submission of information to federal agencies by private individuals and organizations.[36] Equivalent legislation for South Africa should pay heed to lessons learned elsewhere.

Six other aspects of public access to official records seem to demand attention. All of them could be addressed by freedom of information legislation, but they are not conceptually bound to it:

1. Public rights of access to records in the custody of all "offices of record" should be defined in legislation.

2. Public rights of access to SADF records should be established in law. Obviously, due regard would have to be paid to the

longer-term confidentiality required to protect the nation's defense and security interests.

3. If a closed period is to be retained, the question of what constitutes a reasonable period should be debated vigorously. The five-yearly opening of archives, a clumsy and unwarranted procedure, should be dropped in favor of an annual opening, which is common practice internationally.

4. Access to closed-period records in State Archives Service repositories should be provided for in legislation that (a) lays down the procedures for securing such access and (b) defines record categories that cannot be consulted. The State Archives Service's present guidelines for closed-period applications could be used as a basis for such a definition, although a comparative study of freedom of information restrictions in Sweden, the United States, Canada, Australia, and France would be invaluable.

5. Record categories requiring closure periods longer than the closed period should be defined in legislation. It is common practice internationally for extended closure to be used as a means of protecting the reasonable defense, security, and foreign policy interests of the state and the right of individual citizens to privacy.[37] As argued earlier, the current reliance on public policy decisions to secure such protection invites abuse. Moreover, it fails to provide public servants with adequate reassurance that their legitimate interests will be protected. In part, this explains the deep mistrust that surfaced during the debate on the status of classified official records (discussed earlier): officials simply do not trust the Archives Act to secure them a reasonable measure of protection. Extended closure legislation would go some way toward reassuring officials that it is not necessary to destroy sensitive records.

6. There is an urgent need for comprehensive legislation that defines the full scope of the right to personal privacy. Until the new interim constitution recognized the protection of pri-

vacy as a fundamental right,[38] it was recognized in a variety of contexts and laws. State Archives Service employees, while not bound by the Archives Act to protect private information in their custody, had the closed period and extended closure option at their disposal. Ultimately, however, the protection afforded was haphazard and partial. One result of privacy legislation will be to extend individuals' rights of access to information about themselves in the custody of the state, but another result will be a major limitation on freedom of information. The relative values of the right to privacy and the right to information have been the subject of intense debate, notably in courts of law, in countries that have established both rights.[39] The position appears less complex when access to information is sought specifically for research purposes, as Eric Ketelaar has argued compellingly: "In a conflict between the protected freedom for some—the freedom of research—and the protected freedom for all—the right of privacy—the former has to yield."[40]

## CONCLUSION

Apartheid South Africa was secretive to an abnormal degree, and its very survival was to a large extent based on such secrecy. Under these conditions, the press was unable to discharge its responsibility to keep the populace adequately informed. In a democracy, the public should enjoy the right of access to official information. However, this does not translate into a demand for the indiscriminate opening of all official records. On the contrary, there are numerous legitimate restrictions on this democratic right. The great American archivist T. R. Schellenberg captured the leitmotiv that should inform our thinking on access when he said, "Records should be open for use to the maximum extent that is consistent with the public interest."[41] A society that realizes this goal in any great measure will surely also enjoy in its public life the transparency that both demonstrates and fosters democracy. In striving for this goal, it is vital that the process itself should promote a culture of transparency; in other words, broad-based public debate should be a vital element. As Eric Ketelaar has stated so eloquently:

In a democracy the debate about selection and access should be a public debate, subject to verification and control by the public. If one cannot discuss publicly the moral arguments for secrecy, society runs the risk of creating Stasi and KGB archives—archives not for the people, but against the people.[42]

# Endnotes

1 This essay was first published in the *American Archivist* 57, no. 4 (1994). It was derived from separate papers delivered by the joint authors: "Towards a Culture of Transparency," given by Verne Harris at the South African Society of Archivists (Transvaal Branch) seminar "Archives Accessibility: A Limited Right?," Pretoria, 11 November 1993; and "What's Public Is Propaganda, What's Secret Is Serious: Official Secrecy and Freedom of Information in South Africa," presented by Christopher Merrett at the Annual General Meeting of the Western Cape branch of the Library and Information Workers' Organisation, Cape Town, 7 October 1993. The final draft text was prepared during the run-up to the April 1994 general election. It therefore reflects the position that obtained immediately before the introduction of South Africa's new interim constitution.

2 Quoted by Mark Fisher, Labour MP for Stoke Central, introducing the Second Reading of his Right to Know Bill to the British House of Commons, 19 February 1993.

3 *Yes Minister* was reputed to be Margaret Thatcher's favorite television program. If true, this shows either that she has a well-developed sense of humor or none whatsoever.

4 This was compounded by security and emergency legislation that restricted information on civil unrest and protest action, as well as by the views of the liberation movements and any organizations deemed to be "communist."

5 Some of the more notable assassinations involved Richard Turner (Durban, 1978), Matthew Goniwe and three companions from Cradock (Eastern Cape, 1985), and Anton Lubowski (Windhoek, 1989).

6 This involved the covert funding of Inkatha, the governing party in the KwaZulu homeland, through the security police.

7 R. Rumney, "A Little Light on the Oil Industry" *Weekly Mail,* 11 June 1993, 21.

8 *Democracy in Action* October–November 1990, 15.

9 An editorial in *Farmers Weekly* complained that membership of ACLA was based on political appointments and that ACLA's recommendations were secret. It argued that the judicial process should be used to settle land claims in open courts so that justice could be seen to be done.

10 S. Coll and P. Taylor, "Is Pretoria Being Honest on Nuclear Weapons?" *Guardian Weekly*, 26 March 1993, 18; S. Laufer and A. Gavshon, "The Real Reasons for SA's Nukes," *Weekly Mail,* 26 March 1993, 3; P. Van Niekerk, "Whose Information Is It Anyway?" *Weekly Mail*, 26 March 1993, 4; *Guardian Weekly,* 2 April 1993; *Southscan*, 14 May 1993, 138.

11 C. E. Merrett, "Amnesia by Decree," *Index on Censorship* 22, nos. 5–6 (1993): 21–22.

12 H. Bernstein, "Discovering Exiles," *Southern African Review of Books* 5 (July–August 1993): 12.

13 P. Van Niekerk, "The Riddle of the Red Herrings," *Weekly Mail,* 27 August 1993, 27.

14 People discovered that their spouses or children informed on them, information they might have been better without. In South Africa there is also the distinct possibility that false information supplied to the police out of malice or ignorance is now accepted as truth and that the reputations of honorable people will be sullied forever. The irony of freedom of information achieving the ends of a now disgraced and disbanded security police would be complete.

15  In Australia, 28,247 freedom of information (FOI) requests were received in 1991–92, at a cost of AUS$12.7 million. Full-time equivalent staff employed on FOI matters were 203. Most of the requests (92%) concerned veterans' affairs, social security, taxation, immigration, local government, and ethnic affairs. Other issues (about 6%) included education, housing, defense, police, and foreign affairs. Only 4 percent of requests were refused entirely, and 19 percent in part. Attorney-General's Department, Freedom of Information Act, 1982, *Annual Report, 1991–1992* (Canberra: Australian Government Publishing Service, 1992).

16  Little has been written on the topic of freedom of information in South Africa. See, however, M. Robertson, ed., *Human Rights for South Africans* (Cape Town: OUP, 1991), 131–37; A. Sachs, *Protecting Human Rights in a New South Africa* (Cape Town: OUP, 1990), 52, 145; A. Sachs, *Advancing Human Rights in South Africa* (Cape Town: OUP, 1992), 37, 213.

17  P. Van Niekerk, "Banging the Rights Drum (But the Sound Jars)," *Weekly Mail,* 5 March 1993, 6.

18  A. Heard, "Honesty Will Be the Government's Best Policy," *Weekly Mail,* 6 August 1993, 36.

19  V. Harris, "Community Resource or Scholars' Domain? Archival Public Programming and the User as a Factor in Shaping Archival Theory and Practice," *SA Archives Journal* 35 (1993): Introduction, 5.

20  South African Society of Archivists, *Professional Code for South African Archivists* (1993), paragraph 2.

21  SASA, *Professional Code,* paragraphs 4.4 to 4.6.

22  Archives Act (no. 6 of 1962, as amended), Section 9(6). The act's definition of *archives* embraces all records, both current and noncurrent.

23  State Archives Service, *Handbook* (Pretoria: State Archives Service, 1991), 15:35.

24  Archives Act, Section 9(7).

25  Discussion with Commandant C. M. L. Pretorius, SADF Documentation Service, October 1993.

26  Archives Act, Section 6 read in conjunction with Section 3(2)(b).

27  Archives Act, Section 9(2)(i).

28  Archives Act, Section 9(2).

29  These guidelines were modeled on Australian archival legislation.

30  National Archives of Canada Act, 1987; P. Carucci, "The National or Federal Archives: Systems, Problems and Perspectives," *Archivum* 26 (1991): 210–11.

31  Interim Constitution, Schedule 4, Section 9.

32  Interim Constitution, Chapter 3, Section 23.

33  Riksdag, *Constitutional Documents of Sweden: Amendments to the Instrument of Government, the Riksdag Act and the Freedom of the Press Act,* Stockholm (1978), 18.

34  N. Nilsson, "Archives in Sweden since the Second World War," *Archief-en Bibliotheekwezen in Belgie* 1–4 (1984): 33.

35  Riksdag, *Constitutional Documents,* 18.

36  T. H. Peterson, "After Five Years: An Assessment of the Amended U.S. Freedom of Information Act," *American Archivist* 43 (Spring 1980): 161–68.

37  See, for example, Carucci, "The National or Federal Archives," 207–11.

38  Interim Constitution, Chapter 3, Section 13.

39 See, for example, H. MacNeil, *Without Consent: The Ethics of Disclosing Personal Information in Public Archives* (Metuchen, N.J.: Scarecrow Press and Society of American Archivists, 1992), 61–102.

40 E. Ketelaar, "Archives of the People, by the People, for the People," *SA Archives Journal* 34 (1992): 9.

41 T. R. Schellenberg, *Modern Archives: Principles and Techniques* (Melbourne, Australia: Cheshire, 1956), 226.

42 Ketelaar, "Archives of the People," 9.

# CHAPTER 17

## Contesting Remembering and Forgetting: The Archive of South Africa's Truth and Reconciliation Commission[1]

### INTRODUCTION: REMEMBERING, FORGETTING, AND IMAGINING

Under apartheid, the terrain of social memory, as with all social space, was a site of struggle. In the crudest sense, this was a struggle of remembering against forgetting, of oppositional remembering that fought a life-and-death struggle against a systematic forgetting engineered by the state. The realities were more complex. Forgetting was an important element in anti-apartheid struggles—forgetting those dimensions of struggle too painful to remember, forgetting the half-truths and lies of the apartheid regime. Those in opposition also had their secrets and blind spots. Moreover, they allowed their imaginations to play. Memory is never a faithful reflection of process, of "reality." It is shaped, reshaped, figured, configured by the dance of imagination. So that beyond the dynamics of remembering and forgetting, a more profound characterization of struggles represented in social memory is one of narrative against narrative, story against story.

Nevertheless, the tools of forgetfulness, of state-imposed amnesia, were crucial to the exercise of power in apartheid South Africa. The state generated huge information resources, which it secreted jealously from public view. It routinely destroyed public records to keep certain processes secret. More chilling tools for erasing memory were widely utilized, with many thousands of oppositional voices eliminated through informal harassment, media censorship, banning, detention without trial, imprisonment, and assassination. The tools of forgetfulness also were important to the transfer of power, with the state deploying them to secure strategic advantage as negotiations unfolded.

Between 1990 and 1994, the state engaged in large-scale sanitization of its memory resources designed to keep certain information out of the hands of a future democratic government. Soon after the initiation in 1990 of the process toward a negotiated settlement, opposition individuals and structures began to express fears that such sanitization would occur. By 1994, it was clear that these fears were well founded.[2] Not surprisingly, when the Truth and Reconciliation Commission (TRC) was established in 1995 to shine a light into the apartheid system's darkest caverns,[3] one of its specific mandates was "to determine what articles have been destroyed by any person in order to conceal violations of human rights or acts associated with a political objective."[4] The mandate provided the basis for a focused investigation into the destruction of public records by the state.

From the TRC's inception late in 1995 until April 2001 (when I left the employ of the National Archives), I had responsibility for liaison between the TRC and the Archives. When the investigation into records destruction got underway, I was released to become an integral part of the investigative team, an involvement lasting from late 1996 to mid-1998. During 1998, I was contracted by the TRC to collate information gathered by this team and to draft sections of the final report dealing with records destruction. In the period 2001 to 2004, I directed the South African History Archive's freedom of information program, which sought to use the Promotion of Access to Information Act (PAIA) to build an archive of materials released in terms of the act, and whose first project was to target accumulations of apartheid security establishment records identified by the TRC's investigation. I cannot therefore claim to be a dispassionate observer. Rather, my analysis is that of a player in the events discussed below. I begin with an overview of the TRC as process before focusing on the TRC as archive. This space, as with all archives, is always already one in which dynamics of remembering, forgetting, and imagining are at play. My argument is that this space should be made hospitable to contestation and that we should all be vigilant against impulses in it and around it to amnesia, erasure, secreting, and control.

## THE TRC

It is hard to overemphasize the significance of South Africa's TRC in either national or international contexts. Described as the largest survey of human rights violations undertaken anywhere in the world, it became the key instrument in South Africa's interrogation of its apartheid past. Although its mandated focus was on gross human rights violations perpetrated in the period 1960 to 1994, it consistently attempted to position these violations within broader societal processes. A wealth of information on the apartheid era emerged and was fed into a range of other processes committed to shaping South Africa's future through an understanding of its past. The TRC mobilized South Africans across political, racial, and other divides to engage individual and collective memories of the past, and to debate the importance of memory to processes of reconciliation, envisioning the future, and nation building. This has influenced profoundly South Africa's commitment to an identity-formation founded on the confronting of harsh realities inherited from the past. Such commitment is central to the huge challenge posed by the ideal of reconciliation. The TRC's rationale assumed South Africa to be deeply divided, and to need healing—not through a forgetting of the history of division, but through formal engagements with that history. The TRC, then, was an essential instrument in South Africa's endeavor to find a postapartheid reconciliation, so that the TRC's significance is related not only to memory of the past. As significant is its contribution to memory of South Africa's transition to democracy. Future historians of the transition will find the story of the TRC looming large. So that the operational records of the TRC—the documentation of the TRC *as process*—are as important a memory resource as the records of the past that it both reclaimed and generated.

Unlike truth commissions in many other countries, South Africa's TRC was a public forum. From the appointment of its commissioners to the hearing of individuals' stories in public spaces, there was a commitment to the principles of transparency and public participation. Saturation coverage by the media, most significantly the South African Broadcasting Corporation's (SABC) live coverage of public hearings, took the work of the TRC into homes across the country. Public hearings were not restricted to larger centers; instead, stretching itself to the limit logistically, it sought as far as possible to make the hearings accessible to communities in remote areas. Over 22,000 victims of human rights violations made statements to the TRC, and more than 7,000 perpetrators applied for amnesty. Approximately 10 percent of the victims gave evidence at public hearings. At the height of its impact on public discourse, in the period 1996 to 1998, the TRC was being discussed and debated in homes, classrooms, offices, and factories. Of course, disclosure and participation always have their limits. The TRC felt compelled to delete sections of its final report detailing the culpability of ex-president De Klerk and the National Party. It had to fight hard to fend off a last-minute attempt by the African National Congress (ANC) to force changes to its findings on the ANC. Dissatisfaction was heard from many communities at the lack of consultation around public hearings. Some of its hearings were held *in camera*. Many researchers spoke of frustration at being denied access to TRC records. Information on certain TRC decision-making processes and of internal tensions and disputes was jealously kept out of the public domain.

Without claiming for South Africa a unique status, it is not an exaggeration to assert for South Africa's TRC an important contribution to world memories and narratives. The struggles against apartheid, especially in the 1970s and 1980s, marshaled resources in many countries against the apartheid state. The work of national anti-apartheid movements and international sanctions initiatives drew South Africa into the spotlight, where it came to symbolize racist resistance to the forces of democratization. Not surprisingly, then, the transition to democracy in the post-1990 period drew huge attention from the international media. South Africa was on the front pages around the world. Much of this attention focused on the work of the TRC. Its exposures of apartheid atrocities were reported on.

The public hearings were covered extensively. Its contribution to reconciliation was explored. Its endeavors were compared to those of other countries' truth commissions. TRC commissioners and staff participated in numerous international conferences and seminars both in South Africa and outside the country. The TRC Web site disseminated information around the world. Its report, published in 1998, has been acknowledged as one of the twentieth century's most historically significant documents.[5] Foreign academics, students, and journalists bombarded the TRC with requests for access to its documentation. Numerous institutions from many countries offered expertise and resources to ensure that the TRC's archive was professionally managed and made accessible. Moreover, some sought to collect documentation from the TRC to make it more accessible internationally.

Of course, the TRC was not without its flaws or its critics. I have mentioned the limits on transparency and participation. The composition of the commission has been criticized. It has been suggested that its focus on gross human rights violations within a specific period contributed to a skewing of social memory. Its processes of selection and interpretation have been critiqued. Some have gone as far as arguing that it began its work with a metanarrative in place and simply generated an archive to support this metanarrative. It has been accused of political bias. The impact on its work of inadequate research and investigation capabilities has been pointed out. The degree to which the security establishment was able to frustrate its access to extant records has been highlighted. Many of its findings have been questioned. The concept of amnesty has been challenged, and specific amnesty decisions rejected. Its impact on the work of reparation and rehabilitation has been found inadequate. Its contribution to reconciliation has been questioned. And so on, and on. These are important debates, important at many levels, not least in terms of their potential contribution to processes of reconciliation—important if South Africans are to find one another, not simply by forgetting, but by remembering and imagining a way forward that will create spaces for the forgettings which bring healing. It is crucial, then, that space is provided for these debates. Part of this space is constituted by the archive of the TRC. Every interrogation of its work will rely ultimately on access to records *of* the TRC and *about* the TRC.

# THE TRC ARCHIVE

In the broadest sense of the word *archive*, the TRC archive includes not only records generated by the TRC but also the ever-shifting stories in relation to the TRC carried by myriad people. In addition, it includes records used by the TRC, mainly records of state structures, and documentation of the TRC process generated by a wide range of individuals and organizations, within and outside the country. In this sense, the TRC archive is immeasurable. However, for the purposes of this essay, the term is used in a narrower sense to embrace on the one hand the documentary residue left by the TRC as an institution, and on the other the unpublished documentation of the TRC process generated by individuals and organizations within the country. Obviously, the TRC archive can be categorized in various ways, but within this conceptualization we are dealing with two broad categories: records *of* the TRC and records *about* the TRC.

The TRC's own records were generated in its various offices and by its commissioners and officials as they tracked around the country. The result is a vast accumulation of records in a range of media, documenting all TRC processes, from public hearings to vehicle requisitions, from investigations to the purchase of office furniture. Records in TRC custody can be divided into the following categories:

- Paper-based case files for human rights violations, amnesty applications and decisions, reparation and rehabilitation applications, and witness protection.
- Paper-based minutes of commission and committee meetings.
- Submissions, in both electronic and hard copy form.
- Transcripts of hearings, in both electronic and hard copy form.
- Sound and video recordings of hearings. The latter is incomplete, but a full series is in the custody of the SABC, which produced them. The SABC is in the process of providing the National Archives (NA) with an archival copy of the series.
- Office administrative files, in both electronic and hard copy form.
- Various electronic databases.
- The TRC Web site ( http://www.doj.gov.za/trc/ ).
- Maps, plans, books, journals, photographs, posters, news clippings, and artifacts.

Between 1999 and 2001, the TRC consolidated the records in what was its Cape Town head office. Also in this period, with the assistance of the NA, the tasks of sorting, arranging, listing, containerizing, and labeling were undertaken. Yet, this can only be regarded as a preliminary exercise. A further phase of detailed archival processing is required before the materials will be effectively accessible.

How comprehensive are records making up the formal TRC archive? A definitive answer will only be possible when the records are subjected to detailed archival processing. However, significant gaps already are apparent:

- Inadequate control over electronic records led to some loss of e-memory. There were anarchic hard drives among myriad PCs, and e-mails were routinely deleted. Losses were sustained during media conversion.[6]
- Departing staff removed what they regarded as "personal" records.
- A measure of record-keeping chaos in some TRC structures led to data loss.
- Some state documents secured by the TRC were returned to state structures without adequate documentation.
- A substantial collection amounting to over thirty boxes of records of so-called sensitive documents was handed over to the Ministry of Justice in 1999. Both their whereabouts and contents became the subject of an extended legal battle.[7]

The TRC investigation into the destruction of records by the apartheid state located a number of significant accumulations of security establishment records that survived the purge, and we know there are other such accumulations. Arguably, these constitute an integral part of the TRC archive. Small quantities of records from these accumulations are now in the custody of the NA.

A wide range of individuals and organizations has documented the TRC process. Organs of state (in their formal dealings with the TRC, notably the President's Office, Cabinet, Department of Justice, security establishment, and NA), the media, NGOs, academics, and other researchers have generated large quantities of records about the TRC. Private archives are collecting some of this material, and some is available to the public in one form or another, but most remains outside the public domain.

# PUBLIC ACCESS TO THE TRC ARCHIVE

The TRC archive thus constitutes a rich resource for social memory, both in South Africa and internationally, and consequently its optimal accessibility and use is desirable. In its report, the TRC adopted this position unequivocally in relation to its own records.[8] It recommended that "all Commission records be transferred to the National Archives" after the final report was made public and that all these records should "be accessible to the public, unless compelling reasons exist for denying such access." It further recommended that "Government allocate adequate additional funding" to the NA to preserve and maintain the records, including special support to "facilitate creation of decentralised, nation-wide 'centres of memory' at which members of the public who do not have personal access to computers can access details of the proceedings of the Commission, including transcripts and sound and video clips of hearings."[9] How accessible, then, is the TRC archive? The report was published in 1998 in hard copy and CD-ROM, and is accessible on the TRC Web site. The latter site includes transcripts of public hearings and other formal documentation related to TRC activities conducted in the public domain. But there are no linkages between these records and the mass of TRC material from which they are drawn. Moreover, in 2002 the Web site was relocated by the Department of Justice in a process that has been problematic. At the time of writing, the new site address has not been recorded at the old address, and some of the site's functionality appears to have been lost. Sound and video recordings of public hearings are accessible at the National Archives in Pretoria or the SABC in Johannesburg. Unfortunately, inadequate professional processing (such as detailed description, indexing, and cross-referencing) limits their usefulness. Access to other categories of TRC records must be specifically requested. Until the archive's transfer to the National Archives in 2001–2002, TRC officials strove valiantly to meet the growing demand for access, but a range of factors hampered their work. Access under the archival management of the National Archives has proved problematic, with many researchers reporting access refusals and long delays in access decisions. Relevant apartheid-era security establishment records identified by the TRC remain largely in the custody of security structures. Until very recently, with the implementation of the Promotion of Access to Information Act, researchers had little success in securing permission to access the records.

PAIA, passed in February 2000 and operative in March 2001, transforms the information landscape. It expresses the constitutional right of access to information, overrides other legislation providing for such access, and gives criteria for determining access to records of public and private bodies. Significantly, it defines mandatory and discretionary grounds for refusing access—for example, for the former, how records that a body might wish to make available will have to be restricted. With one exception, grounds for refusal are weighed against various other considerations, including public interest.[10] PAIA requires bodies to publicize information about their records, accords them the right to declare records categories and series open (if falling outside the parameters of mandatory restriction), and empowers courts to rule on appeals against refusal. From March 2001, PAIA became the instrument for managing access to the TRC archive.

Clearly, PAIA is welcome. It establishes the right of access to the TRC archive in institutional custody and ensures access management by legislatively defined mechanisms. But the right of access depends on other factors to be efficacious, namely:
- Professional management of records
- Comprehensive and detailed retrieval tools
- Wide dissemination of information about records
- Intellectual linkages between related records
- Imaginative feeding of records into social memory—for instance, through the "centres of memory" recommended by the TRC

In all these respects, the TRC archive requires substantial additional work.

What about access to records *about* the TRC? Some of these—notably those in public (e.g., SABC and NA) and private archives—are available to the public. But most remain outside the public domain. Substantial systemic barriers limit their accessibility:
- Little information on *what* materials exist and *where* they are to be found. No archival audit or survey has yet been undertaken.[11]
- Limited professional processing of materials outside archival custody.

- Much material, notably that in the possession of individuals, is subject to disposal on the basis of personal whim. Stories abound of potentially valuable records either being destroyed or sold or donated, in some cases to overseas institutions.
- Until the bringing into operation of PAIA in March 2001, there was no legislative basis for exercising a right of access to these materials.

## FUTURE SCENARIOS: CUSTODY, PRESERVATION, AND ACCESS

There are, then, many concerns about the custody, preservation, and accessibility of records *about* the TRC. Given their heterogeneity and the degree to which they are dispersed, it is difficult to generalize about possible future scenarios. Conditions applying to relevant Cabinet records, for instance, differ markedly from those applying to materials in the custody of an academic. However, three priorities applicable to all these records accumulations are identifiable:

1. All need to be located and identified by means of an archival audit or survey.

2. Those under threat in terms of preservation should be brought under the protective provisions of the National Archives of South Africa Act (NASAA) and/or the National Heritage Resources Act of 1999.

3. Ways of bringing those not publicly accessible (the great majority) into the public domain should be explored.

There are fewer concerns in relation to the custody, preservation, and accessibility of the TRC's own records. Apart from the above-mentioned gaps (which require sustained and well-resourced attention), the records are in the custody of the National Archives in Pretoria. In terms of NASAA, the TRC is a "governmental body" and its records are "public records." This affords the records the full protections provided for in NASAA and the professional services of the NA. The latter established contact with the TRC early in 1996, and subsequently assisted the TRC with the design of records systems and the training of staff having responsibility for records. Between 1999 and 2002, NA archivists assisted TRC staff with the consolidation and processing of records.

The question of what would happen to the TRC's own records at the end of the process generated intense debate. The TRC's enabling legislation stipulated that when the TRC ceased to exist, all its assets, including intellectual assets, devolved to the Department of Justice, implying that the records would be transferred into the custody of the department until transferred to the NA. NASAA provides for an obligatory transfer of public records with enduring value to the NA when they reach twenty years of age. However, there was a strong case for transferring the records directly to the NA. (A possible exception was records required by the Department of Justice for ongoing functions, like reparation and prosecution). The NA has the infrastructure to provide the records with professional care, is geared to providing public access, and has staff with developed expertise in relation to TRC records: all attributes the Department of Justice does not possess. Moreover, in its report, the TRC recommended that the records should be transferred directly to the NA. NASAA empowers the National Archivist to identify public records that should be transferred to the NA before they have been in existence for twenty years. The question was discussed, sometimes with fierce debate, by the TRC; the Department of Justice; the Department of Arts, Culture, Science and Technology; and the NA from 1999. The NA, to its credit, resisted what appeared to be a determination on the part of Justice officials to exercise direct control over the records in the longer term. The issue was finally resolved in 2001, with all parties agreeing to the transfer of all TRC records to the NA in Pretoria as soon as remaining TRC work was concluded.[12] The transfer began in October 2001[13] and was completed early in 2002.

Resolution of the custody issue is important but several other key questions remain. To what extent will the NA manage TRC records as opposed to being merely custodian? Which state agencies will take management decisions? Will the NA and the Department of Justice simply process access requests as received or will they proactively identify record series and categories and make them available without the need for recourse to PAIA? My view is that the latter approach is essential. Does the NA plan to subject TRC records to its appraisal program, which aims to select for preservation only 5 percent of public records within its ambit? While it is unnecessary to preserve indefinitely records such as office furniture orders, clearly the nature of the TRC as archive demands an unusually generous set of preservation criteria and a selection process open to public scrutiny and participation.[14] What is the status of the TRC's electronic records? The NA has done little to prepare these vulnerable records for archival management, and I know the TRC has experienced difficulties with media conversion exercises that have been a core element of the records' processing and management for the last three years.[15] It is imperative that vigorous efforts be made to address the above-mentioned gaps in TRC records. The scale of the exercise will place huge strain on the already limited resources of the NA, which will find it difficult to dedicate significant resources to the detailed professional processing of the materials and facilitation of access. Without a substantial infusion of energy and resources, the state will manage a resource for a small elite and the TRC's own vision for the records as a community resource will not be realized.

Clearly, these are issues and questions of intense public interest. The degree to which they remain outside the public domain is therefore disappointing. In October 2000, I was invited to give a paper on the TRC archive at a conference in Cape Town. While still in the employ of the NA, I spoke in my capacity as an individual with specialist knowledge of TRC processes and records. In the paper, I addressed the above-mentioned issues. The response of my employer was immediate and disturbing. I was reprimanded for embarrassing the state, placed under a muzzle in terms of my public statements, and threatened with misconduct proceedings.

## CONCLUSION: REMEMBERING, FORGETTING, AND IMAGINING

Between 1996 and 2001, my professional work revolved around the TRC. For much of this time I was seduced by the TRC's dominant metanarrative: that its mission was to promote reconciliation through the bringing of light to dark spaces through the exposing of hidden pasts. It was an exercise in remembering: a quintessentially archival exercise. Yet, as Derrida[16] observed in an address during a visit to South Africa:

> The work of the archivist is not simply a work of memory. It is a work of mourning. And a work of mourning ... is a work of memory but also the best way just to forget the other, ... to keep it safe, in a safe—but when you put something in a safe it's just in order to be able to forget it.... When I handwrite something on a piece of paper, I put it in my pocket or in a safe, it's just in order to forget it.... So, suppose that one day South Africa would have accomplished a perfect, full archive of its whole history ... everyone ... would be eager to put this in such a safe that everyone could just forget it.... And perhaps ... this is the unconfessed desire of the Truth and Reconciliation Commission. That as soon as possible the future generation may have simply forgotten it.... Having kept everything in the archive ... let us forget it to go on, to survive.

By subverting the remembering/forgetting binary opposition, Derrida, I suggest, opens the door to a re-imagination of archival endeavor and a re-imagination of the TRC's work. Crucially, Derrida enables us to understand that the TRC as archive will have no ending. It always will be becoming among us. The central question is the degree to which those who manage the archive will allow space within and around it for contestation. The ultimate test of the TRC as archive is the extent to which it becomes a space for the play of remembering, forgetting, and imagining. This play is always under way in an archive whatever the intentions of those who seek to control it. We have seen such play in and around the TRC archive. However, we also have seen, as noted above, a closing down of this space through instincts of amnesia, erasure, secreting, and control. These instincts must be resisted. As Derrida[17] argues, "Effective democratization can always be measured by this essential criterion: the participation in and the access to the archive, its constitution, and its interpretation."

On all South Africans there is a burden of responsibility to continue giving life to the TRC process, to be always finding the TRC archive, safeguarding, using, promoting, and taking it outside the domains of elites. For the state, there is the added responsibility of acting on the TRC's recommendations and using the TRC archive to implement an effective reparation and rehabilitation program and to prosecute perpetrators of gross human rights violations who failed to receive amnesty or shunned the amnesty process. If we fail to meet these responsibilities, then we will impoverish ourselves. The debt we owe those who sacrificed so much in the struggles against apartheid will weigh heavily on us. The promise of justice we owe generations to come will be compromised. The value of the TRC and its significance will be corroded. Our past, as the archive always teaches us, lies in our future. The TRC is as much about our future as it is about our past.

# Endnotes

1   This essay was first published in *Innovation* 24 (2002). It was based on a paper presented at the "Archives in the Service of International Human Rights" Conference, Tallahassee, Florida, 2001. It draws on my previous work: "'They Should Have Destroyed More': The Destruction of Public Records by the South African State in the Final Years of Apartheid," *Transformation* 42 (2000); "Remembering, Forgetting and the TRC Archive" paper to "Reparations and Memorialisation: the Unfinished Business of the TRC" Conference, Cape Town, October 2000; and "Seeing (in) Blindness: South Africa, Archives and Passion for Justice," paper to annual conference of Archives and Records Association of New Zealand, Wellington, 2001. I record my indebtedness to various people who commented on this work in draft form, especially to Sello Hatang.

2   Between 1988 and 1994, I was an archivist in the State Archives Service (SAS) records management division. Rumors were rife in the public service. By early 1993, I had enough evidence from government sources to know destruction was widespread. When it was clear the SAS was unable or unwilling to act decisively, I leaked information to the ANC, other opposition structures, and the media. The celebrated 1993 Currin case pushed the issue firmly onto center stage in the media and the Harms and Goldstone commissions, as well as the Goniwe inquest, revealed substantial evidence of systematic records destruction.

3   The seventeen-member TRC had four main functions: to establish as complete a picture as possible of the causes, nature, and extent of gross human rights violations between 1960 and 1994; to facilitate amnesty to perpetrators of such violations associated with a political objective; to recommend appropriate reparation for victims; and to report on its activities and recommendations. The TRC final report was submitted to President Mandela in October 1998. However, the work of its Amnesty Committee proceeded until well into 2001.

4   Promotion of National Unity and Reconciliation Act (1995), section 4d.

5   *Truth and Reconciliation Commission of South Africa Report* (Cape Town: The Commission, 1998).

6   In the first phase of archiving, electronic records, contents of hard drives, file servers, and stiffy disks were downloaded onto tapes. This occurred in 1998. Up until then no formal backup procedures had been put in place. The tapes were not properly managed, so that when at a later stage the tapes were converted to CD-ROM, significant data loss was discovered. Moreover, from my conversations with those involved, it seems that metadata losses were also sustained.

7   In 2001, I put in a PAIA request for a list of these records on behalf of the South African History Archive (SAHA). In response, the Department of Justice advised that it held no TRC records, but when pushed claimed that it would first have to consult with the National Intelligence Agency. See Terry Bell, "Burying the Truth, Again," *Mail and Guardian* 11 April 2002. Subsequently, after at first denying that it had custody of the records, the National Intelligence Agency admitted to having them. Subsequent court action by SAHA saw the records transferred to the National Archives and a majority of them placed in the public domain. However, it remains to be established that none of the records have gone missing.

8   TRC, *Report,* vol. 5, chapter 8.

9   TRC, *Report,* 344–45.

10  The single exception relates to information submitted to the state by citizens for taxation purposes.

11  The South African History Archive launched an audit in 2003.

12  Discussions with TRC and National Archives officials, September 2001.

13  *Mail and Guardian,* 26 October 2001.

14  The mechanism for ensuring accountability in the National Archives' appraisal program is the National Archives Commission. In terms of the Archives Act, the commission (a statutory body appointed by the minister via a process of public participation) is empowered to approve the archives' appraisal policy and monitor its implementation. However, the first commission has performed woefully and made no meaningful contribution to the appraisal process.

15  See "The Record, the Archive and Electronic Technologies in South Africa," reproduced elsewhere in this book.

16  Transcript of Derrida seminar on *Archive Fever,* University of the Witwatersrand, Johannesburg, August 1998, published in Carolyn Hamilton, et al., eds., *Refiguring the Archive* (Cape Town: David Philip, 2002).

17  Jacques Derrida, *Archive Fever: A Freudian Impression* (Chicago: University of Chicago Press, 1996).

# CHAPTER 18

## "They should have destroyed more": The Destruction of Public Records by the South African State in the Final Years of Apartheid, 1990–1994[1]

## INTRODUCTION

As I have argued elsewhere, under apartheid in South Africa the terrain of social memory, as with all social space, was a site of struggle.[2] And the tools of forgetfulness, of state-imposed amnesia, were crucial to the exercise of power. These tools, as this essay recounts, were also important to the transfer of power—between 1990 and 1994 the state engaged in a large-scale sanitization of its memory resources designed to keep certain information out of the hands of a future democratic government.

Soon after the initiation in 1990 of the process toward a negotiated settlement in South Africa, a number of individuals and structures in opposition to the state began to express fears that such a sanitization would take place. By 1994, it was clear that these fears had been well founded.[3] Not surprisingly, then, when the South African Truth and Reconciliation Commission (TRC) was established in 1995 to shine a light into the apartheid system's darkest caverns;[4] one of its specific mandates was "to determine what

articles have been destroyed by any person in order to conceal violations of human rights or acts associated with a political objective."[5]
This mandate provided the basis for a focused investigation into the
destruction of public records by the state. Given the complexity and
extent of the apartheid state, adequate coverage by the investigation of *all* state structures and records systems proved impossible,
and the TRC decided to limit the investigation to state structures
subject to national archival legislation,[6] thus excluding *parastatals,*
statutory bodies that had not voluntarily submitted to the operation
of the Archives Act, "privatized" bodies and "homeland" structures.[7]
The "homelands" were responsible for the management of their own
records, in some cases in terms of their own archival legislation. The
investigation further concentrated its energies on the activities of
the security establishment—preliminary research made it clear that
initiatives for systematic destruction of public records originated
and were felt most acutely there.[8]

   This essay relies heavily on the work and findings of the TRC investigation, thus reproducing in large measure both its emphases and its
limitations.[9] From the TRC's inception late in 1995, I carried responsibility for liaison between it and the National Archives. When the
investigation into records destruction got underway, I was released to
become an integral part of the investigative team, an involvement that
endured from late 1996 until mid-1998. During 1998, I was contracted
by the TRC to collate information it had gathered and to draft sections
of the final report dealing with the destruction of records.[10] This essay
also draws on my own interrogation of National Archives documentation of records destruction up to 1994 (all of which was made available
to the TRC) and of subsequent follow-up investigations by the National
Archives.

   I begin with an account of state record-keeping, official secrecy,
and the destruction of records under apartheid, before detailing the
pre-election purge of 1990 to 1994. The question of accountability
is then explored, and in the conclusion I offer an assessment of the
purge's impact—broadly on social memory and more specifically on
the TRC's work—and an outline of lessons to be learned from it by a
democratic state.

# STATE RECORD-KEEPING AND OFFICIAL SECRECY

Apartheid's bureaucracy was huge, complex, and intruded into almost every aspect of South African citizens' lives. Controls over racial classification, employment, movement, association, purchase of property, recreation, and so on all were documented—usually in a multilayered process—by thousands of state offices across the country. This was supplemented by the record of surveillance activities by the Security Police, Military Intelligence, the National Intelligence Service, and numerous other state bodies, including those of the homelands. And large quantities of records were confiscated from individuals and organizations opposed to apartheid. An army of bureaucrats—servicing registries, strong-rooms, and computer systems—managed this formidable information resource.

What the state does with all the information at its disposal, and how accessible that information is to citizens, are key issues. Under apartheid, the state's memory resources were hoarded with a pathological attention to detail. While all governments are uncomfortable with the notion of transparency and prefer to operate beyond the glare of public scrutiny, in apartheid South Africa state secrecy was a *modus operandi*. Interlocking legislation restricted access to, and the dissemination of, information on vast areas of public life. These restrictions were manipulated to secure an extraordinary degree of opacity in government, and the country's formal information systems became grossly distorted in support of official propaganda. The fundamental guideline for public access to public records was provided by the 1962 Archives Act (which was amended in 1964, 1969, 1977, and 1979). The 1962 act—the forerunners of which were the 1922 Public Archives Act and the 1953 Archives Act—established that access was a privilege to be granted by bureaucrats unless legislation recognized the right of access to specific categories of records. The number of record categories covered by such legislation was insignificant; for instance, records older than thirty years in the custody of the State Archives Service[11] and deceased estate files in the custody of Masters of the Supreme Court. On the other hand, the discretionary power enjoyed by bureaucrats was severely circumscribed by a range of legislation containing secrecy clauses.

Even within state structures, the management of information was framed by an obsession with secrecy. Every bureaucrat was graded in terms of a rigorous security clearance procedure, the grading level determining an individual's right of access to information. This procedure meshed with a pervasive system of information grading—commonly referred to as "classification"—defined by perceived security risks. The Protection of Information Act, and various legislative forerunners, promised severe punitive action against individuals defying the system.

The Archives Act charged the director of archives (the chief executive official of the State Archives Service) with "... the custody, care and control of archives...." "Archives" were defined as "... any documents or records received or created in a government office or an office of a local authority during the conduct of affairs in such office and which are from their nature or in terms of any other Act of Parliament not required then to be dealt with otherwise than in accordance with or in terms of the provisions of this Act." So the State Archives Service had wide-ranging powers over the management of public records at central, provincial, and local government levels from the moment of their creation or acquisition. However, the words "from their nature," as I elaborate on below, left the boundaries around the term *archives* far from clear. Also unclear was who should determine the records that by their nature should not fall under archival legislation. Other provisions of the act elaborated on specific aspects of records management—the physical care of records, their management in terms of approved "filing systems," their conversion to microform, and their accessibility, inspection, and ultimate disposal. Comparison with the archival legislation of other countries reveals that the powers enjoyed by the State Archives Service over the active records of the state were among the most extensive of any national archives service in the world.

The legal disposal of public records involved either their transfer into the custody of a State Archives Service repository or their destruction under the terms of a disposal authority. Until 1979, it was the responsibility of the Archives Commission—a statutory body appointed by the responsible cabinet minister—to authorize the destruction of public records. However, while this authority had been vested with the commission since 1926, by the 1960s, the commission had become a rubber stamp for recommendations made by the director of archives. A 1979 amendment to the Archives Act recognized this *de facto* situation by empowering the director of archives to authorize destruction.

The act made it a criminal offense to willfully damage a public record, or to remove or destroy such a record other than under the terms of the act or any other law. As with all national archives services, the State Archives Service was obliged by limited resources to select only a small proportion of public records for archival preservation. To date, no study has been made of the impact on the archival record of the service's selection program. What is clear is that state secrecy ensured that this program was neither transparent nor accountable to the public, and that it was sustained by bodies (the commission and the service) reflective of the apartheid system and shaped by its ideology.

Needless to say, efficacy in implementation is the most important test of powerful legal instruments. In practice, the service was hampered by inadequate resources and by its junior status in government. Empowered legislatively for the first time in 1922, the service had undergone a number of name changes and been moved successively from the departments of Interior; Union Education; Education, Arts and Science; and, finally to National Education. As with all the service's staff members, the director of archives occupied a public service position and was appointed through the standard public service mechanisms and procedures. Only a small proportion of government offices were effectively reached by the service's records management program. The inspection function, crucial to the auditing mandate of the Archives Act, was no more than a token gesture. This, combined with the state's disregard for accountability and the director of archives' relatively junior ranking in the public service hierarchy, rendered the service almost powerless to resist state organs obstructing its legitimate activities and flagrantly ignoring or defying its legal instruments. Especially problematic were bodies located within the security establishment. With the exception of the South African Defence Force and the Department of Prison Services, the service did not subject these bodies' records systems to professional supervision. Indeed, there is no evidence of pre-1990 professional liaison between the service and other branches of the security establishment. It is not clear as to whether this abrogation of responsibility was the result of orders from higher authority or was simply the result of the service's leadership being intimidated by the security establishment's powerful position. The consequence was that the establishment was a law unto itself in terms of the management of its own records.

Also of crucial importance—and devastating in its consequence—
was the vulnerability of the Archives Act's definition of *archives* to
divergent interpretations of the words "from their nature." It is not
clear what the act's drafters intended to exclude from the definition by
these words, although in his speech of 31 January 1962 to the Senate,
the Minister of Education, Arts and Science indicated that the words
were designed to accommodate requirements for secret records.[12]
The authority of the act over various categories of public records was
challenged unsuccessfully on this basis in the period immediately after
the act's passage into law. However, until 1991, the status of classified
(in terms of security grading) records in relation to the Archives Act
received no legal scrutiny. In that year, it emerged that the National
Intelligence Service had destroyed the sound recording of a meeting between imprisoned African National Congress leader Nelson
Mandela and State President P. W. Botha. The State Archives Service
challenged the legality of the destruction on the grounds that the director of archives had not authorized it. On 10 December 1991, the state
president's office secured a state legal opinion (299/1991) indicating
that "sensitive" documents—those requiring secrecy—were by their
nature not "archives" and therefore not subject to the Archives Act.
Subsequently, the National Intelligence Service also acquired a state
legal opinion (308/1991, 17 December 1991), that produced a similar finding. The legal scrutiny underpinning these opinions revealed
that the security establishment had since the Archives Act's inception
regarded classified records as falling outside the act's ambit and had
implemented a governmentwide policy for the routine destruction of
such records.

## RECORDS DESTRUCTION UP TO 1990

In the period 1960 to 1994, first the Archives Commission and
later the director of archives issued a total of over 4,000 record disposal authorities to state offices. As I indicated earlier, it remains to
be assessed to what extent the interests of the apartheid state were
accommodated in this selection process. Within budgetary and other
constraints, the State Archives Service monitored implementation of
these disposal authorities to ensure that public records were destroyed

under archival authorization and only after the lapsing of appropriate retention periods. Numerous cases of alleged or actual unauthorized destruction were investigated. Most involved disasters such as fires and flooding, and in some cases it was clear that negligence had played a role. However, in not a single instance was the State Archives Service able to identify sinister motivation such as the deliberate destruction of documentary evidence. Over many years, a dispute was sustained with Central Statistical Services (CSS) over its routine destruction of census returns and related records without proper archival authorization. CSS's legislative mandate required the agency to ensure the confidentiality of such records, and it adopted the position that only destruction could achieve this. The loopholes in the Archives Act's definition of *archives* gave CSS the space to outmaneuver successfully the State Archives Service.

Incredibly, the service's monitoring activities did not detect a governmentwide policy for the destruction of classified records until 1991. It is not clear when this policy was first implemented, but it was certainly in place by 1978. In that year, all government departments received guidelines for the protection of classified information, signed by the prime minister and empowering department heads to authorize destruction outside the ambit of the Archives Act. The guidelines did not explicitly challenge the Archives Act's ambit. Rather, they simply authorized destruction without mentioning the Archives Act at all.[13] This was in direct conflict with a standing directive of the State Archives Service that indicated that all classified records were to be regarded provisionally as archival until the State Archives Service had physically appraised them. The guidelines were updated in 1984 by the National Intelligence Service under the state president's signature.[14] How widespread or stringent was their implementation by state offices remains unclear. Certainly within the security establishment they were implemented rigorously. The South African Defence Force utilized a similar parallel set of guidelines from at least 1971. Like their civilian counterparts, military archivists in the South African Defence Force Archives appear not to have been aware of their existence.

The great majority of the records generated by the security establishment was classified and therefore subject to the guidelines' provisions for destruction. In essence, the guidelines on the one hand obliged agency heads to destroy certain categories of records in the interests of security, and on the other, gave discretionary power to destroy records that had lost their functional usefulness. The TRC investigation revealed evidence of widespread implementation, particularly rigorous in structures of the National Security Management System, the National Intelligence Service, the Security Police, and the South African Defence Force. The National Security Management System (NSMS) was set up in the early 1980s to coordinate state action against anti-apartheid activities. It was headed by the State Security Council, ostensibly subordinate to Cabinet but by the end of the 1980s, supreme on issues relating to security. The council ran a huge network of substructures reaching into every part of the country, relying mainly on security establishment resources but drawing in almost all organs of the state. When the public debate on the destruction of classified records occurred in 1993 (recounted later in this essay), the head of the Security Secretariat maintained that a full set of NSMS records was being preserved and that only duplicate copies were being destroyed. However, the official responsible for the management of these records from 1980 to 1990 was later to inform the TRC that the guidelines for destruction were fully implemented throughout that period. Not surprisingly, the documentary residue of the NSMS contains numerous and substantial gaps.

The National Intelligence Service (NIS) was established in 1980, inheriting the functions of the Bureau of State Security (1968–1978) and the Department of National Security (1978–1980). The systematic routine destruction of NIS records began at least as early as 1982. On 1 December 1982, the service's top management adopted a set of guidelines (Directive 0/01) that authorized divisional heads and regional representatives to destroy records that no longer possessed security relevance on an annual basis. It proved impossible for the TRC investigation to determine records disposal procedures in the pre-1980 era, but the evidence suggests that NIS procedures were applied to any records that had survived.

The Security Police was a branch of the South African Police (SAP). With the approval of the director of archives, it managed its records in terms of records systems approved by the director for use throughout the SAP but in physically separate record sets classified as secret or confidential. Standing SAP instructions indicated that no secret or confidential records could be destroyed without written authorization from the director of archives. In the period 1960 to 1994, no such authorizations were given. The TRC investigation determined that throughout this period, Security Police records were routinely destroyed in accordance with internal retention and disposal arrangements. In the main this seems to have applied to support function records rather than operational records. Huge volumes of operational records were generated at head office, regional, and local levels. To cope more effectively with them, a microfilming project was initiated, probably in the 1970s. Originals of microfilmed records were apparently destroyed, but not on a systematic basis. From 1983 onward, a computerized database of operational records was implemented. Again, it appears as if certain original records were destroyed after the core data had been captured on the database. Nevertheless, in 1990 the Security Police retained huge quantities of operational records in locations throughout the country, a large proportion still in paper form.

The South African Defence Force (SADF) enjoyed a special status within the framework of the Archives Act. It managed its own archives repository (the SADF Archives) and, from the late 1960s, provided its own records management service (through the SADF Archives) to SADF structures. Both functions were supervised by the State Archives Service. Standing orders required that records only be destroyed in terms of authorities signed by the director of archives and that destruction certificates be submitted to the SADF Archives. However, as I have already indicated, from at least 1971, conflicting standing orders authorized the routine destruction of classified records without reference to the SADF Archives, the director of archives, or the Archives Act. The evidence suggests that substantial volumes of records were destroyed in this way without any archival intervention. There is also evidence of large-scale destruction of records generated by bodies related in one or other way to the SADF. The South West Africa Territory Force was a joint South African / Namibian force established to operate in conjunction with SADF operations in Namibia. Starting in December 1988, its records were subjected to systematic appraisal. Decisions on which records were to be destroyed were authorized by the commanding officer. There was no consultation with the civilian archives repository in Windhoek, the SADF Archives, or the State Archives Service. Records that survived this exercise were placed in the custody of the SADF Archives.

The Civil Cooperation Bureau was a special unit established to disrupt or eliminate persons considered to be enemies of the state. It reported to the SADF's Special Forces division. The Harms Commission of Enquiry into Certain Alleged Irregularities, which reported in 1989, revealed that all the bureau's records had either been destroyed or illegally removed. The records of Koevoet, the notorious counter-insurgency unit that operated out of Namibia, were reported as having all disappeared in transit between Windhoek and Pretoria.

Between 1960 and 1990, through its appraisal function and the monitoring of state offices, the State Archives Service had sought to control the destruction of public records and to ensure the preserva-tion of records with archival value. Nevertheless, by 1990 there was a well-established practice within state structures of routinely destroy-ing classified records outside the ambit of the Archives Act. Within the security establishment there was an ethos in the management of its own records characterized by almost complete autonomy from the interven-tion of the State Archives Service. Nevertheless, throughout the state, substantial and archivally rich classified information resources were being maintained. Particularly in the security establishment, a prevail-ing sense of being in control supported the preservation of records that in more uncertain circumstances would surely have been destroyed.

## THE PRE-ELECTION PURGE

Uncertainty for state structures was heralded by the February 1990 lifting of the ban on the African National Congress and numerous other anti-apartheid organizations, and the subsequent initiation of formal negotiations toward the official dismantling of apartheid. Apprehension about certain public records passing out of the then-government's control became prevalent. There was particular concern about such records being used against the government and its operatives by a future democratic government. The first state agency to act decisively was the National Intelligence Service. In 1990, it decided to replace its 1982 guidelines for records destruction with a far more rigorous process to be managed by an interdivisional Standing Re-evaluation Committee. New guidelines were given to the committee in October 1991. The guidelines required the destruction of paper-based records unless there were very good reasons for their retention. "Security relevant" records were to be kept on microfilm or electronic form, where they were most secure and easier to destroy/erase quickly. Continued retention was to be reviewed on an annual basis. In addition, documentation of covert operations was to be categorized according to sensitivity and security relevance criteria, with references to the most sensitive documentation to be removed from the electronic information retrieval system. None of this documentation was to be kept for longer than six years. Top management elaborative guidelines issued in February 1992 make it clear that one of the purposes of this exercise was to sanitize the image of both the government and the NIS in a new political environment.[15] Initially, the new guidelines did not accommodate Treasury requirements for the management of financial records. However, in 1992, after conferring with the auditor-general and the director of archives, the NIS director-general requested ministerial approval for the destruction of financial authorizations, vouchers, and related documentation. The minister of Justice and National Intelligence gave his approval on 3 July 1992.

Implementation of the new NIS policy gained momentum in 1992, but reached its greatest intensity in 1993. Mass destruction of records took place at this time, embracing all media and all structures. In a six- to eight-month period in 1993, NIS headquarters alone destroyed approximately forty-four tons of paper and microfilm records, utilizing the Pretoria Iscor furnace and another facility outside Johannesburg. The evidence suggests that many operatives took the opportunity to "clean up" their offices, irrespective of the guidelines. Systematic destruction exercises continued until late in 1994, with many of the surviving minutes of chief directorate, directorate, and divisional meetings, and most administrative records covering the period 1989 to 1994 being destroyed at this late stage. NIS's own requirements for the preparation of destruction certificates were seldom complied with. The result was a massive purging of NIS's corporate memory. This was supplemented by the unauthorized *ad hoc* removal of documents by individuals for their own purposes. Any attempt to quantify this phenomenon was beyond the resources of the TRC investigation. Very little pre-1990 material survives in the paper-based, microform, and electronic systems, and the documentary residue for the period 1990 to 1994 has been substantially sanitized. The one seemingly intact record series is minutes of senior management meetings, which covers the period 1980 to 1994.

In 1992, the Security Police followed the example set by NIS. In March of that year, an instruction emanating from its head office ordered the destruction of all operational records, including nonpublic records confiscated from individuals and organizations. The TRC investigation was unable to determine either the precise source of this instruction or its precise content. The evidence suggests that it was received verbally at both regional and local levels. The instruction embraced all media and required the destruction not only of records but also of all documentation about the records. In the months following the issuing of the instruction, massive and systematic destruction of records took place. In some cases, records were removed to the head office for destruction. In others, destruction took place on-site. In yet others, private companies like Nampak (a manufacturer of cardboard containers) and Sappi (a paper and board manufacturer) were utilized. With few exceptions, it would appear that Security Police offices implemented the instruction to the letter. In fact, some offices destroyed most, if not all, support function as well as operational records. But there were exceptions. The investigation revealed that certain operational records from eleven regional and local offices were not destroyed. Several thousand files also survived in what was the Security Police head office, mostly dating to after 1990. Eleven back-up tapes of the head office computerized database were located, seven of which were still readable. And contrary to the March 1992 instruction, three offices kept lists of files forwarded to the head office for destruction.

As early as 1990, NIS's top management expressed the need for coordinated governmentwide action in the destruction of records. The first step taken in this direction related to the records of the NSMS, which was rapidly dismantled after February 1990. NIS was made the official custodian of NSMS records. On 29 November 1991, a circular instruction was sent to all government departments requiring them to transfer to NIS all NSMS-related records in their custody. While the stated purpose of the exercise was to enable the Security Secretariat to assemble a complete set of these records, it was clearly designed to facilitate systematic sanitization. The exercise was less than successful, and in July 1993 the head of the Security Secretariat, with explicit Cabinet approval, sent another circular to all government departments, recommending that they destroy all classified records that had been received by them from other sources, with the exception of those constituting authorization for financial expenditure or "other action." Special mention was made of documentation related to the NSMS. The impact of this circular was immediate and severe. Across the country, government officials began purging the classified records under their care. At the time, I was an archivist in the records management program of the State Archives Service. I had professional contacts in numerous government offices, and some of the more conscientious among them alerted me to the danger. When I briefed the director of archives, I discovered that he knew about the circular and "had the matter in hand." But when nothing was done over the next week to stem what was clearly a massive governmentwide destruction exercise, I leaked the information to the African National Congress, the press, and Brian Currin, then national director of Lawyers for Human Rights. In the public furor that followed, the state maintained that the step was merely designed to eliminate unnecessary duplicate copies of classified records, that all originals would be preserved, and that in any case, classified records fell outside the ambit of the Archives Act. Currin then challenged the circular's validity in the Supreme Court, identifying the respondents as the state president, the minister of national education, the director of archives, and the director-general of NIS. In his application, Currin argued that state legal opinions 299/1991 and 308/1991 were "wrong," and that the nature of "sensitive" records, including classified material, did not exclude them from the operation of the Archives Act. On 27 September 1993, all the parties reached agreement that from then on no public records would be dealt with otherwise than under the terms of the Archives Act.[16] Two days later the minister of justice issued a media statement in which he stated, "Cabinet is of the view that state documentation should be dealt with in terms of the Archives Act."[17]

Hopes that the loophole in the Archives Act had been removed proved vain. The settlement had not incorporated Currin's broader arguments, and the state exploited this to continue its "legal" destruction of records outside the operation of the Archives Act. The 1984 guidelines for the destruction of classified records were not withdrawn. In fact, as late as November 1994, *after* the installation of South Africa's first democratically elected government, NIS issued an updated version of the guidelines that still ignored the Archives Act. This was a direct violation of the Currin settlement. The director of archives challenged NIS accordingly, and the guidelines were revised appropriately and rereleased in February 1995. In the wake of the Currin settlement, for the benefit of the media and oppositional groups, the state staged a charade of abiding by its provisions. A second circular was sent out to government departments qualifying the contents of the first. An inter-departmental working group was established to prepare guidelines for government offices on which categories of public record fell outside the ambit of the Archives Act. When the group produced draft guide-lines, the director of archives (through the director general of national education) sought a state legal opinion on their validity. The opinion (220/93, 2 November 1993), without even referring to the Currin settlement, simply affirmed the findings of opinion 299/91. However, the opinion did assert that decisions on destruction should not be left to individual department heads and recommended that an advisory mechanism should be created. This was never done.

The full extent of the Cabinet's duplicity only emerged during the TRC investigation. Unbeknownst to either Currin or the State Archives Service, on 2 June 1993, a month before the July Security Secretariat circular, the Cabinet had approved a new set of guidelines for the disposal of "state sensitive" documentation. These guidelines had their origin in meetings of NIS top management in 1990 and 1991, where it was decided to use NIS's own destruction guidelines as a point of departure for the preparation of governmentwide guidelines. The proposal was taken to the State Security Council, which adopted the guidelines in May 1993, subject to a NIS investigation of compara-tive practice internationally. There is no evidence that NIS conducted such an investigation. The following month, the council proposed the guidelines to the Cabinet, which duly approved them. They empow-ered ministers to authorize the destruction of financial and related records outside parameters laid down by the Treasury and heads of departments to authorize the destruction of all "state sensitive" records meeting certain loosely defined criteria.[18] The guidelines were dis-tributed to all government departments. Carrying the weight of the highest authority in the land, their impact was severe. For instance, the State Archives Service's own parent body, the Department of National Education, promptly destroyed most of the files in its security-related filing system, despite the fact that the system was subject to a State

Archives Service disposal authority, which had earmarked the great majority of the files for archival preservation. Nevertheless, the evidence suggests that implementation was extremely uneven and shaped directly by an office's positioning in relation to the coercive aspects of apartheid administration.

It is unclear to what extent subsequent destruction exercises were in response to or shaped by the Cabinet-approved guidelines of June 1993. But clearly, senior managers in state structures regarded themselves as having been given the green light to sanitize records in their care. No records of the KwaZulu Intelligence Service (KWAZINT) survived. KWAZINT existed between 1986 and 1991 as a special NIS project managed in cooperation with the KwaZulu homeland. All project records were either sent to or managed by NIS. During 1995, the remaining former homeland intelligence services were integrated into the new civilian intelligence services, the National Intelligence Agency (NIA), and the South African Secret Service. It seems that, before then, very little records destruction had been effected by these services. However, between April and October 1995, a NIA Chief Directorate Research and Analysis Coordinating Committee subjected some of the records inherited from these services to a thorough re-evaluation process. Working both on-site and with records that had been transferred to NIA headquarters, the committee was mandated to identify for preservation records of value to NIA from both operational and historical perspectives. The TRC investigation revealed that less than 5 percent of the records were identified for preservation, almost none of them predating 1990, and that in practice the sole criterion for preservation seems to have been security relevance. The remaining records were subsequently destroyed, the last destruction exercise taking place as late as November 1996. This episode revealed the resilience of attitudes and values from the past. Not only did NIA, ostensibly a structure of the new democratic South African state, implement the sanitization policy of the apartheid state, in doing so, it ignored the State Archives Service and defied moratoria on the destruction of public records introduced in 1995.[19] After completion of the re-evaluation process, large volumes of additional records were secured at NIA headquarters from the offices of the former Bophutatswana, Transkei, and Venda intelligence services. The periods covered by these records are as follows: Bophutatswana Intelligence Service (1973–1995), Bophutatswana National Security

Council (1987–1994), Transkei Intelligence Service (1969–1994), and Venda Intelligence Service (1979–1994).

The South African Defence Force responded decisively to the Cabinet-approved guidelines. In 1992, Lieutenant General Steyn, SADF chief of staff, had been appointed to investigate SADF intelligence activities. On 23 November 1992, all SADF structures had been informed that from then on records were only to be destroyed with the express approval of Steyn. However, on receipt of the Cabinet-approved guidelines, the chief of the SADF ordered their immediate implementation, thus effectively repealing Lieutenant General Steyn's instruction. Two joint teams consisting of Inspector General and Counter Intelligence personnel were appointed to visit all units and to identify records for destruction. A countrywide destruction exercise followed. By and large, this exercise failed to produce the required destruction certificates, making analysis of its impact extremely difficult. The TRC investigation was forced to seek a sense of the impact through probes into what it regarded as hot spots:

- Although subjected to close scrutiny during the 1993 destruction exercise, a surprisingly large volume of Military Intelligence files survived. As one of the South African National Defence Force's (SANDF) legal team commented to me during the investigation, "They should have destroyed more." Another instance of being confronted by a ghost from the past. Three discrete file groups were identified at the SANDF Archives: group number fourteen, comprising 299 boxes of files covering the period 1977 to 1987; group number twenty-one, comprising 254 files covering the period 1975 to 1987; and group number thirty, comprising 529 boxes of files covering the period 1976 to 1996.[20] However, significant gaps were identified. For instance, no record accumulations of the directorate Special Tasks or the Directorate Covert Collection could be found, and only a small accumulation of Contra-Mobilisation Projects (COMOPS).

- No record accumulation related to the Civilian Cooperation Bureau could be found.

- Spot checks revealed that not all personnel files could be made available, raising the question of whether or not such files had been destroyed.

- Spot checks suggested that substantial documentation of cross-border operations in neighboring countries had survived.
- Very little NSMS documentation managed by the SADF has survived. The only significant accumulation comprises fifty-four boxes of files (now in the SANDF Archives) generated in the Eastern Cape and preserved for use in the inquest conducted into the death of political activist Mathew Goniwe. However, some other NSMS documentation was identified in each of the three Military Intelligence file groups described above.
- A task group authorized by the chief of the SANDF in June 1994 managed the acquisition by the SANDF Archives of all extant records of the former defense forces of Transkei, Bophutatswana, Venda, and Ciskei. These forces had been amalgamated with the SADF and nonstatutory forces to form the SANDF in April 1994. Apart from the 1,544 boxes of files secured from the Bophutatswana Defence Force, relatively insignificant documentary traces were secured: eighty boxes of files from the Transkei, 115 from the Ciskei, and 331 from Venda. Excluded from these figures are personnel files, which were integrated with the SANDF's personnel file series. Clearly, then, huge volumes of records generated by the defense forces of the former homelands had been destroyed.

The limitations of the TRC investigation were exposed dramatically in 2001 when the South African History Archive (SAHA) put in a Promotion of Access to Information Act request for a list of all extant apartheid-era Military Intelligence records. Whereas the TRC, as detailed above, had been told about and given access to only three file groups, SAHA was provided with a list of forty-two file groups, including the three examined by the TRC. This discovery carries considerable import. Not only does it provide evidence that broader TRC investigations were hindered by obstruction in the security establishment, it also places a question mark behind the conclusions drawn in relation to the extent of the pre-1994 purge. How many other caches of records are lurking in security establishment facilities?

This reservation notwithstanding, it seems that by May 1994, when the new democratically elected government took office, a massive deletion of state documentary memory had taken place. This enforced

amnesia was concentrated, for obvious reasons, in the security establishment. Unlike their counterparts in the former East Germany,
Kampuchea, and other countries, South Africa's apartheid leaders had
had plenty of time in which to do the job thoroughly. Despite this, surprising pockets of public records survived the process, even within the
security establishment. Some I have already detailed. There were others.
From the perspective of documenting resistance to apartheid, two
are of particular interest. Firstly, the Department of Prison Services,
despite routinely destroying classified records in the pre-1990 period
and acting on all the 1993 governmentwide guidelines, preserved intact
two significant file series: case files opened for every security/political
prisoner; and case files opened for every prisoner under sentence of
death. And secondly, a comprehensive accumulation of records generated by the Department of Justice's Security Legislation Directorate
survived. The directorate was established in 1982 and endured until
1991. Its predecessor was the Internal Security Division, and before
that, beginning in 1949, the function was performed by various individuals in the department. Its function was to make recommendations
to the ministers of justice and law and order concerning the administration of security legislation, for instance should an individual or
organization be banned? Should an individual be restricted? Should
a certain gathering be allowed? Legislation falling within its ambit
included the Suppression of Communism Act, Internal Security Act,
Affected Organizations Act, Terrorism Act, Unlawful Organizations
Act, and the Public Safety Act. It made recommendations on the basis
of investigations initiated by the Security Police. Recommendations
were supported by information gathered on its behalf by the Security
Police, NIS, and Military Intelligence. The evidence suggests that the
directorate's records management was impeccable. Records were kept
in accordance with State Archives Service and departmental directives,
with disposal being performed in terms of disposal authorities issued
by the Archives Commission and the director of archives. While the
directorate did routinely destroy classified records received from other
state offices in terms of the NIS guidelines, it ignored all the 1993
disposal guidelines. The directorate's extant records, kept in excellent
condition by the Ministry of Justice, comprise the following: a series
of case files for individuals, spanning the period 1949 to 1991; a series
of case files for organizations and for publications (the series for orga-

nizations includes files inherited by the directorate dating back to the 1920s); and policy, administrative, and other subject-based correspondence files.

Despite the large-scale destruction of records that had taken place during the negotiation process, as the April 1994 general election loomed, President De Klerk and his Cabinet became anxious about what remaining public records the new government would inherit. Late in 1993, the president's office asked the chief state law advisor whether representatives of De Klerk's government could retain custody of certain records after April 1994. A draft memorandum leading to the formal request cited an obscure British precedent and indicated that one of the motivations was to "keep this information out of the hands of future co-governors."[21] The records referred to were *gebruiksdokumentasie*—working documentation—including Cabinet minutes and the minutes of Cabinet committees, ministers' committees, and the State Security Council. At the time, none of these records had been transferred into the custody of the State Archives Service, on the grounds that their "sensitive nature" excluded them from the operation of the Archives Act. In his opinion 207/1993 of 22 December 1993, the chief state law advisor indicated that such records could not be removed from the state's custody. Also in December 1993, President De Klerk referred the same question to Advocate S. A. Cilliers for an opinion. Advocate Cilliers responded on 13 January 1994, confirming the chief state law advisor's opinion and going further by disagreeing with opinion 299/1991 and its affirmation of the legality of the destruction of "state sensitive" records on the authorization of departmental heads.[22] Subsequently, Cabinet and Cabinet committee records were transferred to the State Archives Service, albeit with a Cabinet-imposed ten-year embargo on access. The service ignored the embargo, with access being managed from the outset under the terms of the Archives Act's access provisions. In 1995 and 1997, the surviving residue of State Security Council and related records was also transferred into archival custody. Why, one must ask, did De Klerk and his Cabinet not simply destroy these records? With approval already given for the destruction of numerous other records categories, why the fastidiousness over these? I suspect that the answer is twofold. On the one hand, they were high-profile records that both the media and the new government would be anxious to see after April 1994. On the other, the destruction of these records would directly involve the Cabinet. Consequently, it would be impossible to blame junior officials for misinterpreting disposal guidelines.

## ACCOUNTABILITY

The routine destruction of classified public records outside the parameters of the Archives Act had begun well before 1990. Sanctioned by the head of state, the process was concentrated in South Africa's security establishment. Between 1990 and 1994, this process was broadened into a systematic endeavor authorized by the Cabinet and reaching into all sectors of the state and embraced categories of records designated as "state sensitive." At the time and subsequently, those responsible maintained that the endeavor was designed simply to protect intelligence sources and the legitimate security interests of the state. The evidence demonstrates that it went far beyond this, constituting a systematic sanitization of official memory resources ahead of the nation's transition to democracy. Those responsible also maintained that the endeavor was entirely legal. They pointed to the state legal opinions secured by the state president's office, NIS, and the director general of National Education in 1991 and 1993, which ruled that "state sensitive" public records fell outside the definition of records that were subject to the Archives Act. This argument is deeply flawed.

Firstly, the legal opinions were disputed by the State Archives Service, Advocate S. A. Cilliers, and Brian Currin, the national director of Lawyers for Human Rights. The basis of Currin's successful legal intervention in 1993 was a rejection of the two 1991 opinions. Secondly, the public position adopted by the Cabinet itself was that all public records should be dealt with in terms of the Archives Act. Thirdly, the state used the legal opinions selectively. For instance, the 1993 opinion's recommendation that an "advisory mechanism" on records destruction be created was never implemented. Fourthly, the Cabinet's approval of the destruction of financial records outside requirements laid down by the Treasury was of dubious legal validity. And fifthly, the legal opinions begged the question: In terms of what law are "state sensitive" records to be destroyed? Several officials involved in such destruction pointed to the Protection of

Information Act, but this act makes no reference to the destruction of documents.

Ultimately, the question of legality is a nonissue. On the one hand, apartheid was characterized by "official lawlessness,"[23] with rules and actions that were perfectly legal but lacked legitimacy and bore little or no relation to the rule of law. On the other, it is clear that the sanitization of official memory resources would have taken place irrespective of legal constraints. As Brian Currin said of the 1993 settlement that followed his legal intervention, the only way to enforce it would have been to "tie up their [the government's] hands and confiscate all the relevant machinery they can use to destroy documents."[24]

Given its legislative mandate, the State Archives Service was the principal state agency responsible for acting against the destruction of public records without archival authorization. In the 1990 to 1994 period of mass destruction, intervention by the service achieved nothing. It followed up by correspondence every allegation of illegal records destruction, engaged the security establishment in debate around the issue, registered its disagreement with the 1991 and 1993 legal opinions, and forced revision of NIS's 1994 *Guidelines for the Protection of Classified Information*. However, it was hamstrung by the apartheid system's disregard for accountability, by inadequate resources, by its junior status in government, and by a leadership that was intimidated by the security establishment and lacked the will to act decisively. I was a staff member of the service throughout this period and remember well how I and some of my junior colleagues pushed for such action while the leadership chose to sit on the fence. Earlier in this essay I recounted the inadequacy of leadership's response to the 1993 Security Secretariat circular authorizing the destruction of certain categories of classified records. To cite another instance, in June 1992, the Department of Foreign Affairs requested authority to destroy certain special projects files. When the director of archives indicated that they should be transferred into State Archives Service custody, Foreign Affairs withdrew its application and claimed that the files were in fact merely empty file covers. The director refused my calls for an investigation. More damning was the director's collusion with NIS in 1992, cited earlier in this essay, to secure authorization for the quick destruction of that agency's financial and related records. Specific instances aside, not once in the period 1990 to 1994 did the director authorize an investigative inspection of an office suspected of illegally destroying records. Not once did the director undertake a face-to-face meeting with a suspected perpetrator. And not once was the Archives Act used to institute an investigation of possible criminal charges in terms of the act.

What about intervention by the liberation movements? I joined the African National Congress (ANC) in 1990, and in 1992 I was appointed to its Archives Committee (a subcommittee of its Commission on Museums, Monuments and Heraldry). Within the committee and other structures I was involved in there was an acute awareness of the danger that the apartheid state was planning a mass destruction of public records. The experience of Zimbabwe in the months preceding that country's independence, when huge quantities of public records were destroyed by the outgoing regime, was frequently cited in discussions. It was felt imperative that the issue be put on the agenda during negotiations with the apartheid government, and that the ANC's leadership should call for a moratorium on the destruction of public records with immediate effect. The first formal recommendation for such a moratorium was made at a meeting of the Commission on Museums, Monuments and Heraldry in March 1992, and at the ANC's 1993 Conference on Culture and Development it was resolved that "there should be an immediate cessation of the destruction of all State records regardless of existing policy."[25] However, it proved impossible to mobilize the leadership behind the issue. It was not put on the table during the multiparty negotiation process. Support for Currin's 1993 legal intervention was limited to a media release backing his endeavor. When the Transitional Executive Council was established in 1993, the liberation movements that participated failed to ensure that the enabling legislation addressed the question of a moratorium. Moreover, the Transitional Executive Council failed to take any action in the wake of the Currin settlement—the council was, in the words of Currin, "just paralyzed and didn't respond."[26] Action was only to take place in 1995. In June of that year the National Intelligence Coordinating Committee introduced a moratorium on the destruction of all "intelligence documents." On 29 November 1995, the Cabinet decided on a moratorium that applied to all records of the state, irrespective of their age and irrespective of whether or not the director of archives had authorized their destruction. This blanket moratorium endured until completion of the TRC's work in 1998, thereafter it was narrowed to the records of the security establishment. It will only be lifted when the TRC's amnesty process is concluded. These moratoria, of course, came too late. It is also not clear how effectively the moratoria were communicated to and enforced within security establishment structures. Certainly NIS and later NIA, as I pointed out earlier in this essay, continued destroying records after their introduction, until as late as November 1996. It could be argued that more decisive intervention by the African National Congress and the other liberation movements would not have prevented, nor even curbed, the mass destruction. Nevertheless, this was a lever that sadly was not utilized.

In its findings on the destruction of public records in the period 1990 to 1994, the TRC distinguished between culpability and accountability.[27] The former implies wrongdoing, the latter shortcoming or negligence. Identified as culpable were

- The Cabinet and the State Security Council, for sanctioning, from at least 1993, a governmentwide purging of official memory resources.
- NIS, for beginning its purging exercise before Cabinet sanction was secured; initiating the process that led to the adoption of governmentwide destruction guidelines in 1993; defying the terms of the Currin settlement by failing to revise its *Guidelines for the Protection of Classified Information;* and of supervising, or at least of failing to prevent, the purging of NSMS records.
- The Security Police, also for beginning its purging exercise before Cabinet sanction was secured.
- The numerous individual state officials and operatives who used the cloak provided by the destruction endeavor to destroy or remove documents without authorization.

Also found culpable were the NIA officials directly responsible for the destruction of records until as late as November 1996, in defiance of the two government moratoria. NIA's top management was held accountable for not preventing this destruction. In terms of the period 1990 to 1994, the TRC assigned accountability as follows:

- The head of the Security Secretariat, for the consequences of his July 1993 circular to all government departments recommending the destruction of certain categories of classified record.

- The State Archives Service, for "the indecisive and ineffective steps it took to halt the destruction endeavor."
- The liberation movements, for failing "to exercise all the leverage at their disposal in acting against the endeavor."

## CONCLUSION

It is far too early to come to any conclusions about the impact of the 1990 to 1994 purge on social memory in South Africa. Our knowledge of the purge relies heavily on the TRC investigation into records destruction, an investigation severely constrained by a number of factors. It operated with limited resources within extremely tight timeframes. Of necessity, it had to rely on highly selective probes into hot spots, and in doing so was dependent to a greater or lesser degree on resources and cooperation made available by state structures still in the initial stages of transformation. While for the most part levels of support appeared to be excellent, cases of overt obstruction did occur.[28] As detailed earlier in this essay, the most blatant case of obstruction that we are aware of was exposed by the South African History Archive in 2001, when it was able to demonstrate the extent to which the TRC was deceived by Military Intelligence. This case of a successful hiding of substantial accumulations of records from the TRC investigation places a question mark behind all its findings. Clearly, much work remains to be done. Nevertheless, in my view, the TRC investigation gave us a sound grasp of the broader processes of records destruction—the big picture—and considerable insight into the impact of those processes within the security establishment. It remains for the National Archives and private researchers to extend these boundaries. What we can say at this stage is that the evidence suggests a considerable impact on social memory. Swathes of official documentary memory, particularly around the inner workings of the apartheid state's security apparatus, have been obliterated. Moreover, the apparent complete destruction of records confiscated from individuals and organizations over many years by the Security Police has removed arguably the country's richest accumulation of records documenting the struggles against apartheid. The overall work of the TRC suffered substantially as a result. In seeking to reconstruct and understand the past, so many pieces of that past's puzzle were missing. As the TRC itself indicated, "the destruction of state documentation probably did more to undermine the investigative work of the Commission than any other single factor."[29] As significant, it now appears, was the degree to which surviving state documentation was successfully hidden from the TRC's purview. For the most part the big picture—the fundamental shape and pattern of process—was as clear as any interrogation of the past can be. But so often the details, the nuances, the texture, and the activities and experiences of individuals, remain absent. On the other hand, TRC investigation teams were often surprised by records accumulations that survived the purge. One has to ask why they survived. Imperfect central control over what was a vast bureaucracy? The presence of individuals with consciences in the lower reaches of the state? Determination to preserve information that could compromise the leadership of the new government? During the course of the investigation, I saw several files that could create severe difficulties for people now prominent in the public and other sectors. At one point I remember one of my TRC colleagues turning to me with the comment, "Perhaps it would have been better if all these files had been destroyed."

More edifying has been the discovery of extensive accumulations of records detailing the apartheid state's dispossession of individuals' and communities' rights to land. The National Archives and the Department of Land Affairs have worked closely with the National Commission for the Restitution of Land Rights to identify substantial records series in state offices around the country that the commission is using to investigate land claims. Clearly, then, much work remains to be done before we have a comprehensive picture of the scale and consequences of the 1990 to 1994 purge.

Imperfect as our understanding of the purge might be, we know enough to have learned crucial lessons from it. Perhaps the most important is the necessity for transparency and accountability in government. As the transition to democracy has gathered momentum, "openness" and "disclosure" have become watchwords both within the state and in broader societal processes. This emphasis is underpinned by the new constitution's recognition of the public right of access to information, particularly that held by the state.[30] However, it remains to be seen how well this lesson has been learned. Already evident is a strong counter-current, fed by state officials and structures that are finding themselves blinded by all the light. There is now awareness within the state—honed by the impact of the records destruction moratoria—that no state has the resources to preserve indefinitely all the information in its systems. Selection procedures—choosing what to remember and what to forget—are essential. This supports both the efficacy of archival programs and the protection of legitimate interests through confidentiality. But beyond the determining of memory's outer boundaries, the state is also becoming adept at crafting the hidden places—the "official secret"—within that memory. Take the TRC, torchbearer of disclosure, as an example. Some of its hearings were held *in camera*. Its records of protected witnesses were secret. Information on certain decision-making processes and internal tensions and disputes was jealously kept out of the public domain. Its archive is subject to various access restrictions. Some democrats accept that a measure of official secrecy is desirable; most accept it as unavoidable. But there are disturbing signs in postapartheid South Africa that official secrecy is beginning to be embraced as a point of departure. In March 1999, the SANDF demanded the return of certain "top secret" documents it had submitted to the TRC—this followed the detention by the police of a Swiss journalist for possessing a copy of one of these SANDF documents, a document that he had been given by the TRC. The state has effected no meaningful changes to the inherited systems of information classification and staff security clearance. Increasingly, the media are running into government communications officials who constitute brick walls rather than gateways. At the same time, heat directed against media freedom by the state is gathering fuel. And "open democracy" legislation—which will provide for freedom of information, the protection of personal information, and the protection of whistleblowers from the state—has been through a protracted gestation cloaked in secrecy.[31] It seems that for South Africans, particularly lawyers, journalists, and activists, learning how to wrestle effectively with the "official secret" will be essential. The degree to which they are successful will be a crucial measure of South Africa's democratization.

The purge also highlighted the need for a democratic state to take appropriate measures to prevent the sanitizing of official memory resources. The cornerstone for such measures is the provision of suitably powerful legal instruments to a state agency responsible for the auditing of public record-keeping and, ideally, for managing public archives services as well. In many respects, the 1962 Archives Act constituted such an instrument, but it possessed four fatal flaws. Firstly, many state offices were excluded, wholly or partially, from its operation. Secondly, its definition of *archives* (public records) contained loopholes that the apartheid state was able to exploit ruthlessly. Thirdly, the penalty for conviction on a charge of destroying a public record without archival authorization was a laughable fine of 200 rand.[32] This did not constitute a deterrent. And fourthly, it provided no mechanisms for ensuring accountability and transparency in the selection of public records for preservation by the director of archives. All these flaws have been rectified by the National Archives of South Africa Act of 1996, and the national government has put in place mechanisms to ensure that archival legislation passed by the provinces follows the same model.

Needless to say, a powerful legal instrument without appropriate executive action is nothing more than a dead letter. This was recognized by the TRC in three of its recommendations:[33]

- The government should provide the National Archives with the resources it requires to give life to the legislation. The power to inspect governmental bodies, for instance, is rendered meaningless if the resources to exercise it are not made available. Current budgetary allocations to the National Archives are woefully inadequate.

- The government should take steps to ensure that the positioning of the National Archives within the state supports its function as the auditor of government record-keeping. Currently, as with the State Archives Service in the past, the National Archives is positioned as a junior subcomponent of a noncentral national department and lacks both the status and the autonomy it requires to perform the auditing function. Unfortunately, this TRC recommendation loses its force through contradictory elaboration—at one and the same time it advocates independent agency status (the ideal) and positioning within either the office of the president or that of the deputy president.

- The security establishment should not be allowed to escape the operation of the National Archives of South Africa Act. While the act brings security bodies firmly within its ambit, it does allow for various exclusionary options.[34] It is conceded that a special status for such bodies appropriate to the sensitivity of the records they generate would be legitimate, but that they should remain fully subject to the professional supervision of the National Archives.

The TRC also made several recommendations related to redressing the imbalances imposed by the purge on official memory.[35] A number relate to ensuring that the National Archives secures control over the records of the security establishment that have survived the purge. To date, only two of the many records accumulations concerned have been transferred into the National Archives' custody, and of the remainder not one has been either inspected or subjected to an archival audit by the National Archives. In addition, the TRC recommended as follows:

- The security establishment should make every attempt to locate and retrieve documents removed without authorization by operatives of apartheid security structures. To my knowledge, nothing has been done in this regard.
- The South African government should acknowledge that, in terms of internationally recognized archival principles, the extant records of the South West Africa Territory Force (currently in the custody of the SANDF Archives) properly belong in Namibia and must be returned to the Namibian government. It was noted that an agreement between South Africa and Namibia covering equivalent civilian records was already in place. To date, this recommendation has not been acted on.
- The National Archives should be given the necessary resources to take transfer of, process professionally, and make available to the public the TRC's own records (which fill many of the gaps in official memory resources). After a long tussle with the Department of Justice, the National Archives has at last been given the go ahead to take custody of the TRC's records when the TRC office finally closes down, probably early in 2002.
- The National Archives should be given the necessary resources to fill the gaps in official memory resources through the collection of nonpublic records and the promotion of oral history projects. To date, the National Archives has not received a significant infusion of resources for these purposes.

I find the TRC recommendations compelling. It remains to be seen what the state makes of them. To date the signs are mixed. Three years down the line there has been no formal government response to the TRC recommendations. It is hoped that this will be forthcoming once the TRC completes its work and submits the codicil to the final report.[36] On the other hand, the National Archives has sought either to promote the recommendations, where its mandate and resources allow, or to implement them. However, in every case, the National Archives is reliant on higher authority to give full effect to the recommendations.

# Endnotes

1   A version of this essay was first published in *Transformation* 42 (2000). A revised version was published in Richard Cox and David Wallace, eds., *Archives and the Public Good: Accountability and Records in Modern Society* (Westport, Conn., and London: Quorum Books, 2002). The present version has been edited from the latter.

2   See "Contesting Remembering and Forgetting: The Archive of South Africa's Truth and Reconciliation Commission," *Innovation* 24 (2002).

3   Between 1988 and 1994, I was an archivist in the Pretoria records management division of the South African State Archives Service. Rumors were rife within the public service, and by early 1993, I had enough evidence from sources in various governmental bodies to know that destruction was widespread. When it became clear that the State Archives Service was unable or unwilling to act decisively, I began leaking information on the destruction to the African National Congress, other oppositional structures, and the media. The celebrated 1993 Currin case dealt with later in this essay pushed the issue firmly onto center stage in the media. And the Harms and Goldstone commissions of inquiry as well as the Goniwe inquest revealed substantial evidence of systematic records destruction.

4   The seventeen-member Truth and Reconciliation Commission was given four principal functions: to establish as complete a picture as possible of the causes, nature, and extent of gross human rights violations committed in South Africa between 1960 and 1994; to facilitate the granting of amnesty to perpetrators of gross human rights violations associated with a political objective; to recommend appropriate reparation for the victims of gross human rights violations; and to compile a report of its activities, findings, and recommendations. The commission's final report was submitted to President Nelson Mandela in October 1998. However, the work of the commission's Amnesty Committee proceeded and is anticipated to continue into the new millennium.

5   South Africa, Promotion of National Unity and Reconciliation Act (Act Number 34 of 1995): Section 4(d).

6   South Africa, The Archives Act (Act Number 6 of 1962). See in particular the definition of a "government office" in section 1.

7   The apartheid government allocated a homeland to each of South Africa's major African ethnic "groups." In terms of separate development policy, these Africans were to exercise full political rights only in these homelands. The ultimate goal was to establish each homeland as an independent country—by 1994 four of them had taken "independence."

8   Each of the security establishment's structures was subjected to close scrutiny by a joint team comprising representatives of the structure concerned, the TRC, the Human Rights Commission, and the National Archives.

9   The work of this investigation is reflected in the following sections of the TRC's final report: Truth and Reconciliation Commission, *Final Report* (Cape Town, 1998), vol. 1, chapter 8 and vol. 5, chapter 8, paragraphs 62, 66, 67, and 100–108.

10  My work was subsequently edited by the TRC editorial team, but I was involved in the editing process. In preparing this essay I had a choice between quoting extensively from the published version or of assuming that my role in its authorship precluded the need for what would be a clumsy nicety. I chose the latter course, working always in the first instance from my first draft for the TRC and only quoting from the published version in instances where that seemed appropriate.

11  The State Archives Service became the National Archives on 1 January 1997. See National Archives of South Africa Act (Act Number 43 of 1996).

12  South Africa, Debates of the Senate (1962).

13  The guidelines were referenced as EM 9-12. The relevant paragraphs are 31 and 32.

14  The updated guidelines were referenced as SP 2/8/1.

15  These elaborative guidelines are reproduced as appendices 2 and 3 to volume 1, chapter 8 of the TRC's final report. See TRC, *Final Report*.

16  South Africa, Supreme Court, Transvaal Provincial Division, Case No. 19304/93.

17  The statement was issued in Afrikaans. This is my own translation of the text.

18  The guidelines are reproduced as appendix 1 to volume 1, chapter 8 of the TRC's final report. See TRC, *Final Report*.

19  The moratoria are dealt with later in this essay.

20  It subsequently emerged that Military Intelligence had hidden the great majority of surviving apartheid-era files from the TRC. See my essay "Using the Promotion of Access to Information Act: The Case of the South African History Archive," in *The Right to Know: South Africa's Promotion of Administrative Justice and Access to Information Acts,* ed. Claudia Lange and Jakkie Wessels (Cape Town: Siber Ink, 2004).

21  The text was in Afrikaans. This is my own translation.

22  Advocate Cilliers's opinion is dated 13 January 1993, but this is clearly a dating error.

23  Christopher Merrett, *A Culture of Censorship: Secrecy and Intellectual Repression in South Africa* (Cape Town: David Philip and University of Natal Press, 1994), 203.

24  TRC, *Final Report*, vol. 1, chapter 8, 232.

25  I quote this from my own conference notes.

26  TRC, *Final Report,* vol. 1, chapter 8, 234.

27  TRC, *Final Report,* vol. 1, chapter 8, 235–36.

28  The TRC acknowledged excellent support received by it from South Africa's National Archives and various security establishment structures, but noted obstruction encountered in work with the SANDF. See TRC, *Final Report,* vol. 1, chapter 8, 202–4, 216. Numerous minor instances of obstruction were not noted by the TRC.

29  TRC, *Final Report,* vol. 1, chapter 8, 204.

30  The new constitution also recognizes the right of access to information held by persons other than the state "that is required for the exercise or protection of any rights." South Africa, Constitution, Section 32(1).

31  The Open Democracy Bill was under consideration by the state for about five years. At the last moment it was decided to exclude provisions for the protection of personal information and of whistleblowers—both to be dealt with in separate legislation. In January 2000, the legislature passed the Promotion of Access to Information Act, which defines the right of access to information held both by the state and by persons other than the state. This act came into operation in March 2001. The Protected Disclosures Act, which provides for the protection of whistleblowers, was also passed in 2000.

32  This was the equivalent of about $24 U.S. dollars at the current exchange rate (August 2001). Section 16(1) of the National Archives of South Africa Act (Act Number 43 of 1996) has changed the penalty to "a fine or imprisonment for a period not exceeding two years or both such fine and imprisonment."

33 TRC, *Final Report,* vol. 5, chapter 8, 345.

34 The act allows for certain categories of public records identified by the National Archivist to remain in the custody of the creating agency rather than be transferred into the custody of the National Archives. It allows for public records to remain in the custody of the creating agency if another act of Parliament requires it. And it allows for a governmental body to be exempted from any provision of the act with the concurrence of the national archivist, the National Archives Commission, and the responsible minister.

35 TRC, Final Report, vol. 5, chapter 8, 346.

36 By mid-2005, it had become clear that no such formal government response would be forthcoming.

# CHAPTER 19

## Using the Promotion of Access to Information Act (PAIA): The Case of the South African History Archive[1]

## THE SOUTH AFRICAN HISTORY ARCHIVE

The South African History Archive (SAHA) is an independent archive dedicated to documenting and supporting the struggles for justice in South Africa. In South African parlance it is a nongovernmental organization (NGO). It is a registered trust, governed by a board of trustees, which appoints dedicated professionals to achieve its mission. Although at its inception in the late 1980s it was closely connected to the United Democratic Front, the Congress of South African Trade Unions, and the African National Congress, it has always been politically nonaligned and committed to collecting material from organizations and individuals across the political spectrum. Its founding mission was to strive to recapture our lost and neglected history and to record history in the making. This informed a focus on documenting the struggles against apartheid. Today there is an equal emphasis on documenting the making of democracy. With its physical positioning at the University of the Witwatersrand, there is a special endeavor to weave the collections into processes of education for democracy. In 2001, SAHA launched its Freedom of Information

Programme, dedicated to using the Promotion of Access to Information Act to extend the boundaries of freedom of information and to build up an archive of materials released under the act for public use.

## SAHA'S FREEDOM OF INFORMATION PROGRAMME

South Africa's constitution guarantees South Africans a right of access to information, and the Promotion of Access to Information Act (2000) gives legislative expression to the right. This act (PAIA), which came into operation in March 2001, defines parameters to the right in relation to information held both by public and private bodies. Effective and meaningful implementation will be hampered by three factors. Firstly, South Africans have been shaped by generations of an absence of the right to information. They have neither the expectations nor the skills to ensure that PAIA is utilized optimally. Secondly, access to records depends on the appropriate creation and subsequent management of records. In South Africa, in both public and private sectors, records environments are characterized by a Wild West approach with few if any rules of the road. And thirdly, the state is not adequately resourced to ensure effective implementation. This applies to governmental bodies (which generate public records), the Human Rights Commission (which must monitor implementation), and the courts (which will be responsible for interpreting PAIA and dealing with citizens' appeals against denials of access).

What South Africa desperately needs in this new era of freedom of information are organizations committed to promoting public awareness of the opportunities provided by PAIA; supporting human rights requests for information; testing the parameters of access restrictions imposed by information-holding bodies; and building up an archive of material released to the public in terms of PAIA. Given SAHA's history and present positioning, the organization is ideally placed to pursue these multiple objectives. It is especially well positioned to take on the last-mentioned, archival objective.

SAHA's Freedom of Information Program (FOIP) is designed to achieve the multiple objectives outlined above. As shown in appendices A and B below, in the period 2001–2002, a total of 120 requests to state agencies were submitted by FOIP in terms of PAIA. These requests fell into four broad categories: 1) those submitted in terms of the "Gays in the Apartheid Military" special project—here the objective has been to access state documentation on the apartheid military's policies and programs relating to homosexuals; 2) requests for access to Truth and Reconciliation Commission (TRC) records; 3) requests for access to surviving apartheid-era security establishment records; and 4) requests submitted on behalf of individuals or organizations doing apartheid research or seeking information to support human rights endeavors—fifty-nine of the requests fell into this category. SAHA offers a range of services under FOIP:

- SAHA has a growing collection of materials released under the Promotion of Access to Information Act. Finding aids are available, and SAHA staff members offer full user support, either by distance or in the reading room of the Historical Papers Department at the University of the Witwatersrand. Copies of materials can be made for members of the public.

- Through its use of PAIA, SAHA has generated considerable documentation around the act's operation. Access to this documentation, and to the database utilized for tracking individual requests and all follow-up actions, is available to researchers free of charge.

- SAHA staff members have expertise and experience in the operation of PAIA, record-keeping in government, and the broader access to information regime in South Africa. They offer support and advice in all these areas. Customized training is also available.

- To those wishing to make requests for access to records, SAHA offers specific guidance and assistance. The organization is equipped to assist with the preparation of requests and is willing to submit and track requests on behalf of researchers and other members of the public.

## OVERVIEW OF PAIA USE BY SAHA

Use of PAIA by the public in its first two years of operation has been extremely limited. Overarching statistics are not yet available, but it is clear that very few South Africans are using the legislation. A number of factors can be identified. Freedom of information, as an idea and as a culture, has not yet taken root in the country. The media have given very little coverage to PAIA. And the fact that very few section 14 and section 51 manuals have been published means that the public does not have ready access to information about the resources available to it. In this context, statistics published by SAHA on its use of the act are especially significant. Appendices A and B give detailed breakdowns of the 120 requests submitted in 2001 and 2002.

SAHA's experience in 2001 was very encouraging. Of the twenty-four requests submitted to four state agencies, eleven resulted in the release of materials, only two were refused, and eleven were pending at year-end. While average response times were not good, the Department of Defence (including the South African National Defence Force), to whom ten requests had been directed, came in with a respectable average of four months.

In 2002, state obduracy in dealing with requests was far more pronounced than in 2001. This is reflected in the statistics—of the ninety-six requests submitted to twenty-one state agencies, twenty-seven resulted in the release of materials, forty were refused, and thirty-seven were pending at year-end. Average response times remained way over the statutory period of sixty days. SAHA took eleven refusals on internal appeal and six to the High Court. The single High Court action finalized by year-end saw SAHA succeeding in reaching an agreement with the Department of Defence to release Military Intelligence information on the apartheid state's dealings with other countries. A formal complaint against the Department of Justice, related to thirty-four boxes of "sensitive" TRC records, was lodged with both the Human Rights Commission and the Public Protector.

As in 2001, the best performer in 2002, statistically, was the Department of Defence. The cumulative statistics for 2001–2002 show that by far the highest number of requests were directed to them (40), and of the twenty-nine requests responded to by them at 2002 year-end, only nine of them were refused. Moreover, their average response time for 2002 (three months), especially in the light of both the volume and complexity of requests directed to them, was very good. As is recounted below, the department was also a quality performer in other respects.

Despite the problems outlined above, PAIA has enabled SAHA to build up a substantial archive of released materials. It has been arranged and described, and an inventory of the collection has been published in both hard copy and on the organization's Web site. In 2002, the archive was the most heavily consulted of the SAHA collections.

## LESSONS LEARNED BY SAHA

On a positive note, SAHA has demonstrated that PAIA can be an effective tool for ensuring public access to records held by the state. The substantial archive of released materials built up by it in less than two years attests to this. Two highlight experiences, one in 2001, the other in 2002, provide further evidence.

The potential efficacy of PAIA was most dramatically demonstrated in 2001 by SAHA's work on Military Intelligence records. A large part of the TRC's work involved accessing records in the custody of state structures. As was noted at various points in the commission's report, the attitudes of these structures ranged from extremely cooperative to obstructive. However, the degree to which obstruction might have affected the commission's work only became apparent in 2001 when evidence of large-scale concealment of records from the commission by the South African National Defence Force (SANDF) emerged. In 1997 and 1998, the commission's investigation of records destruction by the apartheid security establishment included a study of surviving Military Intelligence records. As was noted in the commission's report, the SANDF's nodal point disclosed only three series of Military Intelligence files. These were subsequently used selectively by various other commission investigations. However, in 2001 SAHA submitted a request in terms of PAIA to the SANDF for lists of all surviving apartheid-era Military Intelligence files. This request revealed not three series, but forty-one series embracing thousands of files. In other words, the existence of thirty-eight series of files had been concealed from the commission. It is not clear what impact this might have had on the commission's work. Nor is it clear whether this was an isolated incident or part of a broader pattern of obstruction. Nevertheless, it raises serious questions about the degree to which the commission was permitted access to the records it required in order to fulfill its mandate comprehensively.

The highlight experience of 2002 adds further evidence of the potential utility of PAIA and foregrounds the potentially progressive role of the High Court appeal mechanism. During 2002, the SANDF released certain Military Intelligence file lists to SAHA with various categories of information masked. Included in these categories was information on countries and firms having dealings with the apartheid military during the international arms embargo of the 1980s. SAHA's internal appeal against these maskings was unsuccessful, and consequently papers were filed in the High Court. The SANDF quickly offered SAHA an out-of-court settlement in terms of which fresh copies of the lists were made available with this information unmasked. Seen together with the successful High Court action of Richard Young in relation to documentation on the arms deal investigation, this raises hope that use of the court appeal mechanism will broaden the scope of freedom of information in South Africa.

Also encouraging has been the professionalism demonstrated by a number of state agencies in implementing the act. Worth singling out here is the SANDF, which has appointed deputy information officers, secured training for staff, created an effective mechanism for dealing with requests, and displayed diligence and courtesy in all its dealings with SAHA. A third of all SAHA requests have been directed to the SANDF. Key issues highlighted by SAHA's experience with the SANDF are as follows:

- In at least one case, the SANDF created a record in order to satisfy a SAHA request. This goes beyond PAIA requirements.
- In several cases the SANDF released a record with certain pieces of information in it "masked" (information restricted in terms of PAIA). In other words, the existence of restricted information in the record did not place the whole record outside of SAHA's reach. This has important implications for interpretation of PAIA's provision for the separation of restricted from unrestricted material.
- Initially the SANDF charged SAHA for time spent by its personnel in declassifying classified records. This was successfully appealed against by SAHA, but subsequent revisions to the PAIA regulations saw the SANDF reinstituting charges. Fruitful discussions between SAHA and SANDF personnel then saw agreement reached that the time taken to assess records in terms of PAIA should not be recorded as declassification time. The latter is actually a straightforward and relatively quick procedure. This links in to the following point.

- In two instances SAHA was refused access to certain records on the grounds that they are classified records. The public bodies concerned were the SANDF and the National Archives. SAHA appealed against the SANDF refusal on the basis that PAIA does not recognize the fact of classification as a legitimate reason for refusing access, and that records classification is effected in terms of the 1982 Protection of Information Act, which is subordinate to PAIA. After a number of discussions between SAHA and SANDF personnel, the latter clarified the situation to SAHA's satisfaction—the refusals were decided on grounds defined by PAIA and not on the basis of classification; and records to which access was refused would not be declassified.

SAHA's experiences with other state agencies have not always been as positive. SAHA has experienced problems resulting from government offices ignoring the act's procedural requirements. Notable is the fact that very few SAHA requests have been responded to within prescribed timeframes. Many responses have not complied with prescribed informational requirements. An example is the National Archives, which has averaged an eight-month turnaround on SAHA requests and has consistently failed to show good reason for refusing access.

Lack of implementation capacity in government is clearly a serious problem. By and large, existing officials have simply been given additional responsibilities under the act. Few have experience and expertise in record-keeping. Training by the Justice College and other institutions is touching the tip of the iceberg. The Human Rights Commission, with its manifold duties and responsibilities in terms of the act, is just beginning to develop capacity. And underlying all of this, the overall quality of records management in government is poor. In some sectors, a Wild West scenario prevails. What value is the right of access to records, when records are not created in the first place, or are submerged in chaos, or are lost or destroyed without authorization? For instance, SAHA is accumulating evidence of apartheid-era Security Police records seen by the TRC now being lost or having been destroyed. In another instance, SAHA has not even been able to establish the whereabouts of thirty-four boxes of "sensitive" TRC records despite using PAIA to this end since May of 2001. The Department of Justice and the National Intelligence Agency each point to the other as being in possession of the records, and in desperation SAHA was forced to take the matter to the High Court at the end of 2002.

What general lessons have been learned through SAHA's use of PAIA? Among many others, the following are the most important:

- For PAIA to be implemented effectively, sound record-keeping in government, supported by adequate resourcing, is essential.
- It seems that many government departments lack capacity to implement PAIA effectively.
- The length of time being taken by departments to process requests will severely impede the media and other PAIA requesters requiring a quick response urgently.
- It is not clear what sanctions can be imposed on bodies that fail to meet their statutory obligations in terms of the timeframes prescribed for responding to requests.
- There are a number of areas of uncertainty in relation to PAIA, all of which require clarification.
- Access under PAIA can be an extremely expensive business. For example, in one instance access to thirty files cost SAHA over 5,000 rands (including the access fee, search and preparation fees, and copying fees).
- SAHA's expert knowledge of government record-keeping has facilitated the request process. But what of those without such knowledge? Here the issue of the manual, which each body subject to PAIA must publish, becomes of crucial importance. Up to now, very few manuals have been published. As worrying is the lack of guidance in the act and the regulations on the minimum content requirements for the manual. It is essential that each manual provides a comprehensive and meaningful disclosure of record-keeping systems.

## THE IMPORTANCE OF THE MANUAL

The manual, it is argued, is a key provision in PAIA's emphasis on the need for proactive action on the part of bodies holding records. The content of the manual, then, is highly significant. Here the requirements in relation to the manual for public bodies (section 14 of the act) are focused on.

Section 14 provides detailed provisions concerning contextual information, which must be included in the manual. But when it comes to the core information—the information about records—it is extremely vague. The section's title raises the expectation of requirements for an "index of records," but this is not fulfilled in the section's text.

Section 14(1)(d) requires that the manual contains "a description of the subjects on which the body holds records and the categories of records held on each subject," with "sufficient detail to facilitate a request to a record of the body." There are three problem areas: 1) There is no mention of an index and no suggestion of information that would constitute an index. 2) The word *subject* is anything but precise. It could be interpreted broadly or narrowly. 3) The same with the word *category*. Clearly, regulations are needed to indicate precisely what is required here.

What is clear is that the objective is to facilitate public access to records. So that the gradient of the provision pulls compilers of the manual toward greater rather than less detail, and toward narrower rather than broader interpretations of "subject" and "category." But is this going to be enough to compel bodies to produce effective and user-friendly manuals? SAHA would argue that to achieve this goal, the manual will also have to make good business sense by providing bodies with a useful management tool. The manual, in short, should facilitate effective records management. For public bodies, this would mean a manual that facilitates compliance with the National Archives of South Africa (NASA) Act, which regulates the management of public records.

For public bodies, NASA compliance rests on a thorough knowledge of what records systems a body sustains and how each of these systems articulates with the functions and structures of the body. A management tool that captures this information would be of great value. And such a tool, SAHA would argue, would have the same value to private bodies. Now, section 14 (subsection (1)(a)) already requires bodies to include in the manual a description of the body's structures and functions. SAHA would like to see regulations that require bodies to integrate this description with records system descriptions.

SAHA is proposing that for each function (the largest unit of business activity in an organization), the manual should provide an account of the records systems (information systems that capture, maintain, and provide access to records over time) supporting it. This account should comprise the following:

- The name of the system
- The nature of the system in terms of records media and form
- The scope of the system in terms of main business activities
- The system's search facilities (classification system, finding aid, etc.)
- The structure(s) utilizing the system
- The person/official directly responsible for managing the system
- The system's connections with other systems

Joined to an index, this model would give meaningful expression to the terms *subject* and *category,* fulfill the requirements of section 14(1)(d), and meet the needs of both management and requesters.

## CONCLUSION

So, based on this SAHA case study, how successful has PAIA been as an instrument for freedom of information? Any conclusions must be tentative, with so many dimensions still untested. Experience with the act has been extremely uneven, ranging from the very encouraging to the deeply disappointing. Certainly it has opened up spaces and advanced levels of access to public records, but meeting the aims of its drafters depends on a range of resources and processes being put in place. The evidence suggests that the underlying conditions conducive to freedom of information remain in their infancy. Government is still shaped by an information ethos informed by the 1982 Protection of Information Act. We desperately need case law to establish interpretations of key PAIA provisions. And we need to be working against a milieu—not unique to South Africa—in which state-held information becomes a commodity that only the wealthy can afford to purchase.

## Appendix A: Statistics 2001

| Requestee | Carried over | No. of requests | Requests granted | Refusals | Pending or inadequate response | Internal appeals | Court action | Average response time |
|---|---|---|---|---|---|---|---|---|
| Dept. of Defence | 0 | 10 | 8 | 0 | 2 | 5 | 0 | 4 months |
| Dept. of Justice | 0 | 1 | 0 | 1 | 0 | 0 | 0 | 7 months |
| National Archives | 0 | 12 | 2 | 1 | 9 | 6 | 0 | 8 months |
| Dept. Environmental Affairs and Tourism | 0 | 1 | 1 | 0 | 0 | 0 | 0 | 23 days |
| Total | 0 | 24 | 11 | 2 | 11 | 11 | 0 | |

## Appendix B: Statistics 2002

| Requestee | Carried over | No. of requests | Requests granted | Refusals | Pending or inadequate response | Internal appeals | Court action | Average response time |
|---|---|---|---|---|---|---|---|---|
| Dept. of Defence | 2 | 30* | 12 | 9 | 9 | 1 | 1 | 3 months |
| Dept. of Justice | 0 | 15 | 5 | 7 | 3 | 5 | 3 | 4 months |
| National Archives | 9 | 1 | 3 | 5 | 2 | 4 | | 8 months |
| Dept. of Agriculture | 0 | 1 | 0 | 1 | 0 | 0 | 0 | 1 month |
| Dept. Environmental Affairs and Tourism | 0 | 1 | 0 | 0 | 1 | 0 | 0 | |
| Dept. of Foreign Affairs | 0 | | 0 | 0 | 1 | 0 | 0 | |
| National Intelligence Agency | 0 | 3** | 1 | 1 | 0 | 1 | 0 | 4 months |
| South African Police Service | 0 | 11 | 3 | 5 | 3 | 0 | 0 | 6 months |

*continued*

| Requestee | Carried over | No. of requests | Requests granted | Refusals | Pending or inadequate response | Internal appeals | Court action | Average response time |
|---|---|---|---|---|---|---|---|---|
| SA Council for the Non-Proliferation of Weapons of Mass Destruction | 0 | 1 | 0 | 0 | 1 | 0 | 0 | |
| Nuclear Energy Corporation of SA | 0 | 1 | 0 | 0 | 1 | 0 | 0 | |
| ARMSCOR | 0 | 2 | 0 | 0 | 2 | 0 | 0 | |
| Office of the Auditor General | 0 | 1 | 0 | 0 | 1 | 0 | 0 | |
| Health Professions Council of SA | 0 | 6 | 2 | 4 | 0 | 0 | 0 | 3 months |
| Dept. of Health | 0 | 1 | 0 | 0 | 1 | 0 | 0 | |
| University of Pretoria | 0 | 1 | 1 | 0 | 0 | 0 | 0 | 2 months |
| University of the Witwatersrand | 0 | 3 | 0 | 2 | 1 | 0 | 0 | 4 months |
| Iscor | 0 | 1 | 0 | 1 | 0 | 0 | 0 | 1 month |
| Provinces | | | | | | | | |
| Limpopo | 0 | 7 | 0 | 0 | 7 | 0 | 0 | |
| Mpumalanga | 0 | 4 | | | 4*** | 0 | 0 | 3 months |
| KwaZulu-Natal | 0 | 2 | 0 | 2 | 0 | 0 | 0 | 1 month |
| Western Cape | 0 | 3 | 0 | 3 | 0 | 0 | 0 | 6 months |
| Total | 11 | 96 | 27 | 40 | 37 | 11 | 4 | |

* 2 of these were withdrawn

** 1 request transferred to the Dept. of Justice

*** In this case records were received but could not be used for research purposes as they were either not readable or they could not be connected to the request

## Endnotes

1    This essay was first published in Claudia Lange and Jakkie Wessels, eds., *The Right to Know: South Africa's Promotion of Administrative Justice and Access to Information Acts* (Cape Town: Siber Ink, 2004).

# CHAPTER 20

## Unveiling South Africa's Nuclear Past[1]

*Verne Harris, Sello Hatang, and Peter Liberman*

The apartheid-era South African nuclear weapons program, which built and then dismantled six and one-half Hiroshima-type bombs, is a rarity in international history. But more than a decade after the program's exposure, the historical record of this case remains remarkably thin. A battery of secrecy laws was utilized during the program's lifetime to conceal the existence of South Africa's nuclear arsenal. But though the need for concealment evaporated with President De Klerk's decision to dismantle the program, secrecy laws obstructing fuller public disclosure have largely persisted into the democratic era. While there has been no formal, high-level articulation of official nuclear secrecy policy or justifications, officials of two successive African National Congress–led governments have expressed strong objections to further disclosures beyond those made in 1993 and 1994.

The costs of perpetual secrecy are considerable. As one of the few states to acquire a nuclear weapons arsenal and the only state ever to destroy one, South Africa presents an unusual opportunity to study the causes and processes of nuclear acquisition and disarmament. South Africa's nuclear history is thus a potentially valuable source of lessons for global nonproliferation policy. Its case also bears important lessons in nuclear safety and control procedures, which could help other small nuclear powers, like India and Pakistan, to secure their own arsenals. The value of the South African experience became more widely recognized when, in February 2003, Pretoria dispatched a team of diplomats and former weapons officials to advise Iraq on verifiable disarmament.

The South African government appears to be ambivalent and internally divided about greater openness on apartheid-era history, but there are signs of movement. The new South African constitution, which enshrines access to information as a fundamental right; the 2000 Promotion of Access to Information Act (PAIA); and an interdepartmental Classification and Declassification Review Committee aimed at addressing apartheid victims' demands for access to records have all set the stage for greater disclosure. In response to a PAIA request, the Defence Department recently declassified the first nuclear weapons policy document ever released to the public. But many documentary requests have been rejected or delayed arbitrarily, and the government has yet to put in place the infrastructure and resources needed to implement PAIA properly.

We begin by discussing the status of South African nuclear history and secrecy, including the limited nature and inaccuracies of the De Klerk–era disclosures. Massive shredding of the documentary record under De Klerk has severely constrained the potential for future archival research. But there is evidence that important records survived, notably the recent declassification and release of a March 1975 Defence Force memorandum recommending the acquisition of nuclear weapons. We briefly analyze the significance of the document, as it sheds new light on military attitudes about nuclear acquisition, and about the extent of the South African–Israeli alliance. It provides confirmation that Israel had offered South Africa Jericho missiles by that date and evidence that Israel at least implied it might furnish nuclear warheads as well. This disclosure and other recent signs of greater openness potentially represent a shift from laws and policies formerly prohibiting the release of additional information about South Africa's nuclear history.

We then turn to the incentives for the South African state for greater transparency in this sphere. The South African government may be realizing that disclosures would benefit the global nonproliferation regime, would support South Africa's international prestige and foreign policy agenda, and would enhance South Africa's democratic transparency. As shown by the example of the exposure of Project Coast, apartheid South Africa's secret chemical and biological weapons program, disclosure can be controlled to maximize the benefits and minimize the risks. We conclude by briefly considering steps that could be taken to promote a more effective disclosure process.

## NUCLEAR SECRECY AND REVELATIONS

### A Story Partly Told

At a December 1992 press conference, African National Congress (ANC) representatives demanded that the National Party government "admit the full extent of its nuclear weapons program and weapons-grade uranium stockpile now" and fully disclose all of the program's present and past activities.[2] In March 1993, under domestic and international pressure, South African president F. W. de Klerk announced that his government had already dismantled a top secret nuclear weapons program and six and one-half Hiroshima-type bombs. Nuclear and armaments officials then disclosed a limited amount of information about the program. The head of the Atomic Energy Corporation, Dr. Waldo E. Stumpf, published brief overviews, and additional details were reported in a spate of interview-based articles published from 1993 to 1995.[3] Subsequent studies reported some additional historical detail, but historical knowledge—particularly about South African nuclear decision making—remains fragmentary.[4]

Many observers remained dissatisfied with the extent and credibility of these disclosures. Roger Jardine, then the ANC's science adviser (and now board chairperson of the Nuclear Energy Corporation of South Africa) called De Klerk's March 1993 speech "another can of 'neither lie nor the full truth.'" He disputed De Klerk's claims that the South African bombs were built without foreign assistance, that South Africa never tested nuclear weapons, and that the whole nuclear program cost only R700–R800 million. "Only a democratic government that carries the credibility, moral authority and respect of all South Africans," Jardine wrote, "will be able to convincingly show this dark chapter."[5] Abdul Minty, then director of the World Campaign against

Military and Nuclear Collaboration with South Africa, and now deputy director-general of Foreign Affairs and chief of the Nonproliferation Council, also criticized De Klerk's denials of foreign assistance.[6]

Yet, over a decade later, much of South Africa's nuclear history remains hidden. The most authoritative official published account does not exceed twenty pages in length.[7] The common claim that the whole story—except for proliferation sensitive information—was fully told in 1993–1994 is questionable in light of repeated revelations disproving or filling gaps in the official picture. For instance, De Klerk asserted in 1993 that "at no time did South Africa acquire nuclear weapons technology or materials from another country, nor has it provided any to any other country, or cooperated with another country in this regard."[8] But a secret 1988 court judgment, leaked to the South African press in 1994, revealed clandestine imports from Israel of tritium useful for boosting nuclear bomb yield.[9] De Klerk–era accounts also held that the official nuclear strategy's last resort was a "demonstration through an underground nuclear test."[10] Insiders subsequently admitted that at least two subsequent steps were envisioned had an underground test failed to achieve its desired deterrent or coercive effect: an above-ground demonstration, followed by a threat of tactical use.[11] Moreover, the weapons themselves, originally described as crude gravity bombs, were in fact sophisticated video-guided glide bombs, similar to an Israeli system.[12]

These omissions could have resulted from officials' incomplete knowledge about the program's history. The secretive and compartmentalized nature of the program throughout its lifetime meant that some of the Atomic Energy Corporation and Armscor officials responsible for the 1993–1994 disclosures were unfamiliar with many historical policy details. Dr. Waldo Stumpf, the author of the most detailed account, had conducted a review of the weapons program for De Klerk in 1989, but had not been intimately involved in it until then.[13] The scientists, engineers, and managers who made the 1993–1994 disclosures had had limited exposure to political decision making, which may explain why, ironically, more technological than political history was released. They might also have omitted details because they did not recognize their significance to scholars and the nonproliferation community, or because of political incentives to conceal the past. Whatever the reason, claims that the story has been fully told must be treated with skepticism.

Indeed, a book published in 2003 by three veterans of South Africa's nuclear weapons program revealed additional previously undisclosed historical details. While the authors were vague on many policy matters, they disclosed new information about the structures set up to manage the program, including the involvement in explosives research of the National Institute for Defence Research of the Council for Scientific and Industrial Research, a body that coordinated defense research by academic scientists. The book also revealed some new details about safety, security, and reliability, as well as command and control.[14]

## Archives Destruction and the 1975 Armstrong Memorandum

The ultimate potential of historical research on South African nuclear history is sadly limited by the wholesale destruction of program documentation ordered by De Klerk. Technical documents reportedly were all destroyed between mid-1990 and mid-1991, followed by the policy documents in early 1993.[15] Leslie Gumbi, of the South African Department of Foreign Affairs and Nonproliferation Council, recently stated that "It's not to say that the new government does not want to give out information. But when it comes down to it, we're left with almost nothing."[16]

But it is premature to give up hope. The Department of Defence's release of the first declassified South African nuclear weapons policy document in September 2003 suggests that other documents may have survived the 1990–1993 records-destruction campaign. The destruction effort was apparently focused on records starting from the formal launch of the nuclear weapons program in early 1978, which would have left untouched earlier documents discussing the peaceful nuclear explosives program or the need for a nuclear deterrent.[17] The South African National Defence Force (SANDF), the Nuclear Energy Corporation of South Africa (NECSA, the successor to the Atomic Energy Corporation), and the Department of Foreign Affairs have all now acknowledged, in response to PAIA requests, the existence of archives with potentially relevant documents. Both the military and NECSA have confirmed that none of the case files on individuals involved in the program were destroyed .

Records and reports concerning the dismantling of the program were also probably retained, as these would have been important to the

International Atomic Energy Agency (IAEA) verification inspections. These would include at a minimum South Africa's declarations to the IAEA required for joining the Nonproliferation Treaty and implementing safeguards.[18] Other deliberately preserved documents include De Klerk's official dismantling order, the auditor's final report on the dismantling, and the operating and production records of the uranium enrichment plant.[19]

Some documents might have survived inadvertently; IAEA inspectors reportedly found technical documents that were supposed to have been destroyed.[20] The extensive web of structures involved directly and indirectly in the program also makes it unlikely that the instruction to destroy documents would have reached everyone effectively. Documentation concerning multipurpose technologies, such as delivery systems, would likely have been retained for operational reasons. Records at lower levels of the technological administrative structure—such as worker safety and environmental issues in uranium mining—were undoubtedly saved.

But the first document released was from the upper rather than bottom echelons of the apartheid state, and it sheds light on an issue of great historical importance: early military thinking about whether South Africa should acquire nuclear weapons. In September 2003, the Department of Defence declassified and released a memorandum dated 21 March 1975, from the chief of the Defence Staff (Lt.-Gen. R. F. Armstrong) to the chief of the South African Defence Force (Adm. H. H. Biermann) about "The Jericho Weapon System."[21] It argued that a significant nuclear threat to South Africa had emerged, justifying the acquisition of a nuclear weapons capability. The threat envisaged was that a hostile African nation might acquire a nuclear weapon from China, and that a United States pursuing East-West détente could not be counted upon to come to South Africa's aid. Armstrong contended that the vulnerability of aircraft to modern air defenses, as demonstrated in the 1973 Yom Kippur War, warranted a missile or other stand-off delivery system, such as a guided glide bomb. He concluded: "In spite of the considerable cost involved in acquiring even a limited number of missiles with the JERICHO weapon system, in view of the potential threat which faces the RSA in the foreseeable future, the possession of such a system will greatly add to our ability to negotiate from a position of strength."[22]

This memorandum is significant mainly for what it reveals about Israeli–South African military collaboration and the strategic thinking of certain high-level South African Defence Force (SADF) officers at the time. It does not appear to mark a turning point in South Africa's quest for a nuclear arsenal. Prime Minister John Vorster had already decided in 1974 to proceed with developing nuclear explosives and a test site, though this was still purportedly aimed at commercial "peaceful nuclear explosives." The government officially decided to acquire nuclear weapons only in 1977 or 1978.[23] In addition, while Armscor did eventually acquire Israeli missile technology for a collaborative missile development program in the 1980s, no evidence has surfaced of off-the-shelf acquisition of Jericho missiles as the memorandum recommends. Instead, as mentioned earlier, South Africa adopted a video-guided glide bomb as its primary nuclear delivery system.

Still, this document lends credibility to prior claims, long treated with skepticism, that Israel offered missiles and nuclear warheads to South Africa sometime in the mid-1970s.[24] No source of the proffered Jericho missile is mentioned, but the only known missile by that name is built and deployed by Israel.[25] The memorandum also states that "In considering the merits of a weapon system such as that offered, certain assumptions have been made.... That the missiles will be armed with nuclear warheads manufactured in the RSA *or acquired elsewhere*."[26] There were no other plausible suppliers of nuclear warheads to South Africa besides Israel. Moreover, the memorandum's language about acquiring "missiles with the JERICHO weapon system" implies a warhead already associated with the Jericho missile.[27]

The second significant implication of the Armstrong memorandum is its reflection on the strategic thinking of at least one or two high-level military officers at the time. No evidence had previously surfaced of pre-1977 SADF interest in acquiring nuclear weapons. Limited interview research had indicated that the uniformed services had at best a tepid interest in nuclear weapons, due to cost concerns. The primary military champion of the nuclear weapons program when it was officially approved in 1977–1978 was not the top military brass, but a staff officer, Brig. (later Brig.-Gen.) John F. Huyser.[28] The endorsement two years earlier of a nuclear weapons program by the chief of the Defence Staff, a man who had previously served as chief of the South African Air Force, suggests wider as well as earlier military interest.

Armstrong's strategic rationale for acquiring nuclear missiles also differed from the arguments used later to justify the program, as a deterrent against a Soviet-backed attack from Angola or Mozambique. If the deterrent failed, South African strategists aimed to try to blackmail the United States into intervening on Pretoria's side by progressively threatening to disclose, test, or use on enemy targets its nuclear capability.[29] But the Armstrong memorandum refers neither to the Soviet Union nor to a blackmail strategy, and predates the Soviet aid and Cuban troop deployments to Angola that preoccupied later South African military threat assessments.[30]

Instead, Armstrong argued that "there is a danger that an enemy assuming an African identity such as terrorist organizations, or an Organization of African Unity 'liberation army' could acquire and launch against us a tactical nuclear weapon. China appears to be the most likely nuclear power to associate herself with such an adventure."[31] The memorandum claimed that "the psychology underlying terrorism, modern revolutionary theory and Red Chinese doctrine would not preclude the use of nuclear weapons against the RSA," and referred to a study of the nuclear threat by the SADF director of Strategic Studies (the aforementioned Brigadier Huyser) that apparently drew similar conclusions. But otherwise the memorandum explained neither why China would transfer nuclear weapons, nor addressed the dilemmas even the most ruthless "terrorists" would face in targeting their own country with nuclear weapons.

The memorandum also neglected to explain how South African nuclear weapons would deter the elusive "terrorists." It simply asserted that "should it become generally known that the RSA possesses a nuclear weapon and that we would use it if we were subjected to a nuclear attack, such a deterrent strategy could be used as a positive weapon in our defence."[32] Presumably, the strategy would be analogous to the conventional strategy Pretoria adopted of punishing neighboring states for harboring African National Congress bases. Such a strategy, however, would have raised a host of additional political liabilities, none of which were addressed in the memorandum.

Another interesting element in Armstrong's analysis is his dim view of the prospects for Western support. Western solidarity had been undermined, the memorandum argues, by East-West détente, multipolarity, nuclear proliferation, and "divergent interests and political systems."[33] The apartheid state's fears of Western abandonment and betrayal, typically traced to the late-1975 U.S. withdrawal of support for anti-Marxist forces in Angola, were clearly already percolating through the military establishment.

The overall paranoia, unexamined questionable assumptions, and illogic of the document suggests a generally poor quality of strategic analysis at high levels in the SADF at the time. One possible explanation is a hysterical reaction to the sudden dissolution of Portuguese rule in Angola and Mozambique in 1974 and the ensuing loss of white-ruled buffer states. Another is that this document represented a post-hoc effort to rationalize a strategic program sought for other reasons.

## Nuclear Secrecy Laws and Policies

The release of the Armstrong memorandum, unless merely the result of conscientious administrators acting on their own initiative, indicates a new, more favorable attitude toward historical transparency on the part of the current South African government. So too does the government's acquiescence to the recent publication of a memoir of the program by three former officials. The Truth and Reconciliation Commission (TRC), the 1996 constitution, and the 2000 Promotion of Access to Information Act all represent great overall strides toward openness from the secretive practices of the National Party–ruled state. But anachronistic apartheid-era secrecy laws remain in place, despite many good reasons for the new South Africa to pull back the curtains on nuclear history.

The disclosure of technical, proliferation-sensitive information—anything that could aid foreign states or actors in developing nuclear weapons or fissile materials—is prohibited under South Africa's Nonproliferation Treaty obligations. But the disclosure of nonsensitive information by current and former program employees, with the possible exception of Atomic Energy Board/Corporation employees, is also prohibited by a web of secrecy laws carried over from the apartheid-era.

The basic research, fissile material production, original explosives design, and preparation for an underground test site were conducted by the Atomic Energy Board (AEB), which was renamed the Atomic Energy Corporation (AEC) in 1982, then the Nuclear Energy Corporation of South Africa in 2001.[34] The Nuclear Energy Act 46 of 1999, like prior enabling legislation, "prohibits the disclosure of any information about Corporation activities with respect to 'restricted matter' (i.e., radioactive materials, etc.) if that activity is not yet public without authorization by the chief executive officer."[35] (Unsurprisingly, it was the then-CEO of the AEC, Dr. Waldo Stumpf, who authored one of the most detailed historical accounts of the program.) One could, however, argue that all nontechnical AEB/AEC/NECSA information about the nuclear weapons program has already been de facto declassified by the March 1993 disclosure making public knowledge the "activity" of building nuclear weapons.[36]

No such loopholes exist in the secrecy laws governing the Department of Defence, the Defence Forces, and Armscor. The defense minister's permission is also required for the disclosure of secret or confidential information acquired from the South African Defence Force (now the South African National Defence Force), which became increasingly involved in the nuclear program in the 1980s, under the Defence Act 44 of 1957, section 118. Armscor, the state arms procurement and production agency, was assigned responsibility for weapons design, production, delivery systems, and storage in 1978. Its governing legislation, the Armaments Development and Production Act 57 of 1968, section 11A, prohibits "the disclosure of information relating to the acquisition, supply, marketing, manufacture, etc. of armaments except on written authority of the [Defence] Minister."[37]

Nuclear program personnel were required to sign supplementary oaths pledging to comply with these nondisclosure laws, during and after their employment. An additional, broader secrecy law, the 1982 Protection of Information Act, limits disclosures by all current and former government employees. It is so broad, however, that legal scholars consider it unconstitutional and ripe for judicial challenge.[38]

The Promotion of Access to Information Act was enacted in 2000 to implement the 1996 constitution's right of access to information. It provides a mechanism for citizens to request the declassification and release of specific records, though it has no jurisdiction over information in other forms, such as oral testimony or memoirs. The PAIA overrides all more restrictive acts, but section 41 provides state agencies with the discretionary power to deny access to records whose disclosure would harm the defense, security, or international relations of the country, or that are covered by diplomatic confidentiality agreements. Refusal is not mandatory, so agencies can release such information voluntarily.[39]

The ANC-led government has not yet articulated a clear policy on the declassification of nontechnical nuclear program records, or indeed on other aspects of apartheid-era history. The government has shown considerable reluctance in face of a number of efforts from individuals, nongovernmental organizations, and even public commissions to expose the past. An example relevant to nuclear program history is the case of the apartheid-era chemical and biological weapons program. The TRC began investigating Project Coast in 1997 after police discovered four trunks belonging Dr. Wouter Basson, the former head of the program, containing thousands of pages of Project Coast documents. Many of these documents were highly classified, and all of them were supposed to have been destroyed after being copied onto optical disks for secure storage.[40] TRC investigators helped to inventory these documents, but were then barred from consulting them by the National Intelligence Agency (NIA). Intelligence officials argued that TRC investigators lacked necessary security clearances and that a TRC inquiry would jeopardize ongoing criminal investigations and expose weapons scientists to foreign recruitment and personal danger. They relented only after the Office of Serious Economic Offences, which was investigating allegations of Project Coast corruption, offered to give the TRC access to its copies of the documents. The Defence and Foreign Affairs ministries, the NIA, and the Surgeon-General later sought to block public hearings on the program. Only the political independence and authority of the TRC, and evidence of Project Coast's human rights violations (particularly assassinations using chemical and biological poisons), enabled the hearings to proceed openly.[41] The state also held Basson's bail application hearing *in camera,* but the transcript was declassified after a legal challenge by the Freedom of Expression Institute.[42]

Different perspectives within the state on disclosure in general appear to be emerging. It is perhaps no coincidence that the first nuclear history document ever to be released, the Armstrong memorandum, stemmed from a PAIA request to Defence, which has generally followed a more progressive approach to the implementation of PAIA than has Armscor, the NIA, and the National Archives.[43] Referring to the secrecy provisions of the Armscor, Defence, and Protection of

Information laws, an Armscor official recently asserted that "the South African nuclear programme is still classified except for the information provided by the then President of South Africa, Mr. FW de Klerk to Parliament on 24 March 1993."[44] This is highly regressive since Armscor officials in 1993 and 1994 had disclosed many more details than were revealed in De Klerk's brief speech.[45]

Nuclear science officials appear just as reluctant to open the books. The Department of Minerals and Energy's chief director for Nuclear Policy has contended that "unless new information comes to light, the Department considers the issues involving the Nuclear Weapons Program as having been closed."[46] A NECSA representative wrote recently that "NECSA is committed...to overcoming the secrecy that surrounded nuclear development in South Africa's Apartheid past."[47] But NECSA's negotiation of a nondisclosure agreement with its former head Dr. Waldo Stumpf in 2001, binding him to perpetual secrecy as part of the financial settlement upon his departure, does not exactly inspire confidence in its commitment to openness.[48]

The South African Council for the Nonproliferation of Weapons of Mass Destruction, an interdepartmental body responsible for overseeing South Africa's nonproliferation policies, has indicated a somewhat greater receptivity to information requests:

> Declassification can only be considered if the information is in a tangible form that can be considered against the possible proliferation impact if such information is to be released...
>
> The Council would be in a position to scrutinise any information to make a recommendation on the declassification of it, if requested to do so. However, Cabinet in conjunction with the Department of Defence will have to decide on any declassification of information as the project was originally classified by Cabinet in the previous Government.[49]

While leaving the door open to declassification in principle, the requirement of Cabinet approval in practice will be a daunting barrier to declassification via this route. The reference to any information "in a tangible form," however, leaves the door open for memoirs or transcribed oral histories to be submitted to the Nonproliferation Council for declassification review, something that cannot be easily accomplished using the PAIA.

The South African government is currently reviewing criteria for the classification and declassification of secret state information. In late 2002, the minister of intelligence convened a Classification and Declassification Review Committee, including officials from all relevant departments as well as outside experts, with the purported aim of responding more efficiently to the growing demand for access to surviving apartheid-era documents, particularly by the victims of human rights abuses and their families.[50] There is cause for skepticism, however, that this initiative will significantly liberalize secrecy policy. It is led by the NIA, which has consistently taken an obstructionist position. Besides its efforts to obstruct the TRC inquiry into Project Coast mentioned earlier, the NIA also illegally took possession of thirty-four boxes of sensitive TRC records, concealed their whereabouts, and then blocked access to them.[51] NIA has also sought to obstruct access by the Hefer Commission—investigating certain apartheid-era spy allegations—to state documents.[52] The Review Committee missed at least two self-imposed deadlines to release its findings. Some fear that, far from its originally declared mission of systematizing the disclosure of apartheid-era records, it may develop into a gatekeeping mechanism aimed at preventing "ad hoc" disclosures under PAIA.

Governmentwide, PAIA implementation has also been fundamentally handicapped by a failure to deploy adequate resources. The Human Rights Commission, which has important monitoring and public education functions in relation to the act, is unable to do more than token work in fulfilling this mandate because of resource constraints. Very few records manuals have been published by either public or private bodies, as is required by the act. Even those agencies committed to implementation are crippled by resource problems. For instance, the SANDF is only able to release an average of three files a day with current resources. The inadequacy of this capacity is immediately apparent when considering that just one current request—from the Swiss National Science Foundation researching Swiss collaboration with the apartheid government—involves the declassification of about 1,400 SANDF files. In many cases, the state agencies concerned have not made the deployment of resources a priority. But ultimate responsibility goes back to the highest reaches of government, which has not put in place the infrastructure required to make PAIA an effective access instrument.[53]

# INCENTIVES FOR GREATER OPENNESS

Despite significant governmental reluctance, the declassification and release of the Armstrong memorandum, as well as several less significant Foreign Affairs Department records, suggests a new openness to nuclear declassification. The explanation for this movement lies in the positive incentives for declassification. The primary incentive for secrecy over the nuclear weapons program during the apartheid era ended with the decision to dismantle it. Even unrepentant nuclear powers have found controlled declassification to have beneficial consequences for promoting sound policymaking, public trust, and environmental and health quality.[54] South Africa has compelling foreign policy and domestic political incentives for greater historical transparency, including promoting global nonproliferation and gaining international prestige. These incentives outweigh the risks that disclosures revealing foreign state support for South Africa's nuclear weapons program would irritate the foreign countries involved, as the diplomatic fallout would be minor and fading with time.

## Nonproliferation Knowledge

A primary reason for permitting inquiry into nuclear history is to develop useful knowledge for global nonproliferation policy and responsible nuclear custodianship. As Roger Jardine, J. W. de Villiers, and Mitchell Reiss argued in 1993, "the story of South Africa's acquisition and subsequent dismantlement of its nuclear arsenal holds vital lessons."[55] Much global nuclear weapons history remains shrouded in secrecy, particularly that of the undeclared or new nuclear states Israel, India, Pakistan, and North Korea. The scarcity of knowledge about the politics of proliferation heightens the value of information, however marginal. Although of course much of every case is unique, as an isolated state with limited economic resources, apartheid South Africa resembles current and future nuclear acquisition (and perhaps disarmament) aspirants. Its nuclear policies were surely shaped by factors that will influence the nuclear policies of other governments in the future. Learning why and when states seek to acquire nuclear arsenals—or show nuclear restraint—can help policymakers develop policies to dissuade potential proliferators.[56] Information about how states have managed to acquire foreign technologies and materials is also useful, for improving export control regimes.[57]

Verification of nonproliferation or disarmament agreements is another matter where historical information could bear valuable lessons for the future.[58] The International Atomic Energy Agency gave South Africa high marks for its cooperation with its verification of the dismantling of the weapons program.[59] Thus, as Jardine and others argued, "The manner in which South Africa dismantled its weapons, joined the NPT [Nuclear Nonproliferation Treaty], co-operated fully with the IAEA and accepted comprehensive safe-guards on its nuclear facilities may serve as a useful future model."[60]

Indeed, in early 2003, South Africa's transparent disarmament process was recalled favorably by U.S., IAEA, and South African officials—albeit with different motives—as a standard by which to assess the verifiability of Iraqi disarmament.[61] While U.S. officials aimed to pressure the U.N. Security Council to authorize war on Iraq, South African president Thabo Mbeki sought to give the verification process more time to work. Pointing out that U.N. inspectors had required two years to verify South Africa's disarmament, Mbeki offered the mediating services of the former foreign minister who had handled NPT negotiations in the early 1990s and then dispatched the deputy foreign minister and a team of weapons experts to advise Iraq on disarmament and verification.[62] While war was not averted, a more detailed picture of South Africa's disarmament and verification experience would be useful for future verification efforts, for instance, should North Korea decide to disarm.

For those states that have already acquired nuclear arsenals and cannot be convinced to give them up, nuclear history can provide lessons about safe and secure procedures to avoid theft, accidental or unauthorized use, as well as the avoidance of nuclear postures that heighten the risk of accident or war. Studies of how state officials think about deterrence, formulate nuclear doctrine, and devise command and control systems, have led to proposals for enhanced civilian control over these vital matters.[63] Research in U.S. declassified documents revealed hushed-up incidents of bomber crashes and false-attack warnings, suggesting a need for greater concern about nuclear accidents and for improved safety mechanisms.[64]

Promoting global arms control has been an explicitly prominent goal in the foreign policy of the new South Africa.[65] The ANC had advocated an African nuclear-weapon-free zone before taking power. One of the earliest foreign policy decisions of the first democratically elected South African government authorized the Department of Foreign Affairs to be "an active participant in the various non-proliferation regimes and suppliers groups" and "to support nuclear non-proliferation and to influence African states and Non-Aligned Movement members to support non-proliferation, while ensuring that access to advanced technologies were not denied to developing states."[66] A 1998 Department of Foreign Affairs strategic planning report stressed the government's intention to "continue playing a leading role internationally in disarmament and the non-proliferation of weapons of mass destruction as well as conventional weapons, especially small arms" as a means "to safeguard South Africa's sovereignty and enhance its capability to promote the well-being of its citizens and to contribute towards regional and global peace and security."[67]

Given South Africa's interest in nonproliferation, and its ongoing commitment to the Nonproliferation Treaty, it is understandably concerned about the potential risks of releasing information that could assist other nations or "terrorists" in building weapons of mass destruction. But clear distinctions can be drawn between technological weapon and materials information, which pose a proliferation hazard, and information about nuclear weapons policy, policymaking, and safety procedures, which do not. Systematic declassification reviews can, indeed, reduce proliferation dangers by identifying insufficiently protected sensitive documents. This in fact occurred in a recent U.S. declassification initiative, resulting in improved information security.[68]

The technical requirements for distinguishing proliferation-sensitive from nonsensitive material are not very demanding. Dr. André Buys, a former South African nuclear official, has recommended "instituting a process of controlled declassification. A panel of experts should be appointed to evaluate the proliferation value of the information and advise the government on declassification or not."[69] Other nations' nuclear declassification guidelines would be helpful in the preparation of South African guidelines.[70] According to Roger Heusser, former director of the Office of Nuclear National Security Information of the U.S. Department of Energy, a dozen South African experts, if backed by the government, could "accomplish the release of a mountain of documents."[71] The decimation of archival holdings under De Klerk has undoubtedly left much less than a "mountain of documents." In addition, dismantlement left South Africa with a surplus of nuclear weapons experts, many of whom are still employed by Armscor or breakaway subsidiaries such as Denel, who could advise the government on the proliferation implications of declassification.[72]

The disclosure of nuclear material or technology suppliers might theoretically present a proliferation risk. The passage of time is likely to make information about specific providers obsolete, but caution should be exercised in disclosing such information. On the other hand, information about illicit trade can help identify legal loopholes and patterns of traffic, as well as help mobilize political action against it.[73] Revealing weapon scientists' identities could make them more vulnerable to recruitment by proliferating countries, though public awareness might instead deter covert recruitment efforts.[74] Nevertheless, this risk could easily be met by excising scientists' names from any documents released or interviews conducted.

The case of the exposure of Project Coast shows that a controlled nuclear program declassification and history initiative would not only be beneficial but also administratively feasible. Far more information has been disclosed about Project Coast than about the nuclear weapons program, through the avenues of documentary declassification, oral testimony at TRC hearings and the Basson trial, and a quasi-official history in the form of the TRC's final report on Project Coast.[75] The report was not written by professional historians, nor did it benefit from full access to relevant state documentation.[76] But it provided the most detailed and authoritative account publicly available when published in 1998 and a valuable resource for researchers.[77]

The relatively complete disclosure of Project Coast has provided valuable lessons about the origins of chemical and biological weapons programs and the opportunities for the misuse of state funds in covert military projects. Project Coast's use of front companies to conceal state involvement in illicit weapons research, development, and production also suggests strategies for identifying similar deceits in the future. Another lesson is that instruction in medical and scientific ethics, as well as in relevant international law, might help discourage scientists from participating in such projects.[78]

The process by which Project Coast was disclosed also provides reassurance about the feasibility of safe, controlled nuclear declassification. After the initial governmental resistance mentioned earlier, a workable compromise was reached under which a small group of TRC and government personnel reclassified the documents into three categories: 1) documents that could not be discussed or released by the TRC because they contained details on chemical or biological weapons technology or involved confidential diplomacy; 2) documents containing sensitive information that could be used as evidence but not released to the public; and 3) documents not containing classified information that were declassified. Most of the documents fell into the last category and were released to the public. [79]

Project Coast personnel were instructed not to reveal details of chemical and biological weapons production that would pose a proliferation threat, but otherwise were to answer all questions posed by the TRC investigators. TRC legislation superseded their prior security oaths. Concerned that Project Coast personnel might reveal sensitive information in public TRC hearings, the government arranged to monitor the proceedings and, if necessary, block the release of any proliferation or diplomatically sensitive information. This improvised system worked imperfectly, however, bogging down the hearings with legal motions and delays. Information was improperly released just once, ironically by the surgeon general Dr. Knobel, who passed out classified documents to the media on the first day of the hearing. [80]

No reports have arisen alleging that the disclosures about the program may have led to any transfer of sensitive weapons material or know-how. In fact, police and TRC investigators uncovered sensitive, secret documents that were supposed to have been destroyed; most of these had been kept by Basson, possibly intended for illicit sale or extortion. [81] Nor have there been any reports that the disclosure of the identities of former program employees has led to foreign recruitment efforts. Thus the exposure of Project Coast appears to have been a clear net benefit to the global chemical and biological nonproliferation regime.

## Nonproliferation Diplomacy and Other Foreign Policy Objectives

Prestige from being the sole nuclear power to disarm has helped South Africa to take a leadership role in NPT diplomacy, and a progressive approach to nuclear history would only bolster its prestige in this arena. A South African proposal broke a deadlock at the 1995 NPT Review and Extension Conference, leading to a compromise agreement for the indefinite extension of the treaty while committing the nuclear weapon states to reduce their arsenals.[82] South Africa, along with several other middle powers, advanced aggressive nuclear disarmament proposals at the United Nations and the 2000 NPT Review Conference.[83] South Africa also took a leadership role in negotiating the African nuclear-weapon-free-zone treaty, and more recently has been actively involved in preliminary negotiations on a global treaty halting the production of fissile materials, dismantling facilities, and neutralizing existing stockpiles.[84]

South Africa's arms control status and expertise also lent prominence to Mbeki's criticisms of the U.S. push to war against Iraq in 2003. But its moral authority was not helped by limits to public disclosure about its own nuclear history and verification process, as at least one news story pointed out.[85] Of course, greater transparency would also promote South Africa's broader image as a constitutional democracy and arms control leader, which would help—if intangibly—South Africa achieve a wide range of foreign policy goals, such as a seat on the U.N. Security Council, preferential trade agreements, foreign investment, and so on.

Disclosures involving foreign involvement in the apartheid-era nuclear weapons program could have negative diplomatic consequences. If De Klerk was right that no foreign governments or scientists aided the bomb program, the offers mentioned in the Armstrong memorandum notwithstanding, then further disclosures could not embarrass any foreign government. But even if foreign governmental involvement had taken place clandestinely, the passage of time and change in foreign governments minimize any embarrassment that disclosures now would cause to current foreign governments.[86] Diplomatic repercussions might also be smoothed by an acceptance of responsibility on the part of foreign governments for their past collaboration with a pariah state. It would be a different story if the foreign involvement had blatantly violated international undertakings, such as the Nuclear Nonproliferation Treaty. But this is unlikely. Israel, the only state seriously suspected of such assistance, never signed the NPT.[87] Of course, many South Africans would welcome as "just deserts" the exposure and embarrassment of foreign collaborators with the apartheid state—a form of international truth and reconciliation.[88]

Disclosures of apartheid South Africa's covert illegal acquisitions of sensitive technology from foreign companies would probably be welcomed by foreign governments, for it would assist them to enforce their own export control laws over their own firms. Exposing apartheid-era business relationships between Armscor and covert foreign suppliers would probably disturb those foreign firms. But with the passage of time and the termination of South Africa's nuclear arms illicit foreign procurement practices, there is probably negligible commerce with these suppliers that would be put at risk.

## South Africa's Domestic Objectives

Access to information is generally and increasingly considered a hallmark of modern liberal democracy. Twenty-six countries have adopted new laws promoting access to information in the last decade alone.[89] South Africa's 1996 constitution is the only one in the world that enshrines access to information as a fundamental right. South African citizens, journalists, scholars, and nongovernmental organizations are increasingly seeking information from the government under PAIA.

But in South Africa and beyond, questions on the purpose, scope, and dismantling of the program remain the subject of public speculation. Although denied by every program employee and official, prominent journalists charged that the program produced advanced miniaturized bombs and that, even after 1991, right-wing officials or employees had hidden away components or whole bombs for nefarious purposes.[90] Suspicions remain that the nuclear bombs were built to be used domestically against anti-apartheid revolutionaries, rather than the avowed purpose of deterring Soviet-backed external threats. Further release of information would help resolve and allay these old divisive controversies and uncertainties. It would also contribute to the public's general trust in the current government and its commitment to transparency.[91]

The failure of the state to make the TRC archives fully and promptly available to the public has fostered speculation that ANC officials fear the domestic political fallout from the exposure of colleagues with compromised pasts. This issue was brought to the fore by recent allegations against the national prosecutor, Bulelani Ngcuka, and the ensuing Hefer Commission proceedings.[92] However, these concerns are unproblematic for disclosing nuclear history, except insofar as it would create a precedent and stoke demand for declassification in police and intelligence spheres as well.

## UNVEILING THE NUCLEAR PAST

South Africa has made important strides toward a fuller disclosure of its apartheid-era nuclear history. The Promotion of Access to Information Act of 2000 provides a potential avenue for requesting documents, if not individual testimony. The government retains wide discretion in withholding information involving national security and diplomacy, regardless of its actual sensitivity. The appointment of the Classification and Declassification Review Committee in 2002, with the avowed aim of systematizing the release of apartheid-era records, has been an encouraging sign. The September 2003 declassification and release of the Armstrong memorandum is the most promising sign to date that the government, or at least the Defence Department, is taking a conscientious attitude toward declassification.

In addition to realizing the new South Africa's constitutional right of access to information, these movements can be understood in light of the government's incentives for greater nuclear historical transparency. The potential benefits for global nonproliferation policy, for South Africa's foreign policy aims, and for South African citizens' trust in the government outweigh the miniscule risks of technological leakage and the limited potential diplomatic repercussions. The oft-made claim that all useful history has already been disclosed does not appear sustainable in light of the limited disclosures, and incomplete shredding efforts, of the De Klerk government. At the same time, the current South African government is understandably preoccupied with more pressing priorities, may face foreign pressures to let sleeping dogs lie, and is probably anxious about a disclosure process that could ripple into areas of even greater domestic political and diplomatic sensitivity.

PAIA requests are currently the only way for scholars, journalists, and other interested nongovernmental actors to conduct historical research into the nuclear program. For its part, the state can facilitate this process by promoting conscientious and adequately resourced implementation of the PAIA process in all relevant departments.

Two other approaches, with much greater potential for illuminating this history, would require new laws or policies. The state should offer an amnesty to former program employees who violated secrecy laws by keeping their own copies of secret documents in return for their turning in the documents now. This would likely result in the recovery of historically significant, and possibly proliferation sensitive, documents. While the state took great care to keep track of its records, officials sometimes violate strict and time-consuming secrecy regulations, whether to facilitate working at home, to preserve documents for posterity, or for more self-interested reasons. Wouter Basson's four trunks of documents, which he had stashed in an associate's garage, are an obvious example.[93] If some valuable secret program documents have survived only in private hands, an amnesty could enrich the archives, for the benefit of the state as well as the public, once the documents have been declassified.

A still more valuable historical resource are the recollections of South African officials, scientists, and other program employees. In South Africa, nuclear policy records were never very detailed to begin with, due to the high level of secrecy surrounding the nuclear program, as well as to the characteristic brevity of governmental record-keeping at the time.[94] The subsequent destruction of records has only made matters worse. Conducting interview research and facilitating new oral histories and memoirs will be an invaluable method of recording this important history.

Unfortunately, former officials who could undoubtedly shed new light on the program are discouraged from doing so by the laws and oaths binding them to secrecy. Rather than submitting their book for official clearance, the three program veterans used their own discretion in avoiding disclosing information that would open them to state prosecution.[95] It is likely that this self-censorship approach led to the omission of significant but nonsensitive information. Former officials are probably also hesitant to grant interviews, or discuss formerly taboo topics in interviews that they do grant, for the same reasons. Declassification procedures for oral history or memoirs are not provided for in the PAIA, though they could conceivably be orchestrated by the Nonproliferation Council (NPC) as mentioned above. But the possibility that the NPC would reject a request to review or to declassify a submitted memoir, for a reason unrelated to the sensitivity of its content, would surely discourage anyone from putting much effort into preparing the memoir in the first place.

Unrecorded memories are a wasting asset. Numerous knowledgeable officials have died in recent years, others are quite elderly, and still others have moved on.[96] Scholars, activists, and parliamentarians should press for legislation that would annul apartheid-era secrecy oaths while prohibiting disclosures of weapons technology information. An informal version of this approach appears to have worked well in permitting Project Coast employees to testify in the TRC process and in the Basson trial. At a minimum, the state should conduct its own oral history initiative to preserve the history for internal use by the South African state and possible future declassification.[97]

As it stands, many of the valuable lessons South Africa's nuclear experience holds for other countries remain unshared as a result of official secrecy. Its own citizens remain in the dark about a highly significant dimension of the country's history. A systematic information declassification program, incorporating the controlled release from secrecy undertakings of apartheid scientists and other operatives, and taking heed of nonproliferation obligations, would be a fitting expression of the country's constitutional commitment to freedom of information. Given the uneven progress and divisions within the government over declassification, further transparency will depend on increased political will from the top, and continued requests and pressure from scholars, journalists, and other actors in civil society.

# Endnotes

1   This essay was first published in *Journal of Southern African Studies* 30, no. 3 (2004). Peter Liberman did the bulk of the research and writing.

2   D. Albright and M. Hibbs, "South Africa: The ANC and the Atom Bomb," *The Bulletin of the Atomic Scientists* 49, no. 3 (April 1993): 33.

3   J. W. De Villiers, R. Jardine, and M. Reiss, "Why South Africa Gave up the Bomb," *Foreign Affairs* 72, no. 6 (November–December 1993): 98–109; W. Stumpf, "South Africa's Nuclear Weapons Program," in *Weapons of Mass Destruction: Costs Versus Benefits*, ed. Kathleen C. Bailey (Delhi: Manohar, 1994), 63–81. Interview-based studies include D. Albright, "South Africa and the Affordable Bomb," *Bulletin of the Atomic Scientists* 50, no. 4 (July–August 1994): 37–47; M. Hibbs, "South Africa's Secret Nuclear Program: From a PNE to Deterrent," *Nuclear Fuel* 18 (10 May 1993): 3–6; M. Hibbs, "South Africa's Secret Nuclear Program: The Dismantling," *Nuclear Fuel* 18 (24 May 1993): 9–13; Frank V. Pabian, "South Africa's Nuclear Weapon Program: Lessons for Nonproliferation Policy," *Nonproliferation Review* 3, no. 1 (Fall 1995): 1–19; M. Reiss, *Bridled Ambition: Why Countries Constrain Their Nuclear Capabilities* (Washington, D.C.: Woodrow Wilson Center Press 1995), 7–44.

4   William J. Long and Suzette R. Grillot, "Ideas, Beliefs, and Nuclear Policies: The Cases of South Africa and Ukraine," *Nonproliferation Review* 7, no. 1 (Spring 2000): 24–40; P. Liberman, "The Rise and Fall of the South African Bomb," *International Security* 26, no. 2 (Fall 2001): 45–86; T. McNamee, "Afrikanerdom and Nuclear Weapons: A Cultural Perspective on Nuclear Proliferation and Rollback in South Africa," (PhD diss., University of London, 2003); H. Steyn, R. van der Walt, and J. van Loggerenberg, *Armament and Disarmament: South Africa's Nuclear Weapons Experience* (Pretoria: Network Publishers 2003).

5   R. Jardine, "The Nationalist Party and the Atom Bomb," *Mayibuye* (May 1993), 28.

6   J. Carlin, "De Klerk's Bomb Story 'Incomplete,'" *The Independent*, 26 March 1993, 13.

7   Stumpf, "South Africa's Nuclear Weapons Program."

8   F. W. de Klerk, "Speech on the Nonproliferation Treaty to a Joint Session of Parliament, March 24, 1993," *Joint Publications Research Service, Proliferation Issues*, (29 March 1993), 1–3.

9   The case concerned charges that a retired South African Air Force pilot, who had ferried some of the materials, had attempted to blackmail the government. W. E. Burrows and R. Windrem, *Critical Mass: The Dangerous Race for Superweapons in a Fragmenting World* (New York: Simon and Schuster 1994), 450–52; D. Albright, "South Africa's Secret Nuclear Weapons," *ISIS Report* 1, no. 4 (May 1994): 5.

10  W. Stumpf, "South Africa's Nuclear Weapons Program: From Deterrence to Dismantlement," *Arms Control Today* (December–January 1995/96), 5.

11  Liberman, "Rise and Fall of the South African Bomb," 56.

12  Known as the H2, the South African system was also used for precision conventional bombing in the Angolan War. Liberman, "Rise and Fall of the South African Bomb," 54; Steyn, van der Walt, and van Loggerenberg, *Armament and Disarmament*, 74.

13  P. Liberman interview with W. Stumpf, 27 January 1999.

14  Steyn, van der Walt, and van Loggerenberg, *Armament and Disarmament*.

15  Reiss, *Bridled Ambition*, 18–19, 23–24.

16  N. Lelyveld, "S. Africa Provides Cautionary Tale," *Los Angeles Times,* 13 March 2003, 3. Cf. memorandum (NA 2/1/1) from D. J. van Beek, Secretariat of the Council for the Non-Proliferation of Mass Destruction, to V. Harris, 1 July 2002.

17  Correspondence from A. J. Buys to Peter Liberman, 3 November 2003.

18  A. von Baeckmann, G. Dillon, and D. Perricos, "Nuclear Verification in South Africa," *IAEA Bulletin* 1995, no. 1 (1995): 42–8.

19  Reiss, *Bridled Ambition*, 18–19. The dismantling order is cited in a recent Armscor-commissioned (but still unpublished) history, L. J. Van der Westhuizen and J. H. le Roux, *Armscor: A Will to Win* (Bloemfontein: Institute for Contemporary History, University of the Orange Free State 1997), 181.

20  Reiss, *Bridled Ambition,* 40, n.70.

21  The document is available to the public at the South African History Archive, based at the University of the Witwatersrand (reference AL 2878, A 3.1.1.). Particulars about SAHA and its nuclear history program, other freedom-of-information initiatives, and collections can be accessed on-line at www.wits.ac.za/saha/.

22  Lt-Gen. R. F. Armstrong, "The Jericho Weapon System," 21 March 1975, declassified 25 September 2003.

23  Liberman, "Rise and Fall of the South African Bomb," 50–3; Steyn, van der Walt, and van Loggerenberg, *Armament and Disarmament,* 43.

24  Prior claims had been made by Seymour Hersh, whose source was a disaffected former Israeli defense employee whose credibility was widely questioned, even by Hersh. A more credible source is the former South African Navy commodore—and Soviet spy—Dieter Gerhardt. See R. Bergman, "Treasons of Conscience," *Ha'aretz,* 7 April 2000 (English Internet Edition, accessed from www3.haaretz.co.il); S. M. Hersh, *The Samson Option: Israel's Nuclear Arsenal and American Foreign Policy* (New York: Vintage Books, 1992), 274.

25  The memorandum refers to the missile's 500 km range, which corresponds to the estimated range of Israel's single-stage Jericho 1, first deployed around 1970. On the Jericho 1 and 2, see S. Carus and D. Zakheim, "North Africa/Israel," in *Report of the Commission to Assess the Ballistic Missile Threat to the United States, Appendix III: Unclassified Working Papers* (Washington, D.C.: GPO, 1988); Carnegie Endowment for International Peace, *Missile Proliferation/World Missile Chart/Israel* (2003) at http://www.ceip.org/files/nonprolif/numbers/israel.asp; Federation of Atomic Scientists, *Missile Proliferation/Israel* (2003), at http://fas.org/nuke/guide/israel/missile/index.html.

26  Emphasis added; Armstrong, "The Jericho Weapon System," 1.

27  Armstrong, "The Jericho Weapon System," 3.

28  Liberman, "Rise and Fall of the South African Bomb," 53, 63–8. Huyser had a reputation within the SADF as a prodigious producer of studies and memoranda, most of which were not taken very seriously. Liberman telephone interview with Gen. H. de V. du Toit (chief of staff: Intelligence, 1974–77), 27 October 2003. But Huyser appears to have been a favored advisor of then-defense minister and later prime minister P. W. Botha, perhaps because he (along with Magnus Malan) was also a member of the defense committee of the secret nationalist Afrikaner Broederbond society. I. Wilkins and H. Strydom, *The Super-Afrikaners* (Johannesburg: Jonathan Ball 1978), A52; correspondence from D. F. Gerhardt to Peter Liberman, 15 October 2003.

29  Liberman, "Rise and Fall of the South African Bomb," 58–63.

30 Robert S. Jaster, *South Africa's Narrowing Security Options*, Adelphi Papers 159 (London: International Institute for Strategic Studies 1980); Robert S. Jaster, *The Defence of White Power: South African Foreign Policy under Pressure* (New York: St. Martin's Press, 1989).

31 Armstrong, "The Jericho Weapon System," 1.

32 Armstrong, "The Jericho Weapon System," 2.

33 Armstrong, "The Jericho Weapon System," 1–2.

34 Some early research may also have been conducted within the Council for Science and Industrial Research.

35 Section 31 is the relevant provision. This act replaced the Atomic Energy Act 92 of 1982, which in turn replaced Atomic Energy Act 90 of 1967. J. Klaaren, "Some National Security Non-Disclosure Provisions," manuscript, University of the Witwatersrand, Johannesburg, 2002.

36 Several former nuclear program officials have taken this position; Steyn, van der Walt, and van Loggerenberg, *Armament and Disarmament*, xvi.

37 Klaaren, "Some National Security Non-Disclosure Provisions."

38 J. Klaaren, "National Insecurity? Constitutional Issues Regarding the Disclosure of Information by Public Officials," paper presented at a conference on "Unlocking South Africa's Nuclear Past," University of the Witwatersrand, Johannesburg, 31 July 2002.

39 Section 46 provides for a public interest override of discretionary refusal in certain circumstances. Disclosure in response to a PAIA request is mandated when the harm to defense or diplomacy is outweighed by public interest in disclosures that would reveal a breach of law or "imminent and serious public safety or environmental risk." I. Currie and J. Klaaren, *The Promotion of Access to Information Act Commentary* (Cape Town: Siber Ink Publications, 2002), 107–10.

40 C. Gould and P. Folb, *Project Coast: Apartheid's Chemical and Biological Weapons Program* (Geneva: United Nations Institute for Disarmament Research, 2002), 224.

41 M. Burger and C. Gould, *Secrets and Lies: Wouter Basson and South Africa's Chemical and Biological Warfare Program* (Cape Town: Zebra Press, 2002), 8–9; Gould and Folb, *Project Coast*, 224–28.

42 Summaries of the trial evidence are available at http://ccrweb.ccr.uct.ac.za/cbw/cbw_index.html; the bail hearing transcript is available at http://www.fxi.org.za/.

43 V. Harris, "Using the Promotion of Access to Information Act: The Case of the South African History Archive," paper presented at the Workshop on Transactions of Public Culture, University of the Western Cape, Cape Town, January 2003. However, this represents an apparent recent change of attitude on the part of the Department of Defence regarding nuclear history. A public affairs official stated as recently as early 2002 that "All information regarding this subject that could be declassified and made available was done so when the program was disclosed.... The remainder of the information is still sensitive and classified and still warrants protection.... More information in this regard will not be made available for public scrutiny. The DoD considers this matter as closed." Unsigned, 8 Feb 2002 e-mail from Department of Defence Information Centre to Peter Liberman.

44 Correspondence from L. P. "Bertus" Celliers, Manager: Corporate Communications, to Peter Liberman, 22 July 2002, emphasis in the original.

45 See the sources cited in footnote 2. Armscor successfully obtained a gag order from the Supreme Court in 1994 to prevent sixteen former employees from discussing

their work, reportedly seeking to extort additional pension benefits; "Supreme Court Stops Former Nuclear Scientists from Revealing Information," *South African Press Association,* 29 March 1994.

46  Letter from T. B. Maqubela, Chief Director: Nuclear, Department of Minerals and Energy, 31 July 2002, to Verne Harris.

47  V. Khoza, "Overcoming the Secrecy of the Past," *Earthyear* 1 (2001), 100.

48  The nondisclosure agreement was described in an e-mail from W. E. Stumpf to Verne Harris, 4 June 2002.

49  Memorandum from D. J. van Beek to V. Harris, 1 July 2002.

50  W. Hartley, "Apartheid Era Documents Might Soon Be Declassified," *Business Day* (Johannesburg), 6 June 2002; "Committee Looks to Declassify Top Secret Information," *South African Press Association,* 8 March 2003.

51  V. Harris, "Where Are the TRC Records?" *Natal Witness,* 22 April 2002; G. Dominy, "A Delicate Balancing Act at the National Archives," *This Day,* 17 November 2003.

52  R. Tabane, "Slowdown at the Hefer Commission," *Mail and Guardian,* 14–20 November 2003, 10.

53  W. Ferroggiaro, "Two Years On: South Africa and the Right to Information," (Washington, D.C.: National Security Archive, 2003); Harris; "Using the PAIA," W. Hartley, "State Ignorant of Access Act, Says DA Survey," *Business Day* (Johannesburg), 6 November 2003.

54  R. Dahl, *Controlling Nuclear Weapons: Democracy Versus Guardianship* (Syracuse, N.Y.: Syracuse University Press, 1985).

55  De Villiers, Jardine, and Reiss, "Why South Africa Gave up the Bomb," 109.

56  Recent additions drawing on declassified documents include D. Holloway, *Stalin and the Bomb: The Soviet Union and Atomic Energy, 1939–1956* (New Haven, Conn.: Yale University Press, 1994); W. Reynolds, *Australia's Bid for the Atomic Bomb* (Melbourne: University of Melbourne Press, 2000). Recent comparative analyses include Reiss, *Bridled Ambition;* T. V. Paul, *Power Versus Prudence: Why Nations Forgo Nuclear Weapons* (Montreal and Kingston: McGill-Queen's University Press, 2000); A. E. Levite, "Never Say Never Again: Nuclear Reversal Revisited," *International Security* 27, no. 3 (Winter 2002/03): 59–88.

57  K. Hamza, *Saddam's Bombmaker: The Terrifying Story of the Iraqi Nuclear and Biological Weapons Agenda* (New York: Scribner's, 2000); D. Albright, *Preventing Illegal Exports: Learning from Case Studies* (Washington, D.C.: Institute for Science and International Security, 2002), at http://www.exportcontrols.org/case_studies.htm.

58  For example, K. C. Bailey, *The UN Inspections in Iraq: Lessons for On-Site Verification* (Boulder, Colo.: Westview Press, 1995); Von Baeckmann, Dillon, and Perricos, "Nuclear Verification in South Africa."

59  Von Baeckmann, Dillon, and Perricos, "Nuclear Verification in South Africa"; R. Nessman, "U.N., U.S. Officials Point to South Africa as a Model of 'Real Disarmament'," *Associated Press,* 31 January 2003.

60  De Villiers, Jardine, and Reiss, "Why South Africa Gave up the Bomb."

61  C. Rice, "Why We Know Iraq Is Lying," *New York Times,* 23 January 2003, 25; S. Mulugeta, "Blix: S. Africa Disarmed the Right Way," *Newsday* (New York), 31 January 2003, 55; Nessman, "South Africa as a Model."

62  M. Dynes, "Mandela Denounces Blair over Iraq War," *Times* (London), 31 January 2003, 17; "South African Weapons Experts Arrive in Baghdad," *BBC Monitoring International Reports,* 24 February 2003.

63 Peter R. Lavoy, Scott D. Sagan, and James J. Wirtz, eds., *Planning the Unthinkable: How New Powers Will Use Nuclear, Biological, and Chemical Weapons* (Ithaca, N.Y.: Cornell University Press, 2000); J. L. Gaddis, *Cold War Statesmen Confront the Bomb: Nuclear Diplomacy since 1945* (Oxford: Oxford University Press, 1999).

64 B. G. Blair, *The Logic of Accidental Nuclear War* (Washington, D.C.: Brookings Institution, 1993); Scott D. Sagan, *The Limits of Safety: Organizations, Accidents, and Nuclear Weapons* (Princeton, N.J.: Princeton University Press, 1993).

65 Its top foreign policy goals are trade, development, and regional stability.

66 Department of Foreign Affairs (RSA), "South Africa's Policy on the Non-Proliferation of Weapons of Mass Destruction—The Role of the Department of Foreign Affairs," (Pretoria, 1995), 8, cited in G. Shelton, "South Africa's Nuclear Weapons Experience and the Global Arms Control Agenda," paper presented at the conference on Unlocking South Africa's Nuclear Past, University of the Witwatersrand, Johannesburg, 31 July 2002.

67 Cited in Shelton, "South Africa's Nuclear Weapons Experience.". While arms control was mentioned in the Department of Foreign Affairs' 2002 strategic planning report, however, the report's emphasis was on regional conventional arms rather than global nonproliferation aims. It is unclear whether this represents a downgrading of nonproliferation among South Africa's foreign policy priorities. See Department of Foreign Affairs (RSA), *Strategic Plan 2002–2005* (November 2002) at http://www.dfa.gov.za/department/stratplan.htm.

68 R. Heusser, "From Secrecy to Openness: The U.S. Historical Perspective," paper presented at the conference on "Unlocking South Africa's Nuclear Past," University of the Witwatersrand, Johannesburg, 31 July 2002.

69 A. Buys, "Statement on Secrecy and Disclosure about South Africa's Past Nuclear Weapons Program," paper presented at the conference on Unlocking South Africa's Nuclear Past, University of the Witwatersrand, Johannesburg, 31 July 2002.

70 U.S. Department of Energy, *Draft Public Guidelines to DOE Classification of Information*, Washington D.C, 27 June 1994.

71 Correspondence from Roger N. Heusser to Peter Liberman, 5 November 2002.

72 Correspondence to the authors from P. W. Labuschagne, Denel Group Manager: International Trade in Arms Control, 11 November 2002.

73 Albright, *Preventing Illegal Exports*.

74 We are thankful to Chandré Gould and André Buys for these points.

75 Truth and Reconciliation Commission, *Final Report*, vol. 2 (Cape Town: The Commission, 1998), chapter 6-C.

76 Gould and Folb, *Project Coast*, 225, 92–5.

77 Subsequent work includes Gould and Folb, *Project Coast;* H. E. Purkitt and S. F. Burgess, "South Africa's Chemical and Biological Warfare Program: A Historical and International Perspective," *Journal of Southern African Studies* 28, no. 2 (June 2002), 229–53; S. F. Burgess and H. E. Purkitt, *The Rollback of South Africa's Chemical and Biological Warfare Program* (Maxwell Air Force Base, Ala:. U.S. Air Force Counterproliferation Center, 2001).

78 Project Coast blatantly violated the Biological Weapons Convention, ratified by South Africa in 1975; Gould and Folb, *Project Coast*, 7–9.

79 Burgess and Purkitt, *Rollback*, 68–72; Gould and Folb, *Project Coast*, 224–6, 228, 231. The full TRC records theoretically are accessible by formal PAIA requests from the National Archives, but this process has not yet been tested.

80 Burgess and Purkitt, *Rollback,* 69. The TRC hearing transcripts can be accessed at http://www.doj.gov.za/trc/special/index.htm@cbw and at the South African History Archive at the University of the Witwatersrand.

81 Gould and Folb, *Project Coast*, 222–24; Burgess and Purkitt, *Rollback,* 66–8. This suggests that the inquiries may have actually enhanced the security of truly dangerous information.

82 Dhanapala, "The 1995 Review and Extension Conference of the Nuclear Non-Proliferation Treaty," *Disarmament* 17, no. 3 (1995): 7–8; Z. Masiza and C. Landsberg, "Fission for Compliments? South Africa and the 1995 Extension of Nuclear Non-Proliferation Treaty," *Policy: Issues and Actors* 9, no. 3 (Johannesburg: Centre for Policy Studies, 1996); T. Zamora-Collina, "South Africa Bridges the Gap: Indefinite Extension of Non-Proliferation Treaty," *Bulletin of the Atomic Scientists* 51, no. 4 (July 1995): 30–1.

83 J. R. Burroughs and J. Wurst, "A New Agenda for Nuclear Disarmament: The Pivotal Role of Mid-Size States," paper presented at the Annual Meeting of the American Political Science Association, San Francisco, 2 September 2001; R. Johnson, "The NPT Review: Disaster Averted," *Bulletin of the Atomic Scientists* 56 (July/August 2000), 52–7.

84 See U.N. Conference on Disarmament Press Release, "South Africa Presents to Conference on Disarmament Working Paper on the Possible Scope of a Fissile Material Treaty," 23 May 2002; cited in Shelton, "South Africa's Nuclear Weapons Experience."

85 Lelyveld, "S. Africa Provides Cautionary Tale."

86 Less inflammatory, but possibly still sensitive for other governments, would be the disclosure of confidential diplomatic meetings. During the TRC's inquiry into Project Coast, defense, foreign affairs, military, and intelligence agencies objected that public TRC would harm the government's international relationships, due to confidential communications from the British and Americans on Project Coast in 1993–95. This was ultimately resolved by an agreement between the TRC and relevant government departments that these documents could be used by the TRC but not circulated to the public media. British and American officials subsequently described the content of the talks in interviews, so it is unlikely that their governments would have objected to such disclosures; Gould and Folb, *Project Coast*, 210–13, 25; Burgess and Purkitt, *Rollback,* 67.

87 It would be highly embarrassing to Israel if South African disclosures revealed that the 22 September 1979 flash in the South Atlantic was in fact an Israeli or joint Israeli–South African test. For a recent review of the debate over the September 1979 episode, see D. Albright and C. Gay, "A Flash from the Past," *Bulletin of the Atomic Scientists* 53 (November/December 1997): 15–17. Both countries had joined the Limited Test Ban Treaty banning above-ground nuclear tests, so the test would have violated international law. If any documentation survived, they might theoretically be subject to mandatory disclosure, if public interest in exposing this illegality is judged to outweigh the diplomatic costs of doing so.

88 Such views have been expressed to the authors in off-the-record discussions with South African officials.

89 T. Blanton, "The World's Right to Know," *Foreign Policy* (July/August 2002): 50–4. See also R. Martin and E. Feldman, *Access to Information in Developing Countries,* Working Paper, Transparency International, April 1998, at www.transparency.org/working_papers/martin-feldman/index.html.

90  P. Hounam and S. McQuillan, *Mandela's Nuclear Nightmare: The Mini-Nuke Conspiracy* (London: Faber and Faber 1995).

91  Public distrust of the environmental and health safety practices of U.S. nuclear production facilities was a prime motivation for the U.S. declassification initiative in the 1990s. See Heusser, "From Secrecy to Openness."

92  S. LaFraniere, "South Africa's Ruling Party Struggles Within," *New York Times*, 11 November 2003, A3.

93  Gould and Folb, *Project Coast,* 224.

94  Liberman interview with Stumpf, January 1999.

95  Conversation between Verne Harris and authors Hannes Steyn, Richard van der Walt, and Jan van Loggerenberg, Pretoria, July 2003.

96  Those who have passed away in recent years include Lt.-Gen. R. F. Armstrong, the author of the 1975 memorandum discussed above; Lt.-Gen. Robert H. (Bob) Rogers, Air Force Chief of Staff 1975–79; Brig.-Gen. John Huyser; Gen. A. J. (Kat) Liebenberg, SADF Chief, 1990–93; P. G. Marais, Armscor Chairman 1976–91; Fred Bell, Executive Director, Armscor, 1982–85; A. J. A. (Ampie) Roux, AEC chairman until 1980; Dr. J. W. de Villiers, AEC Chairman, 1980–89. In November 2002, we contacted former SADF chief admiral H. H. Biermann, then eighty-six, about the Armstrong memorandum (which had been addressed to him), but he could not recall anything about it or the issues, apparently due to failing memory.

97  Official histories of mass destruction weapons programs are typically written by professional historians with security clearances, who are allowed to search for and consult all relevant documents, conduct interviews with program veterans and politicians, and write a comprehensive history. Examples include H. D. W. Smyth and L. R. Groves, *Atomic Energy for Military Purposes: The Official Report on the Development of the Atomic Bomb under the Auspices of the United States Government, 1940–1945* (Princeton, N.J.: Princeton University Press, 1945); M. Gowing, *Britain and Atomic Energy, 1939–1945* (New York: St Martin's Press, 1964); M. Gowing and L. Arnold, *Independence and Deterrence: Britain and Atomic Energy, 1945–1952* (London: Macmillan [for the United Kingdom Atomic Energy Authority] 1974). Even if the state chose not to publish an official nuclear history immediately, the project would save testimony-based information for the future.

# SECTION V
# ACTUALITIES

# Chapter 21

## Actualities[1]

## TELLING TRUTHS ABOUT THE TRC ARCHIVE

### (Published under the title "Where Are the TRC Records?" in *The Natal Witness*, 22 April 2002)

If any achive in South Africa should be open, and widely used for and by the public, it is the archive of the Truth and Reconciliation Commission (TRC). While views on the TRC itself diverge dramatically, there is broad consensus in public discourse on the need for all of us—South Africans in particular—to continue interrogating its work and seeking understandings of its significance. For, as the recent Basson trial illustrates, South Africa has barely embarked on the paths of truth, reconciliation, and justice.

There are disturbing signs that the TRC archive is far from open. Numerous researchers speak of their unsuccessful attempts to access TRC records while the records were still under TRC management. In 2001, the South African History Archive (SAHA) was denied access in terms of the Promotion of Access to Information Act (PAIA) to a range of

National Archives records about the TRC archive on the grounds that the records were security classified. The movement of the bulk of the archive to the National Archives in Pretoria has been characterized by National Intelligence Agency (NIA) involvement, with a concomitant prioritization of security concerns and talk of records processing from a security classification perspective. It should be remembered that the bogey of classified information was a well-used instrument of the apartheid state.

Most disturbing is the uncertainty surrounding the thirty-four boxes of "sensitive" TRC records removed from the TRC offices in 1999 and placed in the custody of the Minister for Justice. No one involved has provided a satisfactory answer to the question of why these records were regarded as sensitive. Using PAIA, SAHA has secured a list of the files in those boxes. Analysis suggests that they comprise a diverse accumulation of records, many already in the public domain, very few at face value containing information that needs to be protected in terms of PAIA. Among the latter are records of *in camera* hearings, but the great majority of such records are already in the custody of the National Archives. Why are these being treated differently? There is a list of informers. And a confidential submission by the African National Congress (ANC).

Whatever the contents of these "sensitive" TRC records, they clearly belong together with the rest of the TRC archive in the National Archives. However, it is not clear where they are today.

In May 2001, SAHA put in a PAIA access request to the Department of Justice (DOJ) in relation to these records. Eventually, in December 2001, DOJ indicated that they did not have the records and suggested that SAHA approach the National Archives. SAHA immediately requested clarification in writing from both the National Archives and NIA. To this day, the National Archives has not responded. In contrast, NIA indicated in writing that the records, to its knowledge, were still in the safe custody of DOJ. This view was repeated by the minister of intelligence on 3 April 2002 in a letter to the journalist Terry Bell.

During the week 8–12 April, John Perlman of SAfm (radio) conducted a series of interviews with key role players in relation to the "sensitive" TRC records. On 9 April, the spokesperson for DOJ informed him that the records were with NIA for safekeeping. And on 12 April, the NIA spokesperson finally admitted that the records are indeed with NIA, but emphasized that they will be returned to DOJ shortly.

The truth out, at last? I remain unconvinced. The sorry saga of contradiction and obfuscation outlined above invites vigilance. Clearly the primary concern remains the whereabouts and the safety of these records. But a range of other serious questions are raised by the saga. What is the explanation for the contradictory answers given by state agencies as to the whereabouts of these records? Is anyone going to be held accountable for what constitutes a concealing of public records? Here it should be noted that in terms of PAIA it is a criminal offense to conceal a record to frustrate access to it. Why have the records not been placed in the professional care of the National Archives? And the broader questions: which state agency is going to control the TRC archive; how accessible is the TRC archive going to be; and how effective is PAIA in securing public rights of access to information?

This saga provides an early and profound test for PAIA. If a PAIA request can be frustrated with impunity—through delays, incomplete answers, even concealment—then a dangerous message is being conveyed to state officials. If a PAIA request cannot even identify the whereabouts of particular public records, less secure access to them, what is that saying about the act's efficacy? And if SAHA, with its considerable record-keeping and other resources, can be frustrated so easily, what are the implications for the average member of the public wanting to exercise his or her right of access to public records? Clearly it is vital that the matter be pursued, something SAHA is committed to doing.

While at this stage there are more questions than answers in relation to the matter, two things seem clear to me. Firstly, there are powerful elements within the state with intense, and potentially damaging, sensitivities around access to the TRC archive. And secondly, freedom of information is never something that a society possesses, notwithstanding excellent constitutional and legislative provisions. This freedom, like all freedoms, must constantly be worked for.

# SEX, SPIES, AND PSYCHOTHERAPY: THE STATE SECURITY CLEARANCE PROCEDURE NEEDS TO BE RECONCEPTUALIZED

**(Published in *The Natal Witness,* 17 June 2002)**

Recently there was heavy media coverage of the security clearance questionnaire that journalists aspiring to the presidential press corps would have to complete. Understandably, the focus of this coverage was on the questions related to sex and sexuality that the minister of intelligence withdrew in face of resistance. This was a victory from many perspectives, and it must have brought a smile to the faces of the numerous South Africans who have been forced to submit themselves to the state security clearance procedure.

It's a pity that broader issues highlighted by the incident were given cursory attention. For instance, we need to interrogate the rationale for security clearance procedures. Conventionally, they are designed to identify weaknesses in character and lifestyle—those weaknesses that make a person vulnerable to blackmail, bribery, and temptation to disloyalty. This is fraught terrain, a minefield of assumptions about values, beliefs, and rights. Is it terrain on which National Intelligence spies should determine the rules?

Thousands of public servants are routinely subjected to the state security clearance procedure every year. Astonishingly, the procedure has hardly changed at all since the grim apartheid days of the 1980s. Candidates are still subjected to scrutiny in terms of sex, religion, finances, psychic health, relationships, and so on. Family members, friends, and colleagues are questioned as part of the corroboration exercise. I always found this the toughest dimension in an ethical sense—to answer questions about a friend's or colleague's most intimate spaces. And the measures of strength and weakness appear not to have changed either—what would have been regarded as a weakness in the 1980s is still regarded as such in the 2000s.

Let's take the example of psychic health. Back in the eighties, a person's use of psychotherapy triggered flashing lights. It implied weakness within a framework of values that understood such therapy as merely a means of finding solutions to problems. Today, I would argue, this framework remains in place. During my most recent security clearance, in

2000, I was asked questions about when I had received psychotherapy, from whom, and for what reasons. I believe, along with many others, that psychotherapy should be seen as comfortably within the bounds of the "normal"—one means among many others for assisting human beings to work with the stuff of life, to find the patterns and rhythms that bring meaning and healing. This is especially true in the context of South Africa in transition, with widespread recognition of the degree to which apartheid and the struggles against it disrupted or destroyed these patterns and rhythms. So, to the question of why I needed such therapy, I responded "because I saw it as a huge opportunity not to be missed." Needless to say, my interrogator responded with consternation.

I am not saying that the fact of a person receiving psychotherapy is irrelevant. Indeed, I would concede that much psychotherapy *is* focused on problem solving and that much of it unhealthily lifts the individual out of collective contexts. For many looking to psychologists, psychiatrists, and counselors for help, getting out in the collective trenches would be a far better option than sinking into the shrink's chair. What I *am* saying is that in light of South Africa's huge societal and constitutional changes, the measures of relevance in relation to psychotherapy need to change.

Apartheid patterns remain resilient. Realms of unfinished business still confront us. But our values as a society have changed in fundamental ways. The constitution recasts completely how we understand and engage notions of right and wrong. The legal framework within which we relate to others has been transformed. It is in this context that the present state security clearance procedure should be evaluated.

The procedure, I would argue, is patently out of step. As is the spook culture that informs it. Obviously, there are many complex reasons for this, requiring a far broader analysis than I can offer here. But one very tangible reason is the continued existence of that quintessential piece of apartheid legislation, the 1982 Protection of Information Act. This is South Africa's own expression of official secrecy, which made a lot of sense from the perspective of the state in the eighties, but which has dubious validity under our current freedom of information dispensation.

There is a direct connection between this act and National Intelligence's oversight of the governmentwide Minimum Information Security Standard (MISS) and concomitant security clearance procedure. To say that there are strains between this act and new legislation passed to give expression to the constitution's commitment to freedom of information—notably the Promotion of Access to Information Act and the Protected Disclosures Act—is to understate the case. As I have reported previously in this column, there is evidence of requests for information in terms of the Access Act being evaluated not in terms provided for by the act, but rather in terms of requirements defined in the 1982 legislation. And there are strains in relation to a range of other rights protected in the constitution, notably the right to privacy. If one's reasons for using psychotherapy are not private, then what is?

I am not arguing for a scrapping of the state security clearance procedure. I am arguing that it needs to be reconceptualized, with its assumptions and requirements brought into line with the constitution and relevant legislation. Specifically, I am suggesting that the 1982 act should be scrapped and a new legislative definition of legitimate state secrecy provided. Promising news is that the MISS (an appropriate acronym in both English and Afrikaans), last reviewed in 1996, is again being subjected to review. However, I ask, where is the public scrutiny that should surely characterize such an exercise? And, finally, I am suggesting that any instrument for policing state secrecy should not be left in the hands of an agency like National Intelligence. Interpretations of appropriate character and lifestyle require inputs at once broader and more permeable to public participation.

## CHALLENGING WHAT IS INDIGENOUS: PRISTINE "CULTURE" AND ITS INVIOLABILITY NEED TO BE DEMYSTIFIED

### (Co-authored with Sello Hatang, published in *The Natal Witness,* 1 August 2002)

How often have you heard the protestations "But this is my culture" or "We are Africans" in response to critique? We hear them often. Recently they have been thrown out with increasing frequency in one form or the other as weapons in the hurly-burly of public debate.

A number of voices were heard protesting at the intense media scrutiny of reported rapes of very young girls: "It is not in our culture to discuss these things in public." A similar argument to the one offered in response to media coverage of prominent South Africans who apparently died of AIDS-related diseases. The latter links into South African versions of dissident views on HIV/AIDS that suggest that we should resist "Western" solutions to the crisis and instead plug into indigenous knowledges.

Criticism of black leaders in any sphere of life is frequently responded to with suggestions that such criticism is un-African. Calls for "traditional" leaders to be held accountable to democratic values and critique of the consequences of the *lobola* system practiced outside of traditional contexts receive the same treatment. Outrage at the needless deaths of young men going through initiation ceremonies runs the risk of labeling as cultural insensitivity. At a conference in Pietermaritzburg recently, an archivist speaking of her research into gay and lesbian practice by *sangomas* was told that such practice was not part of African culture. And we need no reminding of denunciations of gays as un-African in Zimbabwe and Namibia.

This short litany could be extended endlessly. We've offered just a few expressions of what constitutes a resilient view on culture and society in our part of the world. This view is founded on a whole range of assumptions, three of which seem central to us. Firstly, that one can inhabit a single "culture." Secondly, that there can be a pristine "culture" fundamentally impervious to influences either in time or over time. And thirdly, that anything identified as part of such a pristine "culture" should be above criticism.

*Culture* is an imprecise term used to describe dimensions of human experience ranging from religious beliefs and social rituals to the clothes we wear and the music we listen to. In a rapidly globalizing world, none of us is impervious to influences reaching across regional and national divides. All of us, to a greater or lesser degree, feel the impact of global mainstream dynamics and values jostling with those of local cultures. More than ever before, we feel the pull of diverse and often competing cultures. Our identities are patchworks rather than seamless cloths.

And it has always been so, even before the turbocharged dynamics of globalization. Culture has never been static. It has always been evolving, in response to tensions within communities and societies and to shifting realities in the worlds "external" to them. It is commonly believed that in Africa colonialism marked the inception of change. And yet scholars have demonstrated the cultural dynamism of precolonial Africa. They have, for instance, unfolded the development of Zulu society in the late eighteenth and early nineteenth centuries. They have traced the evolution of *lobola* or its equivalent in a number of societies.

Critique of culture is a healthy and necessary dimension in any society. The clash of youth cultures with those of adult worlds is essential to a well-adjusted transition to adulthood. Resistance to the dominant white Afrikaner cultures was an important part of the struggles against apartheid. Equally, questioning of resilient precolonial rituals and practices is a crucial element in the endeavors of collectivities to articulate with changing realities. Take the *kgotla* as an example. Without buying into simplistic notions that precolonial African societies were undemocratic, we would argue that the marginalization of women and youth in this ancient Tswana decision-making forum must be confronted. What place should such a forum enjoy in the context of a democratizing South Africa? How can it be encouraged to become permeable to more broadly participative processes?

We realize that our critique might be read as an attempt to dismiss the value—even the existence—of indigenous knowledges. This is not our intention. We would certainly question the notion of such pristine knowledges surviving the impact of multiple fusions over time. And we would resist any clear-cut distinction between such knowledges and those from "outside"—whether they be labeled "European," "Western," "global," or whatever. We would go further and argue that "indigenous" as a concept must always be accorded a relative value. Scholarly research is constantly pushing back the boundaries of our understanding of the peoples and societies that inhabited this part of the world over millennia. We are being forced to shift our question from "Is this indigenous?" to "How indigenous is this?" And that moves us to the question of how long must knowledges have root in a place before they are accorded the label "indigenous"? How indigenous are the knowledges that have found root in the Cape from the time they were brought into the country by slaves from the East?

We believe that simplistic notions of what indigenous knowledge is have contributed to the marginalization of such knowledges. Their very identification as "other" opens them to further marginalization by dominant knowledges. And this marginalization is impoverishing mainstream public discourses across the board, from medicine to heritage, from archives to organizational development. If we are to draw on the richness of ways of thinking and doing available to us in this part of the world, then it is critical that ways be found of increasing the hospitality of dominant knowledges to diversity, complexity, and fusions.

A starting point is to demystify the notion of indigenous knowledge along the lines we have suggested. We need to insist that the imagined age and origin of a way of knowing is of little significance. The critical issues are its rootedness in this part of the world and its capacity to engage shifting realities meaningfully. We need to insist on every way of knowing being given a space in public discourse, in a context of interaction and contestation. We must address the issues of power, of systemic marginalization of the weak and the isolated, but at the same time we need to avoid the danger of romanticizing what we regard as indigenous and as therefore above criticism.

## THE BEST AND THE BEAST: FINDING CRACKS IN ANTIGLOBALIZATION AND ANTI-AMERICAN DISCOURSES

**(Published in *The Natal Witness*, 7 September 2002)**

In the week after the events of September 11 last year I e-mailed all my North American friends to express my concern and wishes that the United States would respond outside of a knee-jerk, antiterrorist agenda. Some were less than enthusiastic about my sentiments. One of them accused me of being instinctively anti-American.

At the recent World Summit on Sustainable Development in Johannesburg, we heard many expressions of outrage at the United States and its role in the processes of globalization. Some of these views could comfortably be positioned within the linked conceptual frames of antiglobalization and anti-Americanism, but others would require more sophisticated labeling. This, in essence, was the point I made in responding to the accusation of anti-Americanism last year—"do some analysis of my views," I suggested, "before you label me as anti-American."

Of course, it doesn't take a genius to delineate the global ravaging wrought by globalization. Any number of voices at the summit have pointed out how the global powers, led by the U.S., are making a mockery of sustainable development as an ideal and are courting ecological disaster on an unimaginable scale. Equally, it doesn't take a genius to realize that the U.S. has become a global power with unprecedented oppressive capacity.

From the 1970s through the early 1990s, as Noam Chomsky has pointed out, the U.S.'s capacity to enforce its will on other countries was constrained by a combination of internal dissent and the dynamics of the Cold War. Now, the latter is over and, especially since September 11 last year, internal dissent is being frozen. The Bush administration, riding a wave of popularity at home, feels free to take overt action against what it regards as terrorist organizations or hostile states in a way its predecessors since the 1970s could only dream of.

The Bush offensive engages domestic issues as much as it does foreign policy. His administration is unraveling inherited policies on protection of the environment, social security, and freedom of information; pouring trillions into the defense industry; building up a huge budget deficit; giving generous tax cuts to the richest 2 percent of Americans; promoting the notion that material success is everything and can be enjoyed without a price to be paid by others; and mobilizing society around "homeland security" imperatives.

The degree to which civil society in the U.S. is lining up (either willingly or unwillingly) behind the "war on terrorism" is worrying. The mainstream media pound out a patriotic beat. Corporations rally to the call for increased surveillance. Academics adjust their research proposals to the homeland protection agenda. Even trusted "political" artists like Neil Young prevaricate. Young, the man who gave us classic howls against the Vietnam War and related oppression, has just released an album including an ode to the passengers who supposedly attacked the hijackers of flight 93 on September 11.

Frightening stuff. All of it feeding concerns that we are facing a juggernaut dressed in the rhetoric of freedom but intent on bending the world to its wishes. A juggernaut commanding the processes of globalization. And, in a sense, I think this metaphor is just right. However, to the extent that it fosters unqualified anti-American and antiglobalization energies, I find it problematic. For if we are to understand the challenges confronting the globe and identify appropriate strategies for resisting the new forms of oppression, then we must avoid reductionist analyses.

As was argued by a number of voices at the World Summit, the world cannot be divided neatly into countries of the global hub and countries of the periphery. The profoundest global divide, between the haves and the have-nots, between the powerful and the weak, cuts across national boundaries. The global elite, with its destructive values and insatiable appetites, is to be found in all countries. Equally, all countries, including the U.S., possess elements of what is rapidly becoming a global underclass. In November last year, I walked the streets of Washington, D.C. and didn't have to walk far to leave the display of American flags behind and find neighborhoods focused on grinding out a living. It is clear that most African Americans in Washington live in poverty, victims of a policy that regards being poor as a personal rather than a collective problem. And in the Adams Morgan neighborhood I discovered any number of restaurants run by expatriate Africans and crossed paths with many residents who hardly speak English.

To be effective, resistance to global oppression has to get beyond particular "problem" countries and address the worldwide structural dimensions of oppression. It has to confront the possibility that countries like South Africa, India, Pakistan, and a host of others, if given the resources of the U.S., would in all likelihood present the world with identical challenges to those being posed by the U.S. It has to confront the reality that globalization cannot be turned back, and to focus on finding ways of harnessing its awesome energies in the interests of justice.

Moreover, it must be acknowledged that as powerful and scary as the U.S. is today, it is neither monolithic nor inhospitable to contestation. Muted as dissident voices are, they are still to be found. Many courageous struggles are being fought within the belly of the beast every day. Freedoms are under siege but by no means lost. More importantly, as I have already suggested, the energies of the global periphery vibrate in that belly. The distance between the rich and the poor is increasing. States are going bankrupt. The health service is in chaos. Race problems are far from solved. Cultural diversity is growing. As is alienation from formal political processes.

I am not anti-American. Too many Americans and too much of what is American inspire my admiration for that label to stick. As Leonard Cohen sang ten years ago: "I'm sentimental, if you know what I mean: I love the country but I can't stand the scene." The U.S. remains, in Cohen's words, "the cradle of the best and the worst." The country that gave us jazz, rock 'n' roll, Martin Luther King, "the personal is political," Toni Morrison, Bob Dylan, and a host of extraordinary creative voices cannot simply be dismissed as an evil empire.

Nor am I without hope that the U.S., indisputably the most powerful empire the world has ever seen, can find again its dream of a justice that is indivisible. In the words of Cohen once more: "From the wars against disorder, from the sirens night and day, from the fires of the homeless, from the ashes of the gay: Democracy is coming to the U.S.A." I would not be completely surprised if the 2010s turn into the twenty-first century's equivalent of the 1960s.

## AN EXERCISE IN FORGETTING: REMEMBERING THE UNFINISHED BUSINESS OF THE TRC

**(Published in *The Natal Witness*, 26 September 2002)**

On a visit to South Africa in 1998, Jacques Derrida, arguably the world's most eminent living philosopher, offended many South Africans by suggesting that the Truth and Reconciliation Commission needed to be understood as an exercise in forgetting. Outrageous! Wasn't the TRC precisely a mechanism for moving into the future through a thorough dealing with the past? Wasn't it a process for remembering and memorializing, one moreover regarded internationally as exemplary— a global symbol of a noble refusal to simply forget and move on?

Derrida was not denying the dimensions of memory that informed the TRC's work. Indeed, he had many positive things to say about the TRC's determination in extremely difficult circumstances to unfold and archive apartheid atrocities. And he acknowledged that the claims to exemplarity were not unjustified.

He was making a point at once very simple and deeply philosophical. Archiving, traditionally understood as an act of remembering, is at profound levels a simple act of forgetting. As he illustrated it at a seminar convened by the University of the Witwatersrand, when we write a note on a piece of paper and consign it to a pocket, we are archiving the information so that we can forget it now but retrieve it when we need it. Moreover, he was suggesting that remembering and forgetting are not binary opposites—light opposed to darkness. All remembering is informed by forgetting; all shedding of light involves the casting of shadow.

It is not my intention here to explore the philosophical spaces opened up by Derrida. I want to consider briefly the dimensions of forgetting (conventionally understood) associated with the TRC as process and as institution.

Scholars, journalists, and commentators have covered extensively the processes of selection that characterized the TRC's work. Its mandate restricted it to a narrow investigative focus, namely, gross human rights violations committed during part of the apartheid era. Practical constraints forced it to focus even more narrowly—for instance, only about a tenth of the victims who came forward were given an opportunity to tell their stories in public. Numerous investigations were hampered by incompetence, internal wrangling, political pressure, and various forms of obstruction. Some of its hearings were conducted *in camera*. All of these, I would argue, are dimensions of forgetting.

The New National Party was able to force the deletion of certain findings from the TRC's report. In 1998, the ANC mounted an unsuccessful attempt to do the same thing. Now we have the Inkatha Freedom Party (IFP) taking the TRC to court to challenge findings related to its alleged involvement in gross human rights violations. Arguably these are expressions of an instinct to forgetfulness.

On a more positive note, a dimension of forgetting was embraced by the TRC's commitment to public disclosure and storytelling. I am not implying simplistic notions of closure, or of forgiving and forgetting. Central to the TRC's endeavor was resisting denial and erasure. But equally central was the bringing of healing—in other words, tell the story not to then forget what happened, but tell it so that the pain, guilt, anguish, hatred, and so on—as lived experience—can be forgotten.

The loss of institutional memory resources is another dimension of forgetting. Here I refer specifically to the incomplete and scattered TRC archive. A thorough audit of TRC records and the surviving apartheid-era security establishment records identified by the TRC has not yet been done, so it is impossible to come to any firm conclusions. But consider the following. We know that the whereabouts of thirty-four boxes of so-called sensitive TRC records is either not known or is being concealed by the state. We know that a large part of the TRC's electronic memory is in a tenuous condition and probably has significant gaps. We know that many TRC staffers removed organizational records when they departed. And we know that at least in the case of surviving Security Police files, there is already evidence of records seen by the TRC now being lost.

Needless to say, the impact of these realities on the public's right of access to the TRC archive is significant. Moreover, securing access to the parts of the archive that are safely in the custody of the National Archives is not easy. Commitment to remembering, in my view, would make this the most public—the most open and accessible—of South African archives. It is not. Access can only be secured through the submission of requests under the Promotion of Access to Information Act. And, as many are discovering, due to a range of factors this is a complex, time-consuming, and often frustrating business.

A final layer of forgetting is to be discerned in the state's response to the numerous recommendations made by the TRC in its report. This aspect has been reasonably well covered by the media. Very little has been done to provide reparations to identified victims of gross human rights violations. There seems to be no will to pursue the prosecution of perpetrators who ignored the TRC's amnesty process or who failed to secure amnesty. The recent presidential pardoning of persons who were denied amnesty by the TRC constitutes, among other things, a grave forgetting of the amnesty process as a critical mechanism in South Africa's transition to democracy. And, despite some brave attempts by the National Archives, the TRC's wide-ranging recommendations on state record-keeping have been by and large ignored.

When we add all this forgetting together, I would suggest, we cannot but come to the conclusion that Derrida's typification of the TRC demands serious consideration. We might even be justified in going further, by coming to the conclusion that for the state the TRC is no more than a tool for providing a nod at remembering in the interests of a profounder forgetting. Those who have come to this conclusion— and there are a growing number—suggest that while the state says it is dealing with the past, in fact it is intent on getting back to business as usual as quickly as possible.

However, as Derrida would quickly point out, there is never forgetting without remembering. And there is never forgetting without the possibility of remembering. As he asserted in 1998: "What we think we have forgotten may come back through a number of ways, unpredictable ways." Fortunately for South Africa, the country has many individuals and organizations committed to troubling processes of erasure and to importuning justice to come. For them the unfinished business of the TRC will never be forgotten.

## GETTING THE OUTSIDERS IN: SOME ON THE MARGINS DON'T WANT TO BE PART OF THE MAINSTREAM

**(Published in *The Natal Witness,* 4 November 2002)**

The harsh realities of power relations, even in democracies, mean that there will always be a mainstream with a bevy of interests, values, and communities jostling around its margins. For some, being in the margins—of an institution, a community, a discourse, or society more broadly—is a choice. They have no desire to be in the mainstream. For most, however, being in the margins is the result of exclusion. They have been marginalized.

I was reminded of these harsh realities in September when I attended a gathering convened by the Pietermaritzburg Heritage Forum, a loose grouping of heritage structures with a presence in greater Pietermaritzburg. Despite the intentions, and efforts, of the conveners, there was little or no participation by community-based organizations. To put it crudely, representation from the townships was a little thin. More crudely still, the gathering was very white.

Much of the forum's deliberation focused on how to rectify this imbalance. To its credit, the forum eschewed quick-fix options for bringing in community-based organizations. There was keen awareness that such options do not address the danger of the margins being further marginalized by the power of mainstream resources, cultures, and competencies.

Also to its credit, the forum found space to consider what is arguably the fundamental question—why is it imperative for every mainstream to engage its margins? Why not simply run with what are systemic processes of privileging and exclusion? Of course, a strong argument based purely on survival could be mounted. Let these processes go too far unhindered, and the whole system might collapse, a lesson the whites of Zimbabwe failed to learn.

Beyond concerns for survival, there is a profounder—a deeper and more enduring—imperative. It is what I would call justice. Of course, as with all those key terms around which we frame value systems, the meaning of "justice" is hotly contested. But whatever it means, I would argue, it must hinge on hospitality to "the other." I am speaking of a call to respect every "other," a call to invite every "other" in. For heritage practitioners (and the forum is keenly aware of this) the call intrudes into all they do. It is not something that sounds only when formal gatherings and processes are being organized. In all professional work, from collecting materials to mounting displays, from staff appointments to public education, the call of justice importunes them to listen intently for the voices of those who are marginalized or excluded entirely by prevailing relations of power.

What the forum did not consider is the broader context within which the challenges outlined above are playing out. Local heritage cannot be dislocated from societal processes, nor indeed from global dynamics. Superficial analysis might suggest that participative democracy has never been easier for South Africans. Apartheid is being dismantled, a formal constitutional democracy is in place, and in so many ways resistance to marginalization is being encouraged. And yet, as the forum is discovering, while things might be easier, they are far from easy. Legacies from our past are clearly a factor. But equally challenging are the tough new realities presented by globalization and corporatization.

Increasingly, power is being aggregated by corporations, many of them multinationals with resources beyond those of smaller states. Unlike states, these corporations escape in large measure the demands of accountability and transparency. Not only do they promote the concentration of wealth in the hands of a small elite, but they exert significant leverage on public representatives and increasingly determine national public policy agendas. The role and the influence of both governments and civil society are diminishing.

As worrying is the extent to which these corporations are promoting the commodification of knowledge, information, and services. All commodities have a price, and in a context of widening disparities between the haves and the have-nots, fewer and fewer people (relatively, and in some cases absolutely) can afford them. It is no accident, for example, that heritage, unquestioningly a public resource, is being turned into an industry. And the logic of industry, as opposed to that of public service, is the exclusion of those too poor to afford its products. It is no accident, to quote another example, that at the very moment when South Africa is given freedom of information (by the constitution and by legislation), the processes I am speaking of turn information into a commodity that only the wealthy can afford.

The Pietermaritzburg Heritage Forum, in short, is confronting huge systemic barriers to participative democracy. And this is only the beginning of its problems. In resisting the forces of marginalization, it is confronted by a range of intractable questions. Committed as it might be to finding those marginalized voices, those "other" voices, how does it begin to invite in what is always beyond the limits of understanding? How to avoid the danger of speaking *for* these other voices? How to avoid reinforcing marginalization by naming "the marginalized"? I remember being alerted forcefully to these issues during a conference presentation in Canada last year—my presentation on marginalization was interrupted by a tall woman who said, "I'm a radical feminist lesbian, and I resent your arrogance in assuming that I would have any desire to be represented in or by mainstream institutions."

Another complexity is that out in the margins are myriad voices we might have no desire to invite in. In fact, we might want to erase them altogether—the voices, for instance, of white supremacists, or of hard drug dealers, pedophiles, rapists, pimps, and so on, and on and on. And yet they are part of our reality, part of our heritage.

It is imperative, I would argue, to avoid romanticizing "otherness." In the memorable words of Gayatri Chakravorty Spivak: "Let us, then, ... arrest the understandable need to fix and diagnose the identity of the most deserving marginal. Let us also suspend the mood of self-congratulation as saviors of marginality." We should fear "otherness" even as we respect it. We must know that as much as it is "outside," it is also "inside." We should know only that justice calls us to engage it, without blueprint, without solution, without answers.

# CARING FOR THE APARTHEID RECORDS THAT SURVIVED: IRREPLACEABLE ARCHIVES ARE DISAPPEARING

**(Published in** *The Natal Witness,* **28 November 2002)**

Between 1996 and 1998, the Truth and Reconciliation Commission undertook an investigation into records destruction by the apartheid state. It discovered that a massive destruction exercise, authorized at the highest levels and concentrated in the security establishment, had taken place in the period 1990 to 1994. Surprisingly, the TRC was able nevertheless to locate and document substantial accumulations of security records that had survived this devastating erasure of state memory resources.

The value of these surviving records to the work of the TRC cannot be overemphasized; nor can their value to continuing research into the inner workings of the apartheid state. Appreciation of their value, together with concern about their safety, led the TRC to make a number of recommendations for their future care. Three recommendations were central: firstly, that the surviving records be brought under the control of the National Archives as soon as possible; secondly, that the National Archives take what was acknowledged as a severely circumscribed and inadequate investigation further; and thirdly, that the National Archives be resourced to undertake this work.

These recommendations for state intervention were modest. Germany, in comparison, acted vigorously after 1989 in dealing with the surviving security establishment records of the former East Germany. For example, it mandated by legislation an extremely well-resourced structure (the Gauck Institute) to secure, preserve, and manage access to surviving Stasi (Security Police) records. South Africa's different approach is informed by resource constraints and the complexities of a negotiated transition from oppressive rule.

Modest as the TRC's recommendations were, there are few signs of the state being willing to implement them. The National Archives has neither been resourced nor specifically mandated to undertake a thorough audit of surviving apartheid-era security records. While it would be unfair to accuse the National Archives of having done nothing, the institution has done very little to extend the TRC's inquiry.

A few examples illustrate the point. Four years after the TRC's report was published, the legal status of the archives being run by the South African National Defence Force (SANDF), Armscor, and National Intelligence has still not been clarified. It took investigations by the South African History Archive (SAHA), a small NGO, to uncover thousands of Military Intelligence files that had been concealed from the TRC. No attempt has yet been made to determine what documentary record has survived of South Africa's nuclear weapons program. And there is no coordinated endeavor to locate and preserve the records of the apartheid-era homeland governments.

Since 1998, only two accumulations of apartheid security records have been transferred into the custody of the National Archives—the Department of Justice Security Legislation Directorate files, and the prison files of former political prisoners. The great majority of the records documented by the TRC remain with the security establishment structures that inherited them, outside the purview of the National Archives, and outside the purview of the South African public.

The critical question, I would argue, is—how safe are these scattered archives? Some, I think, are as safe as any records can be. The professionalism of the staff at the SANDF archives, for instance, inspires confidence. But in other areas there is serious cause for concern. The case of the missing thirty-four boxes of "sensitive" TRC records has been well documented in the South African media. At the time of writing, SAHA's attorneys were preparing High Court papers designed to force the Department of Justice to disclose the whereabouts of these records. This is not an isolated case—in November the family of Ahmed Timol was informed that the TRC records on the death of Timol in police custody had gone missing.

Concern is not confined to the records of the TRC. The bulk of surviving Transkei archives, dating back to the 1800s, have been consigned to a shed in the backyard of the Nelson Mandela Museum in Mthatha. There they are cruelly exposed to the elements and can only be regarded as a disaster waiting to happen. Then there are the surviving apartheid Security Police records. In recent months, SAHA investigations have revealed the following: some of the records inventories compiled in response to TRC interventions cannot be found; no work has been done since 1998 to ensure the readability and long-term preservation of data from Security Police databases; and certain files inventoried by the TRC have been lost. For instance, a request by Dumisa Ntsebeza, former head of the TRC Investigation Unit, for copies of Security Police files relating to himself elicited an affidavit from the South African Police Service (SAPS) indicating that the files could not be located.

These, I would suggest, are warning signals. The surviving fragments, especially valuable in the context of the apartheid state's attempt to obliterate incriminating evidence, are being exposed to further attrition by neglect. Our democratic state owes it to South Africans to revisit TRC recommendations in relation to state record-keeping and to put a mechanism in place for auditing, securing, and ensuring the preservation of surviving apartheid security records. The argument that action must be put on hold until the submission of the codicil to the TRC report has worn thin. Years are passing and irreplaceable archives are disappearing. The state, specifically through the National Archives, needs to acknowledge its obligation to preserve and make available the documentary evidence of a critical dimension of our tortured past.


## THE CRY OF THE ASHES: WHY WOULD PEOPLE WISH TO DESTROY THE ARCHIVAL TREASURES OF IRAQ?

**(Published in *The Natal Witness*, 28 April 2003)**

Until a few weeks ago, Iraq possessed one of the world's most ancient, diverse, and valuable archives. Baghdad's National Archives, Library and Museum contained documents, books, and artifacts tracing centuries of human experience and endeavor in a geographical space which has been, and remains, one of the richest crossroads of national, religious, cultural, and other traditions.

In a few days, this treasure, at once an Iraqi and a world treasure, was destroyed. First the looters came, then the arsonists, and now all that remains are ashes. As so often in history's great human tragedies, we are left with only the ashes. What are they saying to us?

Of course, it would be legitimate to point at the broken bodies, the orphaned, the ashes of the dead, and come to the conclusion that in comparison the loss of archives is of relatively little concern. Only a fool would resist this logic. But on the other hand, only a fool would ignore the significance of the loss and the insights it offers into the bigger phenomenon of Baghdad's sacking.

In a powerful piece posted from Baghdad on 15 April, *The Independent*'s Robert Fisk gave an eyewitness account of the destruction. Horrified and powerless, he repeatedly returned to the question "why?" Why would people want to destroy these treasures? Why would they want to impoverish their society further? Why did the American forces do nothing to stop it?

Clearly American complicity is a fundamental factor. By all accounts the U.S. government had been warned in advance by experts about the vulnerability of Iraq's archaeological, archival, and other treasures. And yet there is no evidence of any attempt by the U.S. to protect them. In contrast, elaborate plans were made and implemented to protect the Iraqi oil industry. Not surprising perhaps, but the values informing this contrast provide the deepest layer of context to any attempt at addressing the "why" question.

One might argue that no invading army in its right mind would prioritize the protection of such treasures. But a willingness, and a determination, to respond to acts of destruction are different things. As Fisk reported, the American forces in Baghdad did nothing when warned of what was unfolding at the National Archives. This can be contrasted with the British force's intervention in Basra to save the Baath Party archives in that city. A cynic, of course, would point to the nature of the Baath Party archives and its value to an army of occupation in, on the one hand, identifying potential collaborators and enemies, and on the other, in demonstrating the reach of Saddam's oppressive regime. The Baath Party archives offered a readily identifiable utility; the National Archives did not.

Commentators have pointed to the composition of the American forces as another factor in explaining their failure to intervene. Unlike a conscripted army, which includes a wider cross-section of society, and which would have at least a sprinkling of intellectuals and those with a liberal arts education, the American forces comprise professional soldiers with little or no education in "culture" and the "arts." This difference is echoed at the political level, where no one would expect any respect for archives and related values from

Bush's hard-nosed gang of philistines. No surprise then that Defense Secretary Donald Rumsfeld made light of the looting in Baghdad in a wisecracking performance at a press briefing.

The harsh reality though is that it was Iraqis, not Americans, who destroyed the National Archives, Library and Museum. Who were they and why did they do it? It is doubtful that we will ever have satisfactory answers to these questions. I have no doubt that the crowd responsible was diverse both in its composition and in its motivation. There would have been individuals aware of the value of the collections and intent on stealing items for their monetary value. There might have been individuals intent on destroying the documentary evidence (among the more recent archival materials) of past collaborations with Saddam's regime. No doubt there were extremists with political, religious, and other agendas; hooligans caught up in the rush of a society's unraveling; and ordinary Iraqis intent on removing any perceived symbol of Saddam's rule. There might even have been *agents provocateurs*, deployed by who knows what forces.

No simple answers. No simple explanations. What is clear though is that in Baghdad there wasn't a sufficient groundswell of appreciation for archival treasures, of a sense of public ownership in them, to prevent the destruction. A salutary lesson for archivists and curators the world over. Failure to turn archives from a haven for an elite of scholars and tourists into a widely used public resource—a failure, ultimately, to secure broad societal ownership—makes archives extremely vulnerable when society is under stress. More dangerous yet (and I don't know to what extent this was a factor in Baghdad) is the temptation for archivists to identify with and express the narratives of their political masters. This might effect short-term advantage, but in the long term, the most effective insurance for archives, indeed for any public resource or service, is their capacity to express and meet the needs of "ordinary" people.

In the broader context of Iraq's suffering, the loss of Baghdad's National Archives, Library and Museum might not register prominently for most observers. But the ashes are speaking to us. And they are raising serious questions about the politics and the values informing our twenty-first–century globalized societies.

# INSIDE THE NUCLEAR WEAPONS PROGRAM OLD BOYS' NETWORK: FRIENDLY GRANDFATHERS DEDICATE THEMSELVES TO NONPROLIFERATION NOW

**(Co-authored with Evelyn Groenink, published under the title "The Nuclear Grandads" in** *The Natal Witness,* **24 July 2003)**

Three former officials in South Africa's nuclear weapons program have just published a book on the program entitled *Armament and Disarmament: South Africa's Nuclear Weapons Experience*. This is the first published "insider" account since F. W. de Klerk made his dramatic disclosure in 1993. That is significant in itself. While it does not provide conclusive answers to many of the questions that have occupied scholars since 1993, it does provide fascinating insights into the operational management of the program.

We were invited to the book launch in Pretoria. The candlelit, strangely cozy cellar is part of a restaurant that is a traditional haunt for South Africa's military fraternity. "The (foreign military) attaches know this place very well," the senior host confides. "And they have all been invited. How come they are not here now?" "Because there are journalists present and they still don't want to be associated with you guys in public?" one of us whispers to the friendly grandfather close by, to be met with an almost boyish, smiling shrug. The three former high-ranking military (white) men (there are only white people here) and their technological and academic friends are grandfathers now. One of them even carries a business card with pictures of his grandchildren on it and his new title: "professional grandfather." They are all disarmingly sweet and welcoming; one asks us if we are "religious," and then we have a nice chat about morality, and how to distinguish between right and wrong in matters military.

The three—the former general manager of research and development at Armscor, the chief of the Air Force, and the general manager of the Atomic Energy Corporation—have written the book not to divulge any secrets on exactly what nuclear weapons were designed and produced in this country up to 1991, but, in their own words, to "give the backroom boys who made the programme possible by their dedication, hard work and sense of responsibility, their due." Even though they state in the very last sentence of the book that it should in no way be perceived as a "defence of the past"—and by inference, of themselves in that past—a certain personal need to explain and defend themselves as good human beings is an undertone throughout the book, even in the most technical sections. They dedicated a large part of their lives to producing weapons of mass destruction; and they produced top of the range, state-of-the-art "devices." Furthermore, they did it all in total secrecy and amid "choking sanctions"—even if, it is conspiratorially said on page 82, "expert inspectors of 'dual use' items must have gained more than a whiff of suspicion at the flow of some sophisticated components into South Africa."

It is clear that the nuclear grandfathers are worried about the perception that they might have liked apartheid. They were and are not, let that be clear, "an evil-minded gang of racist ideologues." "We wanted to get rid of apartheid by the end of the sixties," confides academic and former senior Armscor official Professor Andre Buys, over a glass of port wine and hot peppery lentil soup. "But in the seventies we had the problem that we couldn't give the country to the blacks—not if we wanted to avoid going down like the rest of Africa—and in the eighties we couldn't give up because of the threat of Communism. Only when the Soviet system started crumbling in the late eighties and early nineties did we have the breathing space to contemplate change."

Before that, both international sanctions and rejection by Western governments hurt. But, as the book demonstrates, and as their demure, barely suppressed smiles confirm, they overcame that. They are all undeniably proud of what they accomplished. Armscor was "very creative" when it came to "sensitive procurement"; "technology transfers" to upgrade an inadequate local capability resulted in "trained specialists, an infrastructure of information, laboratories, manufacturing facilities," and even a ballistic missile suited to carrying nuclear warheads. "Of course the West and others dealt with us in spite of the verbal protestations against apartheid," Buys admits. "It actually made you very wary of both politicians and businesspeople. The double standards and the hypocrisy were there all the time." He refers to a trip he made to the U.S. in 1974. "The people there were so eager to deal with us that it made me run away. They were so blatant I feared they were going to put us in trouble. I never went abroad again professionally until the early nineties." The other thing he has to say—and here all the nuclear founding grandfathers concur adamantly—is that "the international cooperation took place outside the nuclear circle. There was cooperation as far as the 'normal' military technology was concerned—there we had foreign collaborators. But not when it came to the nuclear side. We sheltered that inner circle with our lives."

He agrees that some in the West might have wanted very much to know what was going on inside that inner circle by the late eighties and confirms later, when he makes a speech to launch the book, that inspectors from the U.S. and the U.K., when they finally came to see the South African designs at the time when the country signed the Nonproliferation Treaty in 1991, expressed their surprise at the "innovation" of it all. So South Africa did have the much talked about "mini-nuke" after all? He smiles and says that "regrettably, I can't give details of the design as this is expressly prohibited by the NPT."

The founding grandfathers are bitter about the manner in which the plug was pulled on the program in 1991. "State of the art technology" and a "big investment" were lost and "no quid pro quo was given by the international community." Still, they are now, they write and confirm during our chats, firmly committed to nuclear disarmament and nonproliferation. But, as they repeatedly point out, why should some nations not be allowed to have nuclear weapons while others are? Why should South Africa not have nuclear weapons merely because it is regarded as a "third world" country? They point to the fact that international missile control and nonproliferation regimes stop any flux moving, for instance, from the U.S. to anywhere else, but it doesn't at all limit the U.S. from acquiring whatever it wants at any time. They are of the opinion that either nobody should have nuclear weapons, or everybody should have the right to, with the proviso that every nuclear nation must commit to "responsible ownership."

When pressed on the subject, the grandfathers can't really think of any nation that would be an example of such "responsible ownership," beyond, of course, South Africa. This despite the fact that their book lists many warnings and cautions addressed to apartheid government representatives by nuclear weapons officials and scientists at the time, some even going as far as telling the minister of defense at the time that they were "praying for wisdom" for him; another paragraph calls the government leaders who had their finger on the nuclear bomb trigger "unsophisticated."

The scientist, the manager, the air force chief discuss with us arms proliferation in Africa and the so-called red mercury murders of nuclear material peddlers in South Africa in the early nineties. Maybe, they nod, maybe, as long as there are such profits at stake, there can be no such thing as responsible ownership. But what do they know about these things? They were mere officials in the nuclear weapons program. They are not, have never been, and have seldom dealt with, arms dealers. They have only a very vague knowledge of illegal cross-border traffic, "multi-sourced" origins and falsified end user certificates. "Arms dealers?" the three kind grandfathers all agree, "you better stay away from them."

## BRIDGING OLD DIVIDES: ANY SUSTAINED POLITICAL SETTLEMENT IN IRELAND MUST BE INCLUSIVE

**(Published in *The Natal Witness,* 15 August 2003)**

Belfast is a city scarred by centuries of conflict, in particular by the sectarian violence of what was called "the Troubles" from the late 1960s into the 1990s. In those years, Northern Ireland was regularly in the world headlines as layerings of social division—Protestants and Catholics, workers and the ruling classes, loyalists and nationalists—threatened to tear the territory apart.

In July I spent three days in Belfast, capital city and birthplace of personal heroes like George Best and Van Morrison, birthplace of my eleven-year-old son's current obsession, the *Titanic*. Though I walked many streets, talked to many residents, and soaked in the place's confluence of river, sea, green Irish hills, and city, my brief sojourn could, of course, secure me only the most selective of impressions.

Negotiations toward a political settlement have been underway for nearly ten years now. At present they are stalled, and a settlement appears no closer to realization. Although leaders from South Africa's peace process have shared experiences with their Northern Irish counterparts, there is no plan yet for an equivalent of the Truth and Reconciliation Commission.

Residential segregation between Catholic and Protestant remains marked. Walk up the Shankill Road, for instance, and you are confronted by a splurge of loyalist flags, street bunting, and pro-British wall murals. July is the month of loyalist memorialization and street marches. But cross over the "peace wall," a little Berlin Wall, into the Falls Road area, and here are street images of Irish Republican Army (IRA) memory and solidarity with international liberation movements. "Peace walls" is the euphemism for physical boundaries between communities that are designed to reduce the potential for conflict.

Like South Africa's racial legacy, the divide between Catholics and Protestants in Northern Ireland is ubiquitous. They have different mythologies; different names for places—the Protestant Londonderry is the Catholic Derry. They send their children to different schools. They tend to play different sports. Recently a footballer withdrew from the Northern Ireland team after receiving death threats from Protestant extremists.

And yet there are many positive signs and energies. The economy is reviving, evident in job creation and a sprouting of new buildings. The peace is holding. Belfast feels like a very safe place for a stranger to wander in. People everywhere, across divides, seem equally ready to talk. The incomparable Irish humor pops out everywhere. And the city is attracting both tourists and potential immigrants. (Although the latter, almost inevitably, seems to be triggering an equivalent of South Africa's current experience of xenophobia.)

I was in Belfast to visit the city's world-renowned Linen Hall Library, which includes an extensive archive of political conflict in Northern Ireland. This archive draws material from all quarters and has done so for many years, pursuing a line as deliberately impartial as possible. Its documentation of "the Troubles" is particularly impressive, and at present it is focusing considerable energy on documenting the peace process.

Pursuing this line has not been easy. In many cases, materials were collected literally from the barricades. A library director was once arrested for being in possession of seditious material. The library was fire-bombed by the IRA.

We have no equivalent of this archive in South Africa. In the past, political lines fashioned our archives' collecting endeavors, for good reason, and today the imprint of that past remains resilient. Maybe this difference expresses, and speaks to, our countries' divergent paths to democratization.

South Africa's negotiated settlement was arrived at relatively quickly. Today, nearly ten years after 1994, we are struggling to build reconciliation on the foundation of that settlement. The TRC gave a kick-start to reconciliation endeavors, but by almost every measure we are only beginning to tackle the huge legacies of our past.

Though a political settlement for Northern Ireland seems far away, I am hopeful that this troubled land will be successful. In simplistic terms, it is busy with processes of reconciliation that ultimately will become the foundation for a political settlement. The Linen Hall Library, it seems to me, is symbolic of this different approach. Seeing posters of Ian Paisley and Bobby Sands side by side, browsing the materials of loyalists and republicans in the same room, offers a powerful vision of the type of inclusivity that must inform any sustainable political settlement.

Northern Ireland has sought to learn lessons from the South African transition. Emblematic for me was Madiba's image in the Linen Hall Library archive and on the walls of the Falls Road. But I wonder if we don't have just as much to learn from Northern Ireland ...

## TINKER, TAILOR, INFORMER, SPY: "DISLOYALTY" TO THE ANC CAN RESULT IN REVELATIONS OF A DUBIOUS PAST

**(Co-authored with Sello Hatang and Rolf Sorensen, published in *The Natal Witness*, 22 September 2003)**

In 1999, Sifiso Nkabinde left a leadership position in the ANC in KwaZulu-Natal to join the United Democratic Movement (UDM). Within months, a former apartheid Security Police file emerged in which he was named as a state informer. In recent months, the director of public prosecutions, Bulalani Ngcuka, has offended the ANC leadership by his investigations of senior ANC members. Now we have Mac Maharaj claiming that he has documents in his possession that prove that Ngcuka was an apartheid spy.

These incidents could be indications of a pattern—stay loyal, toe the line, and your dubious past, or suspicions of a dubious past, will be suppressed; step over the line, and the can of worms will be opened. They certainly expose the flaws in an approach to dealing with the past that is informed by political imperative rather than principle. And they highlight the dangers of state documents being allowed to move outside formal process when expedient.

The Truth and Reconciliation Commission remarked on the number of former state security establishment operatives who had stolen state documents. And it marked the danger of such documents being used to guarantee immunity or to blackmail individuals and structures. In our view, the Nkabinde and Ngcuka cases are in precisely the same ballpark.

Numerous voices have been raised in response to the Ngcuka case calling on the state to address the problem by revealing all. They argue that it is time for a full disclosure of apartheid spies, informers, agents, and sources. Until this happens, they assert, the worms we have seen crawling out around Ngcuka will continue to corrode the democracy we are trying to build.

There is considerable merit to this argument. It expresses, after all, the rationale on which the TRC was founded. However, it fails to address a range of potentially damaging consequences. Here we flag only the most significant of them.

Because of the large-scale destruction and looting of security records in the early nineties, a full disclosure by the state is impossible. This means, on the one hand, that many individuals who should be unmasked will not be. On the other, it means that many who are innocent but under suspicion cannot be cleared conclusively.

The apartheid intelligence services routinely played the disinformation and false accusation cards. Inevitably, then, systematic disclosure of files will result in the false labeling of innocents. And the specter of "people's justice" for the unmasked must be confronted. South Africa has a tortured history of retribution for suspected informers.

What is current government policy in face of these complexities? Our reading of what is largely an unstated *de facto* regime highlights three core elements. Firstly, the identities of all apartheid-era informers are protected on principle. Promotion of Access to Information Act requests by the South African History Archive, and by individuals and organizations it has assisted, has resulted in the release of numerous intelligence records. But in every case the personal identifiers of informers have been deleted.

The most commonly cited reasons for such protection are the need to avoid breach of confidence, possible prejudice to the future supply of information, and the threat to the safety of the individuals concerned. All of these reasons can be challenged, especially in light of the passage of time and South Africa's transition to democracy.

Secondly, in dealing with access to information, the state recognizes no fissure between the present and the apartheid past. In other words, there is no special access regime in relation to pre-1994 information. So, for example, bizarrely, Cabinet records for the period 1983 to 1994 remain under lock and key. And thirdly, unlike in Germany after reunification in 1989, there is no extraordinary intervention to locate, audit, consolidate, and manage the state records that document this troubled dimension of our past. Indeed, there is already evidence of such records that were used by the TRC now being lost—it is not clear whether this is deliberate or the result of neglect.

In our view the scenario outlined above is insupportable. The time has come for government to grasp the nettle. It is imperative that a coherent policy backed by adequate resourcing be adopted. Such a policy must concede that a conflation of pre- and postapartheid realities is unacceptable. An access to information regime must be fashioned that distinguishes between protections geared to the imperatives of democratic governance and protections geared to the imperative to deal with apartheid-era legacies.

Policy implementation must be founded on the kind of extraordinary intervention undertaken in post-1989 Germany. A dedicated structure with a robust mandate—along the lines of Germany's Gauck Institute, set up to deal with the Stasi files—is essential. Simply leaving the National Archives to grapple with the problem as best it can is not going to work. Already the National Archives has responded to a series of apartheid-era archival challenges with a sickening combination of incompetence and political paralysis.

The dedicated structure we're advocating—and there are any number of foreign funders who would be delighted to resource it—would be responsible for managing access to records in a controlled, transparent, and accountable manner. Thoroughly—and publicly—debated protections would be implemented.

Not all the dangers flagged by us would be averted by such an approach. Not all the messy consequences of a complex and tragic past would be avoided. But at least we would be demonstrating the courage to get our hands dirty in a responsible way. Process would replace the *ad hoc*. And we would be subverting the dubious agendas of those intent on making personal and political capital out of past trauma.

## STORYTELLING AND HEALING: ALWAYS PROBE THE MEANING OF STORIES

### (Published in *The Natal Witness*, 6 October 2003)

When last did you have the unnerving experience of disagreeing fundamentally with someone over an account of something that you both participated in only a day or two before? It happens to us all the time. And usually it's not because one of us is either untruthful or overly forgetful. Usually it's because we're telling different stories about the same event.

Story—or narrative—is ubiquitous. It shapes our most intimate interactions with other people. It informs what we do in the workplace and how we understand what we do in the workplace. Recognizing this, I want to suggest, is fundamental to what we call well-adjusted living.

Narrativity—as Hayden White, Jacques Derrida, Michel Foucault, and others have demonstrated—as much as it might strive to work with actual events, in its form—structurally—brings a certain fictionalization. Listen to Derrida for a moment: "No matter how singular, irreducible, stubborn, distressing or tragic the 'reality' to which it refers, 'actuality' comes to us by way of a fictional fashioning." Those of us who have watched TV "reality" programs, or CNN coverage of the war in Iraq, will know exactly what Derrida is talking about.

For the form of narrativity—like all forms—is not merely a neutral container. It shapes, even determines, the narrative content in significant ways. Every narrative construction of the past is by definition creative, a work of the imagination—it recalls events that in all their particularity, their uniqueness, are irrecoverable, and that flow in a chaotic open-endedness. The construction gives to them a shape, a pattern, a closure. So that all "nonfictional" discourse employing narrativity inevitably invites "fiction" in.

A hard boundary between "nonfiction" and "fiction," then, is unsustainable. On the one hand, narrators of fiction are always addressing "a reality." Moreover, they frequently use their tools to unfold actual events and processes, "facts" of the past. On the other hand, narrators of nonfiction, no matter how dedicated they are to "facts" and to empirical methods, are confronted by documentary records, collective memories, and individual memories shaped by the dance of remembering, forgetting, and imagining. And that dance whirls in their own heads as they construct their representations of the past. History slides into story, reality into fiction.

Anyone visiting the Apartheid Museum will see this "sliding" at work. The museum's big story (or metanarrative) of apartheid pits oppressors against victims, with much of the apartheid system's complex and often contradictory dynamics erased. This is not to say that the curators are telling a lie. Merely that they have allowed the power of their story to overwhelm them.

It has been argued that "good scholarship" and "sound science" avoid the pitfalls I've outlined. They employ, so the argument runs, forms of knowledge construction other than slippery narrative. Well, these other forms have their own problematics in relation to "reality." Crucially, they cannot ultimately escape story. Behind every form, every way of knowing, there is story. Take Freud's psychoanalysis as an example. It was conceptualized as a science, given substance with a rigorously empirical methodology. But this cannot hide the reality that psychoanalysis is built upon a classical myth elaborated into a contemporary myth.

Any number of other examples could be cited. Newtonian physics was constructed within a metanarrative of the universe as God's machine. There is metanarrative behind Marxist historical and social analysis. It is behind the science of Einstein and the deconstruction of Derrida. And it is not only great thinkers who cannot escape story. Life, it seems, has given human beings a need for meaning. It seems also to have given us story as instrument for meeting that need. Throughout history, in all societies, there is story. Steal from people the narratives that give shape to their lives—by exposing the fictions dressed as truths, the inconsistencies, the weaknesses, the lies, and the secrets—and those people will simply replace them with new ones. Soul needs healing, and it finds healing in fiction.

Maybe here lies the biggest mistake of the Apartheid Museum curators. In seeking healing for South Africans they have been tempted by the allure of the big story. All storytelling invites privileging, exclusion, and moralizing judgment. This is seen most starkly in the big story, which also lends itself to becoming an instrument for social control. Hayden White argues compellingly that the big story steals from history and from the world their confusion, their lack of "a meaning." It imposes meaning on them. In doing so it steals from individuals what they need—space, confusion, a sense of meaninglessness—to construct their own meanings.

This might sound like a case of catch 22. We cannot construct meaning without narrative; the same narrative poses a threat to meaning construction. But it also sounds a call to creative engagement. To know always, whether we are practicing science or recounting the day's events to a partner, that we are telling a story—not detaining "reality" or "the truth"—and to make this plain to our readers and listeners. To trouble the narrative form, pushing its capacity to accommodate confusion, contradiction, shapelessness, and partial or multiple closure. To remain open always to other tellings of the story, to re-tellings and to the holding of competing stories.

As the receivers of story, we should be ever vigilant. Cherish what story gives us, but always probe its telling, explore other tellings and other stories. Know that as compelling as it might seem, as seamless and satisfying and healing, it remains story not truth. We should never allow story to be more than a platform to our own search for meaning. The healing of soul, in the end, is never something given to us—it is something we give ourselves.

## IT TAKES AT LEAST TWO TO ACHIEVE BALANCED AND PROFESSIONAL DISCUSSION

### (Co-authored with Sello Hatang, published under the title "Smoke and Mirrors" in *This Day,* 24 November 2003)

We welcome the national archivist's article ("A delicate balancing act at the National Archives," published in the 17 November 2003 issue of *This Day*) on the vexed question of public access to thirty-four boxes of "sensitive" Truth and Reconciliation Commission (TRC) records. It is important that a person in his position engages in public discourses around issues of demonstrable public interest. However, we question whether his contribution encourages the "balanced and professional discussion" that he advocates. What he offers readers is a fine example of the ancient art of smoke and mirrors.

He states that the South African History Archive (SAHA) has argued that the contents of the thirty-four boxes have been "destroyed, concealed or interfered with by government agents." This is to misconstrue SAHA public statements on the matter. What we have demanded is reasonable public access to the boxes in terms of the Promotion of Access to Information Act (PAIA). We first submitted our PAIA request for access to them in May 2001. Although the act provides for a thirty-day period in which an access decision should be taken, we are still waiting for such a decision—by our calculation we have been waiting for close to a thousand days!

In this context, Dr. Graham Dominy's statement that "instant access is being demanded" can only be regarded as disingenuous. We have waited patiently for two-and-a-half years, in the process mandating our attorneys to negotiate three separate access timeframes with the state, all three of which have been reneged on. It is not unreasonable in these circumstances, we would argue, to raise the question of why access mechanisms defined in law have been treated with contempt.

Nor is it unreasonable to point to the dimensions of concealment involved in the case. Dr. Dominy relates how the thirty-four boxes were removed from the TRC in 1999 and placed in the custody of the minister of justice. But he fails to mention that they were later moved to the minister of intelligence, without the knowledge, let alone the approval, of the National Archives.

He also fails to mention that through 2001 and 2002, his own office, the Department of Justice and the National Intelligence Agency (NIA) were either unable or unwilling to tell us where the boxes were. During April 2002, the South African public was treated to the spectacle of the Department of Justice and NIA each claiming on public radio that the other had the boxes. It was only when SAHA filed papers in the High Court that these agencies admitted where the boxes were.

Concerning the transfer of the thirty-four boxes from the minister of intelligence to the National Archives (which took place earlier this year), Dr. Dominy intimates that we should be delighted. Instead of which, our "fury knows no bounds." What he fails to disclose is that we had been pushing for this transfer since early in 2001, and that the transfer only took place after our filing of papers in the High Court. Of course we are relieved that the records are now where they belong. However, we wonder why this couldn't have been achieved without our having to resort to lengthy and costly legal action.

Dr. Dominy asserts that SAHA has conceded that "it has no knowledge of the contents of the boxes" and then wonders how we can insist that "there is almost nothing sensitive therein." Frankly, we find this mind-boggling. He himself gave us (in terms of a PAIA request) a detailed list of the files in these boxes in 2001. We subsequently showed the list to former TRC staffers who briefed us on the nature of most of the files. In the course of this inquiry we were given photocopies of some of the material. Our analysis, which has been publicized and which Dr. Dominy has had access to, is that the vast majority of the files are innocuous from a security perspective. Indeed, a substantial number of the documents are already in the public domain.

In short, far from demanding that everything in the boxes be made available immediately, which Dr. Dominy accuses us of doing "blithely," we are simply demanding that a decision on access be taken strictly according to the provisions of the Access Act. We recognize that certain documents might well have to be protected. Our fury in relation to this case stems from the blatant disregard for legal provisions on the safe custody and accessibility of the records in the thirty-four boxes, and the sorry trail of ineptitude, obstruction, and broken undertakings that has characterized the saga.

Where Dr. Dominy gets it just right is when he quotes us as saying that the National Archives has demonstrated "a sickening combination of incompetence and political paralysis." The sad reality is that the litany of inaccuracies and silences we have enumerated above has become a pattern in the National Archives' approach to dealing with what it regards as "sensitive" matters. Like its apartheid predecessor, democratic South Africa's National Archives has become adept at dancing to the tune of its political and bureaucratic masters, and at deploying smoke and mirrors to try and hide the fact. Dr. Dominy's frustration with SAHA, we would suggest, has to do with our capacity to see through the smoke and mirrors.

Two final observations. Firstly, Dr. Dominy makes the curious claim that "SAHA is staffed by former officials of the National Archives." This is not true. SAHA has nine full-time staffers, only three of whom are former officials of the National Archives. What this has to do with the matter at hand he does not make clear.

Secondly, Dr. Dominy goes on at great length about the International Council on Archives' round table he hosted earlier this year, the theme of which was human rights and archives. We congratulate him on the accomplishment. But perhaps he would like to explain why SAHA, one of a handful of human rights archives in southern Africa, was not invited to participate. Then again, the values and attitudes expressed in his article make it plain why we weren't invited. So much for "balanced and professional discussion" ...

## SO, WHAT WAS THE HEFER COMMISSION ALL ABOUT?

**(Published under the title "After the Hefer Circus" in** *The Natal Witness,* **29 December 2003)**

Mercifully, the public spectacle that has been the Hefer Commission is done. Of course, there remains the tying up of loose ends, but effectively the media circus is over. And it doesn't take a genius to predict the formal findings. So, what was it all about? Did we learn anything meaningful? Were public monies well spent?

Any serious attempt to answer these questions, I would argue, must return to the nature and content of the political settlement negotiated for South Africa in the years between 1990 and 1994. A key element was the deal struck on how to deal with the past, in particular on how to deal with individuals compromised by that past. The deal involved a form of absolution for all except those guilty of criminal offenses or of gross human rights violations. The latter would be dealt with through the Truth and Reconciliation Commission process, the former (including those not given amnesty by the TRC) would face the criminal justice system.

In other words, all other forms of compromise, including spying for the apartheid state, would be buried in the interests of reconciliation. This is why it is possible for Marthinus van Schalkwyk to be prominent in government despite having admitted to being a spy while a university student. This is why it is possible for Inkatha Freedom Party (IFP) leader Buthelezi to be in Cabinet despite the findings of the TRC about his role in the political violence of the 1980s and 1990s. And this is why Judge Hefer, compromised professionally by his role in the apartheid legal system, can preside over a presidential commission of inquiry in 2003.

In this context the question of whether Bulelani Ngcuka was an apartheid-era spy is of no consequence from a governance perspective. Only two questions are critical—has he abused his office, and does a compromised past have anything to do with that abuse? These are questions—perhaps precisely the questions—that the commission has failed to investigate. Serious analysis must ask why this is so.

In my view, the commission was set up not to investigate these questions. The juggling with its terms of reference was all about ensuring that the abuse of office inquiry would only happen if the spy allegations were found to be "true." And the latter was rendered a task impossible from the outset, with the state making it clear that it would not make available to the commission intelligence information under its control. The announcement by the president's office that he has access to all intelligence documentation and that nothing of relevance to the commission exists can only be described as disingenuous. Much of the documentation was destroyed or removed by operatives in the period 1990 to 1994, and much of what has survived is inaccessible to anybody as a result of poor management.

If my analysis is accurate, what *was* the real purpose of the commission? Why spend significant public monies on a fruitless exercise? The answer, I suggest, is rooted in the above-mentioned deal brokered between 1990 and 1994. Linked to the deal was a code—a code expressed in the phrase "we keep silent about compromised pasts." This is the code that Mac Maharaj and Mo Shaik broke. And the commission was about demonstrating what happens to people who break the code. They get hung out to dry.

The fact is that the evidence presented by Maharaj and Shaik could have been shown to be flimsy very quickly by the state, without the need for an expensive commission of inquiry. But the point was that they had to be publicly and painfully discredited. South Africa had to see what happens to people who break the code.

No doubt there were other dynamics at play behind the scenes. Some commentators have suggested links to the arms deal scandal, and to Ngcuka's investigation of Deputy President Zuma. Others have alluded to documentary evidence known to Maharaj and Shaik but suppressed by the state. Yet others have spoken of power plays within the ANC and the settling of scores in relation to Operation Vula (the ANC underground operation that foundered in the early 1990s). Sadly, we are unlikely ever to find out to what extent these dynamics were a factor in the framing of the commission.

My cynicism notwithstanding, I don't agree with those commentators who dismiss the commission as a complete waste of time. Even the most carefully orchestrated public show can issue in unforeseen outcomes. For one thing, it has provided us with evidence of how the 1990–1994 deal and its concomitant code play out in the South Africa of 2003. It has demonstrated how flawed the ANC's intelligence-gathering processes were in the 1980s—Mo Shaik was, after all, a major cog in ANC counterintelligence during the late eighties. And that reminds us of the many activists who were sidelined, tortured, or killed on the basis of such intelligence gathering.

For those able to see past the spectacle, theater, and hype of the commission's public hearings, there are other lessons to be learned. Three are particularly important. Firstly, it gives us a window into a vast swathe of unfinished business from our apartheid past. Through the TRC, the Land Commission, and other institutions, we have just begun to scratch the surface of the challenge facing us in this area. Secondly, it has focused our attention on the question of custody, management, and access to apartheid-era records. The sad reality is that (whether we are talking about intelligence records or former homeland records) they are scattered around the country and desperately in need of a thorough and professional audit.

Finally, the commission has undermined the postapartheid myth of a glorious struggle against apartheid, with heroes pitted against villains. The reality is that there were many struggles, there were struggles within struggles, and few of the heroes were without flaws. It is through embracing this complexity, and refusing to comply with the code of silence around the messiness of anti-apartheid struggles, that South Africa will find its course to a more mature and just form of democracy.

# PINNING DOWN APARTHEID'S PAPERS

**(Co-authored with Sello Hatang, published in *This Day*, 19 January 2004)**

After the collapse of East Germany in 1989, the new German state moved quickly and decisively to secure the records documenting the era of Communist rule. Particular care was paid to the Stasi (Security Police) records, with a dedicated piece of legislation and an implementing agency being put in place to manage them.

During South Africa's transition to democracy, many activists lobbied for a similar intervention in relation to surviving apartheid-era records. They were particularly mindful of the extent to which records had been destroyed by the faltering apartheid state, and the extent to which records were scattered both institutionally and geographically. Their hopes have still not been realized.

Whatever one thinks about the Hefer Commission, it must be conceded that it has foregrounded the issue of apartheid-era records. In particular, it has focused public debate around the questions of authenticity, custody, and access in relation to such records. *This Day* has contributed to the debate by publishing lists of files kept on individuals by the apartheid Department of Justice—for many people this has provided the first opportunity to exercise their right to access information about themselves generated by the apartheid security establishment.

For the most part, however, public debate has skirted the big questions: where are these records, who controls them, and how secure are they? During its work, the Truth and Reconciliation Commission (TRC) undertook a focused investigation into these questions. It found that while large volumes of apartheid-era security establishment records had been destroyed in a coordinated endeavor between 1990 and 1994, surprising quantities had survived. The TRC recommendation was that the surviving records be brought under professional archival control as quickly as possible.

The harsh reality is that very little has been done to effect this TRC recommendation. With the exception of the Justice files detailed by *This Day,* and certain prison, State Security Council, and Security Police records, surviving apartheid-era security establishment records remain dispersed throughout structures of the present security establishment.

In some cases, they are in good order and under sound management—the best example being those records under the control of the South African National Defence Force. In other cases the scenario is bleak. For example, surviving Security Police files were located, secured, and listed under TRC direction in 1997–1998. Today they are in chaos, effectively inaccessible, and in the process of transfer to the National Archives only as a result of sustained lobbying by interest groups.

Another problem identified by the TRC was the extent to which security establishment records had been illegally removed by individual operatives and officials. The best documented cases of this phenomenon were those involving chemical and biological warfare head Wouter Basson and the chief prosecutor at the Rivonia Treason Trial, Percy Yuttar. It is imperative that the state develop a coordinated and sustained strategy for securing the return of such records.

The challenge of dispersal reaches far beyond the case of security establishment records. Ironically, the TRC archive itself has been subject to the same phenomenon. Protracted court action by the South African History Archive was necessary before thirty-four boxes of "sensitive" TRC records were transferred to the National Archives from the minister of intelligence. Numerous records were removed by TRC staffers when they left the organization and remain scattered around the country. A large part of the TRC electronic archive was dumped onto disks when TRC offices closed down and has received no professional attention since.

The records of the *bantustans* raise serious concerns. All *bantustan* military and intelligence records were secured by the SANDF and the National Intelligence Agency (NIA) respectively. The former appear safe, but the TRC discovered that NIA had been systematically destroying the latter as late as 1996. The province of KwaZulu-Natal is making good progress in attempting to secure other apartheid-era KwaZulu records, but the situation in relation to the remaining *bantustans* is worrying. Records are dispersed and often in deplorable condition. The worst case we are aware of is the dumping of Transkei archives in a shed behind the Nelson Mandela Museum in Mthatha, where they were exposed to the elements and subjected to still undetermined damage.

Also of concern are the records of the many statutory bodies and state-owned facilities that fell outside archival control during the apartheid era. The National Archives has compiled an inventory of such organizations, but has made very little progress in auditing the records under their control. The dangers are illustrated by the present High Court case in which a researcher is contesting the claim by Iscor that it has no apartheid-era records in its custody.

Finally, there is the challenge posed by the anti-apartheid records of a wide range of organizations inside and outside the country. The Mo Shaik database disclosed at the Hefer Commission could be the tip of the iceberg in terms of organizational records that have been or are in the hands of individuals. In terms of records created outside the country, the liberation movements have made good progress with the huge task of securing and processing their own records. But no audit has been done of the vast dispersed archive of the international anti-apartheid movement. A few individual collections have been donated to archives in South Africa. Some were utilized by the TRC. But the vast majority remain unknown and inaccessible to South Africans.

Auditing this dispersed and more or less vulnerable archival heritage should be a priority of the state. In the late 1990s, the National Archives and the Department of Land Affairs, with international financial support, demonstrated what could be achieved in this arena when they audited, secured, and made available to the land restitution process all state records of potential use to the process. It is high time that the National Archives, the South African Heritage Resources Agency, and provincial archives and heritage structures demonstrated similar vision and leadership in grappling with the broader problem posed by apartheid-era records.

## A FRIENDLIER BIG BROTHER?

**(Published in *The Natal Witness*, 30 March 2004)**

In February, Minister of Intelligence Lindiwe Sisulu disclosed to the media that she had appointed a commission of inquiry into intelligence gathering by nonstate structures and individuals. To those who have followed her performance as intelligence minister, this came as no surprise.

She has established a pattern of relatively high visibility and public announcement of work being undertaken by the National Intelligence

Agency (NIA)—from investigating information leaks at Durban Metro to reviewing the classification of apartheid-era files, from securing the Truth and Reconciliation Commission archive to countering corruption in the Department of Home Affairs. Last year, NIA even ran media commercials reminding the South African public of the agency's role in ensuring "normality" for society.

In contrast, public knowledge of the workings of the South African Secret Service, Military Intelligence, and Police Crime Intelligence remains slight. More striking is the contrast with NIA's immediate apartheid forerunner, the National Intelligence Service (NIS), which was a shadowy outfit renowned for keeping its cards close to its chest and for shunning the media.

What are we to make of this "coming out" by NIA? And is the apparent expansion of its role something to be applauded? The answers to these questions, I would suggest, should emerge from analysis of the broader post-1994 endeavor to transform South Africa's state intelligence services.

Even the most cynical commentator would have to concede that there have been positive developments in this transformation terrain. The appointment of a Cabinet member responsible for intelligence has fostered greater political accountability. The establishment of the watchdog office of the Intelligence Inspector-General is welcome, as is a wider reporting of intelligence activities to Parliament.

Thorough reviews of policy and procedure driven by NIA have taken place or are under way. For instance, we know that the deeply problematic Protection of Information Act (1982) and subordinate Minimum Information Security Standard are under review. Last year, Sisulu appointed both the Classification and Declassification Review Committee (CDRC), mandated to make recommendations on the declassification of apartheid-era files, and the commission of inquiry announced in February. Both of these structures have incorporated participation by experts from outside the state.

Also encouraging has been evidence of NIA's responsiveness to public debate and pressure. We have seen agency officials participating in conferences, workshops, and other professional gatherings. In 2002, we saw NIA backing down on certain security requirements for the presidential press corps. In 2003, a combination of media attention and litigation by the South African History Archive saw the ministry for intelligence giving up thirty-four boxes of so-called sensitive TRC records to the National Archives.

So there is considerable evidence of a NIA far more transparent than its apartheid forerunners, more willing to engage in public discourse around its work, and involved in a far wider range of "routine" activities. Nevertheless, I would argue, there remains cause for concern and a need for constant vigilance by the public.

Firstly, levels of accountability are not what they should be. Reporting to Parliament, while more extensive than in the pre-1994 era, is not adequate to enable either public representatives or civil society to subject NIA to the kind of accounting that democracy demands. So when NIA media commercials, for instance, claim success for the agency in ending the "taxi wars" and the Cape Town bombing terror, there is no way of assessing whether such claims have any validity. It might as well be claiming to have ended the drought.

We also still need convincing that the office of the Inspector-General is anything more than window-dressing. Substantive evidence of a meaningful role for this office is conspicuous by its absence. And the many reviews outlined above have yet to deliver shifts in policy. The CDRC process, for instance, initially designed to report to the minister in June 2003, has still not issued in a publicly announced set of outcomes.

Secondly, post-1994 NIA performance is characterized by a litany of interventions that raise questions about both the depth of transformation and the values informing it. Let me cite just a few examples. In 1996, the TRC caught NIA systematically destroying records of the former *bantustan* intelligence agencies in defiance of President Mandela's 1995 moratorium on the destruction of any state records for the duration of the TRC's work.

The role played by both NIA and the intelligence ministry in relation to the thirty-four boxes of "sensitive" TRC records bears all the hallmarks of the apartheid era. Documents filed in the High Court recently by the Department of Justice reveal the extent to which the agency blocked that department's attempts to fulfill its legal obligations in relation to the records. And further questions are raised by the facts that one of the files (titled "List of informers") is missing and that SAHA's court action has already forced the majority of the files into the public domain. So much for them all being highly "sensitive."

Numerous commentators have expressed concern at the increased surveillance powers accorded the intelligence services by the Interception of Communications Act. Already there is evidence of human rights activists, pursuing constitutionally protected activities, being placed under state surveillance. And in 2003, the Hefer Commission of inquiry was effectively crippled by the refusal of the intelligence services to cooperate with its investigations.

We must, then, be cautious in our assessment of the transformation of South Africa's intelligence services. Until a surface transparency is married to meaningful accountability mechanisms and a better track record in support of democratic objectives, South Africans should be vigilant. Indeed, vigilance in relation to what are inherently shadowy public services will always be essential. A failure here will raise the specter of a rosy-hued but ever bigger big brother.

## Endnotes

1   These texts are not reproduced from the versions published in the newspapers cited. I have worked from my original drafts together with notes made on the versions published at the time.

# INDEX

These abbreviations are used in the index:
    ANC = African National Congress
    PAIA = Protection of Access to Information Act
    TRC = Truth and Reconciliation Commission
    VH = Harris, Verne

international isolation of South Africa, 3, 191, 203

International Standards Organization (ISO) and electronic records, 118

Investigation Task Unit, 11

Iraq, archival treasures of, 402–404

Iraq War, 2003- , build-up to, 168, 352, 365, 369

Ireland, political conflict in, 408–410

*ISAD(G) (General International Standard Archival Description)*, 149

Iscor, 423

Israel and nuclear weapons program, 352, 354, 356–357, 369, 374n9

Jardine, Roger, 353, 364

jazz, xv, xvi–xxxi, 394

jazzification, 227, 236n1

Jenkinson, Hilary, 29, 56, 59, 65, 193n3

Jericho weapon system, 356–357

journalism and transparency, 272, 276, 284, 292–293

Joyce, James, 25, 30, 73

Jung, Carl, xix

justice
    and accountability, 249–250
    in African identity, 218, 221–222
    and archives, 168, 247–249
    and deconstruction, 234
    and hospitality to the other, 5–6, 76–77, 249, 257, 398
    passion for, 36
    politics of, 256–257
    and story, x–xii
    *vs.* law, 125, 208

Kamuf, Peggy, 256

Ketelaar, Erik
    and archival odysseys, 29
    and Derrida, 83n23
    effect of visit to South Africa, 183, 197n61, 201n92
    on ethics, 204–205
    legal issues, 129n43
    and transparency, 284–285

*kgotla* forums in democratization, 390

King, Martin Luther, 394

Knobel, Dr. Neils, 368

knowing, ways of. *see* ways of knowing, indigenous

knowledge and mystery, 249

knowledge as seeing, 47

knowledge management systems, 114

knowledge managers, 166, 170n22

Kosovo, 110

Kundera, Milan, 193n4

KwaZulu Intelligence Service, 319

KwaZulu-Natal province archives, 185, 193n7, 194n12, 201n91, 422

labels, 111, 127n16, 232, 234
    *see also* naming

Laine, Brigitte, 209, 264n6

Land Claims Court, 107–108, 126n2, 126n4

land in African identity, 218, 221

language in African identity, 218, 222, 224, 226–227

Latin, linguistic hegemony of, 123

Latour, Bruno, 33–34, 144, 241, 248

law. *see* evidence, laws of

Lawyers for Human Rights, 274, 317

Lerner, Gerda, 29

Levinas, Emmanuel, 73–74, 256, 258

liberation
    and archival heartland, 124–125
    and descriptive standards, xx–xxi, 151–152

Liberman, Peter, 351–380

libraries, museums, art galleries, etc, 15–16, 17, 173

Library and Archives Canada. *see* National Archives of Canada

Linen Hall Library (Belfast, Northern Ireland), 409–410

listening, xiii, 258

*lobola* system, 389, 390

Lubowski, Anton, 286n5

Lyotard, Jean-Francois, 61, 73, 192

MacNeil, Heather, 138, 140

macro-actors, domination by, 33–34

macro-appraisal
    overview, 94–96, 99n18
    and Schellenbergian appraisal, 62, 68n20
    and State Archives Service, 97–98, 188, 201n92, 201n94
    and VH, xxv

Maharaj, Mac, 410, 419–420

Mallarme, Stephane, 236n1

and globalization, 393
privileging in, 259
as recordkeepers, 168, 245
resistance to pressures from, 242, 248
oral testimony in South African courts, 107–108, 116, 126n4
orality and oral history
collection of, 189, 201n98, 201n100–101
conversion into material custody, 18
as form of archive, 78
of nuclear weapons program, 372–373, 380n96–97
as record, 251n8
in record-keeping paradigm, 121
responsibilities to, 261
in transformation discourse, 181
and ways of knowing, 230–231
organizational process, 163, 164
original order, 30, 135, 143
originals and electronic records, 12, 117
otherness and the other
in African archival discourse, 220, 233, 234
in archival discourse, 65, 217
and authoritative ideas, 66
in deconstruction, 76
and Derrida, 40–41
and description, 145
embracing, 51
hospitalities to, 4–6, 76–77, 257, 398
and jazz, xv
and justice, 5–6, 76–77, 249, 257, 398
listening to, 258
in National Archives, 225
as ourselves, xi
and outreach, 398–399
in record-keeping paradigm, 121
re-spect for, 36, 147
responsibilities toward, 262
O'Toole, James, 129n43
outreach, 17–18, 181, 189–190

PAIA. *see* Promotion of Access to Information Act (PAIA)
"paper minds," 167, 168
Papon, Maurice, 209
paralysis, 227–228, 236n14
Parker, Charlie, xvi, xvii
passion

in appraisal, 105
in archivists' meetings, 45
in deconstruction, 234
of Derrida, 44, 50, 71
and ways of seeing, 48
*see also* compassion
patriarchy, 32, 56
people's history, 181, 189
*see also* orality and oral history
Perlman, John, 384–385
permanently valuable record, determination of, 88–89
Personal Information Protection and Electronic Documents Act (Canada), 117
Petroleum Products Act under apartheid, 271
photography and ways of seeing, 46, 49
Piasecki, Sara, 126n4
Pietermaritzburg Heritage Forum, 397, 399
Piggott, Michael, 251n11
place of consignation, 42
playfulness of Derrida, 80
poetry of archives, xix, xxvii–xxviii
Police Crime Intelligence, 424
police files, 274, 286n14
*see also* Security Police
policy documentation in State Archives Service, 91, 99n17
political pressure, 240–242, 254
politics
in archives, xiii, 239–252, 244–247
and archivists, 144, 157–158, 166, 168
direction of, 256
as engagement, xiv
and ethics, 158
messiness of, 254
Positivism, xi, 10–12, 16, 19, 20n5
postcustodialism, 111, 113–114, 121, 139–140
postmodernisms
in African archival discourse, 234
in archival discourse, 65, 101–106, 132
circles of knowledge, 76
and Derrida, xxv, 73–74
meanings of term, 61–62, 251n10
and VH, xxiii, xxv–xxvi, 70
postmodernity, 9, 20n2, 123–124
power
and archival description, 139
complicity in, 147

archive as reflection of, 11, 229
changing meanings of, 13–15, 75
nonrecoverability of, 13
and process of record creation, 102,
    259–260
*vs.* actuality, 246, 413
reconciliation and healing, 291
record-keepers. *see* archivists and record-
    keepers
record-keeping paradigm
    and global periphery, 120–125
    liberation of standards from, 151–152
    misreadings of, 62, 68n21, 68n24
    *vs.* recordmaking, 5
recordmaking
    concept of, 5, 157
    messiness of, 249, 254
    politics of, 167–168, 241, 242, 254
    role of archivist, xxiii, 133
records and recordness
    changeability of, 12
    definitions, 64–65, 108, 120, 121,
        128n37
    electronic records as, 112, 127n19
    listening to, 258–260
    in macro-appraisal, 96
    outside conceptual cocoon, 249
    and power, 34, 259
    responsibilities to, 260–263
records continuum model. *see* continuum
    model
records creation
    context for, 260
    electronic records, 112–113
    extension of archival domains into, 15,
        114
    identifying a creator, 102–104, 135
records management
    under apartheid, 175, 176, 194n15,
        308, 309
    as archival function, 114, 185–186,
        199n72–73
    under Government of National Unity,
        184
    at TRC archive, 297, 299
*Refiguring the Archive* (Harris), xxiii
refugees. *see* otherness and the other
Reiss, Mitchell, 364
relativism and postmodernisms, 74
religion

and archives, xxvi
in Derrida, x, 70, 74
and divine capacity to dance, 227
as responsibility, x
remembering and forgetting
    under apartheid, 289
    and appraisal, 104–105
    relation of, 124
    selection of, 330
    and TRC, 293, 394–397
    vs evidence, 121–122
research value of records
    under apartheid, 87, 93, 177
    as appraisal criterion, 96–97
    in macro-appraisal paradigm, 94
    in Schellenbergian appraisal, 90, 99n15
researchers, xxi, 14–15, 41–42
*respect des fonds,* 134–135, 138, 139–140, 143,
    153n6, 154n29
responsibility to the record, x–xi, 260–263
Ricoeur, Paul, 143
right of access. *see* access to information;
        freedom of information; public
        access to records
rights
    African conceptual framework for, 229
    documentation of, 21n24
    protection of, 203–213
rock 'n roll, xvi, 394
Rubin, Jerry, 27–28
Rumney, Reg, 272
Rumsfeld, Donald, 404

Sachs, Albie, 274
sacrifice, 49, 53n25
SADF. *see* South African Defence Force
    (SADF)
"safety" of record-keeping, 122
SAHA. *see* South African History Archive
    (SAHA)
Saleh, Razia, 193n8
Samuels, Helen, 94, 132
SANDF. *see* South African National Defence
    Force (SANDF)
SAPS (South African Police Service), 402
SASA. *see* South African Society of Archivists
    (SASA)
saxophones, xvii
Schellenberg, T. R., 284
Schellenbergian appraisal